GEORGIA
IN PROFI

GEORGIANS IN PROFILE

Historical Essays in Honor of

ELLIS MERTON COULTER

EDITED BY

HORACE MONTGOMERY

Publishers UNIVERSITY OF GEORGIA PRESS *Athens*

Dedicated by the Authors
His former students at the University of Georgia
to
ELLIS MERTON COULTER

In appreciation of his many years of service in
The University of Georgia

CONTENTS

PREFACE

FOR over a third of a century Professor Ellis Merton Coulter has engaged in teaching and productive research in the history of Georgia, the South, and the nation. His former students are pleased to honor him with the dedication of this volume of fourteen biographical essays, the subjects of which belong primarily to Georgia's past. None was obscure; some were two or three ranks removed from their more prominent contemporaries; a few were conspicuous beyond the colonial-state level. Whatever the degree of eminence of their subjects, the contributors to this volume hope it will provide their friend and former teacher a measure of the delight he has so long afforded them.

A native of North Carolina, born in Hickory, on July 20, 1890, Professor Coulter received his academic degrees at the University of North Carolina (B.A., 1913; M.A., 1915) and the University of Wisconsin (Ph.D., 1917). Before coming to the University of Georgia in 1919, he taught in the public schools of his native state and at Marietta College, Marietta, Ohio. In 1923 he became professor of history; in 1941, head of the history department; and in 1948, regents professor, the highest honor within the gift of the Board of Regents of the University System of Georgia. Both Marietta College and the University of North Carolina have awarded him honorary degrees and in 1952 his colleagues in the University's College of Arts and Sciences named him distinguished professor of the year.

In 1921 he was appointed to the Editorial Board of the *Georgia Historical Quarterly*. Shortly thereafter he became editor of this journal, a position he still holds. Professor Coulter has been active in regional and national historical associations, serving as president of the Agricultural Historical Society in 1929-30. Because of his interest in Southern history, he was one of the prime movers in the founding of the Southern Historical Association. In 1934-35 he was its president.

A complete list of Professor Coulter's publications appears in the appendix of this volume. Its length attests to his industry and singular devotion to scholarship. Though his writings have won him an enviable reputation, his former students remember him best for his courses on the Antebellum South and the Civil War. They have long been among the most popular courses offered by the University's history department. His students are widely scattered, for, in addition to long service at the University of Georgia, he has taught in a dozen leading universities in every section of the country except the Far West. In 1944 he was visiting professor at National University, Mexico City, Mexico and in 1952 he gave courses in American history and civilization at the University of Jerusalem.

Of Professor Coulter's many contributions to historical scholarship, two deserve special mention. Since 1943 he has served with Professor Wendell Holmes Stephenson, now of the University of Oregon, as co-editor of the ten-volume *History of the South*. Jointly sponsored by the Louisiana State University and the Trustees of the Littlefield Fund for Southern History at the University of Texas, seven volumes of this work have now appeared, two of them — *The Confederate States of America* and *The South During Reconstruction*—by Professor Coulter. In 1952 he became a member of the Board of Trustees of the Wormsloe Foundation, a non-profit corporation which contemplates the publication of important manuscripts relating to Georgia and the South. This series of works is to be known as the *Wormsloe Foundation Publications*. Professor Coulter prepared the first volume and the University of Georgia Press published it. Titled *Wormsloe: Two Centuries of a Georgia Family*, it was selected as one of the 1955 Southern Books of the Year in the Southern Books Competition sponsored by the Southeastern Library Association.

The editor of this volume is grateful for the cooperation of the contributors and he wishes especially to thank the members of the committee which undertook this project. Serving with him on this committee were Dr. S. Walter Martin, Dean of Franklin College and Professor of History until his appointment as President of Emory University, who originally suggested the volume; Dr. Albert B. Saye, Professor of Political Science;

Dr. C. Jay Smith, Jr., Associate Professor of History; and Mr. Ralph H. Stephens, the able Director of the University of Georgia Press, for whose patience and understanding the editor is especially grateful.

HORACE MONTGOMERY

I

JOHN PERCIVAL
FIRST EARL OF EGMONT

BY RUTH AND ALBERT B. SAYE

THE Earl of Egmont never came to America, but in importance he was second only to James Edward Oglethorpe in founding the colony of Georgia. Oglethorpe's life, full of variety, adventure, and achievement, has been the subject of a number of full-length biographies.[1] As yet, however, no one has attempted a biography of the Earl of Egmont. Just who was this man Egmont, and what did he have to do with the colony of Georgia?

John Percival, who became First Earl of Egmont in 1733, was born at Burton, in Cork County, Ireland, July 12, 1683. His father, Sir John Percivale, Baronet, was nineteenth in a direct line of descent from Robert, Lord of Breherval and Yvery, who with his son, Ancelin Gouel de Perceval, accompanied William of Normandy in the Conquest of 1066. A detailed history of the Perceval family was published in 1742.[2] The author of this genealogical history illustrates variations in the spelling of the family name as follows: "We may observe, that David, the direct Ancestor of the present Earl of Egmont, who lived in the reign of Henry the Eighth, wrote his name *Preceval;* George, his Son and Heir, is entered in the visitations of Somerset, *Percyval;* Richard, his son, Register of the Court of Wards, wrote it in the same manner.—But his Son, Philip Perceval, wrote it *Percivalle;* his Son, Sir John, left out the (e), and retained the double (l); Sir John, his Son, the father of the Earl of Egmont, still varied it again, and wrote it *Percivale.* And the Earl of Egmont is the first that has wrote it *Percival.*"[3] In all, twenty-nine varia-

Albert B. Saye is a member of the political science faculty at the University of Georgia. Ruth Saye is his wife.

1

tions in spelling are noted. As for etymology, one theory is that
the name was originally Perci, and the termination "val" was
added, supposing the original French to have been *le val de
Perci*. Others would have it that the name derives from two
French words, *per* or *par,* and *cheval,* indicating military service
by horseback.[4] The mother of the First Earl of Egmont was
Catherine, third daughter of Sir Edward Dering, of Surrenden,
in Kent, Baronet.

The titles of nobility conferred upon John Percival were all
in the Irish peerage. The name Egmont, used in his highest title,
derived from the name of a place near Burton, in Cork County,
Ireland, where his father was born.[5] His ancestor, Richard Percyval, had been made register of the Court of Wards in Ireland
by James I in 1617, and from that time forward members of
the Perceval family had held lucrative offices in the Irish government. As was a common practice of the day, actual occupancy
of these government offices was farmed out to subordinates, but
the bulk of the remuneration retained by the official titleholder
who spent most of his time in England. By investment and wise
management, the Perceval landholdings in Ireland became so
vast as to resemble "rather a principality, than the patrimony
of a private house."[6] Several of their castles and villages were
destroyed in the upheavals of the Commonwealth period, but
the estate was still sufficiently intact at the time of John Percival
to make him independently wealthy.

John Percival's father died in April, 1686, when only twenty-
nine years old, from some disease contracted while sitting as
foreman of a grand jury at the assizes in Cork County.[7] He had
been married for five years, and was the father of five children.
One daughter, Catherine, died in infancy. Another daughter,
Mary, and two sons, Edward and John, survived him. A third
son, Philip, was not born until November, 1686.

Two months after the death of her husband, Lady Percivale
went to England to Kings Weston, the home of Sir Robert
Southwell, her husband's uncle, who had been named guardian
by his will. The year was an eventful one in her life: in November her third son was born, and in December her second
daughter died. Four years later, in August, 1690, she married
again, this time to a Colonel Butler. On November 9 of the
following year her eldest son, Edward, died, and in February
of the next year (1692) she herself died of a miscarriage.[8] This

left of the immediate Percival family of our present interest only John, age eight, and his brother, age five. As the elder living son, John was now heir of the family estate and title, baronet. Sole guardianship of the two orphans lay with their great-uncle, Sir Robert Southwell.

John remained in the home of his uncle under the tutelage of Dr. Henry Roby, former chaplain to his father, until 1696. In that year at age thirteen he was sent to Mr. Demoeure's Academy, where Latin, French, geometry, music, dancing, fencing, vaulting, quarter-staff, and other hearty exercises were regularly taught; and at leisure hours, an actor was employed to teach him oratory.[9] His brother Philip was placed in the same school, located at Westminster.[10] In a letter to his uncle written after a year and a half in this school, John reported: "I have read the seven first books of the Gaulish war in Caesar; the seventh, eighth, ninth, tenth and eleventh books of Virgil; the History of the Bible—a chapter every morning and evening into Latin. Justin; Ovid's Metamorphosis—four chapters in the Greek Testament. I read Justin and Ovid in the form of Mr. Moeures the son. My brother Philip has read some parts of Eutropius, Corderius' Colloquies and the Rudiments."[11]

His uncle was solicitous that the youth be "perfected in school learning." At age fifteen he was removed to Westminster School, and at age sixteen (in November, 1699) he entered Magdalen College at Oxford University. As a part of his matriculation, he subscribed to the Articles of Religion, took the Oath of Supremacy, and swore to observe the statutes of the university.[12] His course of study was the traditional classical course. The instruction was no doubt superior in quality. A hint as to its personal quality is given in a letter written by the youthful "Sir John" on his fifth day in residence: "I read the first letter of Le Clerc of Incredulity last night with Mr. Smallbrook; he read the English and I followed him with the French, and we concluded that it will bear reading over more than once."[13] Richard Smallbrook, his tutor, later Bishop of Lichfield, had only four pupils. He wrote to Sir Robert Southwell in February, 1701, as follows: "The greatest occasion of Sir John's expenses has been his love of music, which has engaged him to have more entertainments at his chambers than otherwise he would have had, and at the same time I must observe to you that though this has proved expensive, yet I think it has excused himself from drinking more than the greatest part of other conversation would have done."[14]

After a year and a half, in 1701, at the age of eighteen, Sir John left Oxford and went on a tour of England. He had planned to extend the tour into Scotland, but changed his mind after the experience of one day in that country. The accommodations in the village of Langholm where he stopped were miserable indeed. The food consisted of wine, butter, and half-baked bread, made of oats. He ate with gloves on for fear of itch which showed on his landlady's fingers. Describing the experience to a friend, he wrote: "I shall say nothing of the stink which both the woman and the house favoured us with, because the smoke got the upper hand, and to our comfort overpowered it; but at first entrance I thought I should have been struck down. After all this we were forced to thank our lady for our good reception with another kiss, which had certainly brought up my dinner had not the bread been as heavy as lead in my stomach. The bad success of this forenoon made me take a resolution to fly the country, and I never looked behind me till I got again within the borders of England."[15]

The management of his estates in Ireland appears to have been entrusted to Percival before he was of age. In 1702, when he was but nineteen, his uncle gave him much advice in this matter. One recommendation made was that he require all proposals for renting to be submitted in writing. "Declare this to be your standing rule, and they all will acquiesce," advised his uncle. "The true rule should be to let no more to any one tenant than his own stock were able to manage." The practice had been "to let a great deal to some Irish gentleman that has nothing of his own, but so he may bring in his followers, and while he makes them pay double the rent, he lives idly upon the overplus himself."[16]

In 1704 Sir John visited Ireland, and while there was elected Knight of the Shire for Cork County to serve in the Irish Parliament. This was his first public office. In October of that year he was appointed to the Privy Council in England, a position that he was to hold for the next forty-four years.

In August, 1705, Sir John, now of age, set out on a grand tour of Europe, lasting two years.[17] More time was spent in Rome than any other place. He had much interest in painting, architecture, and music.

Upon his return to London in 1707, Sir John sometimes amused himself by attending debates in Parliament as a spectator.[18] He had always combined an interest in politics with his interest in music, art, and the theatre. Two years later he wrote to a cousin: "As to the employment of my time, I am resolved not to be altogether idle, but as well as I can inform myself on our Constitution, no study being so proper for a gentleman to know as the measure of his obedience and the length of their power who rule."[19]

In June, 1708, Sir John again visited Ireland to look after his estates. It was on this visit that he met George Berkeley, then a fellow at Trinity College, Dublin, who became a lifelong friend.[20] Berkeley became well known in the 1720's for his scheme to establish a college in Bermuda that would provide an educated clergy for the American colonies. Percival aided him in securing a charter for the proposed college and acted with William Belitha, Stephen Hales, Robert Hales, and the Reverend Thomas Bray as a member of a trusteeship for disposing of subscriptions raised for the college.[21] Students of Georgia history will recognize in this a suggestion of the pattern to be used a few years later in founding a new colony.

Marriage was a subject of great interest to Percival. In 1708 one of his cousins, Helena Le Grand, recommended to him a young lady as suitable for a wife. He did not like her, however, because she had red hair. In writing to this cousin he set forth six desirable qualities in "a complete wife," namely, good nature, beauty, sense, breeding, birth, and fortune. He set least store on fortune and birth, though he did not despise these qualities. He had particular reason to desire a beautiful wife because, as he put it, "I love home, and intend to be furiously constant."[22]

June 20, 1710, when 27 years old, Percival married Catherine, eldest daughter of Sir Philip Parker, Baronet. Her intellectual interests were similar to his, and the marriage was a happy one. Their first child, John, heir to the family estate and titles, was born a year after the marriage. In all they had seven children, but four of them died in infancy. John was the only son to survive. His sisters were Catherine and Helena.[23]

In 1711 and again in 1713, Percival sat in the Irish Parliament, but most of his time was still spent in England. He served in the procession attending George I from his landing at Greenwich to St. James' Palace in his rank as privy councillor.[24] The

new King, desirous of securing the attachment of men of estate,
not only continued Percival as a privy councillor, but made him
Baron Percival of Burton, a rank that admitted him to a seat
among the peers of Ireland. Eight years later, in December,
1722, he was made Viscount Percival of Kanturk. Earlier that
same year the Prince of Wales had served as a surety at the
baptism of his son George.[25] Literary contemporaries were Addi-
son, Steele, and Pope. Some of the correspondence between Percival and Alexander Pope is still preserved.[26] With interest in
politics, religion, literature, philosophy, art, music, and drama,
these years of Percival's middle life were happy ones. His greatest care stemmed from the ill health of his wife. For years she
suffered recurrently from cholic. Months spent at Bath, Spa,
and other famous watering places had little favorable effect.
Laudanum was the only drug that gave even temporary relief.
One physician, Dr. Herman Boerhave, prescribed "constant exercise on horseback."[27] This, like other remedies, was ineffective. But that Lady Percival's illness was not wholly confining
is shown by the fact she and Sir John spent the winter of 1725-
26 in Paris and visited The Hague the following spring.[28] In
1727 both Lord and Lady Percival and seventeen of their do-
mestics suffered from a severe fever.[29]

In the election of the first English Parliament under George I
(in 1727), Percival was elected a member of the House of Commons from Harwich, in Essex. The borough had less than thirty
voters, but the election cost Percival £800.[30] He was a friend
of both Sir Robert Walpole, Prime Minister, and his brother,
Horace Walpole, also a member of Parliament. Percival's brother-
in-law, Sir Philip Parker, was also a member of the House of
Commons. In most matters Percival supported the Government.
He did not speak often, but went to great pains to record in
his diary what other members said in debate.

Percival used his influence both in Parliament and in the
Government to promote Irish interests. In opposing the English
tax on Irish wool in 1731, he said: "It is the essential mark of
a free people that no taxes should be laid but by a nation's own
representatives."[31] The occasion of the marriage of the Princess
Royal to the Prince of Orange in 1733 brought forth a prolonged
and heated debate in Court circles on the station to be occupied
by Irish peers in the royal procession. There had been examples
of Irish peers taking precedence in England next after English

peers of their own rank and before English peers of inferior rank; but on this occasion the Irish peers got wind of a "conspiracy" to leave them out of the ceremony. At a meeting of eight Irish Lords present in London, Percival was selected to present a memorial to the King asking that the Irish be given their proper rank in the procession.[32] Preparations for the marriage were too far advanced to permit any changes. In indignation, the Irish peers stayed at home and left empty the box reserved for them in the chapel when the wedding ceremony took place.[33] Afterwards the King took steps to restore the rights of the Irish peers. At the funeral of Queen Caroline in 1737, Percival had his station as Earl in the procession, and his eldest son had a place with the eldest sons of Earls, before English Barons. The same was true at the marriage of Princess Mary to the Prince of Hesse in 1740.[34]

Percival was a favorite in Court circles. The King spoke to him almost every time he attended a levee, and from time to time he was granted a private audience.[35] The Queen was drawn to him from their common literary interest. She sought his aid in inducing Dr. Peter Francis Courayé to make a French translation of Thuanus's Latin history of his times. She read Percival's religious tracts, and took pleasure in his printed books of heads.[36] On April 21, 1733, the Prince and Princess went "to dine and pass the day at Charlton," Percival's country home. Catherine, Percival's elder daughter, danced at Court on the Queen's birthday in 1732, and was complimented by both the Queen and Princesses upon her clothes, above all her jewels, "which were some of the finest there."[37] In November, 1732, Percival suggested to Lord Grantham that if the King would advance him to the rank of Earl his children would marry better.[38] In this he also enlisted the support of Robert Walpole. The honor was conferred on August 5 of the following year.[39] Percival used his influence not only to advance his personal interests, but also to secure government jobs and financial benefits for numerous friends.[40]

Percival usually went to bed at ten o'clock and got up at four. He spent the winter months at his home on Pall Mall and the summer at Charlton, only a few hours drive from London. In the fall he and his family usually had a vacation at Bath. Friends for dinner was a daily affair, and some stayed at Charlton for the summer.[41]

Despite a busy life, Percival spent many evenings in his study, and the amount of writing he did was extraordinary. His diary is a masterpiece, constituting the source *par excellence* on Georgia's early history.[42] Numerous pamphlets that he wrote dealing with religion and politics were published anonymously.[43]

While a patron of all the fine arts, Percival was most interested in music. Reference has already been made to the excessive expense occasioned by his musical entertainments while a student at Oxford. We know that he took part in musical performances while on a grand tour of the Continent in his youth. His love of music continued throughout life.[44] On February 27, 1731, at the opera he sat by Lord Baltimore, proprietor of Maryland, who told him that the American colonists were "in a miserable condition, and in a few years will set up for themselves purely from the hardships put upon them. That in New England alone, there is a militia of fifteen thousand foot and three thousand horse, which all the power of England will not in case of defection be able to reduce, and then if we succeeded the planters would all retire, but they would perhaps throw themselves under the protection of the French, and so we should for ever lose our interest and consequently our trade. . . ."[45]

In 1732, when forty-nine years old, he was a member of the Monday Music Club and the Thursday Vocal Music Society. On several occasions he left other members of the House of Commons debating in order to attend a music club meeting. On Friday nights bi-weekly during his residence in London he had a concert at his Pall Mall home, attended by from fifteen to twenty guests. Musicians at his concert on March 9, 1733, consisted of eight violinists (including Percival's brother), two harpsichordists, and three singers (Signor Arrigoni and Percival's two daughters).[46]

A deep religious faith led Percival to take an active part in promoting the Christian religion. On Sundays he attended public worship both morning and evening, and sometimes recorded the content of sermons in his diary.[47] Bishop Berkeley was perhaps his closest friend, and both with him and other friends religious matters constituted a frequent topic of conversation. In 1731 Percival was elected a vestryman of St. James's Parish, a position in which he rendered faithful service.[48] The following year he was selected a trustee for building a new church at Woolwich.[49]

Percival was grieved by the immorality of the Prince in seducing many women and in having a child by a chambermaid.[50] When his own son returned home from Ireland in April, 1732, Percival took pride in presenting him at Court and in introducing him to the speaker of the House of Commons and other men of influence. But a showdown came three days later when an account arrived from Ireland disclosing that the son had spent £1,930 in eleven months. This, wrote Percival, was "a lesson to me for the future, never to trust the discretion of young men when left to themselves, let them promise ever so fair. I immediately put him to an allowance of 300l a year . . . which is enough for him, his man, and his horse (living with me), for all reasonable and handsome expenses. The forfeiture of his character by the ill company he must have kept to squandor so much money away in that cheap country, and my disappointment in him, who I proposed to confide in and trust all things to as my second self, has sunk deep and preys on my spirits. . . ."[51]

A week later in talking with the Queen, Percival spoke of the "cheating and overreaching our neighbors . . . occasioned by riches, trade, and the great increase of the city. . . ." "May be," replied the Queen, "you are for reducing people to poverty to make them honest." "Not so," replied Percival, "but great wealth occasions luxury, and luxury extravagance, and extravagance want, and want knavery. . . . It were better if riches were more evenly divided."[52] Later in the year Percival observed to the Prince that the pleasure of his life "lay in little things." This is borne out by the joy that he took in observing the birthdays of members of his family, comforting sick friends, searching about town for a piece of music wanted by a friend, securing free postage for a religious magazine, and aiding numerous charities. But his pleasure in little things did not prevent him from envisioning major reforms. In talking with the King on March 31, 1732, he commented upon the injustices arising from the rigidity of the common law, and said it seemed "a contradiction that law and equity should be different." "It would" he observed, "be the glory of his Majesty's reign if three or four learned lawyers had great allowances made them to neglect their practice for some few years and apply themselves wholly to reforming the law."[53]

In analyzing his character, it should be noted that Percival, while intelligent, kind, and noble, was pompous and egotistical. He lived in splendor and liked for the world to know it. To illustrate, in setting out for Bath in August, 1730, he records: "Our number was my wife and I, her maid, my gentleman, two footmen, a helper, coachman, and postillion, six coach horses and three saddle ones."[54] And time after time he records that at levee he was one of the few persons to whom the King spoke. Whether he had race prejudices personally is not clear, but he opposed letting Jews into Georgia.[55] An excessive concern for his honor weakened his political strength. He felt that Sir Robert Walpole broke a bargain with him in the fall of 1733 concerning the election of the mayor of Harwich. To show the voters there that he was still first in favor with the Government, he demanded that Walpole dismiss certain officers for having voted the wrong way, with the understanding that they should be reemployed upon his forgiveness and intervention in their behalf. Failing in this, he openly showed coolness toward both Sir Robert and his brother, Horace Walpole, and aired his grievance to all his friends.[56]

A detailed account of the part Percival played in establishing the colony of Georgia would fill a full length book; only a few general statements are possible here. Credit for the idea of founding the colony and for setting it up has rightfully been given to Oglethorpe. Yet Percival's aid and influence were indispensable. Dr. Arthur Percival Newton, editor of the *Calendar of State Papers* for the period, puts it this way: "The most significant happening during the year [1732] was, of course, the founding of Oglethorpe's new settlement in the southern part of South Carolina, the real Georgia. The negotiations between the Board of Trade and the promoters, led by Oglethorpe but usually working under Lord Percival's name, had been going on since 1730. . . ."[57] That the *Acts of the Privy Council* record the petition for the charter of Georgia as coming from Lord Percival, the Hon. Edward Digby, "and others" does not hide the fact, shown by an abundance of evidence in other sources, that Oglethorpe was the real leader in securing the charter, but the fact that he worked so often under Percival's name shows how greatly he relied upon the influence and prestige of the latter.

Oglethorpe first mentioned his plan to Percival on February 13, 1730. A few weeks later he kept Percival three hours in explaining it. Percival approved from the beginning, and soon began an active collaboration. The nucleus of the Georgia Trustees was a group of friends of Oglethorpe and Percival in the House of Commons. The long delay in securing the charter arose from the fact that the Government's policy of the period favored concentration of colonial authority in the Crown and frowned upon private charters. It was largely because a colony in the Georgia region was needed for military purposes and the plan promoted by Oglethorpe promised to secure it without expense to the Government that a charter was eventually granted to the Trustees. Percival attended a hundred meetings and talked to practically everyone in the Government concerned, from the King and Prime Minister on down, before the charter was eventually approved in 1732. In it he was named as first president of the Georgia Corporation. He took the oath of office on July 7, and in the weeks that followed swore in the other Trustees.[58]

Raising funds through contributions was the chief objective set by the Trustees for the first year. Percival was at Bath in October, 1732, when he learned through Thomas Coram of Oglethorpe's decision to set out for Georgia with a hundred colonists. He was back in London on October 28. At a meeting of the Trustees on November 4, some resolutions concerning the government of Georgia were passed, but as Percival records it in his diary, "we were not particular in establishing the constitution, because till we come to that the laws of England take place."[59] Three days later Percival bade farewell to Oglethorpe who was leaving for Gravesend, whence the *Ann* was to sail.

 The success of the new colony depended as much upon the work of the Trustees in England as it did upon the adventure of Oglethorpe and his little band of settlers. Percival attended board meetings regularly, insisted that proper records be kept, aided in the selection of new settlers to be sent over, and sought in every way to promote Georgia interests. Although the impression was at one time prevalent that Georgia was founded largely as a colony for imprisoned debtors, no committee ever visited the prisons to select Georgia colonists, and not a dozen persons who had been in prison for debt ever went to Georgia.[60] Percival described the settlers of Georgia who came from England as belonging to the "middle poor." He kept in longhand a list of the settlers with thumbnail descriptions.[61]

Raising funds was one of the ways in which Percival aided Georgia. At meeting after meeting he reported gifts from his friends for the colony, and it was he who induced such influential men as the Earl of Shaftesbury, the Earl of Tryconnel, and Lord Viscount Limerick to become Trustees of Georgia. He organized support for Georgia in the House of Commons, and got Lord Jekyl to present the petition in 1733 that brought the first £10,000 support from the Government. A few weeks afterwards Lord Jekyl himself donated £500 and Lady Jekyl £100. Nine-tenths of the £154,000 spent by the Trustees on Georgia during the twenty years of their control came through parliamentary appropriations, and Percival was the chief figure in securing these appropriations.[62] After 1733 he was no longer a member of the House of Commons, but he managed to be present when bills appropriating money for Georgia were up for consideration.[63] The arguments used to advantage in securing the parliamentary support were, first, the military strength that the new colony would add to the empire, and, second, the economic benefit that would arise from the culture of wine, silk, and other needed products. With the passing of years, the latter point lost most of its force, and the only convincing argument for the support of the colony left to the Trustees was that Georgia constituted "the Southern Frontier of his Majesty's Dominions in North America."[64]

When Oglethorpe returned to England in 1734 with Tomo-Chi-Chi and eight other Indians, Percival entertained them at Charlton.[65] He described the Indians' clothes as "fantastic," but his relations with them were cordial. Everyone was pleased by the ability of little Tooanahowi to recite the Lord's Prayer both in English and his native tongue. Tomo-Chi-Chi said that he would get a ribbon and hang "at his breast next his heart" the gilt carved tobacco box that Percival gave him.[66]

Oglethorpe was negligent in writing to the Trustees. James Vernon approached Percival in March, 1734, complaining "of the neglect Mr. Oglethorpe shows in not corresponding with us frequently, and thereby keeping us in great ignorance of his proceedings in Georgia and the state of the Colony there, he not having writ to us since December last, and never once in any full and satisfactory manner, though by all accounts from thence writ occasionally by others he is very indefatigable in the settlement of the Colony."[67] Ten days later the Trustees' Committee of Correspondence drew up a letter to Oglethorpe embodying this complaint, and asked him to find a suitable person to correspond with the Trustees, and to assure such person of a fair recompense. Oglethorpe never complied with this request, and his own failure to write fully was to remain a standing complaint raised against him by the Trustees.

Finally despairing of ever getting satisfactory reports from Oglethorpe, the Trustees determined in 1737 to send William

Stephens as "Secretary for the Affairs of the Trust within the Province of Georgia." One reason for the selection of Stephens was the fact that Percival found the journal that Stephens had kept while in South Carolina in the employ of Colonel Horsey to be "excellent." "We shall have from him by every ship an account of the state and transactions of the Colony [of Georgia]," wrote Percival.[68] Stephens was directed, among other things, to take a census, give an account of the number of forts and their strength, report upon the behavior of the people toward the magistrates, send an account of the cultivation of various crops, tell whether the people frequented divine worship, and to urge the other officials to send their reports to the Trustees.

The Trustees, always eager and at times pathetic in their appeals for information, derived more satisfaction from the diary, or *Journal*, as it is called,[69] which Stephens kept than from any other source. He knew the views of the Trustees on land tenure, Negroes, and rum, and was anxious to present the state of the colony in the best light possible; hence he directed his reports toward justifying the policy of the Trustees rather than giving an impartial account of the actual situation.[70] Percival encouraged Stephens in his work.[71]

Considerable friction developed between the Georgia Trustees and Oglethorpe when he established forts below the Altamaha River, and after 1741 the Trustees largely ignored him. Oglethorpe had for years been primarily engaged in military affairs, and was responsible for England's success in the War of Jenkins' Ear. With the spreading of the war into a general European conflict, in 1743 Oglethorpe left Georgia, never to return. The year before (on July 7, 1742), Percival had resigned from the Common Council of Trustees, as he said, "partly by reason of my ill health and partly from observing the ill behavior of the Ministry and Parliament with respect to the Colony."[72] The discontent of the Georgia colonists must also have been a discouragement to Percival. They were soon disillusioned about Georgia's being a Garden of Eden: the sun was hot, and there was malaria in the swamps; they had no success in producing silk or wine. How could they compete with South Carolina where slaves were allowed in the production of rice and lumber? Up rose a mighty protest which dinned the ears of the Trustees. In 1741 the malcontents sent Thomas Stephens, the wayward son of President William Stephens, as colonial agent, and he appealed directly to the King and to Parliament. He clamored so loudly against the policy of the Trustees that they had the House of Commons carry out an investigation which found Stephens's charges to be "false, scandalous and malicious."[73] Apparently Stephens had sought to lay upon Percival blame for the ills of the Georgia settlers.[74]

The system of land tenure is a conspicuous instance of failure by the Trustees, despite heroic efforts and idealistic motives, to adopt measures suited to the actual conditions in the colony. In consideration of the necessity for military defense, the nature of the colonists, and the possibility of profiteering, the Trustees early decided that only fifty acres should be granted to the charity settlers. The charter itself limited grants to five hundred acres for any one person. The fifty-acre grants were more like military fiefs than true possessions, as they involved military service in time of war and guard duty in time of peace. The land granted, either to charity settlers or to adventurers who should pay their own expenses and bring over servants, could be neither sold nor mortgaged, and could be inherited only by a male heir. There were no less than nine distinct grounds for forfeiture, including failure to occupy the land and plant a specified number of mulberry trees for each acre cleared.[75] Inasmuch as the grants were gifts, and could be made on such conditions as the Trustees pleased, no man, it was felt, had a right to complain. "The Board will always do what is right," declared Percival, "and the people should have confidence in us."[76] The Trustees were indeed lenient in the enforcement of their rules, always making special concessions in individual cases where hardships were involved; yet the severe letter of the law drove away many would-be settlers and caused constant complaint in the colony.[77] The regulations for land tenure, adopted from time to time and frequently revised, were never incorporated into any formal law, with the result that great uncertainty always troubled the colonists lest they lose their tenure. One of them is said to have remarked that "the whole laws consist of 'tails' and 'males,' and that all the lawyers in London could not make them plain to a common man."[78]

In disapproval of the Trustees' policy, after his return to England, Oglethorpe seldom attended their meetings. After 1743 Percival also ceased to be a leader in Georgia affairs, though he was more active than Oglethorpe. The two founders of Georgia remained personal friends.[79]

Both Percival and his wife were often sick. The cholic that bothered Lady Percival in earlier years continued in the 1730's and 1740's. Percival visited a physician for relief from rheumatic pains in April, 1731, and he was often confined at home with a cold.[80] Both he and his wife were "cupped" now and then. A painful injury from hitting his shin against a chair at Court kept Percival at home most of the month of November, 1733, and during this period of confinement the rift between him and Robert Walpole grew apace.

As early as June, 1732, Percival told Walpole that he did not intend to run himself in the next parliamentary election, but would seek to have his son elected from Harwich. Walpole soon learned that Percival's son talked too freely, but he did not openly oppose his election. But inasmuch as twelve of the twenty-odd voters in the borough of Harwich held government offices,[81] election without Walpole's assistance was well-nigh impossible. When Percival's candidate for mayor of Harwich was defeated by two votes in 1733, Percival was convinced that Walpole was opposed to his son's election; and in the parliamentary election of 1734, the son was defeated by a vote of 19 to 13. One of the voters was so elated at the outcome that he exclaimed: "Lord, now let Thy servant depart in peace, for mine eyes have seen Thy salvation."[82] At the election in 1741 Percival sought a happier hunting ground in which to pick up a parliamentary seat for his son. He thought he had well in hand the sixty voters of the borough of Haslemere, which had returned General Oglethorpe as one of its two representatives in the last two elections; but as the election drew nigh he found the opposition using funds freely and so many voters departing from the terms he had made with them that it was best for his son to withdraw. Soon after, however, his son was elected to fill a vacancy from Westminster, a post of greater honor as it represented some 6,000 voters.[83] By this time his son, married to Catherine, daughter of the Earl of Salisbury, was himself the father of two sons, John James and Cecil Parker.

After 1745 entries in Percival's diary became increasingly brief. His wife suffered from distressing headaches, and his own health failed rapidly. The diary ends abruptly with a two-line entry for August 30, 1747: "We returned from Tunbridge to Charlton and found no good from the waters." Percival died on May 1, 1748, and was buried at Erwarton, in Suffolk. He was survived by his wife, his son, and his daughter Catherine ("Kitty"), then a widow. Helena, his other daughter, who married Sir John Rawdon and was the mother of one son and four daughters, had died of consumption two years earlier. Few men have lived a fuller or nobler life than did John Percival.

HENRY ELLIS

BY W. W. ABBOT

HENRY ELLIS, an odd and rather wonderful Englishman, arrived in Georgia in 1757. For three years he was governor of the colony, leaving in 1760 never to return. This was but an interlude, and a short one, in an extraordinarily varied and colorful career. Yet Ellis's stay in Georgia is what makes him something more than simply an eighteenth-century English gentleman of rare charm and intelligence. For one time in a long life, the gifted dilettante was faced with a situation which demanded the full play of his powers. The result was that a really first-rate talent for politics and diplomacy bloomed briefly in Georgia. It was Ellis's skill as a politician and diplomat, and little else, that protected the southern flank of Britain's American empire in the last and the greatest of the French and Indian wars.

Brief though it was, Ellis's tenure as governor of Georgia also is an important chapter in the history of the state. The years 1757-60 were critical years. After nearly a quarter of a century, Georgia was still only a shallow beachhead tentatively edging its way into the wilderness south and west of Carolina. At the moment of Ellis's arrival, the colony, threatened by enemies on three sides and wracked by internal dissension, was falling apart. The new governor united the colony under his leadership, held its encircling enemies at bay, and for the first time set Georgia on the broad path to prosperity and growth. And this with no other advantage than imaginative statecraft.

The spectacle of Henry Ellis, the royal governor of the province, walking at midday along the sandy streets of Savannah during the unusually hot summer of 1758 with a thermometer dangling by a thread from his umbrella to the height of his nostrils, must have

W. W. Abbot is a member of the history faculty at the College of William and Mary.

lingered long in the memories of the Savannah townspeople.[1] The
perspiring governor was in fact only displaying for all to see certain facets of his personality — his avid curiosity, his lively and
lifelong interest in all natural phenomena, his passion for exact
scientific data, and, incidentally, his "rational, benevolent, and
pleasant" singularities in character.[2] In this instance, Ellis, an old
tropical hand, was astounded to discover from his thermometer
that it was "highly possible" that the inhabitants of Savannah
breathed "a hotter air than any other people on the face of the
earth."[3]

Governor Ellis had been indulging this penchant for observing
the oddities of nature in foreign places for many years before
coming to Georgia. Born in 1721, he ran away from the home of
his father, "Francis Ellis of Monoghan," in his early youth and
went to sea. (Apparently young Henry, a second son, found the
prospects of sharing in his father's "considerable fortune" not
enough to outweigh his father's "ill-judged severity.") For a number of years Henry Ellis led the life of a sailor. His whereabouts
were unknown to his family during this time, but eventually a
reconciliation between father and son took place. The elder Ellis
thereafter actively promoted the career of his son and at his death
left to him his entire estate, which made the younger Ellis a
wealthy man.[4]

Before he was thirty-five years old, Henry Ellis had seen much
of the world. Although most of his voyages were to the tropics,
three to equatorial Africa and three to the West Indies, his most
famous was to the polar regions. In 1746, Ellis, evidently once
again enjoying the patronage of his father, returned to England
from Italy just in time to learn that an expedition was on the point
of sailing for Hudson's Bay in search of a northwest passage to
Asia. Hearing of his interest in the project, the magnates who were
financing the voyage sent for Ellis and offered him command of
one of the ships, even though a captain had already been chosen.
Ellis refused the appointment because of his insufficient experience with "Northern Seas and Northern Climates" and, instead,
became a patron of the expedition and a passenger in one of the
ships. The explorers failed to discover the Northwest Passage, but
the expedition provided Ellis with the opportunity of writing a
book, on the strength of which he was made a Fellow of the Royal
Society. In his book, Ellis takes note of everything: of the wind,
waves, tides, current, ice, of the stars and planets, of the tempera-

ture — always the temperature — and of the birds and beasts as well
as of fish. And he speculates about everything that he sees. His
deductions and conclusions are always logical, plausible, stimulat-
ing, and delivered with clarity and pungency. Unfortunately they
are nearly always mistaken.[5]

A decade later, in Georgia, Ellis applied these same powers of
observation to the political scene. Fortunately, in this instance
the conclusions that he drew with his usual logic and imagination
were nearly always correct. He was a better politician than scientist,
although to both pursuits he brought pace and style. When Governor Ellis fled the Georgia climate in the fall of 1760, discouraged
and in failing health, he performed one last service for the colony
he had served so well. Alarmed by the turn of events in the southern provinces, he "undertook with infinite hazard in the depth of
Winter and on board a small Shallop, a voyage to New York" for
the purpose of urging General Jeffrey Amherst to send assistance.
After seeing Amherst, Ellis sailed for England and arrived there in
late spring, 1761.[6] He immediately learned that the King had made
him governor of Nova Scotia. Since for some time to come Ellis
was to lead the life of an invalid, maintaining that his arduous
labors as governor of Georgia and the insufferable heat of that
place had ruined his health, he almost certainly left the administration of Nova Scotia to his lieutenant governor. At any rate,
Governor Ellis retired from active government service in 1763,
making "his quietus" by securing "a patent for life of Secretary,
Clerk of the Council, Register, and Commissary of all Canada, and
of Provost-marshall of the four new islands."[7] The duties attached
to these posts were performed by deputies. His public service was
thereafter confined to the penning of letters full of good advice to
the men in the government charged with the direction of colonial
policy.[8]

Immediately upon retirement, Ellis began to allow his life to
take up the rhythm of the man of wealth whose delicate health and
unmarried status leave him free to seek his own comfort and
pleasure where and how he will, with an eye only to the state of
his digestion. Even here, Ellis's instinct for style does not desert
him. Good taste, a perfect sense of timing, and a lively intelligence
save him from either grossness or fatuity. To a life of self-indul-
gent idleness, he gave a certain distinction and elegance. Usually
residing during the summer months in London rather than upon
his estate in Ireland, Ellis each year would set sail for France as

soon as London began to settle down for the winter cold. Once he had paid his annual visit to his famous friend Voltaire, he always turned southward and headed for the warm shores of the Mediterranean, usually going either to Marseilles or to Pisa. Amiable and eccentric, Ellis in time got to be "Known and expected like a bird of passage" along his route through France.[9] Then, in early spring, before returning once again to London, he would make his visit to the Spa in order to enjoy the salutary effects of the baths.

A delightful conversationalist, Ellis became a famous host, known for his "unlimited hospitality" and the great "variety of delicacies" his table afforded. Yet, according to one of his visitors at Marseilles in 1786, Ellis himself adhered "strictly to a singular Kind of Epicurean temperance. . . . His drink is pure water mixed with a small quantity of the richest, most costly, and cordial wines. His diet is very abstemious, yet luxurious, especially in fish dressed with all the ingredients and arts of the nicest cookery."[10] In his last years the old gentleman was marooned in Italy by the wars of the French Revolution where he was an interested observer of Bonaparte's Italian campaigns; but he was unhappy to be separated from his London friends and to be deprived of the special brands of tea of which he was fond.[11] Ellis died in Naples on January 21, 1800.[12]

Henry Ellis's short moment in the mainstream of eighteenth-century life had begun nearly a half century before when on January 27, 1757, he landed in Charleston, South Carolina. He had decided to stop there instead of going directly to Savannah because he was anxious to get "advice and information" from William Lyttleton, the governor of South Carolina, before plunging into the bitter political controversy which he knew awaited him in Georgia. Always alert to exploit every possibility in a situation, he took this opportunity to conciliate the South Carolina governor and to arrange for a regular correspondence with him to assure that in the future the two colonies would work together in harmony.[13]

The weather being bad, it was February 11 before Ellis left Charleston for Beaufort, where he embarked in one of the South Carolina scout boats on the fifteenth. On the next day, Governor Ellis sailed past the crude lighthouse on Tybee Island into the river and on up toward the capital at Savannah.[14] Savannah was a desolate little town perched on a sandy bluff above the river. A few hundred people lived there in frame dwellings. No wall or fortification stood between the houses and the pine forest which pressed in from three sides, cutting off the breeze on sultry summer days.[15] Unprepossessing as it was, Savannah was the metropolis of the colony. To the south along the coast, Oglethorpe's Frederica was already deserted;[16] Darien and Midway were as yet hardly towns. A short distance up the river from Savannah a congregation of Salzburgers lived in a place called Ebenezer, which was little more than a cluster of farm lots hemmed into the mud bottoms of the Savannah River and Ebenezer Creek by the ubiquitous pine barrens. The town of Augusta, farther up the river, at the fall line, consisted mainly of a ramshackle fort used as an Indian trading post.[17] For the rest, the forest lay undisturbed except here and there a clearing where a farmer with his family tilled the soil and during the winter months fed livestock.

Georgia, a tiny remote outpost of the British Empire, was sunk into premature decay. The inhabitants, strung as they were for hundreds of miles along the coast and up the river, numbered hardly six thousand men, women, and children, black and white.[18] And more were leaving than were coming in. Of the seven or eight hundred white men living in the colony, a small number had begun to build their fortunes by acquiring land suitable for rice culture along the streams in the tidewater, and two or three had made commercial connections in Charleston or in England which in a short time would make them prosperous merchants. But most were simply small farmers barely subsisting on the livestock, food crops, and game which their farms and the adjacent woods afforded.

In the winter of 1757, with Britain facing defeat in her great struggle with the French Empire, the fear of Indian attack hung like a pall over the little colony. To the north, to the west, and to the south hovered thousands of Creek and Cherokees warriors, who could expect aid from the Spanish of St. Augustine and the French at Mobile in any move to discomfit the English settlers of Georgia. Despite its obvious peril, Georgia, as Governor Ellis soon discovered, was practically defenseless. The colony was without usable forts or fortifications of any kind. A troop of Rangers and a few hundred militiamen, untrained, poorly armed, and for the most part ready to flee at the first sign of hostilities, stood between the colony and destruction.[19]

To make matters worse, the colony was torn with bitter political strife. Ellis's predecessor, the first royal governor of Georgia, one John Reynolds, a captain in the British navy, had steered a crooked course between stupidity and corruption while in the colony. Not only had the ill-tempered Reynolds failed to take any effective action to strengthen Georgia, but he had compounded his difficulties by unnecessarily offending the neighboring Indian chiefs, alienating most of the leading men of the colony, and by feuding with the governor of South Carolina. Infuriated by this mixture of arrogance and stupidity, the Council at length sent one of its members to London to demand Governor Reynolds's recall. He countered by going all out to secure control of the Lower House of the Georgia legislature. His political manager, William Little, the governor's office-laden private secretary, was entirely successful in filling the House of Assembly with friends of the administration and was himself elected its speaker. Reynolds and Little hoped to destroy the new governor by means of the hostile Assembly they were leaving behind when Reynolds returned to London to face the charges of the Georgia Council.

When he disembarked at Savannah, Governor Ellis was met on the bluff by "loud Huzza's" from all but a very few of the inhabitants. Atop the enormous bonfire which burned that night while the town celebrated was placed an effigy of "a certain Tyrant in himself, a Promoter of it in his Master, and his greatest Enemy" — Speaker Little, Reynolds's crony.[20] Ellis took his oath of office, ordered all officials to carry on as usual,[21] and, "finding a recess would be agreeable at this Season of the Year," thought it "prudent" to adjourn the legislature immediately.[22] After he had removed two of Reynolds's most recent nominees to the Council with "such apparent justice & impartiality that no umbrage was taken even by these Gentlemen,"[23] Ellis played a waiting game while the storm raged about him. The men who had lost out under Reynolds, hungry for revenge and for office, set up a clamor for the new governor to turn the old lot out. Ellis listened; he sympathized and soothed. He took the measure of his would-be friends and of his political opponents. From what he read and heard, he learned and began to understand. But he did nothing; he promised nothing. To his superiors in London he wrote:

Sensible of my own inexperience & of the violence of such Councils fearful of being misled & aiming rather at healing the wounds and extinguishing the flame of Party than stirring it anew, I forebore making any material alteration until I should be qualified to Act from observation & experience in order that the Changes I shall then make may rather be attributed to my own judgement than to the advice of designing and interested people. — This suspense will give time for mens passions to subside & for truth to appear through the cloud of party prejudice that at present obscures it.[24]

While friend and foe alike were waiting for the new governor to show his hand, Ellis was taking a hard look at Georgia and analyzing what he saw. Immediately he perceived that the essential thing was to devise ways and means for bolstering the defenses of the colony.[25] On this, all else depended. Despite distractions of every sort, Ellis never once forgot that every consideration, no matter how attractive or desirable, had always to give way before the great need for building up the defensive strength of the province.

But there was one problem even more immediate. The political tangle left by Reynolds had to be unraveled. As Ellis was fully aware, he had first to gain the support of the inhabitants before he could do much toward reviving the colony. Even the most strenuous efforts of all the settlers would hardly suffice to make Georgia strong, small and poor as it was. He wisely let time work for him in erasing the passions and bitter feelings which Reynolds had left behind, but soon he began unobtrusively and quietly a campaign to reconcile the differences which split the colony into rival factions and to bring the supporters of Reynolds and Little into his camp. Using restraint, treating all fairly and without prejudice, advocating nothing but what was obviously for the general good, he rallied the colony to his support with a deft and sure political touch. Before summer was far gone, harmony reigned.

Ellis quickly grasped the elemental political fact, which had eluded Reynolds, that the Council was the governor's natural ally in colonial politics.[26] Made up of the most substantial men in the colony and appointed on the recommendation of the governor, the Council offered a substantial foundation on which the governor could build his political power. The elected House of Assembly could be courted and bent to the governor's will but, because it had another master, could never be completely depended upon.

From the first, Ellis treated the members of his Council with great deference and respect. He was meticulous in consulting them on all matters of public interest, not only to win their support but because he recognized their superior experience in colonial affairs and valued their advice. By keeping the Council busy with affairs of state during the spring of 1757, Governor Ellis filled its members with a gratifying sense of their own importance.[27] If this unwonted attention were not enough to win over the wariest councilor, Ellis's approach to the Indian problem secured the enthusiastic approval of these old frontiersmen and made of them Ellis's warmest supporters.

While wooing the Council, Governor Ellis was also patching up the weaknesses in the position left him, intentionally or otherwise, by his predecessor. He set out to regain those powers and prerogatives of the governor which Reynolds had allowed to slip away in his open bid for popular favor during the last days of his administration.[28] The concession made by Reynolds to the Lower House of the legislature which Ellis was least willing to countenance was its assumption of the right to audit and pay the public accounts.[29] Not one to make a frontal assault when indirection would serve, Ellis, calling the Council together while the legislature was still recessed, told it that Speaker Little's policy of playing favorites in paying accounts had sorely damaged public credit and suggested that the Council advertise for all holders of public accounts to present them for payment.[30] With this one stroke, he repaired the colony's credit, pleased its creditors, and restored the disbursement of public funds to the governor and Council — and all without any overt challenge to the House.[31] Ellis was also displeased to learn that Reynolds had gone so far as to request the House of Assembly to nominate the new Justices of the Peace.[32] Consequently in March he issued a new commission of the peace, adding new names but carefully including most of the old ones.[33] By this, Ellis pleased some while offending few, if any, and effectively reasserted the governor's right to commission justices without consulting the Assembly.

Ellis complained bitterly that Reynolds before his departure had seen to it that "every publick Office that either existed or were likely to be established, were filled with his Creatures,"[34] even to the staffing of two troops of Rangers which existed only on paper.[35] On May 5, 1757, he tells how he got around this in the case of the militia officers:

I have just been Regimenting the Militia. . . . This step afforded me an opportunity of gratifying some worthy men, who are vain of Military Titles, of putting the Militia in a condition of being useful & I may add of establishing a right that Mr. Reynolds intended giving up to the Assembly that of appointing the Officers.[36]

And the officers were indebted for their commissions to Governor Ellis, not Reynolds. William Little's impending departure did leave vacant a place on the General Court, and, although Ellis distrusted the two remaining justices and suspected that they, with Little, were in collusion with the notorious Bosomworths who were seeking judicial validation of their claim to three of the islands off the Georgia coast, he chose not to disturb them.[37] Instead, in view of the "Business of great Importance to come before the ensuing Court," Ellis persuaded the Council that not one but three new justices should be appointed, thereby giving his appointees a majority on the bench.[38]

By far the knottiest problem left Ellis by Reynolds and Little was the hostility of their hand-picked House of Assembly. Ellis became acutely aware on the very day of his arrival at Savannah that he would have to be "very circumspect" in dealing with the Lower House of the legislature.[39] A "Private Society" greeted him on the bluff with a paper asking him to dissolve the Assembly, and he soon learned that plans were afoot in every district of the colony to forward similar addresses to the governor.[40] Simultaneously he found out that the Assembly "at the instance of Mr Little their Speaker" intended to address him in such a manner as would put him in a false position should he choose to call for new elections. It was at this point that Ellis decided it would be "prudent" to adjourn the Assembly for a month, and he found it "expedient" to extend the prorogations through the spring.[41]

Early in March, while Ellis was busy writing a long letter to England giving his first impressions of Georgia, William Little called on the new governor and, "among other things," dared him to dissolve the Assembly, declaring it would be useless "as he had taken measures to have the same men rechosen."[42] The governor refused to be smoked out by the taunts of the speaker but continued to gather together the strings of his power against the day when he would have to have a showdown with Mr. Little's Assembly.

Ellis pondered whether to form a new legislature, which certainly would be easier to handle, or to stick with the old and try to win it to his side. His policy during these crucial first three or four months was clearly designed not to build up a following

which could overpower the Reynolds faction, but rather to conciliate the men indebted to Reynolds so that the whole colony
would join with Governor Ellis in working out its problems. He
looked on Little's friends in the Assembly as ordinary men, "flexi-
ble weak & ignorant," but "Not dishonest in their private characters but easy credulous & equally disposed to good or evil." The
only real fault that he could find with them was that they were
inclined to oppose him in order to justify "their friends lately in
power," which Ellis considered reasonable enough under the circumstances. He remained steadfast in his opinion that if he offered
only what was "most apparently for their own good," they would
prove "more tractable" than was generally imagined. "But if they
should be obstinate or fractiously inclined," he wrote, "I think a
way is to be found of getting rid of them without appearing to
act from resentments": he would make the formation of a new
legislature mandatory simply by ordering the wished-for division
of the colony into parishes.[43]

All during the spring of 1757, Ellis was taking "great pains" to
get acquainted with the people of the colony and mapping out his
"plan" of action to suit it to their "disposition."[44] By early May
he had decided to call the old legislature back into session on
June 16. Then it was that the details of Mr. Little's plot came
out into the open. When he departed for London late in May,
Little left with a local planter, Patrick Mackay, a letter for the
members of the Assembly giving them thinly disguised instructions to maintain their opposition to the Council and new governor at all costs while he was away.[45] The plan was for Mackay
to get Little's seat in the House where he would be elected speaker, and then head a junto to be formed for the sole purpose of
blocking anything Reynolds's successor should advocate. It was
expected that the disorders inevitably arising from the ensuing
stalemate would afford the legislature the occasion for petitioning
the King to restore Mr. Reynolds to office.[46] When Ellis heard
what was intended, he acted swiftly and effectively. With justified
satisfaction and a touch of arrogance Ellis tells how he put a stop
to this affair before it was well started:

This & other reasons determined me to discountenance his [Mackay's]
being elected, & suspend him from the Bench where he sat as senior
Justice. . . . These steps had all the effect I could wish . . . he lost the
election & is retired with disgust & disappointment to his plantation.[47]

With the defeat of Mackay all organized opposition to the new governor disappeared, never again to plague him as long as he stayed in Georgia. Hereafter the colonists, almost to a man, were Ellis men. Even the House of Assembly fell into line so completely that during its first session it often seemed to be vying with the Council to please the governor.

It is difficult to see how Ellis could have done better during his first months in Georgia. His political technique seems faultless. A keen sense of timing allowed him to act with an economy of motion that made every move count for much; an almost impersonal detachment enabled him to disarm his enemies without giving offense and to bare his fist only when policy, not personal pique, dictated. The smallness of the constituency does not alter the fact that a difficult and delicate situation had been handled with political artistry. Ellis could say of his accomplishments of the spring of 1757: " . . . by address, by bold, but honest arts, & by doing my duty in a way unusual here, I have at length been able to change the temper of my opponents to my wishes."[48]

This virtuoso performance gains meaning from the fact that behind the political maneuvers lay a purpose. During these early months Governor Ellis's mind was continually ranging over the possibilities open to him for giving new life and strength to a colony which had gained precious little of either in the past twenty-five years. Here too he moved slowly at the outset:

I have a variety of designs in my own mind which have for their object the utility and happiness of this Colony.—But perhaps it would be premature to enter upon them before I am qualified to judge of their practicability & whether they are well or ill adapted to our Circumstances.—This knowledge can only be derived from experience & that requires time.[49]

But Ellis was ready with his plan of attack when he called the legislature into session. The bills which he prepared for consideration were designed to blunt the three-pronged dilemma which had the colony pinned to the wall. Inadequate defenses, insufficient wealth, and too few settlers were keeping Georgia small, poor, and weak. Since the solution of each waited upon the solution of both the others, Ellis's legislative program was rather like a formula for lifting oneself by one's own bootstraps and was of necessity limited in its aims. Ellis for the next three years, using whatever came to hand, devoted his considerable energy, intelligence, and even a part of his personal fortune, to bringing to his colony more men, greater wealth, and a stronger defense.[50]

His first concern was to provide the inhabitants with some measure of security from Indian attack.

To this weakness & insecurity may in a great measure be imputed the little progress this Colony has made . . . for in a Country that is exposed to every kind of outrage & injustice within & to every sort of depredation & attack how can we expect that people will trust themselves or their property? Incessantly uneasy incessantly in alarm no person that has anything to lose or is exempt from the terrors of a Jail will come among us.[51]

Realizing that no funds could possibly be forthcoming for a military establishment in 1757, Governor Ellis made the ingenious proposal to the legislature that the labor traditionally given by all the inhabitants to road work be diverted to the building of wooden stockades at key spots about the colony to serve as strong points where the people could gather in time of danger.[52] The only fortification standing in Georgia at the time was the old fort at Augusta, which was in a state of such advanced decay that the guns had to be trundled out of the building on the King's birthday lest the firing should bring the structure's complete collapse.[53] In August and September, 1757, the men of the colony worked for twelve days putting a palisade around the town of Savannah and building one log fort to the north of Augusta and three south of Savannah. By the end of September all of the forts were completed or near completion, and Savannah's palisade was manned with old guns which had been dug up out of the sand on the bluff.[54]

Georgia, Ellis knew, could not place its main reliance for protection on the strength of its own arms, but he was unremitting in his labors to make the local defense establishment as strong as conditions would permit. Naturally he never ceased to importune British military authorities and the Board of Trade for troops and equipment; but, long before the legislature returned to Savannah, he was also working to enable Georgia to make some show of military power on its own. As a beginning he already had the troop of forty Rangers which Reynolds had recently raised, but no provision had been made for its support. Since the colony lacked the means for paying for such a force, Ellis had the choice of disbanding the company or of taking upon himself the responsibility for paying the troopers.[55] He chose to keep the Rangers; and by writing unauthorized drafts on the British commander in North America and then using every argument and stratagem to obtain payment, he held the troop together.[56] He also put all able-bodied men into a new militia organization and demanded equipment for them from Britain. When muskets arrived, he did not hestitate to issue them to the individual militiamen.[57]

Ellis's persistence in demanding that regular British troops be stationed in Georgia soon bore fruit. He announced to the Assembly in July that he had wrung a promise from the commanding officer of the King's forces in South Carolina for "a small Body of Troops" and that one hundred men would be sent if Georgia would agree to pay for their transport and provide weekly rations. Ignoring the Assembly's declaration that it would be utterly impossible for the colony to provide subsistence for such a body of men, Ellis gave instructions for the detachment to be sent ahead, which was done.[58]

With the arrival of the Virginia Blues, the governor might well have taken time out for self-congratulation. But as a matter of fact, he was discouraged. The defenses of the colony were still far from adequate, and he realized that he could proceed no further along these lines, however great the need, until he had induced new settlers to come in. Only an enlarged and productive population could provide the men and funds for further expanding the colonial defense establishment. These considerations made Ellis careful to set against the always urgent need for funds to build up the defenses of the colony the advantages of keeping taxes to a minimum so that the embryo merchant or planter could prosper, pay his creditors in South Carolina, and so increase the productivity and trade of the colony, which in turn would lead other men of means and ability to settle there. Then, in time, the day would come when Georgia would no longer have to cringe and tremble before its enemies. Consequently Ellis concluded that the welfare of the colony would be best served in the long run by his putting the prosperity of the inhabitants first, whenever the requirements of defense would possibly permit.[59]

Although determined to keep taxes low, Ellis knew the importance of placing public finance on as sound a footing as possible. The second request that he made of the legislature in the sum-

mer of 1757 was for it to provide for bridging the gap between
the public debt of £850 and the £260 in ordinary revenue, which
Reynolds' "improvident administration" had left him.[60] The
Assembly renewed the general tax on land and slaves at double
the old rate. Ellis, while admitting that even this would hardly
bring in more than £500, defended it as proof that there was,
"every disposition that could be wished in the people to answer
the most sanguine expectations, but they really are incapable
of doing more than they have done. . . ."[61] To aid the legislature
in making the annual tax levy, he instituted the practice of sub-
mitting to the House each year an estimate of expected expenditures, wisely leaving it to the representatives to decide each year
how heavy a tax rate the people could bear.

The legislature also passed in the summer of 1757 a bill providing for the printing and emission of £630 in paper currency.
This measure was designed to help refund the public debt, to
provide credit, and to put into circulation much needed currency. For years the unfavorable balance of trade against Georgia
and the payments made by many settlers in Georgia to creditors
in South Carolina had combined to drain off all of the colony's
specie. If the Assembly had not taken steps to provide some
means of exchange, it would have been next to impossible for
the colony to carry on business, public or private. On this, both
Governor Reynolds and Governor Ellis were agreed. However,
the Governor's Instructions specifically forbade him to allow the
printing of paper bills without the permission of the Board of
Trade, and the Board was not inclined to give its permission.
Although a bill passed in 1755 which put £7000 in paper currency into circulation had still not been approved, Ellis rescued
this currency from devaluation by accepting it in payment of
public fees. And he approved the new money bill.[62] When the
Board of Trade reprimanded Ellis for accepting the old bills as
legal tender and for permitting a new issue of paper money,[63] he
apologized, and then made a cogent argument in favor of paper
currency:

As the Money lent to the planters was at a low interest they found
their advantage in investing it in Negroes the labour of whom not
only served to improve the lands but added also to the export of
the province and thereby diminished the Balance of Trade against
it. And the Revenue arising from the Interest paid for the use of
that money enabled the Government to undertake several important

and necessary services without any additional burthen to the people.
—A burthen that they would have been still less able to bear had
they been deprived of the profit arising from the money lent them. . . .[64]

The money remained in circulation.

The third bill Ellis prepared for the Assembly of June, 1757,
was aimed directly at the problem of attracting settlers. It was
designed to draw into Georgia some of the less fortunate men
living in the colonies to the northward or on the islands of the
West Indies. In effect, it promised protection for any debtor from
his creditor if he could get across the Savannah River without
being caught, unless the creditor happened to be a South Carolinian.[65] Less fanciful were Ellis's effort to make good land available for newcomers. The securing of land grants was already easy
and simple. What Ellis feared was that it was so easy that a small
number of men would gradually build up enormous holdings.
He argued that the supply of good land was strictly limited by
the treaties with the Indians which confined the colony to the
tidelands and the environs of the Savannah River and that unless some land was reserved for new settlers, Georgia would never
have the white men needed for the defense of the frontier.[66]
After winning the Board's approval of an act declaring vacant
all old grants which had not been taken up,[67] Ellis continued to
insist that a limit should be placed on family holdings so that
frontier Georgia would become a colony of middle-sized farms
with a large white population instead of a colony of large plantations with a large slave population. The Board of Trade informed him that it was not interested in the size of the holdings but rather in their productivity. Ellis's reply attests to his
political sophistication and suggests a moral that rulers of an
empire might well ponder:

. . . that system of policy which may be proper for the middle provinces upon this Continent is not for those upon the frontier. —The
first object with the former is the increase of produce and extension
of Commerce. In the latter it should be security & defence. — The
former are secured from danger by their situation [;] the latter exposed to it from the same circumstance [.] the first might have more
indulgencies of one kind [;] the last more of another.—[68]

Thus it was that Governor Ellis set in motion his colonial
policy in 1757. His general approach was marked out in the legislation of that summer. For the next three years he pushed his

attack upon Georgia's dilemma on all three fronts. But Ellis knew full well that he was living in a fool's paradise with his projects and plans so long as the Indians might any day descend upon the settlements, murdering the unwary and sending the fainthearted flying for South Carolina. Unable to muster much military power or to rely on force alone to defend his province, the governor adopted the wiles of diplomacy to hold back the forces of the red men and to neutralize the influence of the Spanish and French in the area. Relations with the Indians absorbed most of his attention after 1757, and it was as a diplomat that Ellis made his most valuable contribution to the colony and found his greatest talent.

The *sine qua non* of Ellis's diplomacy was the retention of at least the outward forms of friendship between the Creek Indians and the English. By making great display of what little military strength the colony had and by encouraging the impression that the strength of South Carolina and the strength of Georgia were inseparable, he sought to persuade the Creeks of the foolhardiness of arousing the ire of the whites in Georgia. The annual allotment of presents for the Indians and the mutually profitable trade between the Creeks and the colonists he held out as the strongest inducements for them to continue on good relations with the English settlers. He realized that it would be useless or even dangerous for him to attempt to force the Creeks to break completely with the French,[69] but he never missed an opportunity to lessen the French influence in favor of the English, always picturing in the blackest terms French cruelty and French treachery as opposed to the kindness and good faith of the English.

As for his dealings with the Spanish, who had never been particularly successful in their relations with the Indians, Governor Ellis did his best to keep alive the "deep rooted aversion" felt by the Creeks for the men of Spain, all the while keeping up a ceremonious correspondence with the Spanish governor of Florida and maintaining a "discreet and very delicate conduct, always adapted to the circumstances" of the moment.[70] Any disagreement or misunderstanding arising between Creek and Cherokee he considered a boon, and he assiduously encouraged any quarrels within the tribes. The success of his policy is made manifest by the fact that Ellis was able to maintain such a fine balance that Georgia was never actually attacked while he was governor, even when the neighboring South Carolina frontier was laid waste by the Cherokees.

In the early fall of 1756, shortly before Ellis's arrival, Georgia had had an Indian scare occasioned by the murder of two Creeks by a group of white settlers living in the vicinity of Augusta. Everything was beginning to quiet down when Ellis took office; and as soon as the Indians got news that a new governor had come to Savannah, singly and in groups they began to drift into town to see him and to hint for presents. Governor Ellis never failed to receive them with ceremony and politeness. In a year's time he entertained nearly thirteen hundred Indians at his home or in the State House. Though he came to be widely known and greatly admired for his skill and finesse in treating with the Indians, Georgia's Governor Ellis sometimes found the Indian spokesman quite as adept as he in the art of verbal maneuver, in blending the honeyed word with the veiled threat.[71]

When the Indian presents were brought up the river to Savannah on May 18, 1757, Governor Ellis wrote to Governor Lyttleton in Charleston, who had never met the Creek chiefs, suggesting that they jointly call a congress of the headmen of the Creeks and distribute the presents.[72] The advantages of identifying Georgia with South Carolina in the minds of the Indians, Ellis felt, far outweighed any loss of personal prestige which playing second fiddle to the governor of South Carolina might entail. Governor Lyttleton replied that he had already invited the chiefs to Charleston and suggested that they come by Savannah on their return from that place.[73] Ellis readily agreed. On July 20 he got from the Assembly an appropriation of £20 to pay for sending his agent to the Creeks to invite their leaders to a conference in Savannah and "to prepare their Minds to receive and relish those impressions and sentiments that it is incumbent on us strenuously to inculcate upon this Occasion."[74]

The Indians flatly refused to go to Charleston.[75] Ellis's agent, a Mr. Wright, had to enlist the aid of the Indian traders to overcome the reluctance of the chiefs to come even to Savannah because of their unpleasant memories of a conference with Governor Reynolds three years before. However, on October 25, 1757, Ellis received word that a large party of Indians had come together on the Altamaha and were on their way to Savannah. This was the signal for him to set in motion the elaborate show designed for the edification and befuddlement of the Creek chiefs. He immediately dispatched Captain Milledge with his troop of Rangers to Fort Argyle on the Ogeechee to escort the party through the last stage of its journey. On October 29 the troop of Rangers, accompanied by about one hundred and fifty Indians, was seen approaching the capital, whereupon, at the governor's bidding, the principal inhabitants of Savannah got on their horses and went out to meet them in a clearing about a mile from town. The whole entourage, now composed of the gentlemen of the vicinity, followed by the Indians according to their rank, with the Rangers bringing up the rear, halted outside the palisades and was saluted by sixteen cannons mounted for the occasion on several bastions.

At the town gate the horsemen parted and formed two lines, through which the Indians filed into Savannah. Inside, Colonel Noble Jones with his militia awaited them. The colonel and his men then led the Indians through the streets of the town. As the procession passed the governor's house, his battery of seven guns saluted them, at which all of the guns on the bluff and on the vessels in the river began to boom. A little short of the old filature where the Council and Assembly met, the foot militia moved off to the right and to the left in good order, leaving the Indians facing a company of the Virginia Regiment of Blues drawn up in a line before the State House. The Blues, after firing a volley into the air, smartly lined themselves on either side of the Council door. The Indians walked between the lines to be welcomed in the Council Chamber by the governor. After an exchange of greetings, Governor Ellis, hoping that all had been duly impressed, invited the headmen to his house for dinner and gave orders for the lesser chiefs to be shown to the quarters prepared for them.[76]

When the governor and his Council returned to the Council Chamber on November 3, the Indians were again escorted into the room with great ceremony. The Chamber was "thronged with the principal Inhabitants who tended with Anxiety to learn the Events of this Congress upon which the Tranquility of the Province so much depended." After Governor Ellis had read and explained a letter from King George "to his beloved Children of the Creek Nations," which the Indians "relished extremely" and "at every Period declared their Approbation aloud," suitable speeches were made and the presents handed out. When he produced the prepared treaty, "the Council unanimously approved the Whole of His Honour's Conduct and confessed that more had been effected than there was reason to expect. . . ."[77]

The treaty signed by Ellis and twenty-one headmen on this occasion was one of friendship and alliance. All former pacts between the colony and the Nation were confirmed, past grievances were buried, and a conventional alliance between Georgia and the Creeks agreed upon. Of particular importance was the specific provision by which both the governor and the chiefs agreed to accept responsibility for the vagrant misdeeds of any of their people and to mete out the punishment and make the redress that the offense warranted. This provision was included in the subsequent treaties with the Creeks; and, although frequently invoked, neither the whites nor the Indians were ever fully satisfied that the other acted with the dispatch and severity that any particular occasion required.[78]

Governor Ellis was confident that the treaty was the fruit of his talks with his Indian visitors in the spring and summer of 1757. He was especially proud that the Indian chiefs had taken his frequent hints and voluntarily ceded to him the islands of Ossabaw, Sapelo, and St. Catherine's with a formal denial that they had ever given them to that remarkable Indian woman, Mary Musgrove Bosomworth. He had sensibly refrained from pressing for land concessions "above the flowing of the tides" at this time, but he had been eager to do something about the Bosomworth claims on the coast which had for years been a disruptive factor in the Indian relations of the colony.[79] Nowhere is Ellis's statesmanship more apparent than in his decision not to use the cession to destroy the claims of the troublesome Bosomworths. Instead he strongly urged the Board of Trade to let him make some sort of settlement which would satisfy these people and eliminate the influential Mary as a hostile voice in Indian councils. In the end, the Board agreed; Ellis granted the land on St. Catherine's Island to the Bosomworths and promised them £2000 for the renunciation of all other claims. Georgia thus gained an undisputed title to the three islands, while Mary became a valuable ally in future parleys with the Indians.[80]

For over two years after the signing of the treaty Georgia had no real trouble with the Creeks. When in 1758 a party of Indians robbed and murdered a family near Savannah, Ellis got

the Indians themselves to punish the offenders.[81] He perceived
that most of the trouble between the Creeks and the settlers
came from the trade which white men carried on in frontier
settlements or in the Indian villages. Beginning in 1757, he
labored to bring the Indian trade under the strict control of
the government.[82] So that irresponsible traders would be unable
to draw the colony into hostilities with the Creeks, Governor
Ellis and the Assembly ruled that only those with a license from
the governor could trade with the Indians, and then only under
certain prescribed conditions.[83] Enforcement was the great difficulty, of course, especially since the Carolina traders in the
Creek country were not subject to control by Georgia. Shortly
before he left the colony, Ellis came up with a plan which
promised success. Each town of the Creeks was asked to appoint
a headman through whom the traders and the colonial government would channel all of their dealings with the Indians. The
headman's hand was to be strengthened among the Indians by
giving him the custody and distribution of the English presents
for his village. He in turn was responsible to the English governor for the good behavior of his people. By restricting the trade
to a few licensed traders dealing with only one Indian in a town,
Ellis hoped to prevent trouble or, if it should arise, to identify
its source immediately.[84]

In 1758 the warriors of the Cherokee Indians returned from
fighting in Virginia, highly incensed at the treatment they had
received there from the English. The fear that the Cherokees
would join with the Creeks and the two would turn upon the
settlers of South Carolina and Georgia was momentarily allayed
by the news that the Creeks and the Cherokees were themselves
at swords' points.[85] In the summer of 1759, however, the Cherokees made their attack upon the settlers on the South Carolina
frontier.[86] A truce secured by Governor Lyttleton in December
stopped hostilities for only a short time, and the Cherokees again
attacked South Carolina in January, 1760.[87] At the outset Governor Ellis had rushed what forces he could muster to the upcountry and "importunately demanded from the Creeks that assistance
which they promised to afford" should the Cherokees attack the
settlers.[88] He put his carefully hoarded credit for £1000, originally provided for purchasing presents for the Indians, at the
disposal of the agents whom he sent into the Indian country to

induce the Creeks to attack the Cherokees. The militia, which Ellis called to arms, remained on active duty in rotation during the crisis. The Assembly complied with Ellis's request for an appropriation to build several permanent forts, and the town of Savannah was also strongly fortified. Georgia having nearly doubled in size since 1757, Governor Ellis felt that the colonists could now bear the costs of this vital expansion of the defense structure.[89]

The Cherokees continued to leave the people in Georgia unharmed during all of this activity. What did most to restrain them from molesting the Georgians, Ellis believed, was their knowledge of the good relations which existed between the rival Creeks and the province of Georgia.[90] Ellis spent the spring of 1760 trying to stir up trouble between the Creeks and Cherokees[91] and "set every Person of Influence upon endeavouring to create a Rupture between those two Nations";[92] but late in May he learned to his dismay that a party of Creeks had on May 16 killed several Georgia traders near Augusta—traditionally the equivalent of a declaration of war.[93] Still seeing in a war with the Creeks nothing but an invitation to disaster, Ellis chose to "Suffer Justice to give way to Prudence," as the legislature advised, and sought to avoid war with the Creeks by ostentatiously assuming that the French, and not the Creek Nation, were responsible for the murders.[94] He went even further to placate the Creeks, leaving the apprehension and punishment of the murderers entirely to the Indians, and in July he made a move toward reopening the Creek trade. The presence of nearly two hundred Creeks in the settlements at the time of the outbreak lent weight to Governor Ellis's contention that the murders were not sanctioned by the Nation as a whole; and his forebearance was further justified when an envoy from the Creeks arrived shortly and convinced the whites that the Creek Nation as such was not involved.[95]

The great harm done by this incident, to Ellis's thinking, was that it made painfully clear the true weakness of the colony, heretofore "by great Management" partially concealed. Settlers had fled the province by the hundreds, and his conciliatory policy toward the Creeks under such provocation could only bespeak a weakness which would surely discourage "Persons of real Property" from coming into the colony.[96] In his last letter from

Georgia, written a few months later, Ellis gave vent to the bitterness he felt at the British government's neglect of the Georgia frontier:

Meanwhile, I cannot help expressing my surprise that his Majestys Southern Provinces should be suffered so long to continue exposed as they are, considering the vicinity, dispositions, & power of the French, and the Savage Nations connected with them, in this Quarter. Surely my Lords 'tis disgraceful to us that whilst our Arms are every where prevailing over the Forces of the Most formidable state in Europe, a few Tribes of barbarians, are murdering the Kings Subjects, and ravaging his Provinces in America, with impunity. From my soul I wish such inattention may not be productive of the most mischievous consequences.[97]

Despite the bitter note of his valedictory, Governor Ellis had accomplished much. He had succeeded in keeping a firm control over men and events in Georgia. At the end of three years the fruits of his labors were everywhere about him, and they were good. With the Lower House of the legislature in line, all parts of the government were working together in unprecedented harmony under his leadership. The colony had been spared the catastrophe of an Indian war largely through his efforts. A respectable defense structure had been built and maintained. The population of the colony was growing steadily for the first time; and its production and trade had more than doubled. He had gained the real affection and respect of the inhabitants and was highly thought of by the Board of Trade. Yet, by the fall of 1759 Ellis had become discouraged and perhaps a little bored. The "intense heats" of the Georgia summers were more than he could bear. Like a suffering David he mourned that the climate had brought him so low that "very little enjoyment of Life" was left him.[98] Whether Henry Ellis in some way lacked ambition, drive, or seriousness of purpose, or whether malarial attacks actually incapacitated him, he was ready to bow out of public life. At his own wish, he set sail from Georgia in early November, 1760, leaving behind James Wright to act in his stead.

Superficially, Henry Ellis and his better-known successor were hardly distinguishable. Both were of English descent, in their middle years, educated, experienced, and wealthy; both were blessed with the requisite ability, intelligence, and character to make them eminently successful colonial governors. But the differences be-

tween the two — and perhaps they were no more than differences
in emphasis — make them stand out as contrasting figures in Georgia history. The impressions left by Ellis and Wright on the infant
colony were in each instance great and good, but good in very
dissimilar ways. The two men wholeheartedly subscribed to the
contemporary rationale of the British imperial and mercantile systems that whatever was good for either Britain or the colonies was
good for both. How they acted upon it is another story. Ellis consistently spoke and acted as if this meant that whatever was to the
best interest of Georgia should be adopted in Georgia; the resulting increase in the colony's wealth and power would be the Empire's gain. Wright, on the other hand, firmly believed that the
immediate local interests of Georgia had to give way to measures designed for the good of the Empire as a whole. With great devotion
and inflexible purpose he undertook to uphold the hand of King
and Parliament right up until the day revolution engulfed him,
never doubting that the ultimate good of Georgia lay in this direction. Whether the Liberty Boys and the revolutionary mob
could have been diverted from their course by Ellis's tact, sympathy, and political stratagems any more than they were in fact
intimidated by Wright's unyielding opposition and contemptuous
disapproval remains a question.

JAMES WRIGHT

BY KENNETH COLEMAN

THE arrival of Lieutenant Governor James Wright in the small frontier capital of Savannah, Georgia, in October, 1760, to take over the government from Governor Henry Ellis caused considerable interest and excitement on the part of the colonists.[1] Well might Georgians be curious about this man who was to head their government. The colony was just beginning to fit into the pattern established by its older and wealthier neighbor, South Carolina, after a not very productive infancy of sociological and economic experimentation. Its first two royal governors had remained in Georgia too short a time to formulate or carry out any sustained policies.

Georgians knew that Wright had lived in South Carolina for a number of years where his office of attorney general and his planting interests had taught him much about colonial affairs. His residence in England while studying law at Gray's Inn and as South Carolina's colonial agent from 1757-60 had taught him a great deal about the workings of the British colonial system and introduced him to many important British politicians.[2] These experiences on both sides of the Atlantic were good training to fit Wright to be governor of Georgia, a title to which he was to succeed in 1761 and which he retained until 1782.[3] These years would see Georgia's greatest development to date and would be the most productive ones in Wright's life.

Wright was cordially received in Georgia — according to the Charleston *South Carolina Gazette,* Savannah put on the biggest celebration in its history to observe his appointment as governor.[4] From the very beginning he got along well, usually getting what he wanted from the colony, its people, and its Assembly. He was

Kenneth Coleman is a member of the history faculty at the University of Georgia.

always popular with "the better sort of people" — the only kind he desired popularity with — and had few, if any, personal enemies even when the revolutionary troubles began in 1775-76. He conscientiously worked for what he thought best for Georgia and Georgians and summed up his aim as governor when he said, "It has ever been my study to discharge my duty to the King & People with integrity, & to the utmost of my power. . . ."[5]

Wright was interested, both personally and officially, in the economic development of Georgia. Throughout his governorship he acquired and built up holdings of lands, slaves, and plantation stocks. There is no evidence that he acquired lands for speculative purposes or that he held lands he was not entitled to under the colony's headright system, by which every free person or head of a family received an allotment. The evidence is rather that he acquired his lands entirely legally and for legitimate planting activities. He was one of the largest and most successful planters in the colony and by the 1770's shipped two to three thousand barrels of rice a year from his eleven plantations, totaling 25,578 acres and worked by 523 slaves.[6]

The year 1763 was in several respects an important turning point in the development of Georgia. In that year the Treaty of Paris ended the Spanish menace by transferring the Floridas from Spain to Britain. This gave Georgia friends to the south and made Indian relations much easier than they had been before. The Proclamation of 1763 gave Georgia for the first time a really definite southern boundary, the St. Marys River. The Southern governors and Indian Superintendent John Stuart held a conference with the Southern Indians at Augusta in November at which a general peace was arranged and the Indians were impressed with the fact that the Spanish no longer owned the Floridas nor the French Louisiana. The Creeks ceded all lands between the Ogeechee and Savannah rivers from Ebenezer to the Little River above Augusta and a strip of land about thirty miles wide along the coast between the Altamaha and the St. Marys rivers.[7] This increased by three or four times the area in Georgia open to white settlement, which was speeded up considerably by the removal of the Spanish menace.

As governor of Georgia, there was never any doubt that Wright considered himself, and was, the real head of the provincial administration. A governor should, he thought, execute orders from London and help the people of his colony in every way possible.

Wright early and consistently recognized that his Council was his best support in most political affairs. He always consulted the Council on important matters, usually deferred to its judgment and secured its approval of his recommendations, and always retained its friendship and cooperation. He several times said that without the support of the Council, he did not know what he would do in his arguments with the Commons House of Assembly.

Wright and his assemblies usually cooperated and worked together harmoniously. At the beginning of each session Wright recommended desirable actions to the Assembly. These recommendations were generally courteously received, considered, and at least the most pressing ones acted upon. Wright sometimes drafted bills and sent them to the Assembly as recommended legislation, especially when a similar bill had been disallowed in London for legal or technical reasons. The Assembly realized that Wright was one of the better trained of the few lawyers in the colony and that bills drafted by him might have a better chance of legal approval in London. Once Wright pointed out to the Board of Trade that a bill had been disallowed upon incorrect legal grounds and secured permission for the Assembly to reconsider and pass a bill like the one disallowed.[8]

Wright always carried out his instructions from London to the letter, even if he did not agree with them or knew they were incorrect. There was no giving in to the Assembly for the sake of expediency, if royal instructions must be violated. However, Wright always sought to prevent public disputes with the Assembly. When he wanted to influence Assembly action, he usually tried to use his powers of persuasion privately with the speaker and members of the Commons House. He never had any trouble with the Upper House, his Council serving in that capacity. On ordinary legislative matters, Wright was able to get along with the Assembly as late as 1775, though there had been an opposition party in the Commons House since the Stamp Act troubles of 1765. When Wright found that he could not secure the desired action on any major item he usually ended the session and did not call another until the trouble was over. There were few bills passed by the Assembly that Wright did not sign. Usually a session was ended before bills of which he disapproved were passed. He seemed to think that it was his duty to sign bills upon which he might have minor disagreements if royal instructions were not violated thereby.

Wright had somewhat different views from the Commons House as to its powers. He often complained that "The House thinks it possesses all powers and rights of the British House of Commons," or "seeks to thwart the sovereignty of Great Britain, to detroy or weaken the weight of the Council as upper house and to endeavor to assume to themselves improper powers."[9] To this Wright would never agree. At one time he dissolved an Assembly because the Commons House had ordered the deputy secretary of the colony imprisoned for refusal to take an oath when giving testimony before a Commons House committee. Wright maintained that neither the Commons House nor the committee had the right to administer oaths upon their own initiative, something that House of Commons committees in London did not ordinarily do.[10] He always insisted that the basis of the Assembly was the royal instructions which could be changed at any time and that the Assembly possessed no independent powers that could not be taken away by the King.[11] While this may have been legally correct, it was not calculated to win political support and friendship among Georgians.

A good example of Wright's obeying his instructions to the letter despite a demand of the Commons House of Assembly that he act otherwise came in 1769. Four new parishes had been created from the area between the Altamaha and the St. Marys rivers after this territory was annexed to Georgia in 1763. Wright suggested to the British government that these parishes should be allowed representation in the Commons House of Assembly as soon as their population warranted it. On November 15, 1769, the Commons House requested Wright to allow representation of these new parishes. Wright replied that he agreed that they should be represented, that his royal instructions did not allow him to increase the number in the Commons House, but that he would request again royal permission to allow representation. The Commons House stated that it dare not impose a tax bill unless these parishes were represented and exempted them from the tax bill, "they not being represented according to the true Intent and meaning thereof."[12]

When the Assembly met in October, 1770, it again requested Wright to issue writs of election for these parishes. Wright again said that he could not do so without specific instructions from London. This time the Commons House refused to pass a tax bill because the four parishes were not represented. Wright dissolved the Assembly just as instructions were received from England to allow representation for the four parishes, but they were represented in future royal assemblies.[13]

To prevent a repetition of this argument, when Wright took up the political division of the lands acquired from the Indians in 1773 he advised that representation be allowed to the parishes to be created out of this area when they had 100 families or voters. This recommendation was promptly approved in London, and Wright was told to issue writs of election as soon as they were warranted.[14]

Wright as governor revealed himself as a rather typical product of eighteenth-century conservatism, in that he believed that government in the very best of empires was naturally the prerogative of the "better sort of people" who understood and worked for the good of all classes. Wright believed in the political participation of the people through the ballot and accepted the Assembly as an integral part of the government. He believed strongly in the powers and prerogatives of the Crown and Parliament and somewhat less in the right of revolution enunciated by John Locke. Wright believed, as did most of the American political leaders of the revolutionary period, in an aristocracy of merit. Everything and everybody had a correct place in life and should strive to fill that place as well as possible. Those who rose to higher stations through natural ability were to be commended, for they were not considered a threat to the orderly social organization he so ardently desired.

Wright was always restrained and, in his official relations, entirely businesslike and correct. He seldom expressed himself freely or personally to his superiors in England or to his colleagues in America. At times there were hints that he did not think the London government had acted correctly. Sometimes he told his superiors that he did not believe they had acted wisely — always with the proper deference to their authority. He usually attributed such improper action to ignorance of the question at hand, which suggests that his long and detailed letters often went unheeded. Wright had lived in both England and America long enough to understand the divergent viewpoints between the two and constantly sought to bridge this gap. Yet regardless of how grave an error Wright believed had been made in London, he always considered that it was his duty to carry out orders until they were modified. It was his job and that of all colonials to obey and then petition for redress of any grievances that had been imposed upon them.

Throughout his term as governor, Wright was a conservative force in land granting. He opposed the granting of large tracts to be held for speculation, which he said would discourage actual settlement. Instead he always insisted that grants should be made to actual settlers under the headright system of one hundred acres for the head and fifty acres for every other member of a family. Thus could the economic and military strength of the colony be increased. He was able to control land granting to a remarkable degree. Most of the large grants not under the headright system were made over the protest of Wright at the direction of the government in London.[15] Because of his attitude on land granting and also because he felt that Georgia was being taken unfair advantage of, Wright objected strenuously to a number of large grants of land made by Governor Thomas Boone of South Carolina. They were made south of the Altamaha in 1763 after the preliminary peace but before the Proclamation of 1763 annexed that area to Georgia. Wright entered into a long and fruitless attempt to get the Boone grants annulled in London, but eventually he had to acknowledge them.[16]

Because most of the good land of the 1763 Indian cession had been granted by 1770 and the Indians were badly in debt to the traders, Wright favored a new cession of Indian lands. While in England between 1771-73 he secured approval for a cession which he and Indian Superintendent John Stuart secured from the Creeks and Cherokees at Augusta in 1773. Wright had also secured approval of his plan to sell these lands to settlers, instead of granting them free, in order to pay the Indian debts to the traders and to secure funds for adequate frontier defense.[17] He was certainly gratified when settlers rushed into the new lands and thus brought Georgia much-needed settlers and funds.

Tied in closely with the problem of land granting and settlement was that of Indian relations. The exit of the Spanish from St. Augustine and of the French from Mobile and New Orleans eased the difficulties with the Indians, but the red man remained an important problem during Wright's administration. Wright always devoted considerable time to Indian relations and understood how to appeal to Indians through the judicious use of presents, flattery, and a show of military force. Generally he was successful, as is attested to by the absence of any really serious Indian troubles during his administration.

The basic aim of Wright's Indian policy was justice and adherence to treaty obligations for both Indians and whites. He was conspicuous in his efforts to enforce Indian rights, especially doing what he could to prevent illegal and oppressive action on the part of Indian traders and insisting that whites not settle upon Indian lands. He opposed the frontier system of "Indian justice," by which frontiersmen killed Indians indiscriminately to avenge any troubles caused by them. Instead, he tried to punish individual wrongdoers and to convince the Indians that they should police themselves. Wright and Indian Superintendent Stuart usually worked together well in restraining unruly frontiersmen; in opposing land grabbing schemes of frontiersmen and speculators; and in trying to make frontier settlements orderly, to keep peace, and to make defense easier.

Soon after his arrival in Georgia Wright brought some order into the Creek Indian trade by allotting specific towns to specific traders, and thus preventing an oversupply of trade items to the Indians.[18] After the Proclamation of 1763 he cooperated with Superintendent Stuart in his attempt to regulate the Southern Indian trade on a unified basis. The Proclamation specified that colonial governors must grant trading licenses to all who applied and obeyed the provincial regulations. Wright protested that unified trade controlled by the superintendent was the only way that peace could be maintained in the Indian country. He enforced a unified plan which Stuart drew up until the lack of any backing from the British authorities was responsible for its abandonment.[19]

As might be expected, Wright's actions as governor and his recommendations to London were usually approved unless they conflicted with established policies or required the expenditure of large amounts of money. Certainly London recognized that Wright knew Georgia conditions best and could be trusted to look out for the interests of the British government. Tangible proof of this approval in London came with the creation of Wright as a baronet in December, 1772, during his one leave in England between 1760-76.[20]

Wright's attitude toward the place of the colonies in the British Empire is well illustrated by the revolutionary troubles which developed after 1764. He thought some of the actions that led to

the Revolution were ill-advised. He knew that Americans were
very jealous of their rights and sometimes considered that officials
in London failed to recognize this sufficiently and did things
to ruffle American feelings needlessly. Wright, who lived with the
Americans, undoubtedly knew their side better than did most
people in England. When the Georgia Assembly objected to the
economic effect of the Sugar Act of 1764 and the proposed parliamentary Stamp Act, Wright took no action. These were orderly
and respectful protests carried out by a legal body.[21] Wright probably thought the Stamp Act unwise, yet he would enforce it to
the fullest once it was enacted. He would use every means in his
power to keep Georgia from joining the other objecting colonies
or from taking forceful action to prevent the enforcement of the
act. He refused to call the Assembly into session to consider the
sending of delegates to attend the intercolonial congress to protest
the stamp duties.[22]

This was preliminary and general. As November 1, 1765, the
day the Stamp Act was to go into effect, drew nearer there was
more overt objection to the act and considerable excitement in
Savannah. The Savannah Sons of Liberty made it clear that the
sale of stamps or the presence of a stamp distributor would be
unpopular with them. Wright, with the backing of his Council,
determined to protect both stamps and distributor to the utmost
of his power and authority when they arrived in Georgia, which
they had not done on November 1.[23]

At this point news of the actions of the intercolonial Stamp Act
Congress arrived in Savannah. The Commons House of Assembly
adopted Congress' petition to the King, memorial to the Lords,
and petition to the Commons and ordered them dispatched to
England for delivery.[24] There is no evidence that Wright objected
to this legal petition or that he made any effort to prevent it.

After the arrival of stamps on December 5, the act was declared
in effect in Georgia; but all business requiring stamps was halted
because no stamp distributor had yet arrived. Wright refused to
allow loaded vessels to clear the port with a certificate stating that
no stamps were available, as was being done in other colonies, or
to appoint a temporary distributor. Instead loaded vessels were
kept in port for about a month until the distributor arrived.[25]

When Wright heard that 200 Liberty Boys were gathering in
town with the intention of destroying the stamps, he got together
what help he could — Rangers, ship captains and sailors, and

townspeople to the total of about fifty-four — and at their head removed the stamps to the Rangers' guardhouse. A guard of forty men was kept for about two weeks, and Wright said he did not have his clothes off for four days. He was sure that his prompt action was all that saved the stamps from destruction by the Liberty Boys, and it is quite probable that he was correct.[26]

When the stamp distributor finally arrived on January 3, he was kept at the governor's house for about ten days while stamps were sold and the sixty or so vessels in the harbor cleared. After this, however, no further attempts were made to sell or use stamps because of popular opposition. Toward the end of the month several hundred people gathered near Savannah to destroy the stamps, and Wright again used military force to protect the stamps. By now he was convinced that the sale of stamps was impractical and was glad to send them out of the colony when a royal vessel arrived in February.[27]

Wright's action in the Stamp Act controversy has been given at some length to illustrate the kind of a man he was. He could have allowed himself to be intimidated by the mob which objected to the sale of stamps or allowed the stamp distributor to resign and never have tried to sell stamps at all. He could have allowed business to be conducted as usual with the statement that stamps were not available, as was done in other colonies when distributors refused to act. Had he suggested such actions, his Council undoubtedly would have agreed. Yet Wright did nothing of the kind. He enforced the act at considerable personal danger and loss of prestige until he saw that any further attempt to sell stamps was useless. With sufficient military force, there is no doubt that he would have taken even stronger action. But he had only about fifty rangers and was afraid to call out the militia for fear that the militiamen would side with the mob. Once the troubles were over, Wright tried to convince influential people throughout the colony of the error of mob action and reported that most of them agreed with him and would try to influence their neighbors that no such action should be undertaken henceforth.[28]

Though he might have thought the Stamp Act unwise, Wright certainly thought its repeal under pressure from America much more unwise. Repeal would undermine the authority of the British government and demonstrate to the Americans that they could secure their desires by strong opposition. Wright would consider proposed action more carefully in the light of its practicability in the colonies, but once a course had been decided upon he would cling to it with all the force necessary to enforce it.

Upon receipt of the official news of the repeal of the Stamp Act in the summer of 1766, Wright and the Assembly congratulated each other that there had been no loss of property in Georgia and that no statements had been made "derogatory to the Honor of His Majesty's Government or tending to destroy the true Constitutional Dependency of the Colonies on the Imperial Crown and Parliament of Great Britain. . . ." — the Commons House used these words from Wright's message in its reply to him.[29] He had weathered the first storm with flying colors. But more was yet to come which would not be so easily handled by a firm adherence to his interpretation of law and order.

A side light to the Stamp Act troubles was the controversy over the appointment of Georgia's colonial agent in London. William Knox, who had been the agent for several years, defended the Stamp Act and made himself unacceptable to the Commons House. Hence it requested Charles Garth, South Carolina's agent, to present its petitions and memorials against the Stamp Act in England and informed Knox that the colony had no further need for his services.[30] In 1766 the Commons House appointed Garth Georgia's agent. The Upper House refused to agree to the appointment but was forced to accept an appropriation of £105 to Garth for services already rendered or kill the entire tax bill. Wright immediately requested London not to accept an agent appointed by only one house of the Assembly, and the governor and Council refused to pass Garth's voucher for payment when it was presented. In 1768 the Commons House again voted the appointment of Garth and the Upper House again withheld its sanction. A compromise was effected when both houses agreed to the appointment of Benjamin Franklin as agent.[31] Wright's concern in this matter was to uphold the right of the Upper House against the claim of the Commons House. There is no indication that he objected to his friend Knox being deprived of his office, probably because he realized that Knox was no longer useful to Georgia.[32]

The passage of the Townshend Revenue Acts by Parliament in 1767 aroused new colonial opposition. These acts along with John Dickinson's objections, *Letters of a Pennsylvania Farmer,* were published in the *Georgia Gazette* and undoubtedly helped the election of what Wright called eighteen "violent Sons of Liberty" out of the twenty-five members elected to the Commons House of

Assembly in the spring of 1768. Because of the excitement, Wright delayed the calling of this Assembly into session until November, 1768.[33]

When the Assembly met, Wright informed it that the King did not approve the circular against the Townshend Acts sent out by the Massachusetts House of Representatives and had instructed him to dissolve the Assembly if it took up this circular. He urged consideration of ordinary legislative business in which he said he would heartily cooperate.[34] After transacting the more pressing legislative business, the Commons House took up the Townshend Acts on December 24. It adopted a "dutifull and loyal address" to the King objecting to parliamentary taxation and declared that the Massachusetts circular was a proper exercise of the right of petition. Wright immediately approved the bills passed thus far and dissolved the Assembly. In his dissolution address, he said that it was impossible to say that Parliament was the supreme legislative body of the Empire and at the same time say it could not tax the colonies except to regulate trade. The difference between external and internal taxes he called a "Distinction without a difference." All liberty must depend upon the full and uninterrupted course of protection and support of the mother country.[35]

Besides this Assembly action there were several merchant and citizen meetings in Savannah in September, 1769, to protest the Townshend Acts, one of which adopted a nonimportation agreement. After talking with people privately Wright came to the conclusion that the nonimportation agreement would not be offered for signatures, as it was not. Hence he took no further action. He did report to London that there would be continual opposition to parliamentary taxation until there was a real decision as to the proper constitutional relationship of the colonies to the mother country. Mere repeal of the duties would not suffice.[36]

After the Townshend Act excitement there was no further trouble in Georgia until a new Assembly met in April, 1771. The Commons House unanimously re-elected its former speaker, Noble Wimberly Jones. Wright, exercising a power given to him by royal instructions but never used before in Georgia, disapproved this choice, probably because Jones was one of the leaders in the opposition to recent British measures. The Commons House then elected Archibald Bulloch as speaker but the next day passed a resolution thanking Jones for his "Steady impartial and faithful Discharge" of the office of speaker for the past several years. A second resolution stated that the negative of the speaker, elected by the unanimous vote of the House, was a "high Breach of the Privilege of the House, and tends to subvert the most valuable Rights and Liberties of the People. . . ." The House said it chose another speaker so as not to delay the necessary legislative business, "already too much protracted by a hasty Dissolution of the last Assembly."[37]

Wright and the Council agreed that such a denial of royal authority made it impossible to do business with this Assembly. After a fruitless private attempt to get the second resolution rescinded, Wright dissolved the Assembly before it had transacted any business. He wrote to England that the powers of the Assembly must be settled or its members would become "Petty Tyrants."[38] Apparently it never occurred to him that many of the assemblymen and colonists might consider him a "Petty Tyrant." His action was approved in England, and instructions were issued that the next Assembly be informed of the King's displeasure at this action and of his intention to uphold the prerogative. The speaker of the next Assembly was to be disapproved, and the Assembly dissolved if it objected.[39] The end of this contest, a victory for the right of negative of the speaker by the governor, came while Wright was in England and James Habersham was acting governor.[40]

For the next three years there was relative peace in Georgia. The 1773 Indian cession was secured and settlers rushed in to take up these rich lands. But before the hoped-for benefits from these lands could materialize, revolutionary storm clouds again enveloped the colony. After the Boston Tea Party of December, 1773, and the passage by Parliament of the "Intolerable Acts" the next spring in retaliation, the colonies moved quickly toward renewed and united opposition to British coercion. In May, 1774, Virginia sent out an invitation for an inter-colonial congress. On July 27 and August 10 meetings were held in Savannah to protest against the treatment of Boston and Massachusetts. The second meeting, which was attended by representatives from all the parishes in the colony, adopted a set of resolutions against "unconstitutional" action by the British government — the first united statement of Georgia in the growing revolutionary struggle.[41]

Wright issued proclamations against these meetings and complained bitterly of his lack of military support to uphold royal authority. He put most of the blame for the Georgia trouble on the example of South Carolina. Although he did not think it advisable to oppose the resolutions publicly, Wright undoubtedly had a great deal to do with petitions which were circulated throughout the province objecting to the meetings and their resolutions.[42]

The August 10 meeting had debated the sending of delegates to the inter-colonial congress, but had decided not to send any. There is no evidence that Wright had anything to do with this decision. The First Continental Congress met and adjourned with no Georgia representatives. Late in 1774 Wright could report that things were tolerably quiet although he feared trouble again, now that the South Carolina delegates had returned from the Continental Congress. To prevent any troubles, he delayed the scheduled meeting of the Assembly from November 15 to January 17.[43] Georgians were badly divided, and many had not yet decided which side to back in the fast developing struggle.

The Assembly met in Savannah on January 17, 1775, and the next day an unofficial body called a Provincial Congress also met.[44] Wright's opening address to the Assembly was well thought out, moderate in tone, and was a sincere attempt to get on with the ordinary legislative business and to discourage any revolutionary activity. It showed the real concern of a man who believed in the complete power of the British government in America and yet had real attachment and love for the colonies. "You may be advocates for liberty, so am I, but in a constitutional and legal way. You, gentlemen, are Legislators, and let me entreat you to take care how you give a sanction to trample on Law and Government; and be assured it is an indisputable truth, that where there is no law there can be no liberty. It is the due course of law and support of Government which only can insure to you the enjoyment of your lives, your liberty, and your estates; and do not catch at the shadow and lose the substance." Wright insisted that he spoke as Georgia's friend of over fourteen years and not merely as her governor. It grieved him to think that a province which he had seen nurtured from infancy at the expense of the Crown should be plunged into distress and ruin by the impudence and rashness of some inconsiderate people. Both houses of the Assembly replied that they too were worried about British-colonial relations but insisted that the rights of British subjects in America had not been respected in England.[45]

Meeting on January 18 as prearranged, the Provincial Congress felt itself too restricted, being made up of delegates from but five of twelve parishes, to take real action for Georgia. Hence it contented itself with preliminaries which it hoped would be completed by the Assembly. It selected delegates to the Second Continental Congress, drew resolutions, agreed to modifications of the Continental Association (a nonimportation, nonexportation, and nonconsumption agreement affecting all trade with England), and then adjourned on January 25.[46] When it seemed that the Commons House would follow the lead of the Provincial Congress, Wright adjourned the Assembly before it could bring Georgia fully into line with the other rebellious colonies.[47] Since Georgia had not adopted the Association, there was considerable confusion and division of opinion as to what the status of her trade was. In effect, every man must decide for himself where he stood on American rights.

Throughout the first half of 1775 the troubles of royal officials in Georgia increased as the people more and more took affairs into their own hands and ignored any official actions they did not approve. There were several instances of open defiance of customs laws, the usual shipment of Indian presents and supplies that arrived in Savannah in July was appropriated by Georgians and South Carolinians to their own use, courts were temporarily stopped, and the Commons House of Assembly refused to meet despite Wright's special proclamation calling it into session in May.[48] On May 11, the day after news of the battles of Lexington and Concord reached Savannah, the public powder magazine was broken open and most of the powder stored there taken out.[49] On the night of June 2 the twenty-one cannon on the battery were spiked and thrown down the bluff. On the King's birthday, June 4, Wright gave his usual celebration. The next day a liberty pole was erected and a rousing celebration held at Tondee's Tavern with toasts to American liberty, the King, no taxation without representation, and speedy reconciliation between Britain and America upon constitutional principles.[50]

By July both Whigs and Tories agreed with Wright that there was little possibility of salvaging Georgia for the King.[51] Wright said that the royal government was powerless to prevent the insults to which it was subjected almost daily. He went through the form of objecting to each action as it occurred, knowing full well that nothing would be accomplished. Throughout the growing revolutionary troubles, Wright had been begging for troops to

uphold the King's government. When 100 soldiers were ordered
to Savannah in April, 1775, Wright and his Council decided that
they were too late and would do more harm than good. Hence they
never came to Savannah.[52] By July Wright said he could not bear
the insults to which he was daily subjected, that he could accom-
plish nothing in Georgia, and requested leave to return to
England.[53]

By the time the Second Provincial Congress met in Savannah on
July 4, 1775, it was obvious that the royal government's power was
gone. Wright appointed a day of fasting and prayer for a happy
reconciliation between Britain and the colonies, at the request of
the Congress, because he feared it would appoint the day itself if
he did not.[54] This Congress brought Georgia fully into line with
the other revolting colonies, provided for future congresses, and
appointed a Council of Safety to carry on in its absence.[55] It was
Georgia's real government now. Wright realized this, but was
powerless to do anything to oppose it. He and his Council continued to meet, to discuss what they were powerless to prevent,
and to report all happenings faithfully to the authorities in London. In November the Commons House refused to meet. In
December the Provincial Congress took over court functions, and
royal government was completely at an end.[56]

In mid-January, 1776, several British naval vessels arrived at
the mouth of the Savannah River to try to secure provisions for
the British army and navy. Wright tried to convince Noble W.
Jones and Joseph Clay, Whig leaders whom he felt he could trust,
that the vessels should be allowed to purchase provisions peacefully. The Council of Safety decided instead to have no dealings
with the vessels and to arrest Wright, his Council, and other royal
officials.[57] After being threatened with deportation into the back
country to prevent contact with the vessels, Wright and several
members of his Council broke their paroles on the night of February 11 and went down to Cockspur and boarded HMS *Scar-
borough*.[58] The next day Wright addressed a letter to his Council
in Savannah, stating that he was compelled to leave because the
Council of Safety would not allow him to communicate with the
officers on board the vessels. He admitted the hopelessness of royal
government in Georgia by announcing that he was going to proceed to England to take advantage of the leave that had been
granted to him some time earlier. He renewed his request to Sir
Henry Clinton for troops — 500 to 1,000, now — with the statement

that many Loyalists in the back country would return to their
royal allegiance if supported by the military. When no troops were
forthcoming, Wright sailed away with the British to Halifax and
thence to England. Thus ended his first period as governor of
Georgia.[59]

Here it might be well to consider what effect Wright had upon
the development of revolutionary sentiment in Georgia. Certainly
he fought this development with every means at his command,
both public and private. He obeyed his instructions to the letter
and never gave in to the colonials for the sake of expediency. He
was sure the British government was mistaken in giving in to
colonial opposition when it repealed the Stamp and the Townshend acts. Because of his influence with the leaders of the colony
and the high regard with which he was held throughout Georgia,
Wright undoubtedly delayed the rise of revolutionary sentiment.
Yet Georgians were a part of America and would not be left out
of what the other colonies were doing. Wright certainly realized
this fact, as his continual blaming of Georgia revolutionary troubles on South Carolinians indicates, though he preferred not to
admit it. Georgia was going with the other colonies in rebellion;
neither Wright nor any other individual could prevent her.

Almost as soon as Wright returned to England in 1776 he began
to press for the recapture of Georgia. He joined the governor of
South Carolina and the lieutenant governors of Georgia and
South Carolina in a memorial in which they outlined a plan for
subduing the two provinces and returning them to British control.
Wright and his lieutenant governor urged that Georgia be recaptured at once, even if there were insufficient troops to capture
South Carolina at the same time. Georgia, they urged, would make
a good base for operations to regain other Southern provinces;
lands could be assigned to Loyalists still in rebel provinces, and
many needed military supplies could be secured.[60]

When instructions for the reconquest of Georgia were issued,
they were based upon the plans outlined in these memorials. Once
the Loyalists were able to reassert their loyalty to the King, colonial government could be restored to show the other rebellious
colonials the blessings of colonial status.[61] The actual recapture
of Savannah and lower Georgia took place in late December, 1778,
and January, 1779, with expeditions from New York under the
command of Lieutenant Colonel Archibald Campbell and from
St. Augustine under the command of General Augustine Prevost.

After a temporary occupancy of Augusta, the British confined themselves to a radius of about fifty miles from Savannah.[62]

Before the recapture of Savannah was known in London, provincial officials in England were ordered to return to Georgia and resume their duties there.[63] Governor Wright, Lieutenant Governor John Graham, and Chief Justice Anthony Stokes arrived in Savannah in July, 1779, and took over the government from the temporary officials appointed by the military in March. In his answer to the congratulatory address from the loyal inhabitants, Wright assured them that Parliament had conceded the points for which the Americans said they were fighting.[64] Wright found that the people generally thought the re-establishment of civil government had restored the province to the "King's Peace." Hence he issued a proclamation so restoring it, although he was doubtful if that step should be taken so early. Before he left England he had indicated that he did not believe many of the people who had taken the oath of allegiance to the King could be trusted and that such people could probably control any Assembly elected — hardly a rosy picture for the restored province.[65] Wright did not change this opinion after his arrival in Georgia.

Wright set about restoring things to their former status in the part of Georgia occupied by the British. One of his major complaints was that sufficient troops were not sent to subjugate the rest of the province.[66] He worked hard toward restoring normal civilian government, but the insecurity of his position and the questionable loyalty of Georgians prevented him from calling an Assembly, as his instructions had urged him to do as soon as possible. He preferred delay until more troops were sent, until the rest of the province was in British hands, or until conditions were more favorable to the royal government — things which never happened.

In September, 1779, the French under Count Charles-Henri d'Estaing and Americans under Benjamin Lincoln tried unsuccessfully to recapture Savannah.[67] Wright ordered in some four to five hundred slaves to work on the fortifications of the city and opposed any suggestions that it be surrendered.[68] As soon as the French and American failure at Savannah was known, the British army under Sir Henry Clinton sailed south and began a campaign which ended in the capture of Charleston in May, 1780.[69]

After the departure of the French and Americans from Savannah, Wright and his Council took steps to call to account people who had taken the oath to the King after the British return but had given no military help during the siege of Savannah. There were several treason trials at the first session of the general court after the siege, and Wright let it be known that people of doubtful loyalty would be questioned. He was sure that the royal government had been weakened by the military activity and would require time to regain its proper position.[70]

Wright had planned to have the British troops going from Savannah to Charleston to help Clinton march up to Augusta to impress the back country and then to hold the first Assembly election since his return to Georgia. However, the troops went directly to Charleston, and the election was not held.[71] During his Charleston campaign, Clinton issued a proclamation offering pardon for past treasonable offenses to all who speedily returned to their allegiance to the King. Wright objected to this proclamation as being too broad, including many Georgians who had been active in the rebellion. To prevent such people from getting control of a Georgia Assembly, he immediately called an election.[72]

In his opening address, Wright informed this Assembly that the British government had given up taxing the colonies excepting duties for the regulation of commerce, the net proceeds of which were to go to the colonies. He made no specific recommendations to the Assembly, but probably worked privately with its members to secure actions which he favored.[73] The Assembly worked hard to return Georgia to her former status. Three of the nine bills which it passed can be traced directly to the Revolution. One of these declared illegal all actions of the state governments which had existed since 1775, and another disqualified politically all prominent rebels and any who had occupied official position under the state governments. Wright seemed well pleased with these actions, although they did not encompass all he wished done.[74]

By the time the Assembly was prorogued, Charleston was in British hands and there were hopes that peace would soon return to Georgia and South Carolina with both of them restored as British provinces. Many back-country people, who had opposed the British since their return, took the oath of allegiance to the King because they now felt the American cause was futile. Throughout the summer of 1780 the royal government gained strength and territory, reaching its greatest power since the return of the British. By September a full contingent of civilian and militia officials for the entire province were appointed by the governor and Council, but it is doubtful if they ever attempted to operate in the Whig areas.[75] Yet opposition to the royal government continued — active in the back country, more passive nearer Savannah. A state government continued to exist somewhere in the back country of Wilkes County or in South Carolina.

From the time the second session of the Assembly met in September, 1780, Wright found that it was hard to get assemblymen to meet at his call, and harder to get them to remain in session until the necessary legislative business was done. The attitude was one of passive resistance rather than open opposition, but by the end of 1780 Wright was doubtful of the cooperation that he could expect from the legislature. Neither his persuasive powers nor the needs of British Georgia seemed able to persuade the assemblymen to do their duty. Wright reported that several of the members elected since the original election held ideas about legislative independence which he had always opposed.[76]

Wright continued, as he always had, to be the real leader of the royal government. He generally got the complete backing of his Council, more and more made up of appointed colonial officials, and had no fights with the Assembly. The London government continued to approve his ideas, except in military matters. After the passage of an act granting permanently to the British government a duty on certain Georgia exports, London said that Georgia was the prize royal province in America and that Wright deserved high praise for his leadership.[77] But this praise and other approvals were small consolation to an official engaged in endless argument with the military.

When Wright returned to Georgia in 1779 he hoped soon to restore the province to its old and, to him, proper place in the Empire. His first disappointment was in finding only part of it under British control and Whigs engaging in guerilla warfare in the back country. But with the work of re-establishing royal government and with the siege of Savannah and its aftermath Wright was kept busy, and was again the efficient and competent governor of the 1760's and 1770's. Though he could never persuade the military officials to send enough troops to restore all the province to British control, he worked hard to govern correctly what was under his control. Things became more desperate when the province was stripped of troops to aid in the capture of Charleston. These troops were never returned to Georgia, despite continual requests of Wright to the military authorities in America and the civilian officials in London.[78]

The military could not see the defense of Georgia through Wright's eyes and consequently, he said, did not have its welfare at heart. He thought the defense of Georgia should take priority over any other military operations in the South. He was always convinced that there were sufficient British troops in America to send from 500 to 1000 to Georgia to subdue the rebels. If the military commanders did not agree with this, they were short-sighted; and Wright used his choicest tirades against them. He was sure that the generals opposed him because he headed the restored civilian government and thus took away some of the power they thought should belong to them. A commander in Charleston summed up the military view when he said of Wright and his Council, that they were "the most absurd of all people."[79]

Wright especially wanted a troop of horsemen to protect loyal inhabitants from rebel guerilla raids. These raids were widely dispersed and usually carried out on horseback, but Wright could never convince the British military authorities that the horsemen were necessary. The best he could do was to get approval from the Assembly or British commanders to allow the use of mounted militia patrols. The army wanted to control the defense of Georgia entirely and always opposed the creation of special troops which would be under the control of the provincial government.[80] Regardless of what each side wanted or decided to do, it was impossible for Wright and the military to agree on what should be done or why.

After the surrender of Cornwallis at Yorktown in October, 1781, General Nathanael Greene, commander of American troops in the Carolinas and Georgia, sent General Anthony Wayne to command in Georgia. Wayne, despite the fact that he was outnumbered by the British, immediately took the offensive and kept the British penned in Savannah, the only place of any consequence in Georgia they still held.[81] Increasingly pessimistic since the loss of Augusta to the Americans in June, Wright's letters now suggested the despair of a man who knew he was doomed. Yet the requests for additional troops continued as a matter of course.[82]

The steady advance of American troops in 1781 and the stubborn refusal of the British to provide adequate military forces changed Wright's pessimism into a feeling of disgust. If Georgia were to be an example in showing all American colonies the blessings of restored British rule, then Loyalists must be protected from rebels. Wright's letters lost their old force and reason and became increasingly the futile objections of one who was in an impossible situation and knew he would be able to do little about it. The caliber of his work did not measure up to his earlier reputation as a competent governor. Several times he requested leave to go to England, saying that he was of little use in Georgia; but his requests were ignored.[83]

In May, 1782, the British commander-in-chief in America ordered the evacuation of Savannah and Georgia as soon as possible.[84] Wright and his Assembly expressed amazement! They maintained that it was unnecessary and that only a few troops could protect the province. They suggested that the St. Augustine garrison be moved to Savannah, and finally asked that East Florida remain in British hands until the Loyalists could make arrangements to go elsewhere to begin life anew.[85]

Wright left Georgia, the scene of his greatest successes and failures, with the British troops on July 10, 1782. Certainly it was with a great sense of pain and frustration that he sailed down the Savannah River to the Atlantic for the last time and went "home" to an England that he scarcely knew or understood. In an England that was hardly aware of the importance of the small colony of Georgia, he spent the remaining three years of his life, a tired and embittered old man trying to get financial compensation for himself and other Loyalists who had lost their fortunes and their importance by being loyal to a King and government which they felt had not properly supported them. For his claim of £33,000 of property lost in Georgia, the loss of his office, and in consideration for his services to the Crown he was granted a pension of £500 a year, hardly sufficient to live as he thought proper or to indicate any real appreciation for the long years he had so faithfully served the Crown. He died on November 20, 1785, at Westminster and was buried in the north cloister of the Abbey.

IV

ANTHONY STOKES

BY ALEXANDER A. LAWRENCE

GATHERED on a spit of sand at the mouth of the Savannah River in the summer of 1782 were several hundred forlorn subjects of King George III. They were the Loyalists of the province of Georgia. The decision to abandon the effort to subdue the American colonies had brought these Tories and Crown officials to Tybee Island to await the ships that were to take them forever from Georgia. Except for slaves and the few goods they were able to carry off, their property had been left behind. The sojourn at Tybee was a trying one; there was little shelter; the heat was unbearable and scarcely a day passed without a thunderstorm; flies and mosquitoes "abounded beyond description," and the water was unwholesome. Many of the exiles died.

The melancholy tale of the Georgia Loyalists is yet to be written. This is the story of one of them — of his Majesty's chief justice of the province of Georgia, Anthony Stokes, Esquire. It is to Stokes, who was among the evacuees in 1782, that we owe the description of the hardships at Tybee. Suffering from a "nervous atrophy" and despairing of his life, he went ashore one day to receive the Eucharist. However, he survived the ordeal and a few months later reached England. During the ensuing decade Stokes wrote a book and two pamphlets. His treatise on the constitution of the British colonies in North America and in the West Indies was published in 1783. The following year he published a narrative of his official conduct as chief justice of Georgia in which he chronicled "the Dangers and Distresses" he had undergone "in the Cause of Government." During the French Revolution Stokes wrote a pamphlet extolling the stability and advantages afforded

Alexander A. Lawrence is an attorney in Savannah, Georgia.

by British institutions as contrasted with conditions produced by democratic forces at work in France and in America.

In all their titular formidability, the three works[1] are:

A View of the Constitution of the British Colonies, in North-America and the West Indies, at the time the Civil War broke out on the Continent of America. In which Notice is taken of such Alterations as have happened since that Time down to the present Period. With A Variety of Colony Precedents, which are chiefly adapted to the British West India Islands; and may be useful to those, who have any intercourse with the Colonies. (555 pp., London, 1783.)

A Narrative of the Official Conduct of Anthony Stokes, of the Inner Temple, London, Barrister at Law; His Majesty's Chief Justice, and one of his Council of Georgia; and of the Dangers and Distresses He underwent in the Cause of Government: Some Copies of which are printed for the Information of his Friends. (112 pp., London, 1784.)

Desultory Observations, on the Situation, Extent, Climate, Population, Manners, Customs, Commerce, Constitution, Government, Religion, etc. of Great Britain: Occasionally Contrasted with those of other Countries; in order to point out the Blessings which the English enjoy above all other Nations. (70 pp., with an index, London, 1792.)

Stokes's publications throw much light upon colonial and revolutionary Georgia. His *View of the Constitution of the British Colonies* is the only work published in the latter half of the eighteenth century that deals to any considerable extent with the province. The *Narrative* is one of the few eye-witness accounts, by either Patriot or Loyalist, of the revolt in Georgia. In *Desultory Observations* there are frequent allusions to the province as he saw and knew it. The writings of Stokes afford a partisan but interesting view of the era of the Revolution as seen through the eyes of a faithful servitor of the Crown. A study of the chief justice must inevitably focus itself on his relation to the struggle for American independence.

Anthony Stokes was born in Wales in the year 1736, being the eldest son of Nicholas and Florence Stokes.[2] The Stokes family was an old one in Pembrokeshire. The coat of arms displayed on Anthony's bookplate is identical to that of a family said to have descended from Peter de Stok of Normandy, who settled in Wales in the time of King John.[3] Whatever its origin, the Stokes family belonged to the landed gentry of Pembroke County. That Anthony possessed a certain station in life at the time he went to London to study law is attested by a comment he later made. "When I was a student at the Temple," he remarked, "I brought up with me as footman, from the principality, a young man that had been a barber; and whose native language was a corrupt dialect of the Welsh."[4]

Concerning his early education there is no information beyond his comment in *Desultory Observations* that "in my youth I had some classical education." It is not until 1758, when he was twenty-one, that a biographer catches up with his Majesty's future chief justice of Georgia. In January of that year he was admitted as a student at the Inns of Court, being described in the admission register of Gray's Inn as "Anthony Stokes of St. Andrews Holborn Gentln." After a few months study at that Inn he transferred to the Inner Temple where he completed his legal education.

On May 9, 1760, Anthony was called to the bar and confirmed as an "utter Barrister."[5] "For some time afterwards," he tells us, "he went part of the Oxford circuit, and from thence down to the South Wales grand sessions."[6] Progress at the English bar was necessarily slow. He could not await success, for in 1759, while a student at the Inns, Anthony had married Miss Elizabeth Wedgbrough of Middlesex County.[7] The first of their three children was born about the time he commenced the practice of law. After two and a half years of struggle Stokes decided to seek his fortune in the West Indies, and in December, 1762, he embarked for the Leeward Islands.

After practicing for three years at Antigua he moved to the neighboring Island of St. Kitts. Prior to his departure Stokes was appointed to his Majesty's Privy Council at Antigua but he did not take office as his commission arrived after he left. In his six-year sojourn in the West Indies he earned, Stokes states in *Narrative,* "an unblemished reputation as an 'honest man'" — a character he esteemed "before every earthly consideration." In his *View of the Constitution of the British Colonies* he tells us that he came into "considerable practice as a Barrister of Law." He mentions only one case that he handled while he was in the Islands. Representing a candidate for the House, Stokes raised the novel question of the eligibility of the governor and the members of his Council to vote in an election of assemblymen. He maintained "with some warmth" that voting by those officials in such a contest was unconstitutional and that it tended to influence elections. Stokes's contentions failed in the Assembly only after the governor let it be known that he would prorogue that body should the members persist in their attitude on the issue.

If the King's ministers ever heard of Anthony's little brush with the established order in the Isles, the aberration was overlooked in considering his application for the vacancy that arose in the province of Georgia with the death of Chief Justice William Simpson late in 1768. Governor James Wright evidently stressed upon the home authorities the necessity of replacing him with a man of learning in the law. The King "is sensible," he was informed, "how important it is that the Office of Chief Justice should be executed by a Person of Integrity, Ability & Knowledge in his Profession" and he was assured that "all possible attention will be had to those qualifications in the choice of a successor to Mr. Simpson."[8]

Apparently Stokes had influential connections at home. Endorsements were obtained from Sir Richard Aston, a well-known judge of the King's Bench, and from John Pollen, chief justice of the Carmarthen Circuit in Wales.[9] Anthony received the appointment and was instructed to "repair as soon as possible to Georgia."[10] Upon receiving this news Governor Wright wrote, "I shall be very glad to see Mr. Stokes here, as we are much in want of a man of abilities on the Bench."[11]

On August 30, 1769, the *Georgia Gazette* of Savannah reported that "Anthony Stokes, Esq., lately appointed Chief Justice of this province, with his lady and family, landed on Ossabaw on Saturday last from on board a ship, Belton master, from St. Kitts, bound to Philadelphia, and are expected in town from Sunbury this day." He took the oath of office on September 1 under a commission from King George III "for and During our Pleasure."[12] After finding temporary quarters in a house on the Bay the new chief justice was able to look around at his new surroundings.

The inhabited portion of the colony over whose courts Anthony Stokes had been called to preside approximated a great triangle of sparse settlements, which fringed the Atlantic tidewater from Darien to its apex at Savannah and thence along the Savannah River to Augusta and its vicinity. However, the back country was rapidly opening up. By 1773 Georgia would have a population estimated by the royal governor at 18,000 whites and 15,000 blacks. The seat of government — Savannah — was a straggling, wooden-built town of about 750 persons. It consisted, according to Surveyor General J. G. W. De Brahm, of "400 dwelling houses, a Church, an Independent Meeting House, a Council-house, a Court-house, and a Filatur." The new courthouse on Wright Square was a two-story affair with the courtroom and judge's chamber upstairs and the prothonotary's office and the petit and grand jury rooms on the first floor. The omission of a jail from De Brahm's catalogue of Savannah's landmarks is understandable in the light of the observation Chief Justice Stokes made about it. "The present wooden Hutt, improperly called a Goal, was not secure enough to confine an Infant," he complained, warning that if a new one were not provided, "all criminal Justice was at an end." Georgia would become, he predicted, a rendezvous for "all Horse-stealers and Criminals from the neighboring Provinces."[13]

Horse stealing, a crime punishable by death, was the subject of one of the first cases to come before Stokes after his arrival in Georgia. A man convicted of larceny was ordered burned on the hand with the letter R, but a horse stealer, despite the jury's recommendation of mercy, was sentenced to be hanged. However, the chief justice was to find a distinct aversion in the colony to the rigors of English criminal law. The *Georgia Gazette* of January 24, 1770, carried a piece in which an anonymous contributor expounded upon the virtues of mercy in the administration of law. In the same issue of that newspaper it was announced that Governor Wright had granted a reprieve to the culprit; a few weeks later he received a pardon.

The judicial system of the province, established by the grace of George II in the year 1754, embraced two superior courts — (1) the General Court and (2) the Court of Sessions of Oyer and Terminer and General Goal Delivery. Actually they constituted a single tribunal with the same judges and officials but with separate civil and criminal divisions. The General Court dispatched civil business, possessing a jurisdiction similar to that of the courts of the King's Bench, Common Pleas, and Exchequer in England. Criminal justice was administered in the Court of Oyer and Terminer. The governor exercised chancery, probate, and admiralty powers.

The chief justice of Georgia received an annual salary of £500 raised by grant of Parliament. He was also entitled to fees from attorneys for various acts performed by him. These averaged about £500 per year and in one year during Stokes's tenure of office they totalled more than £700.[14] Three assistant judges who were ap-

pointed "during Pleasure" of the governor sat with the chief
justice. They were laymen and received no salary or perquisites
of office.

The provincial bar numbered around fifteen attorneys. Stokes
evinced little pride in it. Practitioners in the American colonies
were, he said, of "three sorts." First, there were those who had
been called to the bar at the Inns of Court in London and who
were admitted by certificate; next, there were lawyers who had
served clerkships in the mother country or the colonies; finally,
there were those admitted to practice "through interest" and who,
in the language of the day, were said to "turn lawyers."[15] "Most
of the questions that arise in the Colonies are founded," Stokes
continued, "in litigation, and not in intricacy," and "as the gentlemen of the bar in general go out there at an early period in life,
before they are arrived at any considerable share of knowledge,
they have it not in their power to gain much experience in the
Colonies." It was the chief justice's observation that "the Advocate, who has the greatest fluency, may sometimes be considered
as the ablest lawyer."[16] It is said that he inveighed against the haste
and carelessness of his own bar as well as of the South Carolina
attorneys who appeared before him, complaining that in some
instances they would annex the several sheets of indentures "hind
side before."[17]

Stokes worked hard to improve the administration of justice
in the province. He took "a good deal of Pains," he tells us, "to
regulate the proceedings of the Superior Courts according to the
laws of the land" and to put them on a "respectable footing."[18]
He rendered "a service to the jurisprudence of Georgia," it has
been said, "which has never been acknowledged or appreciated."[19]
What lasting contribution he made is hard to say, but among his
useful services was the preparation of printed instructions for the
guidance of court officials. They were published in 1771 under
the title: *Directions for the Officers of his Majesty's General Court,
and Sessions of Oyer and Terminer, and General Goal Delivery,
of the Province of Georgia.*[20] This twenty-four page compilation
contained minute instructions to clerks and bailiffs beginning with
the time the cryer proclaimed, "Oyer, Oyer, Oyer, All manner of
persons that have any thing to do before his Majesty's General
Court, for this province of Georgia, draw near and give me your
attendance."

With his salary and the fees of office to which he was entitled the chief justice was able, as he put it, to appear "in the character of a gentleman."[21] Before long he purchased a 200-acre plantation, hired an overseer, and bought additional slaves. Befitting his station, he also acquired a "post chariot" and a "park phaeton," both of modern design and London make. The plantation, called "Pembroke," was located about nine miles southeast of Savannah, "on the Salts."[22] The chief justice had soon learned, according to his *Desultory Observations,* that "the heat is almost intolerable out of the reach of the sea air." He erected a house on the tract at a cost of £338.[23] Eventually his holdings in the province totalled 4,500 acres, mostly in wild lands.

While he resided in the Leeward Islands Stokes had first acquired title to a human being. On his arrival at Antigua he was told that he could not do without Negroes, and a friend purchased one for him and sent her to his house. "For want of reflection," he said, "I bought others from time to time; and when I went to North America, I had nine."[24] In Georgia the number multiplied; by the time of the Revolution he owned thirty-three slaves — "five men, ten women, two boys, and 16 children, from about 13 years of age down to sucking infants." Although enslaving "my fellow creatures" was abhorrent, his conscience was salved by the fact that he "spoiled" his own slaves with "indulgence." It was strange to Stokes to hear a lady in America, without the least "uneasiness" on her part, order "a Negro man, to tye up another and to *lay it on well;* under the penalty of being whipped himself."[25] On leaving Georgia in 1776 he confessed, "I have made no great hand of my trade in human flesh; upon reflection I do not approve of it, and sincerely pray to be forgiven for the share I have had in it."[26] Later he wrote, "I smite my breast, and say, 'God, be merciful to me a sinner!' "[27]

To Stokes, Georgia remained a strange and forbidding land to which he was never acclimatized. He came as an Englishman; he left as one. What seemed to impress him most was the great heat, the sudden changes of climate, the unhealthfulness of the province, the alligators, bears, rattlesnakes and, not least, the "seed ticks." He left few observations concerning the Indians, though he saw something of them at close hand during a congress with the Creeks at Savannah in 1774.[28] To him the red man was not nearly so savage as the breed of whites which overran the western parts of North Carolina and Virginia. "Distinguished by the name of Crackers" and descended in many cases from convicts sent from

Great Britain, they inherited, he asserted, "so much profligacy from their ancestors, that they are the most abandoned set of men on earth, few of them having the least sense of religion." When routed in the other provinces, "they fly," Stokes continued, "to Georgia, where the winters are mild, and the man who has a rifle, ammunition, and a blanket, can subsist in that vagrant way, which the Indians pursue."[29] He was shocked at the common practice of eye-gouging and the inhuman sports in which they took part, such as running spurs down a man's spine while wrestling — "a dreadful operation to a man, who has only a shirt, and carter's frock on, as is the usual dress amongst the lower people in that country."[30]

However, there was a brighter side of life in the province. No other American colony fitted so well into the pattern of British mercantilism. Georgia had not outgrown the imperial system of which it was a part. Under the administration of Governor Wright it made "such a rapid progress in population, agriculture, and commerce, as no other country ever equalled in so short a time," declared Stokes. This is a rather sweeping claim, but all the evidence points to the flourishing condition of Georgia during these pre-Revolutionary years. Later Anthony would comment in idyllic terms concerning the province. "When I went out to America, in August, 1769, no one even suspected that a rebellion would take place in that country for no community could be more free, or happy," he said. He maintained that "no country ever enjoyed a greater share of liberty than Georgia did from the time it became a King's Government" until the "Civil War."[31] Georgia was, continued Stokes in roseate retrospect, under the King's government "one of the most free and happy countries in the world — justice was regularly and impartially administered — oppression was unknown — the taxes levied on the subject were trifling — and every man that had industry, became opulent —."[32]

But across this Utopian possession of King George III a shadow was deepening. "The animosities in Georgia occasioned by the Stamp Tax had not totally subsided," Stokes observed upon his arrival.[33] Scarcely had he set foot in the province when a meeting was held in Savannah to protest the Townshend Acts. But Georgia was the weakest of the colonies. It was more dependent militarily and financially upon Great Britain than the others. Though there was always an articulate resistance to unpopular measures of Parliament, of the King, and of the royal governor, the feeling of attachment to the mother country was stronger there than else-where in America. Born of British benevolence, nurtured by British gold, and preserved by British blood, the colony was under especial obligation to the motherland. The people were "more particularly indebted to the Crown, than those in any other Colony," declared Stokes, pointing out that, among other things, "most of the inhabitants owed every acre of land they had to the King's free gift."[34]

Anthony Stokes has been described as an "acute observer of people and things," who "took a very human and philosophical view of the American revolution."[35] But actually he saw only shal-lowly beneath the surface of the fundamental conflict. He did not comprehend that the ultimate interest and destiny of Georgia were inextricably tied to her sister colonies. He did not realize the ex-tent to which the colonists had come to regard themselves as Americans rather than as Britons and subjects of the King. Stokes had little faith in the capacity of the colonials for self-government. He did not appear to understand how the people in this vast, burgeoning new land could be exercised over taxation by a Parlia-ment 3,000 miles across the water. He presented no analysis of the great constitutional issues that had evolved concerning the status of the colonies. He was wedded to the extreme British position as to sovereignty over the King's possessions. A "warm advocate," as he described himself, "for the authority of the Su-preme Legislature over the whole empire," Stokes believed in the "supremacy of Parliament in all cases."[36] As to "taxation without representation" he had only the following sardonic comment, which he expressed in his *View of the Constitution of the British Colonies:* "The Colony, which was thus taxed by a law enacted by the Trustees Council at a Tavern in London, afterwards denied the right of Parliament to tax the Colonies."

Stokes regarded the American and the French revolutions as being cut from the same cloth. Both represented the ascendancy to power by the lower classes. "The present rage for democracy," he wrote in 1792, "is a conspiracy of all the dissipated, and neces-sitous, throughout the world, to overturn every government; for the purpose of plundering those, who have any property." His observation was that "advocates for democracy, in every country where I resided, have been in general, men of an arbitrary, over-bearing disposition; impatient of all legal restraints; and anxious to reduce every one to their own level."[37]

But Stokes did not close his mind to defects in the colonial system. He had sharp words for absentee government through deputies. He called it a "fatal practice, which greatly weakened the King's cause in all the American Colonies," depriving the royal governors of "every appointment of consequence" and of the means of stopping "the mouths of those demagogues that endeavoured to throw the Country into confusion." Typically, however, the cautious author disavowed any intention in these remarks of reflecting upon the colonial minister, who was merely following precedent, he said, in granting leaves of absence.[38]

An even-tempered, unassuming, religious man, Chief Justice Stokes created a favorable impression in Georgia — certainly in government circles. There is, unfortunately, a total lack of reminiscence or personal anecdote concerning him. We never get to see the sort of individual he really was. There are only generalizations which do not unmask him as a man. A contributor to the *Georgia Gazette* in 1774 described him as "a Gentleman of whose honour and integrity, judgement and penetration, I have the highest opinion."[39] According to James Robertson, he was "universally esteemed both as a Lawyer and upright Judge and a man of Great Probity and Integrity."[40] His "publick Conduct," attested others, was "most unexceptional" while "his private Character as a Gentleman entitled him to and procured him the Esteem of all who had the pleasure of his Acquaintance."[41]

Impressed with the chief justice, Governor Wright recommended his appointment to the Council. "I take him," he informed the secretary of state for the colonies, "to be a gentleman of Knowledge and great Probity, and one who does and will discharge his duty and acquit himself on the Bench with Reputation."[42] Stokes was sworn in as a member of the Council in July, 1772. The chief justice thereby assumed the role of legislator, for in addition to the cabinet or privy council functions of that body its twelve members constituted the Upper House of the provincial Assembly.

Anthony was faithful in his attendance at the Council, and was active in committee work and in the drafting of legislation when that body sat as the Upper House. According to him, there was considerable jealousy of the Council on the part of the Commons House of Assembly. Seldom, if at all, did the latter pass a bill that "originated in the Council, nor would they allow it the title of the Upper House." Stokes expressed the opinion that the Council lost its influence as a legislative body because the "members were appointed only during pleasure, and therefore, the Commons House of Assembly from jealousy, supposed they acted under influence."[43]

His Majesty's government in Georgia was rather remote from the people. Most of the officials on the civil list were Englishmen appointed by authorities across the Atlantic. When crisis came, the King had little to fall back upon in the way of popular support in the province. Stokes was vaguely aware of this failing without realizing that he himself was both a product as well as a symbol of the system. Looking back, he would have had the Upper House separated entirely from the Council. Further, he thought that the members of the former should have been appointed for life with the hereditary title of baronet bestowed upon them. Stokes advanced the idea that if they and some of the leading men had been given baronetcies, the province "never would have joined in the Civil War."[44] Such a policy would have engaged them, he believed, in the interest of the Crown so as to counterbalance the influence of "popular demagogues." It is hardly likely that a Georgia peerage would ever have measured up in his eyes to that of Great Britain which, "without any suspicion of flattery," he could term "the most respectable, and well informed body of nobility in the world."[45]

The most controversial litigation that came before Chief Justice Stokes was the writs of assistance cases. A writ of assistance or assistants was a court order directed to constables requiring them to aid customs officials in collecting duties. Sometimes the writ was in general form, authorizing officers to search any place rather than a specific place. In January, 1772, an application by the attorney-general of Georgia for general writs of assistance came before the chief justice and the three assistant justices: Noble Jones, James Deveaux, and Elisha Butler. His colleagues were planters and old residents of the province. All of them were experienced in public affairs. Stokes entertained a poor opinion of the legal ability of the assistant judges. This type of colonial jurist, he said, was "almost always unacquainted with the law."[46] Deveaux and Butler seldom attended court. One of them was "hard of Hearing; the other almost crippled with the Gout," he complained.[47]

By a 3 to 1 vote the application for the writs was denied by the General Court. While the assistant judges expressed willingness to give their utmost assistance in discovering frauds in his Majesty's customs, they felt there was "not an immediate occasion for such writs." The chief justice dissented, believing that under the statutes of Parliament and English precedent the superior courts in the colonies had no discretion in issuing the writs.

In 1773 another attempt was made by the attorney general to secure the writ. Justice Butler adhered to his former view that the request should not be granted until some necessity was shown therefor. Justice Jones, who previously had voted against the issuance of the writs, announced that he had not been apprised of the new application and was not prepared to give an opinion. Deveaux was absent. Stokes thought, as before, that the writs should be granted. Since the members of the court were evenly divided, the attorney general took nothing by his motion.[48]

An able student of constitutional law during the colonial era has attributed Chief Justice Stokes's position in this litigation to his precarious tenure of office and the fact that his salary came from the Crown.[49] To borrow the expressive phrase of Joseph C. Hutcheson, Jr.: "I had taken the king's shilling and put his red coat on. It was right that I should be the king's man." Commissions issued to chief justices in the colonies were calculated to secure subservience. Later Stokes would pointedly remind those in power in England that he had supported the royal cause by siding with the government in the matter of the writs of assistance. However, the report of the rulings shows that the validity of the general type of writ was not passed upon, the main issue before the court being whether the grant of the application was a mandatory or discretionary matter with the judges.

No one professed to believe more thoroughly in the doctrine of separation of powers and in judicial independence than Anthony Stokes. "The judiciary power ought to be separated from the legislative, and executive powers," he wrote in 1792. If it were joined to the legislative power, a subject's liberty would be exposed to "arbitrary controul," while if the judicial power were combined with that of the executive, "the judge might behave," he continued, "with all the violence of an oppressor."[50]

Georgia was no early comer to the Revolutionary fold. In other colonies she was excoriated as a laggard in the cause of "Liberty." Failure to send delegates to the First Continental Congress brought bitter words from without the province as well as self-reproach within. Governor Wright proved a resourceful antagonist. Stokes gave vigorous backing to him in his efforts to contain the rebellious element. An early Georgia historian, Hugh McCall, states in his *History of Georgia* that "the powerful talents of governor Wright and judge Stokes, and the influence they held over the royal servants, and many other inhabitants of wealth, talents and respectability, were with great difficulty over-balanced." The chief justice prided himself in the fact that "it is acknowledged on all Hands that he exerted himself more in the Cause of Government, and in opposing the Rebellion in America than any other Judge there."[51] Friends of his attested that he was a "zealous and Steady Loyalist," who "both with his Pen and his voice assisted Powerfully the Loyal Party."[52]

"Most of the gentlemen of character, abilities, and property in Georgia, were firmly attached to the British government," asserted Stokes. "For a long time," he recounted, "the peaceable, and well disposed part of the community baffled the attempts of the seditious." "Unfortunately," he continued, the "multitude are easily imposed on, and led into error, by designing, unprincipled men." They "imposed on the common people; and particularly on the Germans, Swiss and other European Emigrants . . . by promoting falsehoods — non importation agreements; and many other mischievous devices." In the end "knaves got the upper hand" and "banished the men of honor and property." Such was Stokes's explanation of the course of events in Georgia.[53]

The chief justice used the bench as a pulpit to preach the gospel of loyalty to the Crown. At a session of court in June, 1775, he recommended "to the audience then assembled, a dutiful attachment to the King's person, and government, and obedience to the laws of the land," arguing that "when law and government were once subverted, no man's life, liberty, or property would be safe."[54] Governor Wright described it as "an Excellent Charge very Properly adapt'd to the Present times."[55] Persuasive argument was the only weapon they had; and it was not enough. All that Stokes and Wright could do was chronicle for their superiors in London the dreary progress of the disintegration of royal rule.

Parliament neither offered nor sought a compromise. Tory intransigence which dominated British actions left no rallying point for the Loyalists in America. With a considerable degree of truth the Provincial Congress could inform Governor Wright in July, 1775: "We are not Acquainted with an Individual in Georgia, who looks upon the Claims of Parliament as just, and all Men Speak with abhorrence of the measures made use of to enforce them." Colonial officials were left to their own devices. The King sent neither affirmative instructions to Georgia nor redcoats. Loyal militia officers appointed by Governor Wright were soon replaced by "men who are ready to take up Arms against the King," said Stokes, "whenever they are Called upon by their Leaders. . . ."[56]

After news of the affair at Lexington reached the province "the People in Georgia hurried fast into rebellion," declared Stokes.[57] "A loose was given," he said, "to the Inferior orders of People" and the reins of government taken over by the Provincial Congress, the Council of Safety and by parochial committees.[58] Royalists were ordered out of the province; some of the outspoken among them were tarred and feathered. The King's writ was set aside and defied. When the chief justice refused bail and the writ of *habeas corpus* for a prisoner charged with enlisting recruits for the "Carolina Service," a mob broke into the jail and released him. The following day the same man passed brazenly by Stokes's doorstep as he openly went about town "beating up for Recruits." "As if it was not thought Sufficient to overturn the Civil Establishment," complained the chief justice, "the Rector of Christ Church hath been Silenced by the Authority of the Provincial Congress, for refusing to perform divine Service, on the day appointed to be kept as a Fast, by the People called the Continental Congress. . . ."[59]

As a result of the diligence of Stokes in recording the statements of royal sympathizers we hear sometimes the very voice of sedition. When a levy was attempted on the property of Robert Woodruff in St. Andrews Parish that gentleman not only threatened the levying officer with violence but added, "Nay even if it was the Chief Justice himself he would serve him in the same manner or any in Savannah for they are all a pack of Dam'd Rascals."[60] On one occasion Stokes had to play the part of constable. One night in August, 1775, he was sitting at home conversing with Hadden Smith, the Rector of Christ Church, when a Negro boy rushed in out of breath and reported that Charles Webb had sent for the chief justice as "fifteen Men were going to kill him."[61] Stokes hurried to the scene of the trouble, where he found a number of armed men, one of whom attempted to engage him in an altercation. After procuring a promise that no mischief was intended, he returned home.

When court convened at Savannah in October, 1775, none of the assistant judges was in attendance. Jones was on his deathbed;

the other two judges were "very far from being Friends to Government" and were "attached to the American Cause," the chief justice reported.[62] Others besides the assistant justices failed to turn up. Out of thirty-six grand jurors summoned for duty only eleven appeared. Of these, two were excused and five refused to be sworn. A similar result was attained when other veniremen were summoned. Though he was usually a man of "amiable and inoffensive manners," Stokes expressed himself "with great Warmth and Indignation at such unlawful and dangerous Conduct."[63] He "spoke in a very spirited and proper manner" and "behaved extremely well," according to Governor Wright, who advised the Earl of Dartmouth that some of the jurors acted "very Insolently."[64] The chief justice ordered the provost marshal to take the delinquent jurors into custody, but a showdown was averted when an attorney called his attention to a provision of the law that gave jurors thirty days in which to purge themselves of contempt by presenting proper excuses.[65] Stokes's threat was an idle one, in any event. In St. Georges Parish the people were determined to "obstruct all law proceedings until the Ports were open'd," and announced, Stokes was informed, that if any bailiff attempted to serve a *capias* or levy a fine on a defaulting juror "they would tie him up & whip him."[66] The attitude in that parish was a general one in Georgia.

On November 30 and December 1, 1775, the Provincial Congress adopted resolutions prohibiting attorneys from proceeding against debtors, save in certain instances. The chief justice promptly announced that if any attorney delayed a client's cause on the pretext of this action, his name would be stricken from the rolls. A few days later a man handed Stokes a paper, which he threw down in indignation. One of his Negroes picked it up; it proved to be a communication from the Provincial Congress warning the chief justice that if he carried out his threat he would be "an Enemy to this Country, and thenceforth be precluded from the Protection of this Congress." The angered Stokes informed Governor Wright: "The Menaces of those People will not prevent me from doing what I declared in Court."[67]

The chief justice met the challenge of the Provincial Congress by preparing a lengthy rule of court. It provided for striking from the rolls the names of any attorney who complied with the Patriot resolves. He issued the rule without conferring with his two assistant judges, Deveaux and Butler, who had not "attended the

Courts for some time" and who "differ widely from me," he explained, "in their ideas of government."

But Chief Justice Stokes was helpless. The tide was running strong against the royal government in Georgia and only the shadow of authority, as he complained, was left to the King's officers. The progress of deterioration is illustrated by an exchange of letters between Stokes and the Loyalist-minded printer of the *Georgia Gazette*.[68] The chief justice requested James Johnston to publish the rule in his newspaper, which had carried in full the seditious resolution of the Provincial Congress undertaking to regulate proceedings in the King's courts. The editor counselled against publication, pointing out to Stokes that to do so would "not only subject some of the King's Officers to Insult, and Ill Treatment, but may involve all his Majesty's well disposed Subjects here, in much Trouble." The chief justice replied that he preferred to practice the "old maxim Fiat Justitia, Ruat Coelum" (Let right be done, though the heavens should fall). Reluctantly, however, he accepted the printer's advice as to publishing the rule.

"Quotations from law books would have had no weight with men who had laid aside all respect for the King's Government," wrote Stokes in explaining a charge he delivered on December 12, 1775. Endeavoring to persuade Georgians that their proceedings were "contrary to that blessed religion which they acknowledged," he took as a text certain passages from the Scriptures, including the one, "in those days there was no King in Israel; every man did that which was right in his own eyes." He concluded his charge by admonishing his hearers, in the words of the Epistles of Peter, to "love the brotherhood. Fear God. Honour the King."[69]

The province had gone too far down the road of sedition to be brought back by homilies. A month later the chief justice abandoned the pretense of holding the King's courts. In spite of the oath of allegiance taken by the members of the bar, a majority of the attorneys were aligned with the rebels and several of them had become leaders of the insurgent cause. In Stokes's words, "when the rebellion broke out many of the lawyers joined in it, and helped to overturn the government of the country."[70] On the afternoon of January 10, 1776, the chief justice convened court for the last time. The armed guard which the Patriots had stationed at the courthouse for several days had been withdrawn that morning. Stokes read a prepared statement to those assembled. He confessed that "however firm, and determined he might act" it was impossible to "enforce the Execution of the Laws in Opposition to a whole Province." The King's superior courts were subordinated, he charged, to "a Set of men, assembled at a Tavern, who are ignorant of the Law"; and, as he could not "in honor or conscience, act under an usurpation," he would cease to execute his office "in every instance, until his Majesty's government is restored."[71]

The last vestige of royal authority in the province soon disappeared. On January 12, 1776, British warships appeared at Tybee. While his Majesty's officials were stripped of all power by the Patriots, they had been permitted to stay in the province, unmolested in person or property. The arrival of the men-of-war at the mouth of the Savannah River threw the town into great commotion and excitement. Fearful that the King's officials at Savannah would communicate with the ships, the Council of Safety ordered the arrest of Governor Wright, the chief justice, and others. On the bitterly cold night of January 18 the Government House was surrounded by twenty armed men, led by Joseph Habersham. Sir James Wright, who was closeted at the time with several members of the Council, was arrested. Stokes was not present, being confined by illness to his place in the country. Seized at his plantation, he was brought to Savannah but on account of the poor state of his health was permitted to return on parole.[72]

Shortly after the arrest of the chief justice the insurgents took over the courthouse for the use of the Provincial Congress. The young prothonotary, Henry Preston, pluckily refused to deliver up the keys despite the threat of George Walton and others that "they were come Vis et Armis & By God they must [have] them."[73] Unable to obtain peaceable entrance, the Patriots forced their way into the building. Later Preston was permitted to remove certain personal papers and while in the courthouse noticed the legal records being packed into boxes and trunks. Unfortunately, it is our last glimpse of the files of the royal courts in Georgia. Stokes reported that the "Rebels" broke into the prothonotary's office "and carried off the Publick Records," noting that it is "not improbable but that they are destroyed before this."[74]

On March 6 the chief justice was arrested again. A party of twelve armed men which appeared at his plantation seized the ailing jurist as a hostage for two Georgia officers detained by the British. After being brought to Savannah, Stokes wrote a strong letter of protest to Colonel Lachlan McIntosh to whose house he was taken. "I flatter myself," he said, "that there is not one man in this province, who accuses me of a single instance of partiality or corruption in my office of Chief Justice." He defied "all the province to say, that I ever dissembled with any of you, or declined to exert myself in my line of duty . . . notwithstanding every threat that was used towards me."[75] Stokes received no answer to this communication and was kept confined for a period of three weeks before negotiations for his exchange were concluded. While in custody, he was permitted to receive company and to go into the yard; in fact, the only incivility shown him may have been unintentional. One of his guards handed him a publication by an author he came to detest, Thomas Paine.[76]

Stokes refused to ask formal permission from the rebel authorities to leave Georgia. He had "determined to have no communication with these People," declaring that he could not in honor do so as "an officer of the Crown, and a native of Great Britain."[77] Whilst he would have no dealings with President Archibald Bulloch, the chief justice did nevertheless negotiate with Edward Langworthy, secretary of the Council of Safety. The correspondence dealt largely with the question of taking his slaves away. Refused permission in that respect, Stokes proposed that the rebel authorities agree in writing not to dispose of any property he left behind. This was sought on a "footing of right, and not of favor," for "I would not recede from my principles, in a single iota," he declared, "to save all the property I have here."[78] In the end they permitted him to take away five Negroes and his furniture and "Sundry Trunks, containing his Books & Apparel." Stokes's departure from Georgia was delayed somewhat by the necessity of raising money "to pay what debts I owe here."[79] Before leaving he took the precaution of securing permission to do so from James Mackay, the senior member of the governor's Council and the only person remaining who "had a Right to Administer Government in the Province."[80]

On May 10, 1776, the chief justice and his wife and children boarded one of his Majesty's vessels at Tybee. It was a great relief to him to reach the protection of the British ships, for, despite the firm front he had put up, he confessed himself to be "a man of weak nerves," who had "laboured under many apprehensions."[81] Stokes was satisfied with his record in Georgia. "Impartial administration of justice, had gained him the esteem of the people at large; and his uniform loyalty, and firmness of conduct, had procured him," he says in his *Narrative,* "the respect of the most violent partizans for the cause of America." Support for this claim comes from John Wereat, a member of the Council of Safety. "I am sorry that this province is deprived of so upright a Magistrate as our late Chief Justice," he informed Stokes in a letter written in May, 1776.[82]

Although Stokes detested "the conduct of some men in America in bringing on the Civil War, and the consequent ruin of their country," he harbored no resentment against Americans. If "Christianity forbids me to wish ill to an individual; how much more then does it forbid the wishing ill to thousands," he said. There would be retribution enough for the rebels. "A man who has observed the misery which the Americans brought on themselves by subverting his Majesty's Government, will put a true value," he declared, "on the inestimable blessings of a patriot King, and the best Constitution on earth."[83]

After a voyage aboard a ship so leaky carpenters "wondered how she got home," Stokes reached England late in June, 1776. He lost no time seeking financial relief from the government. The day after his arrival he left certain papers with Lord Germain, which unquestionably related to the matter of his continuation of his salary as chief justice. The ensuing two and one-half years was a period of watchful waiting for Georgia's exiled Crown officials. Stokes's chief preoccupation, besides importunities concerning his salary, was the gathering of the legal forms and materials which later went into his *View of the Constitution of the British Colonies.*

Late in December, 1778, Savannah fell to a British force sent from New York, and within a few weeks his Majesty's rule had been re-established in a large part of the province. On January 19, 1779, Anthony executed his last will and testament. In it he mentioned the fact that he was "in daily expectation of receiving orders to go to America."[84] On the same day Lord Germain sent him the following dispatch: "The King's Service requiring your presence in Georgia it is his Majestys pleasure that You do immediately prepare yourself to return to that Province."[85] The colony was to be a testing ground to prove how far, in Sir Henry Clinton's words, "the restoration of civil government might operate in calling back the disaffected colonists to the affections and sovereignty of their parent state."

Stokes secured passage on H.M.S. *Experiment,* a fifty gun ship commanded by Governor Wright's son-in-law, Sir James Wallace. The voyage was no routine one. En route, Wallace made a foray into Concalle Bay on the coast of France where two French vessels were burned and a frigate captured. In his *Narrative* Stokes says that the *Experiment* "sustained the heat of the action, having the fire of the four vessels, and also a battery in the town, playing on her at the same time." Forced to put back to England for refitting, she did not sail again for Georgia until late in May. During this interim Anthony revised a manuscript on which he had been working for the past two years. On re-embarking for Georgia he left directions for it to be printed. However, the publisher declined, and it was not until four years later that his *View of the Constitution of the British Colonies* appeared in print.

The town to which Chief Justice Stokes returned in mid-July, 1779, was vastly different from the sleepy colonial capital he had known. War had wrought great change in Savannah. Even the courthouse was taken over by the military. "Filled with Soldiers & their Wives," it was in what he called "a very disagreeable Situation."[86] The jail was once more in a "ruinous state." The provost being crowded with military prisoners, Stokes found it necessary to designate a brigantine in the harbor as a prison for persons committed by the civil authority.[87] Stokes had difficulty locating living quarters in Savannah. Finding that residence in town impaired his health, he soon moved to the country. Evidently he was at his plantation prior to August 12, 1779, and was receiving company there, for in the *Royal Georgia Gazette* of that date appears an advertisement by a Lieutenant Davis of his Majesty's 60th Regiment offering a reward for a cornelian seal, set in gold, which he had lost "between the town of Savannah and the Hon. Anthony Stokes's Plantation." Before long there would be other (and less welcome) visitors there and the chief justice himself would lose some belongings.

Early in September, 1779, a powerful French fleet showed up off Tybee. A plan was concerted with the Americans for an attack on Savannah—"the key of the southern provinces, and the Gibraltar of the gulph passage," as Stokes described it in a letter to his wife.[88] On the evening of September 12 the first contingent of French troops landed below Savannah. Three days later Count d'Estaing, their commander, was at the gates of the town haughtily demanding a capitulation.

There was much discouragement in the British camp. The royal cause seemed hopeless. Stokes had hurried back to Savannah when the French came. He did all he could to cheer the despondent. "I would not suffer the language of fear to pass my lips," he told his wife. When all appeared lost, Colonel John Maitland—that immortal soldier of the Empire—reached Savannah with his Majesty's Beaufort garrison. The demand to surrender was declined. The French and American forces thereupon settled down to a siege of the town.

In the same letter Anthony furnishes a graphic account of the bombardment which began on the night of October 3, 1779. It is a somewhat unjudicial spectacle, that of his Majesty's chief justice huddling in a cellar among puncheons of rum or falling on his face as he crossed the common amidst whistling shells. The climax of ruffled judicial dignity came when Stokes was making his way one night to a safer part of town. In passing the place where Governor Wright's slaves were encamped "I fell down," he recounted, "into a trench which they had dug."[89] If there was a humorous side to the experience, the matter-of-fact Englishman was scarcely capable of seeing it. What befell him, however, on the early morning of October 6 was real tragedy. A shell struck the house where his effects were stored and set it afire. Despite his strictures on slavery when he left America in 1776, he had resumed the proprietorship of slaves on his return. Four of his Negroes were killed on the spot and four others, Stokes said, "so much scorched, that they died in a few days." Up in flames went his personal papers and all of his law books except four volumes.[90]

On October 9 the Allies stormed the British lines. "The French behaved with great bravery," declared the chief justice. As usual, he voiced the British propaganda line about the Americans, reporting in the same communication to his wife that d'Estaing's officers spoke of them "in the most contemptible manner." After the bloody repulse the French sailed away while the Americans retired to Carolina, bringing to a close a siege which, according to Stokes, had "rendered famous a sickly hole." He believed that "with the assistance of God, British valour surmounted every difficulty" and reported that "many who did not think so much of religion before, now acknowledge that our deliverance was miraculous, and arose from the immediate interposition of God in our favour."[91]

During the siege the chief justice had been so "reduced by sickness . . . as not to be of the least service." But when he opened court in December, 1779, he was in good spirits, despite a "rheumatism" which left him scarcely able to turn his head. Congratulating his audience upon the "happy events" of the past year, he stated that "the reduction of this country by the King's arms has relieved his subjects from such tyranny, and oppression as would have disgraced even Asia itself." What the people of Georgia had done in 1775 was to exchange, continued the chief justice, "real Liberty, under a gracious and good King, for the despotick Government of their fellow-subjects, many of whom had neither common sense, nor common honesty." He further asserted that "many men who, before the rebellion, had neither reputation or property, afterwards became rulers in the land, and by fraud and rapine, acquired great wealth."[92]

At the same time, Stokes charged the grand jury at some length on the subject of high treason, characterizing it as "a crime of the highest nature that can be committed against man." Justice Joseph R. Lamar has said that the charge "reads like a page from Howell's State Trials." It became Stokes's task later to prepare an act of attainder and confiscation to be introduced in the Assembly. "I promoted this Bill," he explained, "with a Clause of Banishment, as I wished not for any sanguinary law." Refreshing his memory on the subject in after years, he observed from his diary that the drafting of the legislation affected him so greatly in "point of humanity" and lay "so heavy" upon him that he had "retired, and shed tears."[93]

The Assembly which passed the disqualifying act in 1780 and an act of attainder the following year was convened after the chief justice and the attorney general rendered an opinion that the impracticability of holding elections in parishes under rebel control did not prevent it from being a legally constituted body.[94] Their ruling that it formed as "Complete a Representation, as the Nature of Things will admit of; and must therefore of Necessity be a lawful Representation of the Whole province" was made "without the Assistance of Books," for Stokes's library was no more and Attorney General Robertson had left his law books at St. Augustine.

Difficulty in enforcing his Majesty's writ in the province was not confined to Whig-dominated areas. The chief justice had his troubles right in Savannah where some of the British army officers acted as though they fully subscribed to the maxim, *Inter arma silent leges.* "The establishment of the King's civil government in Georgia, seemed to be disagreeable to some of the military gentlemen," Stokes wryly commented. He complained that the contempt of the civil department was such that it became a question "whether a few rash young gentlemen shall overturn the King's government, by resisting the execution of his laws."[95] But disrespect for civil authority was not limited to junior officers, being shared by at least one of his Majesty's generals.

After the return of Stokes, court had been held in a house occupied by Assistant Judge Martin Jollie. One day Major General Alexander Leslie, who had recently arrived at Savannah, proceeded to take possession of the quarters for the use of himself and his suite. Jollie arrived to find most of his furniture out in the street. When he threatened legal proceedings, he was told that the military was "in possession and would keep possession" and that he "might do as he pleased." The chief justice issued a writ which was served on General Leslie. The latter refused to furnish bail, threatening "to make complaint in England." Stokes thereupon ordered him committed to jail. At this critical point Jollie and the commander came to an "accommodation." A *nolle prosequi* was entered.

The chief justice derived great satisfaction from the outcome of the affair. "The Magistrate who is timorous, or unjust, does more mischief to the community, than an hundred wicked men can encompass in private life," he had informed General Leslie on another occasion. Stokes believed that his "firm conduct had prevented oppression on the part of the military" and that he had convinced "the inhabitants, that the King's government was founded in law and justice."[96]

However, the royal courts moved on to other quarters. The perambulations to which his court was subjected were a source of concern to the chief justice. It was a serious matter, he complained, that the military was in possession of the courthouse and that the best buildings in town had been turned over respectively to a tavern keeper and to a merchant, "whilst the King's Courts are bandied about from House to House to the Great Concern of all who are well affected to his Majesty and his Government; but to the Joy of the Rebels, and their Adherents."[97]

The restored civil government in Georgia was, as has been said, a "mere incident in the military policy of England of reconquering her former colonies, and therefore received little aid apart from this purpose."[98] The government of which Chief Justice Stokes was a part could not have survived the withdrawal of the King's troops by a day. But if doubts ever crossed his mind as to how the American colonies could be permanently subdued, he did not reveal them. It was natural to suppose that military victory would restore the colonies to the King; yet, looking back, one may well speculate whether success of the royal cause was not hopeless after 1776. To Stokes, however, the "fatal blow" was Cornwallis's decision to take the southern army to Virginia. The defeat at Yorktown "occasioned the utmost consternation amongst the loyalists," he stated in his *Narrative*. For him this period of waning British fortunes was a melancholy one. The King's domain shrunk to a small area around Savannah. He was unable to reside at his waterside place and as a result his health declined. "Words cannot express," Stokes said, "the extreme depressions he frequently experienced."

The dignity of his Majesty's courts in the province seems to have suffered from the unruly spirit of the times. In *The Royal Georgia Gazette* of February 8, 1781, it was reported that a constable appeared in court drunk and "unfit to execute his offices," and that while Dr. James Houstoun, a Patriot, was being sentenced by the judge for aiding the rebel cause, the defendant's lawyer made a comment, *viva voce*, which, according to the editor, was "altogether out of season." Stokes had troubles enough without scenes in the courtroom. For one thing, he had heard that his name was among the Loyalists the Americans "intended to put to death."[99] When a rumor reached Savannah that the rebels were marching on the town, he confessed that he "never felt more uneasy in his whole life." The chief justice went so far as to plan his legal defense in the event he were brought to trial.

The King's birthday on June 4, 1782, saw a gala celebration at Savannah. The town was illuminated and there was wining and dining by the military and the civil officials. It was the dying gasp of British dominion over this realm of palmetto and pine. In a few days the sands of empire ran out. On June 14 word was received that his Majesty's troops were being withdrawn from Georgia. A week later we find Stokes where we first met him in this sketch—among the Loyalist refugees at Tybee awaiting the ship that was to carry him away forever. As he gazed at the receding shore-line of the colony in which he had spent nearly ten years it would have little consoled him to realize that he would be neither remembered nor honored there.

"Few men bred to the Law, in the peaceful retreat of an Inn of Court, have experienced," wrote Stokes, "so many vicissitudes."[100] His troubles were not over. En route to England from New York a gale caused a sudden lurch of the ship and he broke his arm. The worst blow awaited him when he reached home after an absence from his family of more than three years. His eldest son had died a few days before. He was "a young man of the most promising hopes, whose moral qualities so thoroughly kept pace with his literary acquirements, that it was doubtful in which he excelled." Compared with this loss his "other misfortunes," added the father, "are become trifles light as air."[101]

The remaining years of Stokes's life were marked by struggle and frustration. In his case, as with many of the Loyalists, there was something in this post-Revolutionary phase of sadness and anti-climax. His tribulations left their impress upon "his countenance and manner" in which friends frequently observed a "tender melancholy."[102] He had made up his mind never to return to the New World. Holding "wanton Rebellion in America, against the best of Sovereigns, in the utmost abhorrence," he declared that he "would rather suffer Distress here, than return to either of the thirteen States on the most advantageous terms."[103] But Stokes, who possessed small prestige in England, must at times have looked nostalgically upon the days before the Revolution when he had been a minor nabob in Georgia.

His efforts to secure a continuance of the compensation he had received as chief justice of Georgia began while he was in New York on his way back to England in 1782.[104] On reaching home he took up the quest in earnest. The claim files of the Georgia Loyalists bulge with petitions and communications written by Stokes during the next seven years. They make a somewhat pathetic display of importunity, self-pity, flattery, and even cajolery. No claim was filed by him for his property losses in Georgia; he desired "nothing more than a continuation of his salary, or some appointment in lieu thereof," declaring, "I attend no Meeting of the American Loyalists, nor have I the

least Concern in any of their Publications." Disappointed in this
effort, Stokes applied for relief to the commissioners appointed
to inquire into the losses and services of the Loyalists. He was
handicapped in prosecuting his claim by the fact that he had
conscientious objections against taking an oath of any kind save
that to support the government and the oath of office. If this
non-conformity seems unlike Stokes, his accompanying declaration has a familiar ring. "I would not purchase the Mines of
Peru, and Mexico," he said, "at the expence of my moral Sensa-
tions."[105]

The Commissioners of American Claims gave him a year
to year handout of £200. It was his principal means of support,
for he was never able to establish himself at the English bar.
"By a long Absence from this Country, I have lost my Connnec-
tions," Stokes explained. It was not for want of trying that he
failed to get ahead, for he maintained a "Set of Chambers in
the Temple," in order "to attend to his Profession," where he
generally spent the whole of each week except Sunday.[106] He
reported that despite attendance at court nearly every day during
one term his fees amounted to only "2 half Guinea Motions."
"Whilst I was serving my Sovereign in the prime of Life, in an
unwholesome Climate, Young Men," he complained, "have got
forward, who were at the Breast when I was called to the Bar."[107]

In 1785 Stokes was appointed provincial agent in Great
Britain for the Bahamas. The arrangement proved a not altogether happy one. The Council in the Islands got in arrears in
paying the compensation promised him and he seems to have
incurred the wrath of some of the inhabitants by his alleged
misrepresentation of the state of affairs in the Bahamas in 1789.[108]
On top of all his troubles he was pressed for a debt by Joseph
Clay, a Georgian. Assuring Stokes of his "personal regard," the
Savannah merchant asked reimbursement for a prospective loss
under a bond he had signed many years before at the behest of
the chief justice.[109]

Stokes's finances were hardly improved by his three ventures
as an author. His *View of the Constitution of the British Colonies,* which appeared in 1783, was primarily a survey of the
governments and legal systems of the British possessions in
America and the West Indies. It was also a form book of legal
precedent used in the colonies. A reviewer predicted that if it
were "received in proportion to its utility and merit, it will

have a good sale."[110] Quite probably Stokes realized small returns from the work. Nevertheless, he proceeded with the publication of his *Narrative* the following year. Written for the "Information of his Friends," this pamphlet was designed to promote his claims on the British government by recounting his loyal conduct in the office of chief justice.

The most interesting of Stokes's writings is *Desultory Observations*. It was published in 1792, being inspired by what the author described as "several seditious publications that have lately appeared, in which the blessings this nation enjoys, are impudently misrepresented." As he states in the title, its object was "to point out the Blessings which the English enjoy above all other Nations." The work is an uncompromising defense and eulogy of England—its soil (Stokes predicted that the population in America between the Appalachian Mountains and the Atlantic would "gradually decrease"); its weather; its lack of noxious animals; the integrity of the merchant class in England; British ship building skill; the peerage of Great Britain; its judiciary; and British justice and liberty. An inveterate champion of the *status quo,* Stokes looked on the democratic trend in France and America with something akin to horror. He defended the borough system in Great Britain and praised the Established Church. He was bitter on the subject of Presbyterianism and had tart words for English Catholicism. The main flaw Stokes discerned in the England of the day was the "neglect of religion, and fondness for public amusements, which have pervaded all orders of men." He complained that "now-a-days almost every one lives beyond his circumstances."

It is unfortunate that Stokes (who was one of the few actual participants in the revolutionary scene in Georgia to write about it) possessed little virtuosity as historian or autobiographer. He was not a talented reporter of events and his style is rather ponderous. But, whatever were his shortcomings as an author, his writings are valuable for the insight they afford into colonial Georgia — its courts, government, inhabitants, and economy — and equally so in their revelation of a Crown official's viewpoint of the rebellion in that province. In Georgia the lot of Anthony Stokes has been forgetfulness and neglect, a common fate of nearly all the Loyalists, who have received, as has been said, "scant justice from the Conqueror's historians."[111] Chief Justice Stokes stands out among them as the foremost apologist for

the royalist cause in the colony. As such and as the author of
the most extensive commentaries on the province of his day, he
deserves something more than the veil of obscurity that has
enshrouded him these many years.

The former chief justice of Georgia died at his home in Kensington Square in London on March 27, 1799.[112] He was in his
sixty-fourth year. "The unaffected excellence of his character,
the purity of his religion, and the goodness of his heart entitled
him," said a Savannah newspaper, "to the regard of all who
had the happiness of knowing him."[113]

Stokes died without the satisfaction of seeing the fulfillment
of his prophecy as to the ultimate fate of the tidewater section
of Georgia and South Carolina. In his *View of the Constitution
of the British Colonies* he had predicted that "the civilized
parts of the rice Colonies, who have not now a common parent
to call to their assistance," would one day be "overrun" by the
Crackers "as the Tartars in Asia have done by the fruitful cultivated provinces in the southern parts of that country."

BENJAMIN HAWKINS

BY MERRITT B. POUND

BENJAMIN HAWKINS was born of Virginia ancestry on August 15, 1754, in what is now Warren County, North Carolina, where his parents had settled a few years before. He was a member of a large family which became prominent and respected in North Carolina. His father owned a gristmill, raised tobacco, and became prosperous enough to send Benjamin and his brother Joseph to the College of New Jersey at Princeton.[1]

Driven out of Princeton in January, 1777, by the advance of the British, Hawkins, because of his demonstrated proficiency in French, became an interpreter on General Washington's staff and served in this capacity for more than a year. He evidently left the service of the Commander-in-Chief because of a super-abundance of officers.[2] Back in his home state Hawkins became commercial agent for North Carolina and a commissioner of the Board of Trade. In these capacities he contributed significantly to North Carolina's effort during the Revolution.

Hawkins's success as commercial agent attracted favorable attention in the General Assembly. In July, 1781, he was elected a delegate to Congress. He served five terms in this body with distinction. He was punctual in attendance and, serving as many terms as he was constitutionally eligible to serve under Article V of the Articles of Confederation, he probably attended more sessions of Congress from 1781 to 1789 than any other member. During a period of ineligibility to represent his state in Congress he represented his county in the Lower House of the General Assembly of North Carolina.

He was present at the session of Congress which called the

Merritt B. Pound is head of the political science department at the University of Georgia.

Constitutional Convention of 1787 and was also in attendance when the Convention adjourned and the Constitution was presented to Congress to be referred to the states for their ratifications. He returned home to participate in the campaign for ratification and though North Carolina failed to ratify in July, 1788, at Hillsborough, Hawkins was a member of the convention which ratified the Constitution of the United States at Fayetteville on November 21, 1789. Shortly after the Fayetteville Convention he was elected as one of the two original senators from North Carolina and drew the long term which expired in 1795. He was considered a Federalist while in the Senate, largely because of his friendship with President Washington, and the Republican legislature of North Carolina did not re-elect him for a second term.

Because of his demonstrated ability, his popularity, and the prominence of his family, Hawkins might have continued a distinguished career, already well under way, had he elected to remain in his native state. His national importance, however, and his importance in Georgia history, are due to his long residence among the Creek Indians in Georgia. It is this phase of his life that will be emphasized in this biographical sketch.

Following the Treaty of Paris, 1783, the Indian policy of the United States was chaotic.[3] During the 1783 session of Congress Hawkins, as a matter of routine, received several appointments to committees dealing with Indian problems which had resulted from the successful termination of the American Revolution. The increasing frequency with which he served on such committees indicates certain abilities which led to many later appointments.

On January 1, 1784, Alexander McGillivray, educated chief of the Creeks and a power among Southern Indians, despite the fact that he was half Scotch, a quarter French, and only a quarter Creek, had written Governor Don Arthur O'Neill of Florida proposing an Indian alliance with Spain. This threat led Congress to appoint a commission to negotiate treaties with the Southern tribes. Hawkins and Joseph Martin from North Carolina, Daniel Carroll from Maryland, and Andrew Pickens from South Carolina were named to the commission.[4]

As soon as it had become evident that independence from England was to be gained, Georgia and North Carolina became interested in opening up their western lands for the benefit of their citizens and were determined to clear the western parts of the states of Indian titles. In 1783 Georgia had signed a treaty with the Creeks at Augusta which McGillivray later repudiated as fraudulent.[5] Georgia, on the other hand, held that the treaty was valid and was determined to enforce it and remove the Creeks from the lands involved in the negotiations. North Carolina, likewise, wanted to move the Cherokees farther west. It was under such conditions that Congress appointed the treaty commission.

In October, 1785, Hawkins, Pickens, and Martin met some of the Creeks at Galphinton, a trading post on the Ogeechee River in Georgia. McGillivray, still under the influence of the Spaniards, kept so many of the Indians away from the conference that the commissioners felt a treaty was inadvisable and on November 8 they left the treaty grounds.[6] Georgia commissioners, who were present to protest the right of the United States to treat with the Creeks in Georgia, immediately signed a treaty with the few chiefs present confirming that of Augusta of two years before.[7]

The United States commissioners journeyed to Hopewell on the Keowee River in South Carolina where treaties were signed with the Cherokees in November, 1785, and with the Chickasaws and Choctaws in January, 1786. William Blount, a congressional colleague of Hawkins, attended all of these conferences as a representative of North Carolina and immediately protested each of the treaties on behalf of his state.[8]

Though all of the commissioners were Southerners, two North Carolinians and one Georgian among them, protests continued from North Carolina and Georgia.[9] Through his prominence in the negotiations Hawkins incurred the displeasure of citizens in both states. Political opposition developed against him in North Carolina and Georgians never entirely forgave him for what was done at Galphinton and Hopewell.

Despite the treaties of friendship which had been signed with three of the Southern nations, the Indian problem continued to plague Congress. Not only had the commissioners refused to treat with the Creeks, the strongest and most warlike of the Southern Indians who were in consequence threatening war, but even those tribes which had signed were restless and constantly reported grievances and trespasses.

Confronted with the almost insuperable problems of the post-war period, Congress considered amity with the Indians a necessity. Accordingly, on August 7, 1786, an ordinance for the regulation of Indian affairs was passed. After reasserting, for the benefit of such states as Georgia and North Carolina, the sole and exclusive right of Congress under the Articles of Confederation (Article IX) to deal with the Indian tribes, two districts were set up with a superintendent for each. The Ohio River was the dividing line. The superintendents, not the governors of any states, were to be the highest administrative authorities in the Indian country. They were to regulate trade and travel, enforce the law relating to whites and Indians, report rumored hostilities, and handle the Indians as their personal wards.[10] Georgia ignored the ordinance, as it had consistently ignored Article IX of the Articles of Confederation, and on November 3, 1786, signed with the Creeks the Treaty of Shoulderbone. Again, only a small body of Creeks, pretending to speak for the Nation, signed and gave up the Indian claims to all lands east of the Oconee River.[11]

On the frontier conditions were serious. McGillivray, who had refused to attend the conference at Shoulderbone as he had the earlier one at Galphinton, now repudiated both of these treaties as well as the one signed at Augusta in 1783. Frequent border conflicts led to complaints by both Georgia and the Indians and gave promise of an early outbreak of a general war. Several attempted negotiations fell through and it was not until September, 1789, that a commission of the United States met the Creeks at Rock Landing on the Oconee River.[12] Due to the absence of McGillivray this conference proved abortive.[13]

Under such circumstances President Washington planned to get McGillivray and other Creek chiefs to New York. Colonel Marinus Willett was chosen for the mission. Hawkins had in the meantime taken his seat in the Senate and the President used him to prepare the way for a cordial reception of Willett and his party of Creeks at the home of McGillivray.[14] After months of negotiations the Treaty of New York was signed on August 7, 1790. Though only Secretary of War Henry Knox signed for the United States, Hawkins served him in an advisory capacity throughout the negotiations. This was the first treaty ever signed between the United States and the Creeks. It seemed to presage a new era in Indian relations, but Georgia was far from satisfied and McGillivray continued to oppose that state until his death in 1793.

Georgia was unwilling to accept the Treaty of New York which was considered a violation of the rights of the state. The two most unacceptable features of the treaty were its failure to confirm the land cessions of Galphinton and Shoulderbone, and the implied permanency of the Indian title in the expressed purpose of the United States to furnish the Creeks with free domestic animals and tools and to convert them to the white man's way of life. One historian has characterized Georgia's reaction as follows:

This treaty shocked the Georgians into a daze, out of which they finally emerged only to enter a rage. It was unthinkable to them that a Government of civilized white people would definitely hand over to the savages for permanent occupation all of Georgia excepting a small eastern strip, and, to fix their minds against ever being induced to move, would attach them to the land as farmers. This treaty marked the entry into the heart of Georgia of a gall-like bitterness against the United States government which tinctured her relations with the Federal government in a deep and lasting way.[15]

As Hawkins's senatorial career was nearing a close President Washington was again concerned with the Indian situation in the South. Georgia was demanding new cessions of Creek lands. Accordingly in June, 1795, Washington appointed Hawkins, George Clymer of Pennsylvania, and General Andrew Pickens of South Carolina to treat with the Creeks.[16] When the negotiations began in the summer of 1796 at Coleraine on the St. Marys River, Georgia commissioners were also present and anxious to clear the title to much land in the state then in dispute. The Georgia commission, composed of James Hendricks as chairman, James Jackson, and James Simms,[17] still maintained that the cessions made at Augusta, Galphinton, and Shoulderbone were valid and that the state was not bound by the restrictions of the Treaty of New York. They also held that Georgia's claim to the region between the Altamaha and St. Marys rivers was not subject to negotiation since an act had already been passed by the General Assembly for occupation of this territory. A desire to prevent bloodshed and to have her claims recognized by the Indians and the United States, however, led the state to defray half the expenses of the treaty negotiations, though she was unwilling to concede that participation in them be considered an acknowledgment that the earlier treaties between Georgia and the Creeks had been superceded at New York. The United States commissioners supported the contention of the Creeks that they were bound only by the agreement at New York and on June 29, 1796, signed the Treaty of Coleraine confirming the Treaty of New York and making practically no concessions to the demands of the Georgians.[18]

As chairman of the United States commission Hawkins, with a storm of protest behind him, left Georgia and journeyed north to report his actions to the President who informed Congress on December 7 that while Georgia's desires had not been accomplished the treaty was a success and by means of it " . . . the general peace may be more effectually preserved."[19] Georgia remained unreconciled and continued to protest, blaming Hawkins for the disagreeable treaty. This feeling of bitterness in the state was not conductive to a cordial reception of the chairman of the commission when it fell his lot to return as agent of the Creeks.

On November 6, 1792, in an address to Congress, President Washington voiced the opinion that " . . . the employment of qualified persons to reside among them [the Indians] as agents would also contribute to the preservation of peace and good neighborhood."[20] When Tennessee was admitted as a state in 1796 the position of Superintendent of Indian Affairs for the Southern District, which had been created in 1786, lapsed, and Hawkins was appointed by the President as Principal Temporary Agent for Indian Affairs South of the Ohio River.[21]

An explanation of Hawkins's appointment was published in the *Republican and Savannah Evening Ledger.*

After Col. Hawkins returned to the seat of government from the treaty of Colerain with the Creek Indians, he represented to President Washington that he thought, that the tribe of Indians might be kept at peace, under proper management, by an Agent of Indian Affairs; but that a great sacrifice must be made by a man of talents, who ought to fill the office and reside constantly among the Indians. General Washington replied, "You have on no occasion heretofore refused your services when necessarily called for by the general government, I wish you to sacrifice a few years of your life in making the experiment which you have suggested, and try the effects of civilization among them." This proposition left Col. Hawkins no room for a retreat. He accepted the appointment. . . .[22]

During the winter of 1796-97 the new agent made a three-months journey through the lands of the Cherokees and the Creeks in order to become better acquainted with his new wards. He stopped frequently to converse with those he met, half-breed traders and Indians alike. He was dependent upon these people for shelter and refreshment, for information and guidance. His journal, often garrulous, replete with minute detail, is a valuable source of information about the country and the people with whom he came in contact.[23]

Among the first duties assigned to Colonel Hawkins after his appointment was the running of boundary lines between Tennessee and the Cherokees and between Georgia and the Creeks, agreeing with treaties between the United States and the Indians. In Tennessee he encountered much opposition from private individuals as well as state officials and obstacles were placed before him by Governor John Sevier. Hawkins was forced to leave Tennessee before the surveys were over but only after the completion of the line seemed assured. The citizens of Tennessee were dissatisfied with Hawkins because of his insistence on the rights of the Indians. A friend of Hawkins reported on November 14, 1797, that two Indians had recently been killed by some whites who had been removed from Cherokee lands. In defense of Hawkins he wrote:

. . . to manifest their disapprobation of the justice of government in forcing them from their plundered possessions—the immaculate government of Tennessee, dissatisfied with the line established by the late commissioners have had it run again by a holy pack of insurgents— who report the line imperfect—and Colo. Hawkins a liar—a set of brutes as they are, to endeavour to smudge the reputation of a man, who has more sense, honor and honesty, than the whole state of Tennessee put together.[24]

After leaving Tennessee Hawkins supervised the running of the line between the Creeks and Georgia under the terms of the Treaty of Coleraine. On February 16, 1798, he reported to Secretary of War James McHenry: " . . . I am happy to be able to assure you that there was no diversity of opinion among us, and that the line was closed in perfect harmony."[25]

He next served as a member of the commission to survey the boundary between the United States and Spanish Florida under the treaty agreement of 1795. Andrew Ellicott had been commissioned as the surveyor on the part of the United States. He had descended the Ohio and Mississippi rivers to New Orleans in 1796, encountered opposition from Spanish officials but eventually reached Pensacola, where he requested Hawkins to meet him in April, 1799.[26] Months were lost before the Spanish officials, who were stirring up the Indians to oppose the line, would agree to complete the survey. During this time Hawkins handled the situation in such a way as to elicit from Ellicott praise for "that firmness, caution, and candour, for which he has been so justly esteemed."[27] Finally, after other delays, Ellicott's party, accompanied by Captain Minor, the Spanish commissioner, with a detachment of Spanish soldiers, was at the mouth of the Flint River when, on September 17, it was threatened by a band of hostile Indians. The next day the surveying party began a retreat to Pensacola, leaving only Hawkins to quiet the Creeks, and the line was never completed.[28]

Ellicott laid the whole blame for the failure on the treachery of the Spanish officials. Hawkins, on the other hand, placed part of the blame on Ellicott inexcusable delays:

It is not yet explained to me why the commissioners made a halt of three months on the Chattahoochee. You know how seriously I pressed them not to remain more than two, and that in that case they might proceed in perfect safety, as they would be moving in the session of the Boos-ke-tah, when all of the discontented would be attending on the ceremonies of the annual festival, which always occurs in the month of August. The baggage I saw at Ko-en-cuh was great, and I was surprised to see Americans, who have been accustomed to travel through the woods, encumber themselves with such unnecessary and useless baggage. One fact I will relate. The flat irons, alone, for the commissioners weigh 150 lbs and it takes four horses to move Mr. Ellicott's washerwoman.[29]

Though the Indian disorder was encouraged by the Spaniards and abetted by the culpable delay of the commissioners themselves, Hawkins, as agent, was responsible for the punishment of the perpetrators. He consistently took the view that most of the Indians would abide by their obligations and that all should not be condemned for the crimes of the few. The chiefs were informed of the crime and satisfaction was demanded. Upon receipt of Hawkins's demands a council was called at Tookaubatchee, the Creek council town on the Tallapoosa River, and it was agreed that all who had taken part in the insults to the survey party should be punished. On October 29 the house of one of the leaders was surrounded, his treatment recorded as follows:

We pulled down and set fire to his house; we beat him with sticks until he was on the ground as a dead man, we cut off one of his ears with a part of his cheek and put a sharp stick up his fundament.[30]

Justice was thus executed in the Indian manner, Hawkins applauding this cruel act and demanding that others be punished likewise. Yet he was normally not a cruel man, neither was he crude. No doubt his sensibilities were deeply offended. The circumstances of the attack inclined him perhaps to sympathize with the Indians. Nevertheless he was responsible to his government for order and law enforcement in a wild domain. Where the justice of the white man did not prevail, and would not have been understood, he could subscribe to the Indian manner of punishment if it were effective. Hawkins unquestionably was a successful agent. No doubt his success was in large measure due to his willingness to compromise with the Indians where there were incompatible differences between their customs and those of the white man.

Hawkins had been in the Indian country only a few months as Principal Temporary Agent when President Washington retired from office. President Adams, as Vice President and presiding officer of the Senate, had known and served with Hawkins in that body. He was therefore acquainted with Hawkins's qualifications for the position he held and continued him in office as a matter of course.

For some years Hawkins did not establish a permanent residence but spent his time among the Indians, in their villages and at army posts in the Indian country. During this peripatetic period he was often at the Creek towns of Cussetuh, Cowetuh, and Tookaubatchee; but he preferred Fort Wilkinson on the Oconee River. Though he had served with Thomas Jefferson in Congress and had corresponded with him at intervals for more than fifteen years, he had no assurance, other than his belief that Jefferson was sympathetic with what he was trying to do, that he would be continued in his position after March, 1801. His original appointment may have been due to his Federalist affiliations, but his continuation in office under four presidents was the result of demonstrated ability.

When his commission from President Jefferson arrived Hawkins was no longer Principal Temporary Agent but Principal Agent for the Creeks on a permanent basis. A new period of his administration of Indian affairs began. He felt that he could establish a permanent location for his agency and build a home. One of the stipulations of the Treaty of Coleraine was that the federal government might set up reservations five miles square on the rivers in Creek country for trading purposes and military posts. Hawkins selected such a site on the Flint River for his home. The agency reservation was marked out on both sides of the river in what are now Crawford and Taylor counties in Georgia. Hawkins's home was on the east bank and on the opposite bank was located Fort Lawrence. There he lived among the Indians as neighbor, as friend, as benefactor, but most important to him, as representative of the United States.

The Flint was an excellent choice of location for the permanent agency. It was in the midst of the country of the Lower Creeks, yet accessible to Georgia and the white settlements. Fort Hawkins on the Ocmulgee, built in 1806 as a factory and military post and named for the agent, was only a day's journey to the east. To the west a slightly longer journey would carry one into the center of the towns on the Chattahoochee, and across the Chattahoochee lived the Upper Creeks. Better still, it was possible to visit most of the Lower Creeks by water; and Hawkins often used this mode of travel. It was not unusual to see Indian canoes or dug-outs pulled up on the banks at the agency; and many hours and days were spent by Hawkins in company with Indian companions paddling along the placid waters of the Flint or up the broader Chattahoochee.

Hawkins was a born dirt farmer with his roots in the soil. On the agency reservation he cultivated a large plantation. It was well stocked with horses, cattle, and other livestock and worked with Negro slaves, some of whom he brought with him from North Carolina. Agricultural interests were natural with him because his early life had been spent on the farm among successful farmers. In much of his correspondence with Washington, Jefferson, and Madison about political affairs he also discussed crops, weather conditions, and insect pests. He was interested in anything that grew. The Indians were his first thought; agriculture was his recreation and hobby, as well as his part-time vocation. Thoroughly convinced that the future of the Indians lay in the cultivation of the soil rather than in hunting, he was especially interested in showing them what their lands would produce under proper tillage.[31]

President Jefferson in his message to Congress on December 8, 1801, reported that Hawkins had introduced sheep among the Creeks and that these Indians were also raising horses, cattle, and goats. Agriculture was "slowly progressive." Among the improvements credited to Hawkins were the settlement of the Indians in villages in new ground, the fencing of fields, and the use of fifty plows. A nursery of peach trees among the Lower Creeks had produced 5,000 trees and another had recently been established among the Upper Creeks. Prior to the establishment of the nurseries, Hawkins had raised peach trees and distributed them at his own expense. Short-staple cotton was grown in small quantities and some had been marketed in Tennessee. Experiments in the growing of sea-island cotton were carried on. Flax, rice, wheat, barley, rye, and oats were introduced. "Apple trees, grape vines, raspberries, and the roots, herbs, and vegetables, usually cultivated in good gardens, have lately been introduced, they all thrive well."[32] Hawkins also had a personal patch of tobacco.

Frequent public references were made to the advance of the Indians during Hawkins's incumbency, not only in agriculture but in industry as well. Several of Jefferson's messages commented upon this advance. In 1807 he wrote: "The great tribes in our Southwestern quarter, much advanced beyond others in agriculture and household arts, appear tranquil, and identifying their views with ours, in proportion to their advancement."[33]

Madison also, as President, made similar references in his messages to Congress, and favorable editorial comment in the Georgia papers was not lacking. On January 24, 1806, the Savannah *Georgia Republican* commented:

Our readers are no strangers to the enlightened and indefatigable exertions of Colonial Hawkins to ameliorate the conditions of the aborigines of the Country, by introducing among them the blessings of civilization. The success with which these efforts have been attended in the short period of ten years is without parallel in the history of savage nations.

In the summer of 1808 the report spread that Hawkins had been driven from the agency by the Indians.[34] He learned of this report and as evidence that he was at home and that the Indians were still practicing the arts of civilization under his tutelage he wrote:

The plan of civilization is progressive. We are clothing and feeding ourselves. The tin ware we use; the hats, shoes and boots, and the saddle I ride on, are made in the Agency; and all the leather we use or want is tanned at the Agency. My family of eighty persons are all clothed in homespun.[35]

Though Hawkins was unmarried when he took up his abode with the Indians and it was customary for white men living there to take Indian women as wives or mistresses, there is no evidence that he ever did so. He was critical of such arrangements only when the white men mistreated their women or deserted their Indian children, but he felt that for the United States agent to take an Indian wife would lessen his influence among these people. Most of the white men had no association with the women except those they lived with. Hawkins, however, visited with them, treated them kindly, and occasionally invited them to dine at his home. He held no high opinion of them nevertheless, observing that:

They have a great propensity to be obscene in conversation, and they call everything by its name, and if the concurrent testimony of the white husbands can be relied on, the women have much of the temper of the mule, except when amorous, and then they exhibit all the amiable and gentle qualities of the cat.[36]

Hawkins took for his common-law wife a white woman named Lavinia Downs. Just who she was, where she came from, and when she first began to live with him is unknown. In 1812 his chronic ill-health led him to fear he would not long survive. Accordingly he was married and his will distributing his estate among six children, a wife, and a nephew, was drawn up on the same day.[37] The absence of a publicly spoken and legally recorded vow did not lessen his feelings of obligation and responsibility toward his wife and children.

Hawkins spent much of his time in removing from Indian lands white men who had come there, without proper authority, to prey on the Indians. His hospitality, however, was well known, and the legitimate traveller was accorded a cordial welcome. Visitors were frequently entertained and transients of any race were assured a cordial reception and excellent fare in abundance. Traders, Indian Department officials, and army officers were so frequently at the agency as to cause little comment. The French General Jean Victor Moreau spent some time there in the spring of 1808, and when he left he was escorted through the Nation towards Charleston by the agent himself.[38]

There is little in Hawkins's correspondence to indicate his religious philosophy. He certainly did not think of himself as a missionary. He often cooperated with Quaker societies which were interested in Indian education; but he did not attempt to force his religious views upon the Creeks. He was to them teacher, friend, lawgiver, judge — but never priest. He wrote Secretary of State Madison on July 11, 1803:

Tell Mrs. Madison we are all Quakers in the Indian Agency and there is little or no difference now between our annual meetings and the annual meetings of our white brethren, we are full as silent, as grave, and circumspect here as in Philadelphia. We are under the guidance of reason, and they under the light of the gospel, in pursuit of the same object. . . . If our doctrine of hereafter is unformed in the opinion of our white friends, we will exchange our *guide* for their *light* and subscribe to whatever they recommend provided they will assist us here, to preserve the birthright portion of the planet we inhabit. To this end the little that we require is, that the followers of the meek and humble Jesus will believe we are their neighbors, and treat us accordingly.[39]

Prior to the administration of President Jefferson, Hawkins had jurisdiction over, and responsibility for, all of the Indians south of the Ohio River. His charges included Cherokees, Choctaws, and Chickasaws as well as Creeks, and he was called *Iste-chate-ligeosetate-chemiste-chaugo* (Beloved man of the Four Nations). In 1798 the Mississippi Territory was created and Winthrop Sargent was appointed governor. This appointment was a continuous source of embarrassment to Hawkins. Sargent was succeeded in 1801 by W. C. C. Claiborne; and, though Hawkins's jurisdiction was then limited to the Creeks alone, the conflict of powers continued. On February 23, 1802, Secretary of War Henry Dearborn informed Claiborne that under the presidential regulations governors of the territories were Indian agents and all subagents should correspond with them. He added, however: "Colo. Hawkins and the Agents of the Factories at Tillico [*sic*.] in Tennessee and in Georgia will communicate with the Secretary of War as usual."[40]

The laws of Georgia did not extend into the Indian country

and, except for Hawkins and his assistants, the only officers in
this region were the military. He, at times, exercised legislative,
executive, and judicial functions over both Indians and white inhabitants. In addition, he served as diplomatic agent for the
United States and his copper-colored wards. Among his many
duties the following were routine: he issued passes to travellers
and licenses to traders; distributed goods and annuities to the
Indians; apprehended and returned runaway slaves; returned
stolen slaves, cattle, horses, and even dogs; adjudicated disputes
of ownership between Indians, between Indians and whites, and
between whites living in Indian country; demanded, and secured,
punishment for criminal offenses; directed posses and military expeditions; officiated at conferences; settled disputes between Indians and the states; and, in his capacity as a federal officer, performed marriage ceremonies.

It is needless to say that all of his duties were not executed
with uniform perfection or with satisfaction to all concerned. His
territorial jurisdiction extended over a wide area, his assistance
was inadequate, and his charges varied from the simple and primitive to the extremely vicious and incorrigible. He also stood in
the way of individuals who wished to take advantage of the Indians, and of the states which wished to extend their boundaries
and territorial jurisdiction. On the other hand, he insisted upon
the Indians living up to regulations; and with impartiality he
demanded that wrongs be atoned for. Naturally he made enemies.
Under such circumstances it is doubtful if anyone could have
failed to do so, but it is difficult to escape the conclusion that but
for his sincerity and honesty he could not have retained the affection of the great majority of the Indians and the respect of
the whites who knew him for his long tenure of office.

Among the Southern Indians the Creeks were the strongest,
the most warlike, and most often and most seriously embroiled in
difficulties with the white men. In their relations with Georgia
and the United States they had been led by more astute and capable leaders than had other tribes. When Hawkins came to
Georgia he found two divisions among these Indians and a further
decentralization of control because of the comparative independence of each town of the Nation. Under such conditions it was
well-nigh impossible to locate responsibility for crimes and depre-
dations. One of the great sources of conflict between Georgia and

the Creeks had been the refusal of some chiefs and towns to recognize agreements made by others.

During the year 1798 Hawkins presented a plan of government to the Creeks which they accepted. The new scheme was so successfully inaugurated that it was made a part of the message of Jefferson to Congress in December, 1801. As described in this message, the national council met once a year, usually in May, at the call of Hawkins. Each town was asked to send deputies. The first order of business was a report on the state of the Nation by the agent. Next the agent advised the council as to what action it needed to take and demanded punishment for crimes committed and compensation for treaty violations. In many respects the relationship of the agent to the council was similar to that of the President to Congress.[41]

Such an arrangement made the agent tremendously effective in the internal affairs of the Creeks and gave him power over them that had not been approximated since the death of McGillivray. He became, in fact, the first chief of the Nation and his influence was paramount over the native chiefs. Conflicts between Georgia and the Creeks continued but Governor Jared Irwin had confidence in Hawkins's desire "to do ample justice to the citizens on all occasions."[42] He supported the agent's efforts to keep peace on the frontier, yet conditions were often such that Chief Tuskeegee Tustunugee could truthfully say to Hawkins: "Your situation for a while was of that sort, which got you blaim [sic.] from both sides. . . ."[43]

After the Revolution the notorious adventurer William Augustus Bowles, Maryland native and Revolutionary soldier who had deserted to the British, appeared among the Creeks and became a serious rival of McGillivray. In 1792 he was captured, turned over to Spanish authorities, and taken to Spain. He was either freed or he escaped and made his way to London. There he was received cordially by British officials and was returned to Florida on board His Majesty's schooner Fox in 1799.[44]

Styling himself "Chief and Director General of the Creeks," Bowles insisted that the Indians were an independent Nation and subject neither to the United States nor to Spain. A contest for Creek control was thus on between Colonel Hawkins and General Bowles. In 1799 Hawkins addressed to "Mr. W. A. Bowles, Styled by Himself, Director General of Muskugee," the following letter:

The plan of the government instructed to my Agency is benevolent in the extreme — it is to introduce the wheel, the loom and the plough, to turn the attention of the Indians to raising cattle hogs and horses and to facilitate to them the means of procuring them; to promote civilization among them and peace toward their neighbours. If in executing my orders faithfully I am considered as a dangerous man I assure you I shall be extremely so, as I omit no opportunity to execute this plan with zeal and fidelity.

I hope it is a farce you have been acting and not a tragedy, that you have played the last act, made your exit, and returned to your employees. If you have not, it becomes my duty to inform you that you are together with your aiders and abettors on or before the 25th of this month to quit the territory of the Creeks, and not to return again under penalty ordained by the laws.[45]

Bowles at first confined his operations to Spanish Florida and secured most of his Indian support from the Seminoles but made some headway with the Upper Creeks. As a result the Indians became restless, sullen, and difficult to manage. He even caused the defeat of a proposed treaty in 1803 and persuaded the Upper Creeks to deny in writing the authority of Colonel Hawkins.[46] In 1803 a council was assembled at Tookaubatchee at Hawkins's persuasion and delegations from the Cherokees, Chickasaws, and Choctaws joined the Creeks. On May 24 Bowles arrived at the head of a band of Seminoles and accompanied by some Upper Creek chiefs friendly to him. Hawkins's influence prevailed and the next day Bowles was arrested, placed in chains, and delivered to Governor Vizente Folch of Florida.[47] He was confined in Morro Castle and died there in 1806.[48]

There had been some signs of resistance to Bowles's arrest, but due to the efforts of Hawkins and the Lower Creek chiefs the discontent subsided and the council drew up a declaration that they were resolved "on eternal peace with all the world, that when they were dead and gone their children might grow up in peace, repeat and remember this talk and take it to the end of the world."[49]

It was Jefferson's expressed purpose to keep Hawkins as one of the commissioners at every treaty conference with the Southern tribes. He accordingly was a member of the commissions which signed treaties with the Chickasaws in 1801, and with the Creeks in 1802 and again in 1804.

The agent's duties between 1806 and 1810 were principally routine. On the whole the Indians were quiet and Georgia was comparatively acquiescent in regard to its boundaries. Thefts, illegal trading, and mutual trespasses created minor disturbances and Georgians were constantly clamoring for the return of stolen properties.

As the War of 1812 drew near, wagon roads into Indian country became necessary for military purposes. President Madison instructed Hawkins to overcome Indian opposition to their construction, and two roads were laid out, one from Athens, Georgia, to Fort Stoddert, near Mobile on the Tombigby River, and another from the Tennessee River to the same terminus. The road from Athens was completed on November 30, 1811, and Hawkins wrote Governor David B. Mitchell of Georgia a few days later: "I find some difficulties in restraining our wild young men from taking toll unnecessarily and very unjustly from our travellers."[50]

After calling the Lower Creek towns together Hawkins secured the promise of protection to all travelers. The road became popular as it became safe, Hawkins reporting that between October 16, 1811, and March 16, 1812, a total of 233 vehicles and 3,726 persons had passed the agency en route to the West.[51] By the time the road was opened the war clouds were darker and soon troops and artillery took the place of traders and covered wagons. The voice of commerce was drowned by the war-whoop; and dripping scalps replaced calicos and ginghams in the marts of Indian trade.

With the approach of war in 1811, Tecumseh, the Shawnee chief and leader of the Indians of the Northwest, was persuaded by the British to seek the alliance of the Southern tribes. He accordingly set out for Tookaubatchee and the meeting of the Creek council in October. The rumor that Tecumseh would be present caused an unusual attendance and about 5,000 Indians were on hand. Causes of discontent among the Creeks were numerous. The hatred engendered by the conflicts with Georgia, the schemes of land speculators, and the wagon road "filled from one end to another" were enough to induce some of them to listen to Tecumseh. When he delivered his war talk he prepared calendars of bundles of small sticks painted red. In each bundle there were sticks corresponding to the number of days before the attack on the settlements was to be launched. Each morning the chiefs to whom the bundles were given were to throw away a stick. When all were gone the attack was to take place.[52]

Tecumseh's mission did not end with the Creeks. He made contacts with the Seminoles, Cherokees, and other Southern Indians, and at the head of six-hundred picked warriors from the Northwestern and Southern tribes he defied the power of the United States in the Southwest. Big Warrior and certain Lower Creek chiefs, notably William McIntosh, stood out against him but failed to counteract his influence.[53]

Hawkins was now faced with a handicap similar to that he had overcome in his contest with the notorious Bowles. He was agent of the United States and was attempting to carry out a permanent policy of Indian control. He had spent long years in trying to wean the Indians from their expectations of constant gifts and favors. He therefore could not meet the offers of the British and Spanish agents when, by a system of bribery, they courted Indian support. The affection for and confidence in Hawkins held by the older chiefs kept them loyal, but the young warriors listened to the siren song of the prophets.

During the fall and winter of 1812-13 Hawkins's health was very poor. Often confined to his bed, he was under the necessity of sending assistants to represent him at important councils at the time when his influence was most needed. If he was lulled into a feeling of false security, it does not necessarily follow that he was guilty of incompetence or neglect of duty. The leaders among the Creeks were also confident of the peaceful intentions of the majority of their warriors. As late as May 28, 1813, the Augusta *Chronicle* reported: "Our Indian frontier is at present tranquil. . . . The Nation generally are disposed to peace. . . ." Three days later Hawkins wrote Governor Mitchell: "From the present disposition of the Creeks there is nothing hostile to be apprehended from them.[54]

Before the end of June, however, Hawkins was forced to admit to the governor that the conflict among the Creeks had commenced and a crisis was rapidly approaching.[55] The hostiles were mostly Alabamas, who belonged to the Creek confederation but were not Creeks, and they were under the direction of the British and Tecumseh. Tuskeenehau of Cussetuh, a friendly Creek chief, had organized 190 warriors for the protection of Tookaubatchee and wished Hawkins to send white troops to their aid so that they might "put an end to these hatchers of war and mischief."[56]

All information received by Hawkins was transmitted to Governor Mitchell, even when the agent had a "gouty hand" and wrote with much pain. Mitchell, therefore, knew that the friendly chiefs had requested aid of Georgia and he was ready and eager to send it. He was, however, forced to await positive authorization to send Georgia troops into federal territory, which Hawkins would not give. It is not entirely clear whether he was inclined to discount the apprehensions of the friendly chiefs or whether he felt that his influence was sufficient to stop hostilities. His critics blamed his procrastination on the jealousy of Governor Mitchell and his unwillingness to share the credit for subduing the hostiles. It is certain that he confined his activities in the crisis to demanding of the fanatical chiefs explanations of their actions. He answered the friendly chiefs' requests for aid by advising them to attack the hostiles.[57] He explained his inaction to the secretary of war on the belief that the Indians would spend their time in fighting among themselves and would not attack the whites.[58]

On July 22 Hawkins was informed by the war department that the governors of Georgia and Tennessee had been ordered to organize 1,500 men each to march separately or in cooperation into the Creek country.[59] On August 6 the Augusta *Chronicle* announced that news from Milledgeville indicated that Governor Mitchell had 3,000 men ready to march. Fifteen hundred volunteers from Tennessee and the 3rd Regiment of United States Regulars would cooperate with Georgia troops. Hawkins had requested only 300 men. "If the hostile Indians are 2,500 strong," asked the editor of the *Chronicle,* "of what avail will 300 men be as an auxiliary corps? This request is exactly in character with the whole conduct of Col. Hawkins; it shows a deadly jealousy of the people of Georgia."[60]

On July 28 the friendly chiefs, impatient at Hawkins's delay, made a direct request of Governor Mitchell for 2,500 men, two field pieces, and plenty of ammunition.[61] When Hawkins heard of this he wrote Mitchell, insisting again that the reports had been exaggerated. He admitted that some of the Creeks were on the warpath and that casualties had been suffered by the friendly Creeks, but he maintained that the situation was not out of hand.[62] He reported to the secretary of war:

This department has long been assailed by calumny and misrepresentation; but it has been left to the Governor of Georgia to usurp all authority of the General Government, except what relates to commerce. . . . As he is a man of legal knowledge, he must be operated upon by a policy of his own.[63]

Governor Mitchell at last assumed that the emergency had

arisen which would authorize his calling out the militia for the protection of the state regardless of Hawkins's attitude. He had, therefore, assembled 2,500 men, 500 of them cavalry, at various points on the frontier.[64] While Hawkins continued to contest with the governor the exclusive right of the United States to regulate Indian affairs, he did not further protest Georgia's threat to invade Indian country under the stress of circumstances.

The most horrible event of the war took place on August 30, 1813, when Peter McQueen massacred the inhabitants of Fort Mims on the Tensaw River. It has been estimated that ". . . hardly two dozen escaped of the five hundred and fifty men, women and children in that stockaded ground."[65]

By this time Hawkins was willing to cooperate with the Georgia troops. After General John Floyd took command Hawkins kept in frequent communication with him and gave him all the information he possessed as to the activities and hostile movements of the Indians. By October the agent was so impressed with the strength of the Red Sticks that he feared the fighting would be brought to Georgia instead of being confined west of the Chattahoochee as he had at first hoped.[66]

Now that Hawkins was willing for the offensive against the hostile Creeks to be pushed, it was found difficult to get it underway. Tennessee troops were entering Creek country under Generals Andrew Jackson and John Cocke and were offering to cooperate with General Floyd, who was powerless to move beyond the Flint because of the breakdown of his lines of supply. On November 8 Floyd's command was no farther west than Fort Lawrence on the Flint opposite the agency.[67]

Georgia was anxious to fight. The honor and safety of the state were at stake and, probably of more importance, many of its citizens saw in the war an opportunity of ridding themselves of Creek occupancy of choice lands without the necessity of negotiating treaties of purchase. Hawkins had anticipated such an attitude on the part of some Georgians and wished to keep Georgia troops out of Indian lands until he was sure there was no other method of stopping the war. He could not condone landgrabbing as it was directed at driving out friendly, as well as hostile, Indians. In November General Floyd finally moved out toward Cowetuh; Hawkins then offered his services, writing Floyd:

As soon as I know that the friendly Indians are to cooperate with your command, or who is the commander in chief of the expedition

I will be ready to take charge of them. And if you should deem my cooperation with you necessary immediately and without delay I shall be with you.[68]

Late in November Major General Thomas Pinckney arrived at Fort Hawkins to take command of the army operating against the Creeks. Hawkins was naturally willing to cooperate with an officer of the United States army and from his knowledge of the Indians was able to give valuable aid. He ordered the friendly chiefs to send a detachment of Indians, including an interpreter familiar with the Tallapoosa country, to act as scouts and runners for the Tennessee troops operating in that area. On December 12 a mounted detachment of twenty warriors and four runners under William McIntosh departed in obedience to these instructions.

General Floyd continued west into the Upper Creek lands. Here, on January 27, 1814, he met and defeated the Red Sticks at Camp Defiance. In his official report he cited Timpochee Barnard, son of Hawkins's assistant Timothy Barnard, who was at the head of a band of friendly Uchees, for gallantry under fire.[69]

With armies converging on the Indians from north, south, and east, an early victory was anticipated. On March 17, 1814, John Armstrong, secretary of war, appointed General Pinckney and Colonel Hawkins to conclude a peace as soon as the Indians showed any desire to end the war.[70] Three days later, however, Armstrong decided that the treaty should take the form of a military capitulation and instructed Pinckney that he alone was to make it. He added that Hawkins could be "usefully employed" in the negotiations.[71]

On March 27, 1814, General Jackson defeated the Red Sticks at Horseshoe Bend on the Tallapoosa River. Of 900 Indians engaged in the fight scarcely 300 escaped. Jackson continued his campaign down the Tallapoosa to its junction with the Coosa and there built Fort Jackson.

On April 23 General Pinckney conveyed to Hawkins the terms upon which peace would be granted to the hostile Creeks with the request that he communicate them to the Indians.[72] These terms were by no means extremely severe on the hostiles and were very specific in their guarantees of protection and indemnities for the fidelity of the friendly Indians. When Hawkins made the conditions known to the friendly chiefs he was told by them that the hostiles were not ready for peace and until they were more severely punished would not abide by any promise they might make.[73] With the promise of munitions and supplies at Pensacola, the Red Sticks were not yet subdued. In the meantime, Hawkins, as a preliminary to peace, had allowed those who professed a desire for it to return to their homes. General Jackson complained to General Pinckney:

I am truly astonished that Colo. Hawkins is permitting the Indians to settle down on their former habitations. I did tell him the territory I had assigned them. I did tell him that no Indians should settle west of the Cosee [*sic*.] or north of the allabama [*sic*.]. At this point is the strength of the frontier of the union to be established by . . . wealthy inhabitants, unmixed by Indians.[74]

On July 11 General Jackson informed Colonel Hawkins that he himself had succeeded General Pinckney as the commissioner to sign the treaty, and had set August 1 as the date for the Creeks desiring peace to meet him at Fort Jackson. Hawkins was ordered to report at the same place without loss of time but was first to notify all chiefs of the conference.[75]

On August 9, 1814, the Treaty of Fort Jackson was signed, with General Jackson the sole commissioner of the United States. He experienced "considerable difficulty" in getting the Indians to sign because of the generous terms which Hawkins, upon General Pinckney's instructions, had offered the Creeks in the spring.[76] Nevertheless, Jackson in his official report acknowledged himself under "great obligations to Col. Hawkins for his aid."[77]

As late as August 7 the Indians appealed to Hawkins: "We are again in trouble and need your advise [*sic*.]." Jackson, they complained, had disregarded the terms offered by Pinckney and had punished the friendly Indians more than the hostiles. He had not consulted them but had drawn the lines to suit himself.[78] Hawkins, unquestionably, was sympathetic with the complaints of the friendly chiefs. If he took any action on the request it is not revealed, but from that time on he had little regard for Jackson.

Most of the hostile Creeks were not parties to the treaty; in fact, there is evidence that only one such chief was on hand. The hostilities, therefore, did not cease immediately. The British continued to promise the Red Sticks aid and invited them to Pensacola for supplies. Jackson advanced into Florida and in November captured Pensacola. Hawkins, under orders from Jackson, began to enroll the friendly Creeks for service.[79] He eventually got together a force of about 800 Indians of which he took personal command. Though they saw little fighting, they were able to protect the frontier against hostile attacks and in January, 1815, they marched to and floated down the Flint in a campaign against Appalachicola.[80] A month later Hawkins was at 115 Mile Camp and was preparing to attack a white, red, and black force entrenched there behind artillery support, when the news of the Treaty of Ghent arrived.

Following the treaty Hawkins was practically the sole agent between the United States and the British, Spanish, and Indian forces in Florida. The British did not evacuate Florida according to agreement. In the spring of 1815 Colonel Edward Nicholls, who commanded the British forces at Appalachicola, addressed an insolent letter to Hawkins in which he stated that he considered the territories of the Creeks to be as they were before the war despite the Treaty of Fort Jackson. Colonel Nicholls further arrogated to himself the entire control of the Creeks and warned citizens of the United States neither to enter Creek territory nor to attempt any communication with the Indians. He appended to this letter a paper signed by three chiefs agreeing to the ninth article of the Treaty of Ghent on which he based his assertion that the boundaries were the same as in 1811. This was evidently an attempt to deter commissioners of the United States who were about to run the boundary line agreed upon in Jackson's treaty. Hawkins replied to Nicholls:

. . . the documents you enclosed signed by three chiefs, purporting to be the agreement to the 9th article of the treaty of peace, I shall lay before the chiefs of the nation at a convention soon to be held at Coweta, and send you the result of their deliberations on it. The result of my reflections with due reference I give you, as on the envelope it purports to be on his Britannic majesty's service. It is within my knowledge one of the chiefs is a Seminole of East-Florida and has never resided in the United States; and that neither of the three has ever attended the national councils of the Creeks, or are in any way a part of their executive government. If the four witnesses had signed as principals, and the three chiefs as witnesses, it would have been entitled to equal respect from me.[81]

In due time the British troops were removed from Florida and quiet again settled down on the frontier. Hawkins was to spend the latter days of his life on his farm at the agency, surrounded by his family and his friends, the Indians. The harsh treatment of the Creeks by General Jackson was a bitter disappointment to him.

He did not long outlive the war. The closing months of his life were filled with suffering, and his illness was aggravated by heartsickness at the condition of his beloved Creeks. Criticism piled up on him and made its impression. Discouraged, he tried on several occasions to resign.

When the Augusta *Chronicle* accused him of treason and deceit[82] he wrote Secretary of War Armstrong:

. . . if the President can find a man, who can fill this office, in his judgement, more for the public interest or convenience than I have done, he owes it to his high standing, and to me to send him on; in doing so he will do me no injury, or excite the least resentment. . . . This department has always been strewed with thorns.[83]

In 1857 General Thomas S. Woodward praised Hawkins extravagantly as a student of Indian life, writing:

He knew more about Indians and Indian history and early settlements and expeditions of the several European nations that undertook to settle colonies in the South and Southwest, than all the men that ever have or will make a scrape of the pen upon the subject.[84]

Such extravagance must, of course, be discounted. Hawkins, unquestionably, was studious and applied himself seriously to a study of the Indian dialects. Jefferson called on him on several occasions for instruction in the Indian tongues. When the Empress of Russia wished to make a comparison of the languages of the American Indians and the Siberian tribes she asked General Washington for Indian vocabularies. Madison heard of this request and sent Washington the Cherokee and Choctaw vocabularies prepared and presented him by Hawkins.[85]

Hawkins was a keen observer and put on paper much of what he had seen. Shortly after his death his home burned and great quantities of historical materials were destroyed. Nevertheless, much was saved. In the library of the Georgia Historical Society are eight manuscript volumes of letters and journals in Hawkins's handwriting. These volumes cover much of his activities from 1797 to 1806 and were published in 1916 as Volume IX, *Collections of the Georgia Historical Society* under the title *Letters of Benjamin Hawkins*. His chief claim to recognition as an author, however, is due to the publication in 1848 of his *Sketch of the Creek Country 1798-1799*, as Volume III, Part I, *Collections of the Georgia Historical Society*. This monograph was written originally in a bound notebook. Because of the natural interest in its subject matter, the desire for information about the country on the part of land owners, military leaders, and speculators, and the generosity of the author, many handwritten copies were made of this manuscript. The Georgia Historical Society has three copies (one complete, and one nearly so) in Hawkins's handwriting, and a beautiful copy made by General Floyd while he was campaigning during the War of 1812. There is another copy in the Library of Congress, and one made by John Howard Payne from the original manuscript in 1835 is in the Edward Ayer Collection in the Newberry Library in Chicago.

Hawkins died on June 6, 1816, leaving a fortune from his inheritance and his farming operations estimated as high as $160,000 to be divided among his wife, six daughters, and a son. The fortune was quickly dissipated and there resulted many bitter disputes and law suits among his heirs.

In 1931 congressional appropriation made possible the erection of a monument to the memory of Hawkins in Roberta, Georgia, about six miles from his grave. At the time of his death many extravagant eulogies were written and uttered by his contemporaries. Reputable historians have recently found his career as Indian agent praiseworthy, Marquis James appraising him "as an anomaly among such officials, being both honest and able."[86]

WILLIAM McINTOSH

BY JAMES C. BONNER

LATE in the afternoon of May 2, 1825, a nondescript Indian pony bearing a fatigued rider ambled into the town of Milledgeville from the Monticello road. The rider was a Creek Indian of mixed blood but attired in the clothing of a white man, and he must have attracted little notice as he splashed along the muddy streets of the frontier capital of Georgia. The visitor was Chilly McIntosh, the twenty-four year old son of a half-breed chief of the Coweta Indians. Accompanying him was a group of five tribesmen who in two days had ridden from their village on the Chattahoochee River.[1]

In English which revealed a Muscogean accent the Indian sought directions to the house of George M. Troup. The tidings which he bore the Georgia governor inspired an extra edition of the *Southern Recorder,* sent messengers scurrying back and forth between the Georgia capital and the Creek Nation, and from Georgia to Washington. On the same day John Crowell, the Creek agent, wrote the secretary of war from Fort Mitchell that "If Governor Troup puts into execution his threats, the whole Creek Nation will be overrun by his troops before this reaches you."[2]

A crisis in the four-sided diplomatic relationships involving Georgia, the federal government, and two factions of the Creek Nation was entering its final and most acute stages. It ended a few years later only after the Indian title to the last remaining acre of their original tribal lands in Georgia had been extinguished. In the meantime there had been a monotonous barrage of charges and counter-charges, of threats and counter-threats, and, on one occasion, an order for the mobilization of state militia against the threatened intervention of federal authority.

James C. Bonner is head of the history department and chairman of faculty research at Georgia State College for Women.

The story which Chilly McIntosh related to the governor, and which was soon corroborated by other eyewitnesses, concerned the violent death of his father, Chief William McIntosh, which occurred two days before on the west bank of the Chattahoochee River. To the Upper Creeks, defiant of the white man and his civilization, the event was a lawful execution of an Indian who had betrayed his people. To a faction of the Lower Creeks who had recognized McIntosh as their leader, it was an assassination by disgruntled enemies. Georgians of the Troup following characterized it as a foul murder. The department of war, under whose jurisdiction Indian affairs then lay, was maintaining a cautious neutrality, for the federal government appeared to be far less interested in the developing Georgia-Creek controversy than was either Georgia or the Creek Nation.

The intense diplomatic crisis touched off by the drama on the Chattahoochee had been long in the making. It was closely identified with the unusual career of Tustunugee Hutkee, who was known among his white friends as William McIntosh. Although a half-breed whose life was spent entirely among Indians, the white blood of his Scotch father gave him a peculiar standing among the leaders of two races. This cultural dualism, combined with a shrewd and sagacious mind, conspired to make him as controversial a figure perhaps as Georgia history has produced. The Lower Creeks of the Coweta towns along the Chattahoochee elevated him to the rank of head chief and followed his leadership in blind and often pathetic confidence. The Upper Creeks, living in the villages along the Tallapoosa and the Coosa, were his bitter adversaries. Little Prince, the head chief of the Creek Nation, on one occasion claimed that he used his ability to write to defraud his people of their government annuities.[3] Judgments of his character by Indians varied just as widely among his white American contemporaries. Daniel Newnan, adjutant general of Georgia, believed him to be a greater man than Alexander McGillivray. He was described by a federal official as "very humane" and exceedingly intelligent. On the other hand, Thomas P. Andrews, a special agent sent to investigate Creek affairs in 1825, described the Coweta chieftain as "avaricious, unjust, and oppressive" in his relationships toward his own people.[4]

Despite these conflicting appraisals of his character, William McIntosh could lay claim to as high a degree of wilderness aristocracy as the Creek country could produce. His paternal grandfather, John McIntosh, had come to Georgia in 1736. This Scotch adventurer who was royally descended married Margaret Mc-Gillivray who bore him six children. One of these was Captain William McIntosh who, as a Tory officer in the Revolution, commanded a contingent of Creeks allied with the British. It was during this period that he formed a rapport with a Coweta woman who became the mother of William McIntosh, the subject of this sketch. Neither his Tory loyalties nor his reputation for indiscriminate fatherhood prevented Captain McIntosh from returning to Georgia after the end of hostilities and marrying his distant relative, Barbara McIntosh. Barbara's brother, General John McIntosh, had fought for the Patriot cause. The youngest daughter of John McIntosh, Catherine, became the mother of George M. Troup whose governorship of Georgia became closely identified with the career of his first cousin, William McIntosh, the head chief of the Cowetas.[5]

The mother of Chief William McIntosh was a Creek woman of unmixed blood about whom very little is known. In addition to William, she bore at least two other sons, one of whom was a full Indian and the other a half-breed. In addition to these filiations of Creek blood, McIntosh also possessed half brothers and half sisters who were full white men and women, one of whom, William R. McIntosh, was in 1817 a member of the Georgia legislature.[6]

The intricate web of McIntosh genealogy is complicated by polygamous marriages, which had become a common practice among the more affluent Creeks. McIntosh had three wives, the oldest of whom apparently was Susanna Coe, a Creek woman, and the youngest was a Cherokee girl known as Peggie. In 1825 Susanna and Peggie lived at the principal McIntosh residence situated on the west bank of the Chattahoochee River in what later became Carroll County. This residence, a large two-story house of hewn logs, was the seat of a plantation known variously as Lockchau Talofau, Acorn Town, and Acorn Bluff. This plantation consisted of a large tract of very fertile river bottom land cultivated by Negro slaves. Nearby was the site of an old Creek town, Chattahoochee, from which the river is said to have derived its name.[7]

Fifty miles west of Lockchau Talofau, on the Tallapoosa River, McIntosh maintained another plantation on which resided a third wife, Eliza, the white-blooded daughter of Stephen Hawkins. The oldest child of this marriage was Chilly McIntosh, who was perhaps the most illustrious of the eleven McIntosh children. Born in 1800, he became in his early twenties the official clerk of the Creek Nation. He spoke and wrote fairly good English, being one of the few literate Creeks of the McIntosh family. His residence was at Broken Arrow, on the west side of the Chattahoochee River, near Fort Mitchell.[8]

William McIntosh was born probably at Coweta town in 1778.[9] It was in this vicinity, near the present site of Columbus, that he was living nineteen years later. On May 15, 1797, he sold the government twelve dollars' worth of beef for a public meeting at Cusseta.[10] From this modest beginning he appears to have pursued a similar type of business activity throughout his life. As late as 1822, his cousin, George M. Troup, spoke of him as "being much in the habit of trade." He asked the Creek agent, David B. Mitchell, to forward to him a request to purchase a dozen "Indian Tackies" to use as plow horses on his plantation in Laurens County. McIntosh possessed an unusual talent for pecuniary gain, whether by legitimate enterprise or parasitic avocation, for he accumulated a reasonably large estate.[11]

By 1800, at the age of twenty-two, McIntosh had become an underling chief among the Cowetas. Five years later, in 1805, he emerged somewhat suddenly as an important figure in the diplomatic negotiations between the Creeks and the federal government. He had not been present at Fort Wilkinson in 1802 when the whites at considerable expense had gained a foothold on the west bank of the Oconee River. The year 1802 was a significant date in the history of the Georgia Indians, for that year the Georgia Compact was signed pledging the United States government to extinguish all Indian claims to lands within the chartered limits of Georgia. Also by the terms of the agreement Georgia transferred her Alabama and Mississippi domains to the federal government. Now, just three years after the compact, McIntosh was included in a carefully chosen delegation of young chiefs to go to Washington for a conference with the President.[12]

Accompanied by Timothy Barnard, an interpreter, and Benjamin Hawkins, the Creek agent, this party of six chiefs held interviews with President Thomas Jefferson on November 2 and 3. The President wanted a re-cession of the lands between the Oconee and Ocmulgee rivers at a lower price than that stipulated

in previous treaties. He also requested the right to cut a horse-
path (which eventually would become a wagon road) through
the Creek territory from Fort Wilkinson to Fort Stoddart, near
the present site of Mobile.

McIntosh must have impressed Jefferson with his bargaining
ability. He stated that the road was unnecessary because of existing communications with the Southwestern region, citing the
road from Nashville to Natchez and the navigable Tennessee
River. The proposed road, he argued, would only bring trouble
between the Indians and their white neighbors. As to the re-
cession of the Oconee-Ocmulgee region, he insisted on the original price, and stated that the Indians now knew the real value
of these lands.

Two weeks later the six chiefs signed the new treaty of cession
extending the limits of Georgia to the Ocmulgee River. The
treaty also provided for the horse-path through the southern
part of the Creek country, together with the rights of Americans
to fish in the Ocmulgee River and to establish a military post
on the east bank of that stream. In exchange for these concessions the Creeks were to receive a total of $206,000 to be paid
as annuities over the next eighteen years.[13] On a per acre basis
this price was considerably in excess of that agreed to in previous
negotiations. It is significant to note that McIntosh acquired
considerable authority in the disbursement of the Creek annuities.

The horse-path which the treaty provided was cut by a party
of federal soldiers and opened in 1806. From four to six feet
wide and commonly known as the Federal Road, this path soon
became filled with white travelers moving toward the Southwest. The Creeks did not provide ferries and inns for travelers
as the treaty stipulated, and these operations fell into the hands
of white men who invariably engaged in commerce with the
Indians. As McIntosh had predicted, this road brought the Creeks
into intimate contacts with Americans and led eventually to a
realization that more and more of their land would be required
by the white men.[14]

As Creek relations with white men increased in scope, Mc-
Intosh must have recognized the opportunities which these events
afforded him. He increased his knowledge of the white man's
tongue and he acquired the art of letter-writing. He combined
his public function as distributor of Creek annuities with his

private role as Indian trader with the result that a large and profitable credit business was afforded him. He operated a ferry on the upper Chattahoochee, near his principal residence at Lockchau Talofau where his house became a tavern for the entertainment of white and Indian travelers. Now cast in the role of an opportunist, he cultivated friendship with the white man's political and military leaders.

Somewhat indicative of his propensity for the white man's civilization and of his efforts to promote closer ties with the government of Georgia was his appearance in Milledgeville in July, 1811. In company with fifty-seven leading Creeks of the Lower towns, they camped for three days on Fishing Creek, a short distance from the statehouse. They impressed the townspeople with their orderly and attentive presence at Sunday services of the Methodist Church. On the following day they assembled in the statehouse for a public meeting with Governor David B. Mitchell. The purpose of this assembly was to give reciprocal assurance of amity and friendship and "to cultivate a more close attachment between white and red men." The talk, said McIntosh, was designed to show that the young Creeks were anxious to cultivate a good understanding with their white brothers of the new generation. After the meeting about twenty of the leading chiefs had dinner with the governor.[15]

Far less enthusiastic about strengthening ties of friendship with their more civilized neighbors was a resentful group of Upper Creeks who lived along the Coosa and Tallapoosa rivers. McIntosh and other Indians in the Lower towns situated along the Federal Road had accepted with complacency the agricultural and sedentary life long fostered upon them by Benjamin Hawkins, who served as a Creek agent from 1796 to 1816.[16] The Upper Creeks of the back country, however, under the leadership of older chiefs possessed a conservative resentment toward civilizing influences. Among the leaders of this reactionary movement was the Okfuskee chief, Ogillio Heneha, commonly known as Menawa.

To the primitive and unprogressive towns of the Creek back country in 1811 came the Shawnee leader, Tecumseh, who appealed for a return to the primitive customs of the Indians and a denial of further land cessions. He arrived at Tuckabatchee in September on the eve of the meeting of the Creek National Council where several thousand Indians had assembled. There he delivered an address which McIntosh heard and reported to Hawkins at his agency on the Flint River.[17] This address seems to have consisted largely of the orator's conversation with the Great Spirit concerning the affairs of his children of the forest, rather than an exhortation to war. The spiritual tone of his discourse, however, introduced the factor of primitive religion into the growing schism between two factions of the Creeks.[18]

This schism was widened by a series of events which occurred the following year. In March some drunken Creeks from Autassee, in the up-country, had killed a white man named Meredith. Two months later William Lott, while on his way to the Mississippi Territory, was murdered by a brigand of Tallasee Indians near Warrior's Stand; and in June some settlers on Duck River, in Tennessee, were massacred by Indians from the Hillabee villages.[19] As soon as the news of these murders reached Hawkins he sent his assistant, a German named Christian Limbaugh, to the Coweta country to contact William McIntosh. The two went to Broken Arrow to see Little Prince, the head chief of the Nation, and thence to Tuckabatchee where they conferred with Big Warrior, the principal chief of the Upper Creeks.

As a result of these conferences McIntosh was placed in command of a party of Coweta, Cusseta, and Tuckabatchee Indians, each under a lesser chief, and sent in pursuit of the murderers.[20] By the end of August six of the ring-leaders had been overtaken and shot, and several others were whipped. Since McIntosh and his party of executioners belonged to a separate faction of Creeks from those executed, the tension between the two groups was greatly increased by these events.[21]

The precursor of the Creek civil war was a weird demonstration of religious fanaticism under the leadership of one Seekabo, who had come to the Nation with Tecumseh. He remained with the Creeks and soon began to imitate Tecumseh's brother, the famous Shawnee Prophet who had upset the equanimity of the Northwestern tribes. A half breed living at Autassee, named Josiah Francis, became Seekabo's leading disciple. Claiming supernatural powers and demonstrating a passionate eloquence, the two won a large following among such Creeks as were unable to resist their primitive evangelism. In June, 1813, they began a holy war of burning and murdering the unbelievers along the Alabama and Tallapoosa rivers. On announcing their intention of destroying Tuckabatchee, this town fortified and sent a frantic call for help from the Lower Creeks.[22] To their assistance went McIntosh, Joseph Marshall, Timpochee Barnard, and a few other chiefs from the Chattahoochee region with a force of two hundred well-chosen warriors. With only minor skirmishing they entered the loosely besieged town and took the inhabitants back with them to the Chattahoochee and Flint rivers where they remained until the arrival on the scene of American soldiers.[23]

Being in need of guns and ammunition the revolting Creeks sent an expedition to Florida to obtain this equipment from the Spaniards at Pensacola. By the time the party returned, fifteen of the Upper Creek towns had been enticed to join in a war on the Cowetas, and the rebel chiefs sent out small bundles of red sticks, known as "broken days" to indicate the time of the attack.[24] Before the attack was launched, however, it was learned that a number of half-breeds and their families had taken refuge at Fort Mims. These much despised half bloods, rather than the Coweta towns, became the immediate targets for their initial major attack. In the Fort Mims attack some five hundred men, women, and children were slaughtered by the Indians without discrimination. Congress in July, 1813, authorized the raising of a militia force of 3,000 men from Georgia and Tennessee to move against the hostile Creeks. Thus a civil war by a group of Creek fanatics became a war against the people of the United States.

The Creek agent, Hawkins, regarded the conflict as wholly a Creek internecine affair and he wisely suspected its unhappy consequences to his Indian charges. He had no choice except to cooperate with his government in what to him was an ill-advised venture, and he entered into his duties without enthusiasm. He instructed the friendly chiefs to send a detachment of Indian scouts and runners familiar with the Tallapoosa country to serve with the Tennessee troops under Andrew Jackson already moving southward. In obedience to these instructions, a mounted unit of twenty warriors and four runners left Coweta under the command of McIntosh.[25]

In the meantime General John Floyd and his Georgia militia were moving slowly toward the Chattahoochee where the friendly Indians were encamped about Coweta. The chiefs of the Lower towns began making forays against the Red Sticks, as

the hostile Upper Creeks were now called. A force under Mc-
Intosh destroyed one of their towns and began plundering in
other parts of the territory.[26] Floyd with less than a thousand
Georgians and 450 Creeks now under McIntosh and other chiefs
arrived at the Red Stick stronghold at Autassee around December, 1813. McIntosh and his Creeks accompanied the Floyd
expedition more as tolerated on-lookers than as fighting allies.[27]
At the battle which followed, however, McIntosh's Indians at
a crucial point threw themselves into the ranks and fought with
such bravery as to win the commendation of Floyd in his official
report of the battle. In this engagement and that at Horseshoe
Bend in March of the following year, McIntosh made his name
well known to Andrew Jackson who recognized his unusual
bravery and courage in battle.[28]

Horseshoe Bend was the virtual end of the Creek phase of
the war. On August 9, 1814, at Fort Jackson, near the present
site of Montgomery, General Jackson exacted the inevitable
treaty. The terms of Jackson's bargain failed to distinguish
between his Creek friends and his Creek enemies and it also
failed to satisfy the state of Georgia. This state's discontent resulted from the unsatisfactory location and the poor quality of
the ceded land, as well as from the fact that it was taken from
the friendly Lower Creeks.[29] In Georgia the ceded territory was
a tract nearly ninety miles wide extending across the southern
portion of the state from the Chattahoochee eastward to within
fifty miles of the coast. In the Alabama region the treaty confirmed to the possession of the United States a wide corridor
running from the Cherokee boundary southward to the Florida
line. The tract lay approximately between the Coosa and the
Tombigbee rivers.[30] In addition to despoiling the Indians of
over twenty million acres the treaty left the Creeks isolated from
all other Indian tribes except the unfriendly Cherokees to the
north.

Significantly, no responsible chief of the Upper towns signed
the treaty of Fort Jackson. Of those who signed for the Lower
towns, many were half-breeds such as McIntosh, Timpochee
Barnard, John O'Kelly, Noble Kinnard, John Carr, and Alexander Grayson. It is significant to note that McIntosh signed
the treaty in four places, first as "Major of the Cowetas" and
again as proxy for his uncle Chehehaw Tustunugee and for two
other chiefs. One of the principal witnesses was the ailing and

disillusioned Hawkins who already had made up his mind to resign his agency. His death in 1816 spared him the bitter experience of witnessing further injustices to his red friends. Big Warrior, in language which must have touched deeply all who heard him, made a dramatic protest against the taking of so much land from the Lower Creeks who had fought with the Americans in the campaign. Jackson was unbending before his primitive eloquence, and the Tuckabatchee chief reluctantly placed his mark to the treaty.[31]

Probably because of his reluctance to sign the treaty Big Warrior's defection to the British was suspected by Jackson whose eyes were now turned to Florida. Activities of British agents in the Spanish territory were bringing to a focus the next phase of the war. On August 25, McIntosh took a message to Hawkins from Big Warrior concerning British and Spanish activities at Pensacola, which indicated that Big Warrior had fallen somewhat under British influence. McIntosh, however, whose enthusiasm for continuing the war was unfaltering, sought permission to go to Pensacola to investigate the report that the British were using that Spanish post for arming runaway Negroes. The communication which Jackson sent to the secretary of war containing McIntosh's report of his observations on Pensacola indicates Jackson's final determination to move his troops into Spanish territory. "The report of Major McIntosh," he wrote to Monroe, "will shew you this is the moment to strike the enemy in his strong hold." In the meantime Jackson had written to McIntosh from Mobile, whither he had moved with his army after the Treaty of Fort Jackson, to raise a force of Creeks and destroy the British establishment on the Apalachicola.[32]

The Apalachicola establishment was an old British fort near the mouth of the Apalachicola River which the British had refitted and turned over to a black leader of that vicinity. From this stronghold runaway Negroes, Seminole Indians who had sided with the British, and hostile Upper Creek refugees were harrying the countryside and causing conditions intolerable to Georgians.[33] Colonel Duncan L. Clinch in July, 1816, was ordered to take his command into Florida and destroy this stronghold. Upon his arrival he found McIntosh and 200 Coweta warriors already there. The settlements in the vicinity were ravaged by Clinch's troops and his Creek allies who destroyed crops, confiscated livestock, and drove the inhabitants into the fort. On July 26, a heated cannon ball struck the fort's well-stocked magazine, demolishing the entire establishment and destroying its inhabitants, including three hundred women and children.[34]

This event, occuring after the Treaty of Ghent which officially ended the war with England, was the prelude to the fourth and last phase of the fighting which had begun with the Creek civil war in 1813. Seminole Indians and the defeated Red Sticks from the Upper Creek towns had taken refuge along the Florida border. These had refused to vacate the lands in the extreme southern part of Georgia which were ceded under the treaty of 1814. Under the influence of the British and Spanish these Indians had become emboldened and threatening. Among the Creek exiles now in Florida were Couchatee Micco, or the Red Ground Chief, Peter McQueen, and the prophet Francis. In December, 1817, the new secretary of war, John C. Calhoun, ordered Jackson to Georgia with broad orders to terminate the conflict.[35]

On January 22, 1818, Jackson was at Fort Hawkins with 2,000 soldiers. Two days later he was at Hartford, Georgia, the seat of Pulaski County, whence he moved by Chehehaw village near the present site of Leesburg on the Flint River. Here he was supplied by the friendly Chehehaws with corn and provisions and here every able warrior of the town accompanied him.[36]

In the meantime McIntosh, now a brigadier general, had arrived at Fort Mitchell where he began enrolling the Creek brigade of 2,000 warriors to join Jackson at Fort Gadsden, built at the site of the old Negro fort on the Apalachicola destroyed in 1816. While Jackson was waiting at Fort Gadsden, McIntosh, on his way thither had already begun the fighting against his old enemies, the Red Sticks. Below the fork of the Flint River a party of these Indians had ambushed a supply boat loaded with army provisions from Mobile and carrying a number of passengers, among whom was a cousin of the Creek general. Only three of the passengers escaped death, one a Mrs. Stewart, who was taken captive by the attackers. On March 2, McIntosh notified Jackson of the capture of three of these marauding Indians. "I have got them in strings, carrying them to Fort Gaines," he wrote, "and expect to catch some more before I get there." On reaching Fort Gaines and delivering his captives to the commander of that post, he was told by that officer to deal with them by Indian law. "I did not want them to stand on our land, and I have taken their lives," was McIntosh's succinct explanation to Jackson of his disposition of the matter.[37]

Hearing that hostile Indians had gathered under the Red Ground Chief about forty miles from Fort Gaines, McIntosh moved after them as rapidly as possible. On March 10 he informed Jackson of his successful pursuit of the Red Sticks. "On the Sunday, in the evening, there was about fourteen of our old enemies came and gave themselves up to us, with their women and children. I sent the women back with some of our people to Ufaula. . . . About one hour ten more came into our camp with white flags and joined us. . . . Tomorrow about nine o'clock the fight will be ended with us, if I conquer the Red Ground Chief." It was not until April 1 that McIntosh finally joined Jackson who was then at St. Marks sixty miles east of the Apalachicola River.[38]

From St. Marks Jackson with his new reinforcements, on April 9, headed for Suwanee, the town of Chief Boleck (Bowlegs) more than a hundred miles to the southeast.[39] During the night of the twelfth sentinels heard the barking of dogs and the nervous lowing of cattle, and McIntosh was sent forward to scour the country for hostile Indians. On the following morning he encountered a party of Seminoles under Peter McQueen, the Negro-blooded Red Stick who had escaped to Florida in 1814.[40] While the engagement which resulted was a running fight of three hours, it was perhaps the most important skirmish of the entire campaign. Among the prisoners taken was the white woman who had been carried off from the Flint River massacre. McIntosh, who personally directed her rescue, slew three of the enemy with his own hands. His coolness and personal courage in this fight won for him almost worshipful admiration by the few white officers who witnessed the struggle. Major Thomas Woodward described him as "one of God's make of Generals."[41]

The Seminole War was over by the end of April, 1819. Among its accomplishments was the destruction of the troublesome Creek exiles and the execution of many of their leaders. The prophet Francis and the Autassee chief were among those hanged by Jackson's orders, which occurred at St. Marks.[42] Peter McQueen, Hossa Yoholo, and other leaders were in hiding and many of their followers were dying of disease and starvation.[43] With one or two exceptions none of those chiefs who had been Red Sticks in 1814 was now in power in the Creek Nation.[44]

On April 24 McIntosh and his brigade of Indians were mustered out of service. On reaching Coweta he was apprised of the massacre of his aged uncle, Chief Howard, and of the unprovoked destruction of Chehehaw village by Captain Obed Wright of the Georgia militia. At McIntosh's insistence, Jackson sent a letter of apology to the Chehehaw warriors in his command and ordered Wright arrested and brought to his headquarters. This incident touched off a bitter controversy between Jackson and Governor William Rabun, in which the latter challenged Jackson's jurisdiction in the case. Wright went unpunished for his deed but Congress provided an indemnity to the survivors of Chehehaw.[45]

This somewhat novel action by Congress advanced the prestige of McIntosh among the Lower Creeks. In striking contrast to the Coweta chieftain and the distinction which he now enjoyed in the Nation, stood the former Red Stick leader, Menawa. Wounded at Horseshoe Bend, he had covered himself with the clothing of a dead squaw and, under cover of darkness, had escaped to the falls of Cahawha where he remained in hiding for more than a year. After the fervor for punishing rebels had subsided he returned to the villages, but he had soured on the whites and on McIntosh in particular. The Chehehaw indemnity must have increased his grievance against the latter, for he believed that McIntosh in the Creek War had falsely charged some of his Okfuskees with murder to provide an excuse for burning one of his villages.[46]

The rebellious remnant of the Upper towns, divested of their old leaders, now turned to Big Warrior (Tustunugee Thlucco) of Tuckabatchee. Being the ranking chief in the Nation, and Tuckabatchee the "capital," Big Warrior's influence was formidable. He was of tremendous size physically, and somewhat corpulent, though agile in his movement. His face was disfigured with large spots resulting from a severe case of smallpox. Though a full-blood Indian, he was somewhat enlightened and wealthy. Near Tuckabatchee he cultivated a large plantation with more than fifty slaves and his house was furnished in plain civilized style.[47]

It is not certain to what extent Big Warrior flirted with

British agents after the Treaty of Fort Jackson but the spoliation of that treaty certainly cooled what little ardor he may
have had for the white man's civilization. He is said to have
upbraided Hawkins for having prevailed upon him and others
to remain neutral in the war with the British. His attitude in
this matter was in direct contrast to that of McIntosh who now
was his most formidable rival for leadership among the Creeks.
The Cowetan's popularity with influential white leaders following
the Seminole conflict must have created both envy and jealousy
in the heart of the Tuckabatchee chief.[48] A Creek warrior's rank
in government was still measured somewhat by his skill and
courage in battle, and by this yardstick McIntosh had few peers.

The animosity between Big Warrior and McIntosh, which is
discernable as early as the Treaty of Fort Jackson in 1814, was
accentuated by the events which immediately followed. Late in
the following year, when the surveyors assembled to draw the
lines of the cession, a dispute developed between the Creeks and
Cherokees concerning their boundary on the west side of the
Coosa River.[49] The Cherokees who, like the Lower Creeks, had
fought with General Jackson were angered by the commissioners'
plan to encroach on their own territory in fixing the northern
limits of the Creek cession. No definite boundary between the
two Indian nations had ever been recognized, but McIntosh
contended that the Creeks had loaned the Cherokees the land
which they now laid claim to at a time when the latter had
lost much of their land by warring with the Americans. A vi-
tuperative encounter resulted between McIntosh and Dick
Brown, one of the Cherokee representatives.[50] Following this
misunderstanding the two nations agreed to fix their boundary
on the east side of the Coosa. McIntosh headed the Creek delegation which in collaboration with the Cherokees established a
boundary line from Buzzard's Roost on the Chattahoochee west
to Will's Creek on the Coosa, a line which in Georgia later
became the northern boundary of Carroll County. This treaty
was concluded at Lockchau Talofau on December 11, 1821.[51]

Since the eastern boundary of the Creek cession of 1814 lay
entirely within former Creek territory, there was no controversy
with the Cherokees concerning this line. It followed the course
of the Coosa River to a point below Tuckabatchee and then
turned southeastward to a point on the Chattahoochee.[52] The
commissioners began running this line in the fall of 1815, start-

ing on the upper Coosa. Accompanying the surveyors were Mc-
Intosh, Big Warrior, and other Creek chiefs. As the party moved
down the Coosa, a growing crowd of sullen and protesting Upper
Creeks followed them, for they had already learned what the
rattle of a surveyor's chain meant to their rights to tribal lands.
When the surveyors reached the Chattahoochee River, Big Warrior who was now joined by some of the Lower Creeks, declared
that the line should not be extended eastward across southern
Georgia. Their demonstration was useless in the presence of eight
hundred soldiers at Fort Mitchell.[53]

The more primitive or hunting element of the Creeks who
had been discredited in the recent wars fell naturally into Big
Warrior's grasp. The Lower Creeks, however, among whom the
half-bloods were numerous, were more inclined to recognize the
leadership of McIntosh, and to part with their lands in exchange
for money. Partly as a result of these circumstances, a treaty of
cession made with the Lower Creeks in 1818, at the Flint River
agency, was obtained with little difficulty. Two relatively small
tracts on the northeastern and southeastern extremities of the
Nation were ceded at this time.[54]

A cession three years later, in 1821, proved more difficult to
obtain. By this time Georgia was increasing its pressure on the
federal government for the execution of the compact of April
24, 1802. This compact stipulated that the western limits of
Georgia were to run along the west bank of the Chattahoochee
River north to Uchee Creek, where the line was to leave the
river and extend north to the Cherokee village of Nickajack on
the Tennessee.[55] Because this line from Uchee Creek to Nickajack cut through unceded Creek and Cherokee lands, it had
never been run. Partly as a result of this situation, the Georgia
authorities now wanted the cession of a corridor which would
run eastward to Alabama across the entire northern half of the
Creek lands and separate the Creeks from the Cherokees. This
Georgia corridor would encompass the principal residence of
McIntosh at Lockchau Talofau.

When the Creeks met the United States commissioners at
Indian Springs early in 1821, the conference was jolted by a
trumped-up claim of Georgia against the Creeks for nearly a
half million dollars allegedly due them under old treaties dating
as far back as the Revolution. The chiefs present for the negotiations were few in number. McIntosh, the principal negotiator

for the Creeks, was inclined to recognize the Georgia debt.[56] The treaty resulted not in a cession of the northern corridor, but of an extension of Georgia's entire western boundary with the Creeks from the Ocmulgee to the Flint River. The Indians were to receive $200,000 for this cession together with payment by the federal government of the Georgia claims, which an auditing commission later scaled down to $25,000. Significantly, the commissioners agreed to set aside a thousand-acre reservation at Indian Springs and one square mile on the west bank of the Ocmulgee at the site of old Fort Hawkins "so as to include the improvements . . . in possession of the Indian chief William McIntosh."[57]

The covetous hand of Georgia together with a suspicion of conspiracy and bribery are thus seen in the Indian Springs Treaty of 1821. In subsequent negotiations with the Creeks the issues became increasingly involved with national and local politics. They also became hopelessly confused with personal animosities and with factional strife among the Indians. Somewhat at the center of these problems stood the Coweta chieftain whose cousin, George M. Troup, assumed the governorship of Georgia in 1823, and whose relationships with influential white men were becoming increasingly obnoxious to Big Warrior.

At this time the Creek towns numbered slightly less than sixty in both the upper and lower regions. The Coweta towns were the most numerous in the Nation and they lay along both sides of the Chattahoochee extending from Broken Arrow to the Cherokee boundary. There were estimated to be about 10,000 Indians in the Georgia portion of the Nation and the same number in Alabama.[58] Little Prince who lived at Broken Arrow was the principal chief of the Nation. Already ninety years old, he was interested mainly in preventing friction with the whites to whom he was neither friendly nor hostile. McIntosh, a capable, though a shrewd and unscrupulous half-blood was only a chief of fifth rank, yet he was recognized as the leader of all the lower towns. Big Warrior, who ruled the Upper towns in which the old hunting element dominated, was perhaps second in actual rank to Little Prince.[59] McIntosh and his supporters insisted that the authority of the Coweta chief was paramount over that of all the Creek towns, since Coweta, they claimed, was the original town of the whole tribe.[60] While there seems to have been a special thread of authority resident in the Coweta chief, it amounted to little more than a certain amount of prestige. In general, the authority of Creek leaders did not come from inheritance or caste, but rather from qualities of leadership.[61]

The strained and complex fabric of personal relationships inherent in the bi-racial character and cultural dualism of McIntosh's personality is illustrated by his association with each of the two Creek agents from 1817 to 1825. When Agent Hawkins died in 1816, the government tendered the' position to David B. Mitchell who was then the governor of Georgia. It is possible that it was the Creek indemnity of $85,000 which was then about to pass Congress, together with Creek annuities all of which Mitchell would be the dispenser, which caused him to resign the Georgia governorship to accept the agency. A year after Mitchell succeeded Hawkins the fort on the west side of the Chattahoochee and the government store, or factory, were abandoned by federal authorities.[62] About this time McIntosh expanded his business interests which included a trading establishment at the house of his son near Fort Mitchell. He employed as clerk his brother-in-law, a white man named George Stinson.[63] Agent Mitchell, whose son, William, took to wife a daughter of McIntosh, appears to have become a silent partner in this trading firm. McIntosh and Mitchell furnished Stinson with goods and encouraged him to go into the Creek Nation and sell them to the Indians on credit. Mitchell then permitted the Indians to receive their annuities in goods or in credit at the McIntosh establishment.[64] In 1821 through the instrumentality of Andrew Jackson and his followers, Mitchell was charged with misappropriation of Creek indemnities and of smuggling slaves across the Florida line into Georgia. He was subsequently dismissed from the agency.[65]

Mitchell's successor was John Crowell, who had been the first congressional delegate from Alabama Territory and he became affiliated in Georgia politics with the Clark or anti-Troup faction.[66] The new agent's unfriendliness to McIntosh was soon apparent and it was fed from other sources than Crowell's political opposition to McIntosh's relative, Troup, and his former colleague and in-law, Mitchell. Upon assuming the agency, Crowell forthwith forbade McIntosh to distribute the annuities. His brother, Thomas Crowell, and other relatives were granted licenses to trade with the Indians in competition with McIntosh.[67]

The McIntosh establishment continued to provide the Crowells with formidable competition, however. When the 1823 annuities were brought to Broken Arrow, Crowell refused to honor McIntosh's drafts on the Indians and proceeded to pay them in cash.[68] He became incensed when McIntosh went among the Indians at the public square and took from them by violence $8,000 which he claimed they owed him. Crowell retaliated by charging McIntosh's associate, Stinson, with selling goods without a license. He ordered him arrested and his goods confiscated. Crowell seized the goods and took them to his brother's establishment. McIntosh, invoking his prerogative as a chief, refused to permit Crowell's men to take Stinson into custody, and ordered Chilly McIntosh to assemble a force and seize the confiscated goods. Crowell hurled bitter oaths at McIntosh and threatened him with ultimate vengeance.

Crowell's animosity toward the Coweta chieftain was further intensified at the latter's interference when the agent drew a knife and threatened to cut the throat of a Creek named Srells. The legal phase of these differences between Crowell and McIntosh was settled with the trial of Stinson in federal court. McIntosh gave bond for his appearance to answer Crowell's charges. At the trial held in Savannah, Mitchell and McIntosh were the principal witnesses for the defense. Stinson was acquitted of the charges, apparently because he was represented as a clerk rather than a partner in the McIntosh firm.[69]

The gyrations of this feud reached in one direction all the way to Milledgeville and Washington, where plans were already under way for a new amputation of Creek territory. In the other direction it extended far into the Creek back country where determined opposition to any further cessions of land was rapidly crystallizing. The nucleus of this opposition apparently centered among those Upper town warriors and underling chiefs whom McIntosh had helped to punish and whose relatives he had put to death as enemies of the whites. Already under the domination of Big Warrior these now found an additional ally in Crowell, and the agent was doubtless happy to nourish their grievances. McIntosh probably saw clearly this intractable combination against him and the dangers with which he was menaced.

Crowell in his conduct of agency affairs frequently appeared to be courting the favor of the old Red Stick conservatives. This is illustrated by his opposition to the Creek mission schools

established by the Methodist and Baptist churches. Suggestive
of the religious aspects of the Creek civil war, the Upper Creeks
were less inclined toward the white man's faith than were those
of the Lower towns. The missions were located in the vicinity
of Coweta town.[70] McIntosh was among those who encouraged
these missions among the Lower Creeks and he sought an additional school to be located on the upper Chattahoochee where
he resided. Crowell, on the other hand, denied the missionaries
the privilege of preaching to the Creeks, either at the mission
or elsewhere in the Nation. In protesting this move, the Reverend William Capers in a letter to the secretary of war cited Big
Warrior's devotion to Crowell which he attributed to the latter's enmity toward McIntosh. Capers accused the agent of such
vices as the use of profanity and of neglecting his duties to attend cock fights.[71] Crowell admitted his addiction to profanity
and his refusal to encourage the Indians in religious instruction,
but the rule prohibiting such teachings he attributed to Big
Warrior and the Creek National Council. Secretary of War
John C. Calhoun interceded in behalf of the missionaires, and
he requested Crowell to modify his policy.

In Crowell's alliance with the Indians in their determination
not to make further cessions of land, he was somewhat more
cautious but no less ardent than in other of their causes which
he espoused. Whether this attitude was derived more from his
contemplation of a permanent and somewhat lucrative personal
establishment at the agency or from his personal enmity toward
Governor Troup and the Coweta chieftain, it is impossible to
determine.[72] Crowell justified his position on the grounds that
he was sincerely interested in the welfare of the Indians and
was protecting their interests against those of avaricious individuals.

If Crowell's interest in the welfare of the Indians included
a sincere interest in their permanent rights to the land which
they occupied, he was amply justified in his hostility toward
McIntosh. As the year 1823 opened, the governorship of Georgia
was occupied by George M. Troup whose opponent, Matthew
Talbot, Crowell had supported with blunt incaution.[73] Troup's
insistence upon the fulfillment of the Georgia Compact was soon
to become the major characteristic of his administration. In an
attempt to comply with his government's twenty-year old com-

mitments to Georgia, President James Monroe directed commissioners to New Echota in July 1823, to secure a cession from the Cherokees. Finding the Cherokee National Council not disposed to make a further cession, the commissioners employed McIntosh in an effort to bribe some of the leading Cherokee officials. In a letter dated at New Town (New Echota), on October 21, 1823, McIntosh wrote to John Ross, president of the Cherokee National Committee as follows:

My friend I am going to inform you a few lines as a friend, I want you to give me your opinion of the treaty, whether the chiefs will be willing or not. If the chiefs feel disposed to let the United States have the land part of it, I want you to let me know. I will make the United States commissioners give you two thousand dollars, A McKoy the same and Charles Hicks $3,000 for present and nobody shall know it. And if you think the land wouldn't [be] sold. I will be satisfied. If the lands should be sold I will get you the amount before the treaty sign, and if you got any friend you want him to received they shall received the same amount. Nothing more to inform you at present . . . the whole amount is $12,000. You can divide among your friends exclusive $7,000. . . .[74]

At the New Echota conference McIntosh had hinted to the commissioners that, since they had failed to obtain a cession from the Cherokees, they might succeed in obtaining land from the Creeks. However, the Cherokee chiefs, scenting a three-sided conspiracy to despoil both the Cherokees and their Creek neighbors, ordered McIntosh out of their Nation and excluded him forever from their councils. They dispatched a runner to inform Big Warrior and Little Prince of what had transpired at New Echota, warning them of McIntosh's intrigues and speculative designs. "We have lost all confidence of his fidelity towards the interests of the red brothers," they wrote, and advised the Creek leaders "to keep a strict watch over his conduct, or, if you do not, he will ruin your nation."[75]

This communication from the Cherokees inspired Big Warrior, with Little Prince apparently giving his consent, to assemble a meeting of the chiefs of the Upper towns at Tuckabatchee in May. At this rump council the chiefs adopted a resolution never again to cede another acre of their land. During the following month the resolution was presented to the full council of the Creek Nation at Broken Arrow where McIntosh was present and where he made a vigorous protest of the Tuckabatchee resolution. Big Warrior led the coalition in favor of the resolution, and it was adopted.

Apparently in order to frighten McIntosh into compliance and perhaps to bring him into contempt of his own people, a third council was held at Pole Cat Springs, in the Creek back country, where the resolution was enacted a third time.[76] At Pole Cat Springs the council dug up and re-enacted an earlier law which decreed death "by ropes and guns" to anyone who should dare to sell a foot of land without the consent of the Nation.[77]

Many observers soon detected the shadow of Agent Crowell in these proceedings. It was discovered that Crowell's official representative in the back country, sub-Agent William Walker, had written the original resolutions. The final meeting, at which was added the death penalty clause, was actually held in his house at Pole Cat Springs. The sub-agent had also sent copies of these proceedings to newspapers in Georgia and Alabama. Walker had taken to wife the daughter of Big Warrior whose "Dukedom of Pole Cat Springs" may have been an additional inducement to his espousal of the Indians' cause.[78] Since the policy of Monroe's administration was to remove the Indians from their eastern tribal lands, this duplicity on the part of the Creek agents was soon brought to the attention of the secretary of war. Calhoun ordered Walker relieved of his duties as sub-agent and reprimanded Crowell for his own conduct toward the negotiations then pending. He urged upon him the necessity for better cooperation with the administration in the future.[79]

While the Pole Cat Springs proceedings were taking place McIntosh was on his way to Indian Springs where he had recently built an elaborate hotel on the property which he had acquired there in 1821. Later when shown a newspaper account of the "Pole Cat Law" as it came to be called, he denied its validity on the ground that it was not enacted by the whole council of the Nation. When he returned to the Nation, however, McIntosh seems to have faltered from the course he had been pursuing. Apparently he acceded to the Pole Cat law when, according to witnesses, he proclaimed it publicly at a gathering of Indians to witness a ball play held near the Methodist Mission.[80]

His conduct during the opening phase of the conference be-

tween the United States commissioners and the full council of
the Creek Nation gives further evidence of weakening from his
previous position. This conference, which was in preparation for
more than two months, was called into session in December,
1824, at the National Council Square at Broken Arrow. Here
the commissioners, Duncan G. Campbell and James Meriwether,
demanded a cession of lands in exchange for territory in the
West. They stated that, because the Creeks had been conquered
in past conflicts with the United States, they were tenants-at-will
on the lands which they presently occupied. A note of legal finality was introduced which, for practical purposes, almost changed
the plea to an ultimatum. This was the statement that removal
was necessary because of the Georgia Compact.[81]

In a reply to the last statement McIntosh, in his new role as
speaker of the Nation, signed an address with Little Prince and
two other chiefs, which claimed they were unaware of this agreement with Georgia and, if it existed, they did not believe the
President would permit it to ruin his red children. The bargaining instinct of McIntosh asserted itself again when he wrote "That
ruin is almost the inevitable consequence" of a removal to the
West. "What assurances have we," he asked, "that we would not
be encroaching on the people of other lands?"[82]

On December 14 the Creek Council announced to the commissioners its firm refusal to make any cession, and it remained adamant throughout the remaining four days of the assembly. As a
final offer the commissioners promised to exchange land in the
West, acre for acre, and to pay for improvements on presently
occupied lands together with the cost of removal, in addition to
a bounty of half a million dollars. For only that portion of the
Creek territory within the chartered limits of Georgia, the terms
would be the same except the bounty would be $300,000. To all
of these offers the Creeks were unyielding. In desperation Big
Warrior's deputy declared that he would "not take a house-full of
money" for his interest in the land. In this manner the official
negotiations at Broken Arrow ended.

Four days before the close of the assembly the commissioners
had realized that their efforts in open council were useless. They
then resorted to the more practical method of negotiating directly
with individual chiefs, and employing intermediaries to offer them
special inducements. In this stratagem the commissioners, both of
whom were citizens of Georgia, had ample reasons to regard Mc-

Intosh as the most likely if somewhat costly mediator.[83] The
Coweta chieftain lodged at his son's house near the Council Square
where some white men in the employ of the commissioners also
were quartered.[84] Soon rumors of secret meetings were circulating
among the Indians. These conclaves held late at night, in the
woods and behind houses and fences, indicated close collaboration
between McIntosh and the commissioners. McIntosh was quoted
as saying that three thousand dollars would take his Creek friends
anywhere. Later investigations substantiated most of the rumors
concerning these nocturnal meetings.[85]

At length Agent Crowell, who had suspected McIntosh's duplicity if he did not actually know of it, began to connive with Big
Warrior and Little Prince to have him broken both as speaker of
the Nation and as a chief.[86] Because of his influence with the
chiefs of the Coweta towns and perhaps also with Little Prince,
McIntosh was permitted to continue as head chief of the Cowetas.
Before the Broken Arrow council adjourned, however, he was subjected to the humiliation and disgrace of being deprived of his
office as speaker.[87]

This event may well have been the turning point both in the
course of the negotiations and the career of McIntosh. He was
unmistakably angered by having been placed in contempt before
the assembled mass of two thousand warriors and head men of
the Creek Nation. When threats were made upon his life he made
a hurried departure at night from his son's house, escaping
through a window. He went to Coweta where he was guarded by
his own warriors. He never again appeared in the Council Square
of the Creek Nation. The next time he is found in an official act,
he is openly and brazenly playing the role of traitor to his people.

From Coweta McIntosh apparently went to his house at Lockchau Talofau, at the upper ferry. Here some sixty miles from
Broken Arrow and the scene of his disgrace, he may have met
again with one or more of the commissioners. It was here that
final plans were laid for the renewal of negotiations in February,
at Indian Springs, within the limits of Georgia.[88]

Shortly after the close of the Broken Arrow Council, McIntosh
began to organize his friends among the Lower Creeks for the next
act of the drama which was rapidly approaching its climax. He
secured the allegiance of approximately forty more or less influential Creeks from the Lower towns of Coweta, Cusseta, Talledega,
Broken Arrow, and Hitchita. Approximately half of these were

mixed-bloods and many of them were his own relatives.[89] The great majority were not chiefs at all, but in the loose designations of the Creeks they were head men and warriors. A few did not justify even this small degree of prominence.[90] McIntosh secured from this group a power-of-attorney, as it were, to continue negotiations. He also obtained their approval of his appointment to head a delegation of eight to visit the President of the United States.[91]

Late in January McIntosh, Sam Hawkins, and the remaining six of the delegation went to the home of John Broadnax in Pike County and engaged him to draw up a letter to send to Washington.[92] This letter, purported to represent the great majority of the Lower Creeks, was an exposition of McIntosh's case against Big Warrior's threatened punitive measures. The enmity of Big Warrior and the group which he led, it was claimed, resulted from events of the Creek War when Big Warrior's principal adherents had been enemies of the Americans beside whom the McIntosh party had fought. This was the faction which he claimed was now meeting in council and passing death sentences without the consent of the entire Nation.[93]

On their journey toward Washington McIntosh and the delegation stopped at Milledgeville to see Governor Troup. Here he was informed that Campbell had already preceded him to the federal capital and that he would return shortly, fully authorized to negotiate a treaty. After remaining in Milledgeville a short time, McIntosh and his entourage repaired to Indian Springs to await developments.[94]

While Campbell was in Washington, Troup, in a letter to Monroe, assured the President that a treaty could be immediately signed upon the conditions which would be disclosed by the commissioner. Campbell asked the President to authorize a meeting within the limits of Georgia where he could negotiate exclusively with the Lower Creeks. This request being refused, the President was again requested to permit a re-convening of the whole Creek Nation and, if this failed to produce a cession, to permit them to conclude a treaty with the Georgia faction alone, subject to the approval of the Creek Nation. President Monroe stood firm in his decision to authorize no treaty, except in the usual manner and under the principles with which Indian treaties were generally made. However, Secretary of War Calhoun did permit Campbell to negotiate with McIntosh, subject to the approval of the

Creek Nation, and extended to him discretionary power to hold the council at Indian Springs in Georgia.[95] It is significant to note also that Agent Crowell was cautioned to give to the commissioners that cooperation which he withheld from them at Broken Arrow. Since the commissioners' procedural instructions remained unchanged from those employed at Broken Arrow in December, it may be safely assumed that they were possessed with ample means of persuasion.[96]

Campbell and Meriwether were later to admit that "a competent fund" had been placed in their hands "to defray costs of the treaty."[97] A large amount of this fund apparently was made available to Campbell's brother-in-law, William Williamson, who was one of the most active unofficial agents in the employ of the commissioners immediately preceding the Indian Springs conference. Major Thomas P. Andrews, the special agent sent later in the year to investigate the Indian Springs proceedings, stated his belief that Williamson had used twenty-five or thirty thousand dollars of these funds to speculate in Negroes and that he offered a bribe of eight thousand dollars to the interpreter, Hambly. Other forms of bribery were highly suspected if not actually proven, such as promises of a share of profits in the disbursement of removal funds and annuities, and of special reservations of land in the ceded territory.[98]

In all of these surreptitious procedures, it is worth noting that McIntosh, if anything, was a recipient of bribes and not a dispenser as he formerly had been. Just before the convening of the Indian Springs conference, the Cowetan bought from Richard J. Nichols, a Milledgeville merchant, six hundred dollars' worth of merchandise which he promised to pay for ten days later. David B. Mitchell assured Nichols that the treaty would put about fifty thousand dollars in McIntosh's pocket.[99] Meriwether, one of the commissioners, signed his name to a note for the payment of the indebtedness. "I had long known of his character, entertained no doubt of his solvency, and had no fears that he would throw upon me the burden of the note," explained Meriwether. After the treaty McIntosh paid into his hands the money with which he discharged the note.[100]

The Indian Springs assembly was slated to begin on Monday, February 7. Because of late arrivals and a small attendance it did not convene until the following Saturday. Big Warrior, Little Prince, and their principal adherents were conspicuous by their absence. Their failure to attend may have resulted as much from the short notice given them and the great distance involved as from their opposition to reopening negotiations.[101] They did send a representative, Poethla Yoholo of Tuckabatchee, whose only contribution to the conference was a warning that the death sentence would be inflicted upon those who sold land.

The treaty itself is significant both for the conditions under which it was made and for the terms which it proposed. Its main point was the cession of all Creek lands between the Flint and Chattahoochee rivers together with Creek lands on the Tallapoosa and Coosa rivers lying somewhat north of the meridian passing through the Coweta falls on the Chattahoochee. These lands were to be exchanged for an equal acreage in Arkansas. To compensate for improvements on their ceded lands and to cover costs of removal, the United States was to pay $400,000 "to the nation emigrating." Of this amount, $200,000 was to be paid "as soon as practicable" after the ratification of the treaty, $100,000 at the time of removal, and the remaining $100,000 was to be paid over a period of twelve years after settlement in the West. The Creeks were guaranteed protection "against encroachments, hostilities, and impositions of the whites and of all others" prior to removal, and they were to be provided with certain inducements toward the pursuit of husbandry on their western lands. They were given until September, 1826, to vacate the ceded territory.[102]

During the night previous to the date set for the signing, a part of the Cusseta and Soogwagloo delegation, becoming apprehensive of the proceedings, broke up their encampment and fled to the Flint River.[103] The departure of these together with the refusal of Poethla Yoholo and seven of his followers to sign reduced in size what at best had been an irregular and highly unrepresentative assembly of the Creek Nation. Nevertheless the treaty was read in its complete form article by article with the half-breed Hambly interpreting slowly but in a low voice. At the conclusion of each article assent was expressed by an Indian grunt or exclamation.[104]

The fifth article of the treaty later became the object of considerable controversy. This article, which many claimed was never interpreted to the Indians, provided for the payment of $200,000 of the purchase money by the commissioners negotiating the treaty. When it was read in English several witnesses noted a pained expression on the face of Agent Crowell.[105] It was the opinion of General Gaines that the entire procedure "was the design of a few desperate half-breeds and white men" to obtain by fraud this sum of money.[106]

The final article of the treaty was also controversial and there is no doubt about its surreptitious nature. The article was a grant of title from McIntosh to the United States of two reservations which he held in Georgia under the treaty of 1821 and for which he was to receive the sum of $25,000.[107] One of these reservations was a thousand-acre plot around Indian Springs on which McIntosh had built the large tavern in which the conference was being held. The other was a tract of 640 acres on the west bank of the Ocmulgee River on which there were some improvements.[108] This article was not presented to the assembly until February 14, and then added as a supplementary clause. It was signed "by all the principal chiefs present," which apparently included McIntosh and eight others.

The total number who signed the treaty was fifty-one persons exclusive of American officials. Fourteen are known to have been mixed-bloods. McIntosh signed first, followed by Etome Tustunugee, chief of Coweta town.[109] Of 56 towns in the Nation, representatives from only eight were signatories. Of the total, only McIntosh was a ranking chief of the Nation and he was but a chief of fifth rank. There were five underling chiefs, all of whom were Cowetas. Twenty-six belonged to the category known as "law menders," seventeen were Indians of no official standing whatever, although fourteen of them had been broken as chiefs. Two were of such obscure reputation as to defy identification. When one of the signers was about to make his mark, Crowell asked McIntosh if he were also a chief, whereupon the Cowetan replied, "Me chief." The final entry in the journal of the proceedings, on February 14, is as follows: "The Commissioners then convened the chiefs, distributed some presents, ordered them furnished with rations to take them home, advised them to temperance and unanimity, took final leave, and adjourned."[110]

After the signing of the treaty McIntosh, in company with Etome Tustunugee and other chiefs, went to Milledgeville where they stated to Governor Troup their apprehensions of danger from the Upper Creeks and invoked the protection of Georgia. This the governor promised, and accordingly he dispatched his aid-de-camp, Colonel Henry G. Lamar, to Cusseta and Tuckabatchee to warn the Upper Creeks against taking punitive action against McIntosh and his party.[111] Early in March the United States Senate ratified the treaty and it was approved by President John Quincy Adams, whose inauguration had occurred three days previously.

On his return from Tuckabatchee Colonel Lamar stated his belief that the Indians would submit peacefully to the treaty, now that it had been approved by the President. He gave as his reason the Indians' unlimited confidence in the wisdom, virtue, and power of the President.[112] In the meantime, however, Crowell had rushed to Washington a cautious protest to the treaty's ratification, a protest which became increasingly vigorous in the closing days of Monroe's administration. Chilly McIntosh, who after the Indian Springs meeting had ventured no farther toward his home at Broken Arrow than the Flint River, learned there that his father and six others had been appointed to die. He sent a runner to Lockchau Talofau warning his father to leave home at once and to meet him at Newnan.[113]

McIntosh remained at his home at the upper ferry. Apparently the developments at Washington, together with Troup's assurances, had lulled him into a feeling of security. At Lockchau Talofau a series of letters was exchanged between him and the governor concerning Troup's plans for an immediate survey of the ceded lands. On April 10 McIntosh held a council of the friendly chiefs at Lockchau Talofau, where in the presence of a large gathering of white people they agreed to permit the land to be surveyed at any time the legislature thought proper. Subsequently Troup sent out a call for the legislature to meet in extra session, in May, to deal with the matter of surveys, to organize the territory into counties, and to authorize a land lottery.[114]

Rumors of an early land lottery involving millions of virgin acres produced a speculative fever among Georgians, and a "Sooner Movement" was the inevitable result. White men crossed over the line in large numbers seeking to acquire some kind of claim to such Indian improvements as houses, cleared fields, and mill sites.[115] In order to bring this confused situation somewhat under control, McIntosh with Troup's approval issued a notice requiring white persons who wished to buy Indian improvements to file their names and other details in McIntosh's register at Lockchau Talofau.[116]

Troup's plans for the immediate survey and organization of

the ceded territory were premature and ill-calculated to reduce the rage of McIntosh's enemies. On three different occasions since the Creek War ten years before, a surveyor's chain had been stretched across their lands, and each time it had been a final and irrevocable act confirming the white man's possession. Crowell was quick to seize upon this action to bring McIntosh into further contempt with the hostile Creeks and to discredit Governor Troup with the federal authorities. On April 27, the agent wrote to James Barbour, the new secretary of war, accusing Troup of usurping the prerogatives of Barbour's office, and McIntosh of playing the role of Indian agent under him. He cited the presence of Troup's aid-de-camp in the Nation, and told of his holding meetings with the Indians, of Troup's threatening messages to them, and of his issuing state papers in relation to the surveys.[117]

Troup's haste in the matter of surveying the territory was dictated largely by political considerations, for 1825 was an election year and Troup was anxious to justify his candidacy for re-election. The free distribution of the surveyed land to Georgia citizens through this lottery offered a prospect for patronage of gigantic proportions.[118] It was this question of surveys which eventually brought Troup into violent conflict with the federal government, and it also doubtless helped to strengthen the Upper Creeks in their determination to take vengeance on McIntosh. Soon after the governor issued his proclamation, on April 18, reciting the ratification of the treaty and announcing the extra session, the outraged Nation finally invoked the law of Pole Cat Springs. At a council meeting at Tuckabatchee, in which the Upper Creeks dominated, several executions were ordered. Big Warrior had recently died and the Indians' concept of vengeful justice now more than ever called for the death of McIntosh.[119]

Near the end of April an execution party of nearly two hundred warriors was dispatched from Okfuskee and Tuckabatchee under the command of Menawa, one of the few surviving leaders of the Creek civil war. They arrived in the vicinity of Lockchau Talofau in the afternoon of April 30, and concealed themselves in the woods near the McIntosh residence. Some of the Indians in the party wore war paint in keeping with their ancient tribal traditions and reminiscent of Tecumseh and the prophets.[120] About three o'clock in the morning, on Sunday, May l, a rising chorus of whip-poor-wills broke the stillness of the night. Ironically enough, this was the season of the year in western Georgia when this moonbird was accustomed to appear at the Indian's door-stone before daylight, to turn his mind once again to the soil and to remind him that the time for planting corn was at hand.

When McIntosh awoke, flames from a burning outbuilding illuminated his house which already was surrounded by his appointed executioners. Occupying the dwelling were white travelers from the upper part of the Creek Nation whose stay there had been prolonged by heavy rains which prevented their crossing the Chattahoochee River. Near the main dwelling was a small house for the accommodation of extra guests where Chilly McIntosh, a half-breed named Mooty Kennard, and a white pedlar were sleeping. Chilly and Kennard escaped through a window and succeeded in crossing the river in a small boat. Other members of McIntosh's family and the white guests were permitted to leave the dwelling which was then fired with lightwood.

Etome Tustunugee was shot as he appeared with McIntosh in the doorway. McIntosh retreated upstairs where he fired several times from a window but was forced by the flames to abandon the building. His body was pierced with several bullets as he descended the stairs. He fell to the floor and was dragged by his feet some distance from the house. He raised himself on one elbow and gave his enemies a last defiant look as the knife of an Okfuskee warrior plunged into his heart.

McIntosh's son-in-law Sam Hawkins, who lived on the Little Tallapoosa River near the present site of Carrollton, was seized and executed on the same day. After his escape from the scene of his father's execution, Chilly McIntosh went to Milledgeville and thence to Washington where he urged the payment of annuities and money due under the terms of the Indian Springs Treaty. President John Quincy Adams's suspicions were aroused, and after an investigation he refused to execute the treaty, which he believed was obtained by bribery. Treaties made during the following year and in 1827 finally extinguished the Creek claims to all of their remaining lands in Georgia.[121]

WILSON LUMPKIN

BY ROBERT G. MCPHERSON

In THE nation's capital, in the spring of 1838, a phrenologist recorded his impressions after examining the head of Senator Wilson Lumpkin of Georgia. It was, he thought, a most remarkable head. Its conformity suggested to him that its owner was possessed of great *"force & power* of mind and character," great singleness of purpose, and no small degree of self-esteem.[1] To the layman unskilled in the mysteries of phrenological analysis, these qualities might not have been apparent from the dimensions of Lumpkin's skull, but they were quite obvious in his career by 1838.

So were other qualities. Lumpkin was devoted to his large family, and often lamented that his public career deprived it of the close attention he would have preferred. He had an intense feeling of loyalty toward his friends, and spared himself no labor in their behalf. The phrenologist wrote that Lumpkin "is surpassed by few for his general understanding of men & things [and] for plain common sense, for practical judgment & matter of fact talent." He "has the most astonishing memory of *facts* and minute transactions long since past . . . [and] is one of the most systematic men I have ever seen. . . ." Possessed of "great boldness, enterprise & energy," Lumpkin was always sure that he was right, allowing no appeal from his judgment.[2] In general these qualities served him well. He needed to be aggressive and persevering to win the objectives he sought.

Descended from seventeenth-century settlers of Virginia, Lumpkin was born in that state on January 14, 1783. Within a year his family brought him to live in that part of Georgia soon to

Robert G. McPherson is a member of the history faculty at the University of Georgia.

be designated as Oglethorpe County. There he was reared in a frontier environment, his education supplemented at home by his father, a jurist of local eminence, who exposed his son to the best books and endowed him with an abiding intellectual curiosity.[3]

Lumpkin was married at the age of eighteen to Elizabeth Walker, who was "something over fourteen," the daughter of a Baptist clergyman of the locality. She and her husband were particularly devoted, and though Lumpkin remarried after her death in 1819, his correspondence many decades later gives evidence of his deep affection for Elizabeth. Of their eight children, five survived their mother and grew to maturity.[4]

For the next few years following his wife's death Lumpkin farmed, occasionally assisting his father in legal duties, and at the age of twenty he began to teach school. His popularity increased steadily, and ultimately effected his unsolicited election to the state legislature in 1804. Most Georgians were supporters of Thomas Jefferson, political parties within the state in this dawning "era of personal politics" consisting of an aristocratic faction led by General James Jackson and William Harris Crawford, and a democratic small-farmer group under Elijah Clarke and his son John Clark.[5] Lumpkin "imbibed a disrelish to becoming a partizan to either of the factions," forswearing political strife based upon personal considerations. Having already been admitted to the bar, he was the next year appointed a magistrate in Oglethorpe County, and for several years served in this as well as in his legislative capacity.[6]

In 1811, together with four neighbors, Lumpkin embarked on an extensive reconnaissance of the lands to the west of Georgia, with a view to relocating his family. Traveling through territory later to become the states of Alabama and Mississippi, they went down the Mississippi River to New Orleans, then crossing that river they went up the Red River into the Louisiana Territory for about a hundred miles. Proceeding northward, they returned to Georgia by way of Kentucky and Tennessee. This four-month venture "through the wild wilderness and savage men of the forest" was not without hazard, though no harm befell the party. Lumpkin mentions spending a day at a great Indian council "at Tuckabatchee in the Creek Nation," where he later learned it was decided that the Creeks would join Tecumseh and the Northern Indians in aiding the British

against the United States in the impending War of 1812. He
described the Creeks as "unaccommodating, stubborn and insolent." He found the western country impressive, but saw nothing to surpass Georgia as "a favourable land to prepare for an
abiding home."[7]

Lumpkin again represented Oglethorpe County in the state
legislature, serving during the first two years of the war. He
then relocated his family in Morgan County, where he was elected
to Congress in 1814. The War of 1812 was over when Lumpkin
arrived in Washington, but the city still bore the marks of
hostilities. In temporary buildings the Congress debated the public debt, the currency, the national bank, the tariff, and internal
improvements shown to be needed during the recent war. Lumpkin observed that the tone of Congress supported a broader
construction of the Constitution than had been manifested before the war.[8]

Confused by the sight of old opponents of the Bank of the
United States, of protective tariffs, and of federally-supported internal improvements now arguing for their adoption, Lumpkin
also abandoned his usual strict construction and voted for the
charter of the Bank and for the Tariff of 1816. The latter he
believed a means of raising revenue to pay the national debt
without having to resort to a direct tax. He did not think of
it as enriching one group at the expense of another. Writing in
1852, he said that he had then been ill-informed, that funda-
mentally he was most strenuously opposed to any development
of federal power beyond the limits set by the Constitution.[9]

This was the same Congress which saw fit to raise its own
salary from six dollars a day to fifteen hundred dollars a year,
thereby precipitating a violent reaction throughout the country.
Lumpkin opposed the principle of the change from a per diem
allowance to a stated salary, and voted against the measure, as
did the rest of the Georgia delegation. Nevertheless, after the
measure was made law by a small majority, Lumpkin was among
those who were indignantly swept from the House in the next
election.[10]

Returning to his home in Morgan County, Lumpkin resolved
to turn his back on politics. But in the fall of 1818 President
James Monroe named him a commissioner of the United States
to designate the boundaries of the treaty made with the Creek
Indians in January, 1818. This proved to be a momentous oc-

currence. Through his experience in this connection, Lumpkin acquired a vast store of information pertaining both to Indian character and white relations with the Indians. It was the beginning of an interest in Indian affairs which was to dominate his political life.[11]

In October, 1818, Lumpkin was appointed a commissioner for the purpose of delineating the boundary between Georgia and Florida. He made a study of the problems involved, and preparations for the undertaking were well advanced when he was ordered to suspend his operations because of the menace of hostile Indians. As far as Lumpkin was concerned, the project was never renewed, though in later years he deplored its having remained unsettled for so many decades.[12]

Lumpkin's services had so pleased the federal government that following the acquisition of Florida from Spain, he was informed that he might have any office in the prospective territorial government which he might desire. Accordingly he traveled to Florida and reconnoitered its western parts. He was particularly impressed by Pensacola, which he expected someday to develop into a seaport to rival Mobile and even New Orleans. But he resolved not to leave Georgia, which all his life, sometimes to the irritation of his Washington friends, he loudly proclaimed the best of all lands.[13]

In February, 1819, a treaty was signed between the Cherokee Indians and the United States, and again Lumpkin was appointed commissioner to perform the same duties as he had in relation to the Creek treaty the year before. This second extensive connection with Indian problems was overshadowed late in the year by the death of his wife at the age of thirty-four.

The following year, feeling the necessity of changing his daily life under these altered circumstances, Lumpkin again decided to enter politics, and accordingly was sent by the people of Morgan County to the state legislature.[14]

A few months later, his private life rehabilitated by his marriage to Annis Hopkins on January 1, 1821, Lumpkin was yet again appointed Indian commissioner by the President for the purpose of designating the boundary lines of the Creek treaty of January, 1821. There being convened at the same time a special session of the Georgia legislature for the purpose of dealing with the survey and distribution of lands concerned in the treaty, Lumpkin was compelled to resign from the legislature in order to retain his appointment as Indian commissioner.[15]

From the end of 1821 to the end of 1824 Lumpkin took no active part in politics. In the presidential election of 1824, however, he was an active supporter of Jackson, a fact which identified him with the democratic Clark faction in Georgia politics.

The next year the legislature created a Board of Public Works with a view to systematic development of river, canal, or railroad communications in Georgia.[16] The governor presided over the bi-partisan six-man board, which was chosen by the legislature. Hamilton Fulton was appointed state engineer, and Lumpkin, having been elected to the board as a Troup man, was authorized to accompany him on the proposed reconnaissance of the state. This was because of his extensive experience as Indian commissioner, and the fact that he worked well with Governor George M. Troup, for whom he had high admiration, though he admitted they did not always see eye to eye on political matters.[17]

In pursuit of his duties, Lumpkin had occasion to visit most of the head men of the Cherokee Nation: "Charles Hicks, their principal chief, the Rosses, the Vanns, the Ridges and Boudinot, the Adairs, the Rodgerses, the McNairs, &c, &c." He was already convinced that the Cherokees had no future in Georgia, and that removal beyond the Mississippi was their only alternative to extinction. He found the Indians generally opposed not only to emigration, but even to the presence of his surveying party in the region.[18]

Lumpkin and Fulton carefully reconnoitered the country between Milledgeville and Lookout Mountain, and found the possibility of water communication very doubtful. However, although railroads were still in their infancy, Lumpkin recommended to Troup the feasibility of rail communication over the route they had selected.[19] Soon after this, Fulton was accused of dishonesty and was dismissed late in 1826, crippling the Board of Public Works. Nothing was done for a decade to continue this work.[20]

After his experiences among the Cherokees, Lumpkin became increasingly convinced that emigration to the West was the only solution to the problem which they posed to Georgia's development. He was also sure that he personally had something to contribute to its solution, and that it could best be handled from Washington. Accordingly he became a candidate for Congress in 1826, and was elected.[21]

When Lumpkin entered Congress in 1827, less than 15,000 Cherokees occupied between five and six million acres in northwestern Georgia, and smaller areas in North Carolina, Alabama, and Tennessee. Despite the federal government's contract in 1802 to remove all the Indians from Georgia in return for the cession of the state's western lands, its contradictory Indian policy only encouraged them to stay. Lumpkin pointed this out to the House of Representatives early in 1828.[22] So did President Jackson in his first annual message to Congress in 1829.[23] Led by intermarried whites (estimated at 220 in 1825)[24] and men of mixed blood, and faced by the threat of removal, the Cherokees in the third decade of the century took a number of steps calculated to confirm them in their possession. They set up a representative government, adopted a written language, a legal code, founded a national capital, and declared themselves a sovereign nation immune from all other law. It is difficult to determine how deeply the Cherokees as a whole were affected by this sudden assumption of the paraphernalia of civilization. But certainly they expected it to set them apart from the rest of America's aboriginal inhabitants, and to preserve them from similar eviction. Lumpkin was determined that Georgia should not be so penalized. Nevertheless the Cherokees' leaders succeeded in arousing sympathy from some Americans whose lands had already been cleared of Indians and who were often sufficiently remote from the problem to view it abstractly. Among these were many of the defenders of the Indians.

Thomas Jefferson had advocated the eventual removal of all Indians west of the Mississippi as early as 1803, and a group of Cherokees had left to reconnoitre the region in 1809. They returned with a highly favorable report which moved some of them to emigrate, followed in 1817 and 1819 by larger groups comprising perhaps one-third of their people, mostly from Tennessee.[25] But by and large the Georgia Cherokees were reluctant to depart, and were stiffened in their resolve by men who stood to profit from their remaining. Georgia reacted formally and at once to their establishment of a Nation within the state's limits. On December 27, 1827, the state Senate approved resolutions which positively stated that the Cherokees were Georgia's tenants at will, and that the state could whenever she chose, extend her laws over the Cherokee area and force all people residing there to conform, "be they white, red or black." The resolutions foreswore violence until all other means of securing Georgia's rights should have been exhausted.[26]

On taking his seat in the House of Representatives in 1827, Lumpkin was placed on the Committee of Indian Affairs. On December 13, despite the protests of the Georgia delegation that he was presumptive, he initiated a resolution that the Committee be instructed to inquire into the question of removal of "all the remnant tribes of Indians within the limits of the States or Territories of this Union to some eligible situation west of the River Mississippi." The Committee was so instructed. Lumpkin said that he was motivated first by a desire to relieve Georgia and other states of their encumbering Indian populations, and secondly by a desire to better the prospects of the Indians themselves. He knew nothing could stop the white inhabitants of Georgia from occupying all of their state, and that clashes with the Cherokees would be inevitable unless they were removed to the West. There they could govern themselves as a political entity, and receive the beneficient civilizing influences of the federal government and eleemosynary institutions. Lumpkin went so far as to envisage the Indians becoming "an interesting and worthy member of our great confederacy of states," once the civilizing process was complete.[27]

The Committee on Indian Affairs secured the appropriation of $15,000 to finance a commission of three men to explore the western lands with a view to removal of the Indians. Their report was favorable, and after much debate, and much behind-the-scenes persuasion by its advocates, it was sustained by Congress.

Lumpkin enjoyed no little popularity and fame as a result of his efforts on behalf of removal, both in Washington and in Georgia. He was re-elected to the next Congress with ample support. But there were more complications yet, before the way was clear for the exodus. Countless petitions from people in various parts of the country, however remote from the controversy, deterred the Congress from acting with decision. The Cherokee leaders employed lawyers, who fattened on the controversy by fighting emigration. But Lumpkin observed that the sentiment in Congress favoring removal was steadily growing, and was confident that once Jackson became President in 1829, the necessary action would be taken regardless of opposition.[28]

Lumpkin's confidence in Jackson was not misplaced, for the new President had very definite views upon Indian affairs, and in general they coincided with Lumpkin's. Naturally there was strong support of removal in Georgia. In December, 1828, the legislature, after preliminary appeals to President John Quincy Adams the year before had failed, adopted laws annexing the Cherokee country lying within Georgia's boundaries, and extended Georgia law over it, invalidating that of the Cherokee government.[29] This in effect added a third set of laws affecting the same area to that of the Cherokees and that of the United States, with many points of conflict existing between them.

The Cherokees registered a protest in Washington, but found the Adams administration, on the way out of office, difficult to interest. Jackson made his position clear by appointing a Westerner, John Henry Eaton, as secretary of war. A month after the inauguration, Eaton informed the Cherokee delegation that the government would not support them against Georgia.[30]

Jackson's first annual message to Congress, on December 8, 1829, was definitely favorable to Georgia's position. He reviewed the Indian problem, pointing out the illegality of the Cherokees' action from the constitutional point of view. He advocated removal or submission to the laws of Georgia on grounds of Cherokee interference with the rights of a sovereign state.[31]

On taking his seat in this same 21st Congress in December, 1829, Lumpkin was again appointed to the Committee on Indian Affairs, which proceeded to act upon the President's recommendation. On February 24, 1830, it made an elaborate report to the House, accompanied by a proposed bill authorizing removal. After two readings, and over strong opposition, the supporters of the bill succeeded in having authorized a distribution of 10,000 copies of the report and bill throughout the country.[32]

Heated debate followed throughout the winter, heightened by a flood of pro-Cherokee correspondence, elicited by the emotional appeals of the opponents of emigration. Nonetheless, the majority of Congress gradually responded to the arguments of its adherents. It was not a novel idea. As Lumpkin argued before the House in May, 1830:

Jefferson gave to it the first official impulse; Madison, Monroe, Adams, Jackson, Calhoun . . . and a majority of the Senators and Representatives . . . have, in their official capacities repeatedly sustained the principles and policy of the bill. . . .[33]

The majority opinion having been won, the bill was finally passed by the House on May 24, 1830, and two days later by the Senate.[34] The authorization now provided, it became necessary to conclude a new treaty with the Cherokees to arrange the terms of the removal. Here the opponents of removal expected to make a successful stand.

At this juncture Lumpkin exchanged the national legislative halls for the chief executive's chair in Georgia. In the winter of 1830-31, he was persuaded by the Clark, or Union party, to run for the governorship despite his own preference to remain in Congress to expedite the removal of the Cherokees.[35] Georgia newspapers of the Clark group published editorials strongly supporting his candidacy. His popularity throughout the state arising from his connection with the effort to remove the Cherokees made Lumpkin a likely prospect for governor at a time when Georgia herself might need to seize the initiative. Thus convinced, Lumpkin belatedly announced his candidacy in the spring of 1831.[36] At once the opposing press of the State Rights faction, which eventually backed the re-election of Governor George R. Gilmer, accused him of vacillation, a deplorable characteristic in a chief executive.[37] This was augmented by the fact that his alignment politically was not completely with either party. At heart a State Rights man, he was at the same time an advocate of moderate Union principles.[38]

The backing of the two parties finally settled solidly behind the two candidates by late summer. The tenor of the times was sympathetic toward democracy, giving the Clark group the advantage over their opponents. They were further aided by the fact that Lumpkin's frontier upbringing and his support of Jackson sustained his role as their candidate.[39]

The campaign was not characterized by any large issues, despite the efforts of the newspapers to arouse feeling. The nullification controversy had begun, but Georgians were as yet apathetic. Agitation from South Carolina was slowly awaking some response, and the adherents of each candidate accused the other side of supporting nullification. But the opinion of the people was that no issue existed here. When the votes were cast, the traditional aristocratic and democratic divisions seem to have been adhered to by the voters, and Lumpkin became governor by a small majority with the backing of the latter group.[40]

The problem of removing the Cherokees from northwestern Georgia naturally continued to be uppermost in Lumpkin's mind. Almost immediately upon assuming the duties of his new office, there came a challenge from the Cherokee country.

The discovery of gold in northeastern Georgia in July, 1829, precipitated an influx of hard-bitten men to the Cherokee country, estimated to have numbered 3,000 within a year's time.[41] As a means of controlling these and all other whites living in the Indian territory over which she had claimed full sovereignty, Georgia in 1830 required all whites residing in the area to obtain a permit from the state to do so, and to take an oath to support the constitution and laws of Georgia. Among those affected were the missionaires who had worked among the Cherokees since the beginning of the century. These men encouraged the Indians to resist the pressure for removal, and denied the state's jurisdiction. Several of them were arrested for illegal residence, but were released on a technicality while pardons were offered them by Governor Gilmer if they would accept a license or leave the state. Most accepted his clemency, but two missionaries, Samuel A. Worcester and Elizur Butler, chose to become martyrs instead. Refusing the pardons, they were again arrested, tried in the superior court of Gwinnett County in September, 1831, and sentenced to four years imprisonment in the state penitenitary.[42]

The missionaires left the state no choice but to imprison them. They hoped thereby to obtain assistance for the Cherokees from the United States Supreme Court, as yet not forthcoming from any agency of the federal government. In 1830 Georgia had deliberately hanged a Cherokee named George, or Corn Tassel, convicted of murder in Hall County, in defiance of a writ of error issued by the United States Supreme Court. Four years later she was to repeat her action in the case of James Graves. In the case of *The Cherokee Nation vs. Georgia* in 1830, the Indians had sought to test the constitutionality of Georgia's extension of her law over the Indian territory. Chief Justice John Marshall ruled that the Cherokees had no right to sue in the court because they were neither citizens nor a foreign nation.[43] Now in the missionaries' case in 1831, *Worcester vs. Georgia,* the Cherokees hoped at last for a ruling that Georgia law had no validity within the bounds of the Cherokee Nation. The Supreme Court issued citations to Georgia through its governor to testify before the Court as to the validity of its contentions. Lumpkin ignored the summons, as had Gilmer in the case of Corn Tassel, regarding the affair as an attempt to override the state's jurisdiction in a criminal case, in violation of both the state and federal constitutions. He transmitted the citations and a statement of his action to the legislature on November 25, 1831, confident of its approval. The message concluded:

In exercising the authority of that Department of the Government which devolved on me, I will disregard all unconstitutional requisitions, of whatever character or origin they may be, and to the best of my ability will protect and defend the rights of the State, and use the means afforded me to maintain its laws and Constitution.[44]

Marshall's decision in the case was that Georgia's acts were invalid, and that Worcester should be released. President Jackson having made his opposition to Marshall known, Lumpkin elected to ignore the decision. It was not until 1833 that Worcester and Butler relented, seeing that they could expect no aid from Washington. They communicated their intention to Lumpkin to discontinue their court action, and considering the danger of their organizing the Cherokees against Georgia as having passed with the occupation of the country by numerous whites, he ordered their release.[45] Lumpkin indicated that he had been willing at any time to release the men upon their agreeing to accept his clemency.[46]

As a means of encouraging whites to take up residence in the region of Cherokee Georgia, Lumpkin proposed to survey the country and distribute by lottery all lands not actually occupied by the Indians.[47] The legislature had authorized the survey and distribution in 1830, but it had never been carried out, possibly due to Governor Gilmer's reluctance to occupy the Indian country before it was ceded by a formal treaty.[48] In November, 1831, Lumpkin communicated privately with President Jackson, expressing his proposal and inviting Jackson's comments. But the President had no desire to incur further criticism as a party to forcible eviction of the Cherokees, and withheld comment. Later, however, when Lumpkin pressed his objective, he and Jackson "came to an understanding, and cooperated harmoniously to the end of the chapter."[49]

Through Lumpkin's initiative the land act was amended in December, 1831, and the date for beginning the survey set at April 1, 1832. The agents were under special instructions to go about their work as quiety as possible so as to avoid any disturbance among the Indians.[50] The militia under General John Coffee was alerted in order to afford protection of the surveyors if needed.[51] In general the survey proceeded without violence, though one of the surveyors, F. A. Brown by name, sent Lumpkin a detailed report in September, 1832, recounting his arrest by Cherokee agents for violation of the federal Intercourse Law of 1822 by surveying in Indian country. He was taken under guard to Athens, Tennessee, for trial, but was able to obtain his release under a writ of habeas corpus.[52] General Coffee believed Ross had engineered the arrest, hoping to get the Indian question into the courts of Tennessee.[53]

Desite criticism of the work both within and without the state, it was completed in 1832. At Lumpkin's urging, ten new counties, were created: Forsyth, Lumpkin, Union, Cobb, Cherokee, Gilmer, Cass, Murray, Floyd, and Paulding.[54] The land was divided into forty-acre gold lots and one hundred and sixty-acre land lots, and distributed among Georgia citizens through the customary lottery system the following year.[55] Occupation of the lands was to begin at once, and in the first annual message of his second term, on November 5, 1833, Lumpkin reported:

We now have a settled freehold population on every part of our territory competent to the administration of our laws, so far as to secure most of the blessings of our system to those whose enterprise has led them to become settlers in that interesting section of our State, hitherto the abode of a people wholly unquallified to enjoy the blessings of wise self-government.[56]

Many Indians were induced by these developments to emigrate voluntarily, especially since the state would pay for improvements to their land. These payments were made at the stations of enrollment for emigration, with a view to encouraging the Indians to so commit themselves.[57]

Meantime the federal government was trying to obtain a final treaty with the Cherokees. Two factions had appeared among the Indians, one favoring emigration and one opposing it. The latter was headed by John Ross, a man of Indian and Scottish ancestry, possessed of education and ambition, who had been elected principal chief in 1828. The leaders of the group who

believed that the only salvation of the Cherokees was to join
their brethren in Oklahoma were Major Ridge, his son John,
and Major Ridge's two nephews, brothers known as Elias Boudinot and Stand Watie. The elder Ridge, a full-blooded Cherokee,
lacked the education of his relatives, but like them, was a man
of superior intelligence.[58]

In 1834-35 a number of efforts were made with these factions
to secure the desired treaty. Some, including an offer of Ross
to sell the Cherokee lands for $20,000,000, were never seriously
considered. Others went much further toward completion before
collapsing. It was not until October, 1835, that John F. Schermerhorn and William Carroll, as federal commissioners, were able
to make positive headway in settling with the Indians.[59]

In that month they called on the Cherokees to meet them at
the Cherokee capital, New Echota, to conclude the treaty, giving
wide publicity to the fact that those absent would be assumed
agreeable to the treaty. Nevertheless, Ross and his agents, by
various persuasions managed to dissuade large numbers from attending. The council was convened on December 21, attended by
several hundred Cherokees, mostly favoring emigration. The commissioners dealt with a committee of twenty of their leaders to
arrange the details of the treaty.[60] It provided that the Cherokees
should receive $5,000,000 in cash, should share the seven million
acres given their Western brethren in 1828, and should receive
other benefits, such as an additional $600,000 for "claims for
spoliation" of their individual holdings, and for transportation
West. The removal was to occur within two years of the signing
of the treaty, and the federal government was to maintain the
Indians for one year after their arrival at their destination. The
proceedings were approved by a delegation from the Western
Cherokees, who expressed their willingness for the Western and
Eastern factions to be reunited under the terms of the treaty.[61]

The Ridge faction, being responsible for the conclusion of the
New Echota Treaty, forever after bore the enmity of the frustrated
Ross group, which felt itself cheated of a rich prize. This group
offered resistance, preparing a petition of highly doubtful authen-
ticity purported to have been signed by 12,000 Indians. Federal
authorities discounted it, particularly since a census taken in
December, 1835, showed the entire Nation to number only slightly
more than 16,000.[62] Despite Ross's efforts, the majority opinion
in the Senate swung irrevocably in favor of the only practicable

course of action. The treaty was ratified by the Senate and signed by the President on May 23, 1836.

In July, having completed his second term as governor, Lumpkin was appointed a commissioner to supervise the execution of the New Echota Treaty. He records his inclination to refuse the job, but was persuaded by a personal letter from President Jackson to accept. Governor William Carroll of Tennessee was also appointed a commissioner, but resigned and was replaced by Judge John Kennedy of Tennessee. Benjamin F. Curry was appointed superintendent of Cherokee Emigration. Brigadier General John E. Wool commanded federal troops in the area, with a view to preventing disorder.[63]

Ross continued his resistance to the treaty, hoping by some means to nullify its effect. By encouraging the Indians to ignore the treaty and encumber its execution, and by continually seeking to reopen negotiations with the government, he incurred the wrath of many officials, including that of the President.[64] A chief complaint was that the treaty had not been approved by a majority of the Cherokee people. Lumpkin commented on this in a letter to Jackson in September, 1836:

Nineteen-twentieths of the Cherokees are too ignorant and depraved to entitle their opinions to any weight or consideration in such matters. They are incapable of self-government. They have been, and are still, governed by the opinions of their leading men upon the subject of removal, just as much as the slave is governed by the opinion of his master. If Ross had entered into a treaty last winter, to suit the selfish purposes of himself and his friends, on his return home his whole party would have received him with acclamations of approbation and applause.[65]

A letter to Schermerhorn signed by such pro-emigration leaders as William Rogers, Elias Boudinot, John Ridge, and Stand Watie, expresses similar sentiment, accusing Ross of "manifest equivocal and double-dealing with an ignorant people," and admitting that most Cherokees did not know the difference between five million and five thousand dollars, but merely followed blindly the influence of their leaders.[66]

The treaty stipulated that the United States was to pay all just debts and claims of Cherokees against their own Nation, and those of United States citizens for services rendered to the Cherokees. The Indians' property was to be evaluated by federal agents, and fair compensation made for all improvements.[67] It was principally the execution of these provisions that occupied the attentions of Lumpkin and Kennedy. Claims were first screened by a Cherokee committee authorized by the treaty, and composed of John Ridge, Elias Boudinot, William Rodgers, John Gunter, and William Chambers. The claims which they approved were then adjudicated by the government commissioners.[68]

Arriving at New Echota on September 2, 1836, Lumpkin familiarized himself with the task confronting him, and notified all having claims arising under the treaty to prepare them for presentation by October 10. In addition to the paper work involved in his duties, Lumpkin traveled extensively in the Cherokee country, being the only commissioner actively at work until the arrival of Kennedy in December. Of the ensuing year Lumpkin says, "no men ever labored with more untiring assiduity, met with, subdued and overcame more obstructions" than did he and his colleague.[69]

Lumpkin was particularly disturbed by the array of parasitical lawyers who advanced heavy claims against the government for having rendered legal services to the Cherokee Nation in combatting emigration. Most of them had been employed by Ross, under the dubious authorization of the Cherokees in council. Lumpkin noted that each of these lawyers protested against the fraud and injustice of all the claimants except himself.[70] He stated that these men, for selfish reasons, gained mastery over John Ross himself, and through him obstructed emigration for reasons of financial gain.[71] Their claims amounted to $150,000, which the Cherokee committee reduced to $36,000, a figure still considered exorbitant by the commissioners but which was accepted and paid in order to end dispute over an interminable matter.[72]

In the fall of 1837 Lumpkin was elected by the legislature to complete the unexpired term of John P. King in the United States Senate.[73] Therefore he left to Judge Kennedy the burden of completing the administration of the Treaty of 1835 in New Echota. In a letter of suggestions requested by Kennedy prior to his departure, he said:

The spirit of fraud is every day becoming more manifest. There cannot now remain very many omitted valuations. The attempts to establish such hereafter will in nine cases out of ten prove to be fraudulent. In all cases represented by white men, fraud may justly be suspected. Applications for increase of valuations should be resisted ninety-nine cases out of every hundred — because in that proportion they are unfounded.[74]

Lumpkin carefully indicated that his responsibility ended on

October 23, 1837, and at the point in the record books of the
commissioners at which his decisions cease. He did this, he said,
in order to "shield his character from censure which is justly
chargeable to others" — specifically to deny responsibility for
awards made on the basis of fraudulent claims subsequent to his
departure.[75]

The conditions of the actual removal were stipulated by Article
8 of the treaty. The United States agreed to move the Indians to
their new home, and to "subsist them one year after their arrival
there," to provide "a sufficient number of steamboats and baggage
wagons . . . to remove them comfortably," and that "a physician,
well supplied with medicines, shall accompany each detachment
of emigrants removed by the Government."[76] The last groups of
emigrants were not removed until December, 1838, under pressure
from federal troops commanded by General Winfield Scott.

Lumpkin entered the Senate in December, 1837, and served
until March 4, 1841. He considered it his main duty there to see
that the New Echota Treaty was expeditiously carried out — the
reason that the legislature had placed him in the Senate.[77] In
the early part of 1838 he made a number of speeches in defense
of the treaty, which Ross and his associates were still actively trying to subvert. He served as a member of the Committee on Indian Affairs, and employed his experience in Indian matters to
best advantage.[78] Nearly all of his speeches in the Senate dealt
with Indian affairs.

One objection fostered by the opponents of the treaty was that
it was not negotiated by Cherokees duly authorized to represent
the whole people. Lumpkin contended that not only was democratic procedure not present in past federal relations with the
Indians, but that among a savage race it meant little. The signers
of the treaty were representatives of the most enlightened faction
of the Cherokees. Lumpkin believed the best possible action was
for the government to legislate directly for the Indians as for
minors or others incompetent to exercise their own rights.[79]

Lumpkin felt that Ross, primarily for the selfish reason of re-
taining his importance in the East, encouraged resistance to the
treaty and sought to profit from the confusion. Even if he failed
in his primary objective, he would become more prominent and
facilitate his assumption of control of both the Eastern and Western Cherokees, after the emigration had occurred. Nearly all of
the federal authorities except Jackson took the position of trying

to mollify Ross, and by money and conciliation win his cooperation. This was particularly true under the Van Buren regime.[80]

It was while Lumpkin was in the Senate that General Scott was
sent to take command of federal troops in the Cherokee country
with a view to facilitating the emigration.[81] He and Joel Poinsett,
Van Buren's secretary of war, requested that Lumpkin submit to
them his views on the best means by which Scott could carry out
his mission. Accordingly, on April 7, 1838, Lumpkin submitted a
document containing a number of suggestions. He urged Scott to
adhere to the provisions of the treaty, already liberal, without
variation; to discount Ross's claims to legal supremacy over the
Cherokees; that if resistance to emigration should continue, the
Indians be gathered in compounds prior to their movement West;
that in this event, they should first be disarmed, their guns to be
returned to them upon reaching their destination. These general
comments were supplemented by more detailed discussion on
certain points.[82]

When it became obvious that the execution of the treaty was
inevitable, by military force if necessary, the resistance at last gave
way, and the movement occurred without actual force or bloodshed. Georgians were now enabled to occupy the remainder of
their state without the evil consequences which experience had
shown must occur if the Indians were allowed to remain. Lumpkin, a prime advocate of their removal, was sincerely motivated
by consideration of the Indian interest as well as that of the state.

Upon arrival in the West, the Ross faction peremptorily ignored
the existing thirty-year-old government of the original Cherokee
settlers, and asserted its control over all. One of its early actions
in June, 1839, was formally to condemn to death the leaders of
the faction which had signed the New Echota Treaty, though
Ross's group had themselves offered to sell the lands at a higher
price. The aged Major Ridge, his son John, Elias Boudinot,
former editor of the *Cherokee Phoenix,* and several others were
systematically hunted down and murdered.[83] Lumpkin avers that
protests registered with the United States government by himself
and three of the signers of the treaty aroused promises of retribution but that nothing ever came of it, and the murderers remained
unpunished.[84]

Lumpkin was so intimately involved in all that transpired
relative to the Cherokee problem, that he was moved to comment,
toward the end of his career, "I would put a higher estimate on

the many years of toil spent in connection with Indian affairs than any one branch of my public labor."[85]

But even if this was the main concern of Lumpkin's public career, it was by no means the only one. He was connected with and expressed his opinions upon many important issues of the day. The question of nullification, for example, was one on which he took an uncompromising stand. He led the majority opinion of the state in opposing it, though he and his supporters by no means condoned the tariffs or the principle of protection. After the adoption of the Tariff of 1832, numerous meetings were held throughout the state, but they came to naught.[86] Lumpkin denied that Georgia had ever used nullification to maintain her rights, and urged that she take no action uncoordinated with other Southern states of identical interests. The course advocated by South Carolina would only "engender strife and disunion, anarchy and confusion among brethren of the same principles."[87] Lumpkin was distressed that the value of the federal union should be questioned in this respect.[88] But he was equally loyal to the state:

I shall constantly bear in mind that we are all citizens of Georgia, as well as citizens of the United States — that we owe our allegiance to both governments — that both governments are ours, and are equally indispensable to our happiness, prosperity and liberty. That each should be kept strictly within their respective constitutional spheres, and, finally, that he who would destroy the sovereignty of the States by *consolidation,* or the Federal Union by *nullification,* is a traitor to liberty, and deserves the universal execration of mankind.[89]

Lumpkin considered mass education essential to the circumvention of tyranny and the preservation of national liberty. He envisaged a system which would give the working man an education sufficient to make him intelligent, virtuous, and useful, and enable him to participate in his nation's governance.[90]

At the time of Lumpkin's governorship Georgia's educational facilities fell far short of this, and he was well aware of the fact. With some supplementation, the basis of the system had been created in 1783, when the legislature authorized an academy for each county. Ninety of these were in operation by 1829.[91] The state maintained a "poor school fund" to assist indigent children, but most impoverished parents preferred to deny their children schooling rather than incur the stigma attached to such relief. Lumpkin felt that not only did Georgia fail to get full value for the forty thousand dollars which was spent each year in this connection, but that the whole system was inadequate. The legislature empowered him to compile all state laws on education, and to appoint a committee to devise a new system of "academic and free school education."[92] In 1832 he reported the laws compiled, but that he had been unable to induce three qualified men to undertake the second task. He stated that although a number of states had successfully placed responsibility for educating their populations upon their legislatures, such a system was "by no means suited to the feelings and habits of our people." Nonetheless, he urged that Georgians be shown the "practicality and importance of each member of society contributing some humble share" to the furtherance of education as a national duty.[93]

Lumpkin had great confidence in the association of manual labor with intellectual discipline in any new system devised, so that the means of earning a useful living might be afforded the masses. Only so, he felt, could the poor be successfully included in the state's educational system.[94] This idea of utilitarianism pervades all of Lumpkin's pronouncements on education, and is observed even in his generally laudatory comments on Franklin College, as the University of Georgia was then known. He suggested that the popular belief that the *"almost exclusive* object of college education is to multiply *lawyers and doctors"* was unhealthy. He proposed a broadened curriculum to prepare teachers to staff the public educational institutions so that they might in turn "prepare our sons to become scientific artisans and agriculturists." He denied that it required "less mind or less learning to make an accomplished farmer or artisan than would be considered requisite to make a current lawyer or doctor."[95] Of the ultimate importance of education Lumpkin said:

We may not reasonably calculate a continuation of the liberty and national prosperity hitherto vouchsafed to us as a people, without providing amply for the diffusion of knowledge commensurate with the increase of our population, and for corresponding improvements in all the arts and sciences calculated to elevate and adorn the human character.[96]

Georgia's militia system provided by colonial and Revolutionary enactments had degenerated by the 1830's into farcical and irregularly held exercises of no practical military value. Lumpkin pointed this out to the legislature in 1832, as had earlier governors, and asked for provision of a new system to replace that which had become obsolete. He championed the militia system over a standing army, which he said was highly incompatible with the national tradition, but elicited only a small response from the legislature in this and subsequent appeals. He could but wonder at their inaction, which he believed would inevitably necessitate a standing army.[97]

In 1831 the state penitentiary, completed in 1817 in keeping with the trend toward more humane criminal laws and treatment, was badly damaged by fire. Since it had failed to pay its own way in most years, a strong movement now began for its abolition. A joint judiciary committee probed the question and issued a strong report favoring retention of the system. But despite its argument that the expense of maintaining the penitentiary was less than the collective local ones, and that the reforming effect of the central institution was infinitely superior to local influence, public opinion was adamant. Therefore the system was abolished in December, and the penal laws of 1816 declared again in force.[98]

Lumpkin was a firm supporter of the penitentiary, and began at once to seek its restitution. He argued that with legislative cooperation and careful management it could easily become a source of profit, that in fact it had between fifteen and twenty thousand dollars in outstanding debts at the time. He said that since the abolition of the penitentiary the number of requests for exemption of convicted prisoners from punishment had vastly increased. These requests were made not because of the brutal nature of the punishments meted out locally, but to relieve the county of the expense of housing prisoners, even when there was nothing to extenuate their guilt.[99]

The legislature became convinced of the need for restoration of the institution, and so voted in November, 1832.[100] It further authorized the governor to appoint a committee to draw up a new plan of operations to place the penitentiary on a paying basis, and relieve the rest of society from the necessity of "laboring to support the convicts."[101]

In his annual message of 1834 Lumpkin reported that the restored penitentiary was operating most successfully under the revised code, and that during the preceding year it had been self-supporting as far as its ordinary needs were concerned. He was especially pleased that it was "not only a house of correction but of reformation"; and that it was able "to reclaim many of the most vicious from habits of vice, and turn them to paths of virtue and usefulness." Of fifty-four convicts discharged during the preceding three years, only one had been recommitted.[102]

Although Georgia had been an avid participant in the banking boom that occurred in the early decades of the century, and although thirty banks existed in the state when Lumpkin became governor, the process of disillusionment was well under way. The founding of the state-owned Central Bank of Georgia in 1828 expressed this uneasiness.[103] Lumpkin was particularly disturbed by the tendency of the highly variable paper currency issued by the banks to drive specie out of circulation. To check the trend he urged that specie replace all bank notes below five dollars. He charged the legislature with responsibility for seeing that the banks were sound, and did not exceed their charters. He advocated caution in granting charters to see that the wealthy were not benefited unfairly over the poorer classes. The legislature responded by requiring all banks to render semi-annual reports to the state government.[104] Lumpkin continued to voice his misgivings over the security of the banks through both his terms as governor, and in his last year in office the state gave its support to Jackson's war on the Bank of the United States.[105]

Ever after his reconnaissance of northwestern Georgia as a member of the Board of Public Works in 1825, Lumpkin was a champion of railroads. He envisaged a rail artery connecting the coast with mountains in the northwestern part of the state, which would serve the entire state and would build a great seaport as well. Ultimately it would be extended to draw upon the Western states as well, which would find their closest and cheapest route to the sea through Georgia.[106] He vigorously defended this plan against those seeking a similar route terminating at Charleston, and even urged that state funds might be used to hasten its completion.[107]

In 1835 he presented to the legislature an elaboration of this scheme which would connect the Ohio valley with the coast of Georgia. Besides the incalculable economic benefits to all concerned, the system would produce a general felicity:

The people of the two extreme regions would every summer meet together in the intervening mountain region of Georgia and the Carolinas (one of the most delightful climates in the world), exchange opinions, compare their sentiments, and blend their feelings, the North and the South would shake hands *with each other* as united brethren yield up every sectional and political prejudice . . . and part as friends. . . .[108]

Georgia's first notable success with internal improvements began after the completion of a railroad from Charleston to Hamburg, South Carolina, just across the river from Augusta, short-circuiting the river route to Savannah. In the 'thirties, numerous proposals from railroads within the state were made, and many charters were issued by the legislature. The Georgia Railroad and Banking Company was chartered in 1833, with Lumpkin a director, and successfully connected Augusta and Athens by 1841. The Central of Georgia Railroad and Banking Company, chartered in the same year, connected Savannah and Macon by 1843.[109]

The Western and Atlantic Railroad, though long being built, was the final link in the Georgia system. A survey of the country between the Chattahoochee River and the Tennessee state line having been made in the summer of 1837, the legislature authorized the construction of a state railroad in December.[110] The southern terminus was selected in DeKalb County near White Hall, and the name "Terminus" was soon applied, to be replaced in 1843 by "Marthasville," in honor of Lumpkin's daughter, and in 1847 by "Atlanta."[111]

Construction got under way the next year, but the Panic of 1837 worked great financial hardship upon the project. Late in 1841 work was halted, the supervising commission replaced by a "disbursing agent," who was to order the affairs of the road and continue construction on the lower half of it. Lumpkin was the agent.[112] He found the affairs of the railroad in hopeless chaos. With vast duplication of effort, the whole road had been under construction at once. Over two and a half million dollars had been spent without a single mile being completed. The records were so disordered as to "forever render them unintelligible."

Gradually Lumpkin was able to place the road on a business-like basis, firing and hiring personnel, exposing fraudulent claims against the state, and replacing defective deeds of cession for the right of way with authentic titles. Legislative acts in 1841 and 1843 provided for continued construction, though at any time between 1843 and 1850 the road would have been sold for one million dollars.[113] Lumpkin's quarterly reports to the governor testified to the difficulties which "cast a thick cloud over our great State enterprise." He expected to have the first half of the road in operation by November, 1843, but it was not until 1851 that the first train ran to Chattanooga.[114] Lumpkin's connection with the project ended in 1843, but he had made possible its completion, and earned the title of "Father of the Western and Atlantic Railroad." He was particularly gratified that its route so closely approximated that which he had selected in 1825.[115]

Lumpkin had intended to retire from public life when he finished his senatorial service in 1841. It was with great difficulty that Governor Charles McDonald had persuaded him to assume the duties of disbursing agent for the state railroad. As soon as these duties could be laid down, Lumpkin, at the age of sixty, retired to Athens where he designed and constructed a large stone house which was to be the scene of his activity for nearly three more decades. These years he filled usefully by farming, writing his memoirs, and serving as trustee of the University of Georgia and as local elder statesman.

Lumpkin had served his state well, showing his devotion by deeds as well as words. Of his service he once wrote:

The ardour of my youth and the best days of my riper years have been faithfully devoted to the public service; and yet I feel that I have discharged but a small portion of the debt of gratitude I owe to the people of Georgia for their generous confidence and support, under all the vicissitudes of an eventful political period of thirty years.[116]

On the national scene, Lumpkin was a consistent supporter of the federal union, and a strict constructionist. He regarded the Constitution as the "anchor of hope for the perpetuation of our beloved Union." But on the other hand he said, "The constitutional relations existing between the several States of the Union . . . must be respected by the several States, both in their separate and united capacities, or the Federal Union cannot be preserved."[117]

He was grievously disturbed over the widening schism between the Northern and Southern states, but in supporting the Southern viewpoint, he expressed a certain optimism that the schism might yet be resolved: "The constitutional rights of the Southern States in regard to slave property . . . cannot be controverted; and I feel disposed to cherish an abiding confidence in the virtue and patriotism of our Northern brethen. . . ."[118] But as the hope for peace faded, Lumpkin advocated secession as preferable to the alternative of constitutional subversion and the loss of state rights.[119]

Lumpkin survived the war, and in his eighties saw the difficult days of Reconstruction commence. He died in Athens, in December, 1870, surviving most of his political contemporaries to see the catastrophe of defeat.

JOHN McPHERSON BERRIEN

BY C. JAY SMITH, JR.

IN MANY ways John McPherson Berrien occupies a unique place in the history of Georgia politics, since he was almost the only successful Georgia politician who ever played a prominent role in a national conservative party. To be sure, Georgia has produced many conservatives who have been important in national affairs, but almost without exception they have been affiliated on the national scene with the party of Jefferson, Jackson, Wilson, Franklin Roosevelt, and Truman. Berrien, on the other hand, was a *rara avis* who, during the major part of his career, sailed frankly under the colors of the Whigs, successors of the Federalists and ancestors of the modern Republicans.

Because of this fact, a study of his career serves to bolster a reassessment of the political history of the Old South which has been moving steadily forward of late. Increasingly it is coming to be recognized that the notion of irreconcilable economic differences between North and South in the years from 1789 to 1861 needs considerable modification.[1] It has been shown, for example, that just as the Northern economy had an agricultural as well as a commercial-financial-industrial base before 1861, so the South was not as wholly agrarian as has been supposed.[2] There was in the Old South an important urban *bourgeoisie* of merchants, industrialists, bankers, railroad men, lawyers, etc., which had the same interests as similar groups in the North, and which had its spokesmen in politics. Essentially, Berrien was a leader of this group, and hence sought, unsuccessfully, to establish the parties of Alexander Hamilton and Henry Clay on Georgia soil.[3]

The fact that Berrien was not a native Georgian or even a native Southerner may be of some help in understanding him,

C. Jay Smith, Jr., is a member of the history faculty at the University of Georgia.

though it is certainly not a vital point. Of French Huguenot and
Scottish descent, he was born in Princeton, New Jersey, on August
23, 1781, the son of a major in the Continental Army and grand-
son of a justice of the supreme court of New Jersey. His father,
Major John Berrien, saw service in Georgia during the Revolution, and moved to Savannah in 1783, when the future jurist,
senator, and cabinet minister was only two years old. It would
appear that though the major acquired plantations in coastal
Bulloch and Burke counties, he always maintained a residence
in Savannah, and later, John McPherson Berrien, his son, would
be regarded as one of Savannah's first citizens.[4]

It seems that the Berriens found the unwashed, rough-and-
tumble, enthusiastically egalitarian Georgia frontier of the 1790's
and early 1800's most distasteful, and preferred the more orderly
and civilized life of Savannah. The major was a member of
the Cincinnati Society, and supported General "Mad Anthony"
Wayne, likewise a newcomer from the North, in the latter's battle
with James Jackson, leader of the Georgia Jeffersonians in the
1790's. The elder Berrien described Georgia in a letter to Wayne
in 1792 as "our turbulent young state," and sent his son back to
New Jersey and New York for schooling and for eventual graduation from Princeton in 1796. Thereafter the younger Berrien
studied law in the Savannah office of Joseph Clay, and was admitted to the bar in 1799.[5] It was established later that in 1800
the Berriens opposed the election of Thomas Jefferson to the
presidency, not a very popular gesture in a state where almost
everyone claimed to be a Jeffersonian.[6]

Thus, by background, environment, and training, John Mc-
Pherson Berrien was clearly marked out for the role of a conservative leader, for a future stand on the side of stability and
order. During the first twenty-five years of the nineteenth century
he began to rise to significant heights in the legal profession which
not only suited his talents, but which was also a bulwark of conservatism. During precisely the period when the federal judiciary
developed under John Marshall as a centralizing, consolidating
force over the entire infant republic, Berrien helped mightily in
causing the state judiciary to exert somewhat the same influence
in Georgia.

After some ten years' practice, he was elected solicitor general
of the Eastern Judicial Circuit in 1809, and in the next year,
1810, when not quite thirty, was made judge of the same circuit.

Even in 1810 this was evidence of unusual qualifications, and although he retired from the bench permanently in 1822, he was ever afterward called "Judge Berrien." In 1815 he attracted state-wide attention. At this time the state legislature, elected annually, dominated by upcountry men, and deeply suspicious of the judiciary, refused to create a state supreme court. The most it would permit was an annual meeting of superior court judges to settle common points of law. Following the end of the second war with Great Britain, and the resulting depression, it heeded a popular clamor and passed an alleviating law suspending the payment of private debts for three years. Berrien, to whom the obligation of a contract was sacred, was outraged. At the judicial convention of 1815, he persuaded his colleagues to follow the example of Marshall's Supreme Court and to declare the alleviating law unconstitutional. The legislature was now outraged and passed resolutions censuring Berrien and his colleagues. But judicial review had come to Georgia to stay, and Berrien had gained much prestige among the followers of George M. Troup, who disputed with John Clark the mantle of James Jackson after the latter's death in 1802.[7]

In Georgia politics of 1800-25, both Troup and Clark claimed to be Jeffersonians, and the political battles of their followers were more distinguished by barbecues, fist-fights, and eye-gougings than by a clear division on matters of principle. But behind it all there does seem to have lurked the idea that Troup vaguely represented the larger interests, and Clark, just as vaguely, the vanishing frontier democracy. In any event, Troup emerged clearly triumphant, and when the legislature elected him governor in 1823, he proceeded to strengthen the executive in 1824 by leading a successful fight for popular election of governors. Berrien retired from the bench in 1822, and entered Troup's first legislature in 1823. The two men became firm political allies. In the state Senate, Berrien sponsored legislation leading to the first digest of the Georgia law, and thus further enhanced his reputation as an upholder of stability. When one of the Georgia seats in the United States Senate became vacant in 1824, the legislature elected him to it, at Governor Troup's bidding. Thus, at the age of forty-three, was Berrien launched upon the national political scene.[8]

In 1825 the Revolutionary generation had passed completely from the Washington scene, and as in Georgia at the time, politics was intensely personal. The old Republican-Federalist battle was

over, since the Republican administrations of the preceding decade had been busily passing most of the legislation which Hamilton had favored in the 1790's. It was difficult to discern precisely
what principles divided the Adams-Clay and Jackson-Crawford
groupings which emerged out of the inconclusive presidential
election of 1824.

As a Senator between 1825 and 1829, Berrien seems at first
glance to have become clearly a Jackson-Crawford man and a
vigorous advocate of state rights. Four years later, his inclusion
in President Andrew Jackson's first cabinet would be cited as
evidence that he was a devoted follower of John C. Calhoun, and
this is the position taken by some of the Jackson biographers.[9]
However, Berrien's record in Congress, when added to fragmen-
tary correspondence, suggests strongly that he was pushed into
opposition to the administration of John Quincy Adams more as
the result of a temporary Georgia problem than out of personal
conviction, and that his decision to enter Jackson's cabinet in
1829 probably suggests more an ambition to reach the Supreme
Court bench than a desire to push the principles with which
Jackson was becoming identified.

The particular Georgia problem which engaged Berrien's attention between 1825 and 1829 was that of the Creek Indians,
and requires some explanation. It should not be confused with
the problem of the Cherokee Indians, which arose later and with
which Berrien was not prominently identified.

In 1825 Georgians felt themselves wronged because the federal
government had failed to carry out a promise made in 1802 to
obtain the removal of the Creeks and Cherokees from the state.
On the basis of this promise, Georgia had relinquished her claim
to the territories which became Alabama and Mississippi. Determined to achieve the removal, Governor Troup took direct action
in 1825. A treaty between Georgia and the Creeks was negotiated
at Indian Springs providing for the cession of Creek lands to the
state. William McIntosh, a half-breed Creek chieftain and kinsman of Governor Troup, arranged the treaty. However, a group
of Creek chieftains who were not consulted, and who opposed
the treaty, murdered McIntosh and appealed to President Adams.
Convinced that the treaty had been negotiated in an atmosphere
of liquor and bribes, the President disallowed it and began work
on a new treaty in Washington with the disaffected chiefs. Governor Troup chose to regard this action as a violation of state

rights, and in 1826-27 he took action to seize the disputed lands, regardless of the outcome of the Washington negotiations. Since Adams all along intended to gain the lands for Georgia, the real issue became the prestige battle between President and governor.[10]

Berrien seems to have realized this from the start. He had begun his career in the United States Senate by voting against the confirmation of Henry Clay as secretary of state, an action applauded in Georgia, where the "corrupt bargain" version of the presidential choice by the House of Representatives in 1825 was widely believed.[11] However, Adams states in his memoirs that Berrien "frequently shared the hospitality of my house and board."[12] Moreover, while in Georgia in 1825, Berrien publicly denied a claim by Troup that the Adams administration was seeking to interfere with slavery in Georgia.[13]

When the 19th Congress met for its long session in December, 1825, Berrien originally approached the Creek question from a moderate point of view. With his Georgia colleague, Thomas Cobb, he entered into communication with James Barbour, secretary of war, who was handling Creek matters, and a conciliatory correspondence ensued. As late as April, 1826, there was a chance that Barbour and the Georgia senators would agree on the Creek question. About this same time Berrien was advising Troup to take a less belligerent attitude, warning the governor that he was making matters difficult for those senators who sympathized with the Georgia viewpoint. These were, as revealed in Berrien's correspondence, the future presidents Martin Van Buren of New York and William Henry Harrison of Ohio, as well as Thomas Hart Benton of Missouri, chairman of the Committee on Indian Affairs, and Hugh L. White of Tennessee.[14] It should be noted that though Van Buren and Benton would later become Democrats and were already Jacksonians, Harrison and White would become Whig candidates for the presidency. These facts demonstrate that the Creek question is not a good one for testing Berrien's political principles.

Adams finally negotiated a treaty by the terms of which all but a small fraction of the Creek lands were surrendered to Georgia. Berrien fought the treaty, but the Senate ratified it because, as Berrien wrote Troup, it did not wish to become involved in a long investigation of the rights and wrongs of the matter. However, Berrien satisfied Georgia's honor by obtaining from the Senate an indemnification of the survivors of William McIntosh and a mode of compensation for the Creeks which differed from that recommended by Adams and which imputed fraud to the Treaty of Washington. Further revenge on the Adams administration was taken when Berrien delivered a strong but unsuccessful attack in May, 1826, on an administration-sponsored proposal to send envoys to a Pan-American meeting in Panama.[15]

Nevertheless, mere opposition to the Adams administration is not a reliable index to the whole range of Berrien's political thinking in 1826. During the same session of Congress in which he led the fight against the Washington Treaty, he strongly defended Marshall's Supreme Court during debate on a bill reorganizing the federal judiciary:

It is said, too, that the uniform tendency of the decisions of this tribunal [the Supreme Court], from the very origin of the Government, has been to strengthen the Federal arm — and what then . . . ? The increased and increasing strength of the Federal Government, is the inevitable consequence of the development of its powers, of its action upon the People of the States, of its own multiplying resources and extended patronage. It is time which has strengthened the Federal Government, by calling into action those powers of which the full effect could not be discerned by the Sages who formed our Constitution.[16]

That Berrien's opposition to the Adams administration was designed only to please his Georgia constituents and thus did not represent deeply held convictions is further proved by his position on a uniform bankruptcy bill discussed at this session of Congress. Though the Constitution specifically delegated to Congress power to pass such a bill, Jackson's supporters in the Senate, notably Benton, heartily disliked a measure which had the firm backing of the Eastern financial community. Berrien, on the other hand, perhaps mindful of the Georgia alleviating law of 1815, just as heartily defended the measure.[17]

In the short session of the 19th Congress (December, 1826-March, 1827) Berrien was again preoccupied with the quarrels of Governor Troup and President Adams. He paid off his political debt to the former by securing from a select committee of the Senate investigating the squabble a report white-washing Troup.[18] (There can be no doubt that Berrien breathed a sigh of relief when the Troup administration finally expired in 1827.) During this session Berrien and Benton clashed again on the uniform bankruptcy bill, and the latter finally triumphed, though by a close margin.[19] At about the same time, however, Berrien's relations with Adams further deteriorated because of the refusal of the President to reinstate the senator's younger brother in the West Point Military Academy, from which the latter had been expelled for participation in a student riot.[20]

The 20th Congress (1827-29) was given over mostly to the passage of a new tariff act, which would later become anathema to most Southerners. It is true that Berrien attacked the tariff law, but the point was frequently missed by earlier biographers that he delayed this action as long as possible. The record of debates on the bill during 1827 and 1828 fails to disclose a single Berrien speech in opposition. Not until the bill was safely passed, and not until the Georgia legislature had forwarded to Congress res-' olutions of protest, did he rise to the attack. His discourse in the Senate on January 12, 1829, moreover, had a curiously ambiguous ring. It was more a warning that the South must not be pushed too far than a ringing denunciation of the tariff act as unconstitutional. Apparently it lost him no friends in the North.[21]

We now arrive at the period of Berrien's service as attorney general in the first cabinet of Andrew Jackson. How did it happen that Jackson picked a man who would be so obviously out of place in his administration? The usual explanation is to attribute the selection to the influence of John C. Calhoun.[22] Another version is to connect it with a desire by the President to reward the followers of William H. Crawford of Georgia who, like Jackson, had been disappointed by the results of the 1824 election.[23] No doubt these factors were involved, although Berrien's closeness to Calhoun has been overemphasized. Jackson's over-all views on Indians in general, and the Creeks in particular, no doubt caused Berrien's controversies with Adams to loom large in the new President's mind.[24] Moreover, as already indicated, Berrien had been on good terms with Van Buren in the Senate, and his intellectual abilities and oratorical powers had attracted wide attention. Both before and after his appointment as attorney general he was mentioned in Washington and New York as a good potential successor to aged Chief Justice Marshall.[25] Whatever the final cause of the appointment, it was tendered to the Georgia senator through John Henry Eaton in January, 1829.[26]

However, we may believe Berrien's own later statement that he hesitated before accepting the appointment, and finally did so only after a conference with Jackson in Washington just before the inauguration. The two men had never met before. We need not, however, accept at face value Berrien's later assertion that he entered the cabinet only to advance the interests of Georgia. He was almost certainly more influenced by the possibility of a later Supreme Court appointment than by anything else.[27]

In any event, doubts as to the wisdom of the appointment seem to have afflicted the new administration as early as the spring of 1829. In April an effort was made to persuade Berrien to take the post of ambassador to the Court of St. James rather than that of attorney general. But he declined, alleging personal affairs which required his presence in the country.[28]

As early as November, 1829, the attorney general found himself at odds with the President on a question of national importance. Jackson had determined to attack the Bank of the United States in his first annual message to Congress, and requested an opinion of Berrien both as to the constitutional law connected with the Bank and the advisability of making a communication to Congress on the subject at that time. On the first point, the attorney general said there was the greatest diversity of opinion. However, he declared that "the existence of the power [to charter a Bank of the United States], has at various times, and in different forms, been affirmed by every department of the Government. If this power is not granted by the Constitution, it is very certain, that no series of usurpations can give it a legitimate existence in that instrument. Since however an ins [ti] tution now exists, questions of constitutional power may be wisely left to rest on the footing on which anterior decisions have placed it, so far as the Executive department is concerned. . . ." As to the expediency of making the proposed communication, he advised the President that no obligation to do so fell within the scope of the executive duty. The charter of the existing Bank did not expire until 1836, and it could not be foreseen that this would be within Jackson's term of office. Therefore, Berrien warned, to bring forward the question so early would cause great agitation and place the Bank and those who controlled it in the ranks of the opposition. To lose the support of Congress at this early stage, he feared, might prevent the administration from putting over the rest of its program.[29] It was hardly the sort of reply which Old Hickory wanted, and it indicates just how far Berrien was from sympathizing with the coming attack on the Eastern financial community.

Shortly thereafter the Peggy O'Neal Eaton affair arose. It cannot be determined with any finality whether this celebrated episode was (1) the result of a deep, underlying conflict between Van Buren and Calhoun for the presidential succession; (2) proof of Jackson's irascible, domineering disposition; or (3) merely proof that the affairs of the virtuous young American republic could be affected by sex scandal in high places quite as much as could those of the bad old contemporary monarchies of Europe.[30] All three explanations have some basis in fact. At all events, the affair did serve to bring into focus some inherent contradictions within an administration which, despite its reputation for forthrightness, had actually straddled a great many important issues.

The Eaton affair went through several stages, and those involved are by no means agreed on what happened at each stage. It would appear unfair to Berrien to classify him definitely with Vice President Calhoun, Secretary of the Treasury Samuel Ingham, and Secretary of the Navy John Branch. For one thing, he had apparently been on good terms with Secretary of War Eaton, and had attended the latter's wedding to the glamorous Mrs. Margaret O'Neal Timberlake just before the 1829 inauguration. Moreover, he was, like Jackson and Secretary of State Van Buren, a widower, and hence could have evaded, had he tried, the troublesome problem of having to entertain Peggy. He did not, for his daughter, as his hostess, declined to receive the pariah. However, if we are to believe his own version, he was not present when the President delivered his first ultimatum to Ingham and Branch in January, 1830, and he asserts that Jackson later apologized for an ultimatum delivered by Senator Richard M. Johnson of Kentucky. By the spring of 1830 it seemed the incident had blown over.[31]

But it burst into flame again the following summer, when Jackson broke at last with Calhoun. By February, 1831, Jackson had definitely come around to the view that Berrien, Branch, and Ingham were seeking to discredit Eaton in order to advance Calhoun's interests. Berrien's denial of this charge is supported by the recollections of Thomas Hart Benton. Shortly after came the resignations of Eaton and Van Buren from the cabinet in anticipation of its general re-constitution. Then, at the demand of Jackson, Ingham and Branch retired, breathing forth streams of sulphurous invective toward their former chief. Van Buren had hastened to London as ambassador, but Eaton lingered to challenge in vain his former colleagues to duels.[32]

Berrien had gone to Georgia after the end of the January, 1831, term of the United States Supreme Court. In Savannah, he found the President to be at the peak of his popularity, because of his refusal to back the Supreme Court in its quarrels with Georgia over the seizure of the lands of the Cherokee Indians. He used the occasion of this visit to try to calm some of the agitation against the Tariff of 1828. When he returned to Washington in June, the President asked for his resignation.[33]

Berrien could hardly have expected anything else, but his departure was made in a dignified manner which greatly impressed Jackson. Moreover, Eaton's honor was satisfied at first by a courteous exchange of letters which did not immediately provoke a challenge. It seems highly possible that during the first two weeks after his departure, Berrien might well have looked forward to further preferment within the administration.[34]

However, he decided to make the break with Jackson clean and permanent. No doubt both wounded pride and an honest desire to separate himself permanently from Jackson both played some part in the decision. In July he was asked by Jackson's ally, Frank P. Blair of the Washington *Globe,* to confirm the President's version of the cabinet break-up and thus to give the lie to Ingham and Branch. Not only did he refuse, but in July and August he engaged in a heated newspaper battle between the pro- and anti-administration press, in the process of which he produced a long "Address to the Public," published early in August. It substantiated the idea that Jackson had tried to dictate the private lives of his cabinet members, and caused the President to regard him with disgust. Eaton finally sent Berrien a challenge, but it was declined on the ground that the former secretary of war had already expressed himself as satisfied with Berrien's attitude toward Mrs. Eaton.[35]

Delight in Jackson's stand on the Cherokee question prevented any serious repercussions in Georgia over Berrien's dismissal. However, the former attorney general had already taken steps to ensure his political survival by involving himself definitely in the anti-tariff movement. On the heels of a new "Address to the Public" on the subject of Eaton's challenge to a duel, he appeared in Philadelphia in September, 1831, as a Georgia delegate to the Free Trade Convention.[36] The question of the tariff would occupy him for the next two years, and it is difficult to avoid the conclusion that he was interested mainly in counter-balancing the effect of his departure from the cabinet.

In June, 1831, Berrien had, in a speech on the tariff in Savannah, told his audience that

Difference of opinion will exist, and conflicting interests will arise in our widely extended empire, but the principle of mutual concession, which gave birth to our fundamental charter, will reconcile these jarring pretensions — and the profound attachment of the people to the government of their choice, will rebuke the spirit of discord, wherever it may arise. In one sentiment we are all agreed, it is that which inculcates as a primary duty, the preservation of the union of these free and independent states. . . . Vigilant in the assertion of the rights of state sovereignty, the people of Georgia have ever been prompt to rally round the general government, in vindication of its claim to the full exercise of its constitutional authority.[37]

This was the keynote of Berrien's attack on the tariff after his dismissal as attorney general. On September 30 he joined a delegation of 129 Southerners who met 66 Northerners in Philadelphia for the Free Trade Convention. Charged with presiding over the committee which drew up an address "To the People of the United States," he sought to find some formula which would please both Northern and Southern delegations. However, the over-representation of the South made it necessary to attack the unconstitutionality of the tariff, which the Northerners, led by Albert Gallatin, could not accept. For all that, Berrien managed to impress both groups as a public-spirited moderate.[38]

Back in Georgia in November, Berrien had a third tilt with the Jacksonian press. He had praised the President publicly for supporting Georgia on the Cherokee question, and was now accused of trying to worm himself back into the favor of the administration. He rose from a sickbed to defend himself from this attack, but did so in mild terms. Jackson's popularity in Georgia was at an all-time high, and the state would go for him overwhelmingly in the election of 1832.[39]

However, there was still the tariff issue, and it was compounded in 1832 when Congress passed a new measure which to the South retained all the obnoxious features of the law of 1828. By midsummer of 1832, Berrien was neatly side-stepping the presidential election by helping to organize anti-tariff meetings all over Georgia. These finally culminated in the crucial Anti-Tariff Convention held at the state Capitol in Milledgeville on November 12, just after Jackson's victory in the presidential race.[40]

It was a tense moment. South Carolina had a representative present, seeking support for her doctrine of nullification. Former Governor George R. Gilmer, a close friend of Berrien, presided. Governor John Forsyth, destined to become secretary of state under both Jackson and Van Buren, was also present, and determined that the convention should do nothing to embarrass the President. On the second day, Forsyth led a walkout of nearly half the delegates on the ground that the convention did not represent the people of Georgia. Berrien remained and took a prominent part in the further work of the rump convention. However, much to the disappointment of the South Carolina representative, he and his fellow delegates skirted the dangerous ground of nullification, and issued only another wordy blast at the tariff. It vaguely mentioned the possibility of a Southern convention. Both before and after the Milledgeville convention, Berrien publicly denounced the doctrine of nullification.[41] No doubt he was very happy to see the whole business ended at the national level by compromise in the spring of 1833.

At intervals during the tariff controversy of 1831-33 Berrien had found time to resume the practice of law in Savannah. In 1832, when he was fifty-one years of age, he married for a second time, and proceeded to have a new family by his young bride. These purely private concerns seem to have occupied most of his time during the second Jackson administration, but, while temporarily in eclipse, he was working quietly towards the formation of the Georgia State Rights party.[42]

The fact that this party ultimately evolved into the Whigs would seem, on the surface, to support the idea that the Southern Whigs represented only planter interests and sectionalism. And it is true that Berrien, as a prime mover in the development of the party, did produce such shibboleths of sectionalism as the Force Bill of 1833 to rally opposition to the administration in Washington. But that sectionalism was, in his mind, more a means to the end of ousting the Jacksonians in Washington than an end in itself was to become quite clear eventually. At any rate, the new State Rights party was strong enough, despite the prominence of Secretary of State Forsyth in Jackson's administration, to prevent Van Buren's receiving Georgia's electoral votes in 1836. They were cast instead for Senator Hugh L. White of Tennessee, who had broken with Jackson and was one of a group of candidates opposing Van Buren.[43]

Berrien felt, shortly after the election, that it was already time to tie in the Georgia State Rights party with the national opposition to Jackson. That he had already approached and made his peace with Whig leaders by 1836 seems clear from a passage in John Quincy Adams's memoirs.[44] In any event, he sought to persuade the Georgia State Rights electors pledged to White to cast their votes instead for General William Henry Harrison, already picked by the Northern Whigs as a good figurehead. Berrien failed in this effort, but it tends to bear out the idea that he was anxious now, above all, to achieve the metamorphosis of his followers from Southern sectionalists into conservatives on a national plane.[45]

The next year, 1837, which saw the panic resulting from Jackson's fiscal policies, likewise saw Berrien's friend, George R. Gilmer, back in the governor's chair in Georgia. In the language of the National Republicans of twenty years before, Gilmer urged the legislature to examine the problems of internal improvement and public education in the state. In 1838 he appointed Berrien to a commission which was set up by the Georgia law-makers to consider state revenues with an eye to further efforts along the lines recommended by the governor. The report of the commission, which thought that more money could indeed be found for internal improvements and public education without raising taxes, produced little legislation, but it served to bring Berrien back into the public eye. As the election of 1840 approached, much of his former prestige had been restored.[46]

Berrien's correspondence during the early part of 1840 indicates that he was busily at work on his task of swinging the State Rights party definitely into the Whig camp in the interest of William Henry Harrison's nomination for the presidency. There was some opposition, but it was overcome, and Berrien was elected chairman of the party's convention in Milledgeville on June 1. After a two-day convention, Harrison was nominated for President, and a complete congressional ticket was chosen.[47]

At long last, and for the first time, Georgia had a genuine two-party system paralleling the national organization. The Democrats denounced Harrison as an incompetent soldier and statesman and as an abolitionist, while defending the future Free Soil candidate, Van Buren! But all to no avail. The Whigs won a sweeping victory, carrying the state for Harrison and winning most of the congressional races.[48]

Speculation that Berrien would receive a cabinet post or a foreign embassy was widespread even before the election, but he scotched such rumors by indicating clearly his candidacy for the United States Senate as early as October 30, 1840. The legislature, controlled by the Whigs, met in November, but its Democratic minority, aided and abetted by a Democratic governor, sought for some time to prevent Berrien's election. These efforts proved unavailing, and on December 4, the leader of the Georgia Whigs was chosen for his old seat in Washington.[49]

It is Berrien's record as a senator from 1841 to the sectional controversies of 1848-50 which provides the acid test of his Whiggishness. Let us assume that despite all the contrary signs, his positions on the Creek question and the tariff had marked him as merely a spokesman for Southern planter interests and that his flirting with the enemies of Jackson was evidence merely of subtle opportunism and wounded personal dignity. Such an interpretation does not explain his ardent espousal of Clay's economic legislation in 1841, nor his subsequent break with President John Tyler, nor his opposition to the annexation of Texas. No, the Berrien of the 1840's was unquestionably a sincere believer in the principles for which simon-pure Whigs like Clay and Daniel Webster stood. He was wholly opposed to the stand of Calhoun, who during Tyler's administration was to find his way back into the Democratic fold.

Berrien appeared in Washington triumphant on inauguration day, March 4, 1841, and lingered on to claim his patronage rewards from President Harrison and to enjoy, among the minor delights of victory, casting a vote to dismiss Frank P. Blair as congressional printer.[50] But a month later, Harrison was dead, and John Tyler had been sworn in as the first vice president to succeed to the presidency.

The special session of Congress, called by Harrison to erase Jackson's fiscal policies, met on May 31. The position which Berrien then held within the Whig party may be judged by the fact that he was made chairman of the Judiciary Committee and a member of the select committee chosen to revive the Bank of the United States. He was, indeed, working hand-in-glove with Clay.[51]

Debate on the Bank bill went on throughout June and July, with Berrien clashing on the floor of the Senate with his Democratic Georgia colleague, Alfred Cuthbert. While the debate was in progress, Berrien succeeded, after a heated floor battle with Senator Benton, in pushing through the same uniform bankruptcy bill over which he and Benton had clashed fifteen years before.[52]

However, the smile of victory faded from the faces of the Whigs, including Berrien's, when it was learned in August that Tyler would veto the Bank bill. From the beginning, Berrien was very distressed. He wrote to a friend in Georgia on August 15:

> We have the veto of the Bank bill and we are going to meet in Whig caucus to determine what course we will pursue. I trust the Whig party will stand firm in Georgia, even if we have to divorce ourselves from Mr. Tyler.[53]

Nevertheless, the Whigs finally bit their lips, after receiving the veto message, and decided to frame a new Bank bill which would be pleasing to the President. Berrien took a large part in all this and called at the White House on numerous occasions to save the favorite Whig measure. He was appointed chairman of a new select committee to frame another Bank bill. On September 1 he introduced it and spoke for two hours in its support. But all to no avail. The second bill was vetoed like the first, and on September 13 Congress adjourned. Two days prior to adjournment Berrien served on a Whig committee which read President Tyler out of the party.[54]

Berrien returned to Georgia to enter upon a storm of controversy with Democratic editors and politicians. During the special session just ended, he had pushed through an amendment to the land distribution bill providing that if the tariff compromise of 1833 were tampered with, land distribution should cease. The Democrats, incited by Frank Blair, claimed the amendment was prejudicial to the South. Berrien was accused, among other things, of being "still a Northern Federalist at heart, notwithstanding his migration to the South."[55] But worse was to come, for the Democrats recaptured control of the state legislature in the fall of 1841. A Georgia Democratic legislator wrote Calhoun in November that "We shall not adjourn without paying proper attention to the acts of the call session and our faithful Senator, Berrien."[56] What he meant shortly became apparent, for the legislature passed resolutions censuring Berrien for his votes on all important legislation before the special session of Congress and instructing him to change his course. The resolutions produced yet another newspaper battle but had no effect at all on Berrien's actions in Congress.[57]

In fact, in the long session of 1841-42, he was, if possible, even more the impeccable Whig than he had been earlier in the special session. He waged a long, arduous, and ultimately successful fight to save the bankruptcy bill, whose repeal was threatened.[58] He supported, in long orations, quite useless efforts by Clay to push through constitutional amendments which would have vested the power of appointing the secretary of the treasury and the treasurer in Congress, which would have made it possible to pass a law over the presidential veto by a simple majority of Congress in certain cases, and which would have made congressmen ineligible for civil appointment by the President during the whole period for which they had been elected.[59] He worked with Secretary of State Webster on a bill extending the power of federal courts at the expense of state courts.[60] In a speech in New York just after the adjournment of Congress, he praised the Whig Tariff of 1842 and its protective features.[61]

Meanwhile, the breach with President Tyler widened. On June 11, 1842, Berrien wrote to a friend whom Harrison had appointed Minister to Sardinia:

You have been very fortunate in being absent from the country at this moment. The year through which we are passing, has been marked by much national, and individual suffering, and promises to be so at its close. The defection of Mr. Tyler, has been productive of very great embarrassment to the country, and has forcibly illustrated the truth of the proposition, that a man may be *impotent* to effect any great or salutary measures, who is nevertheless (humanly speaking) *omnipotent* to thwart the best devises and most important counsels of others.[62]

Again, on July 2 he wrote to the same correspondent that he was

. . . sometimes tempted to give up in absolute despair when I think of the long and dreary prospect before us. Mr. Clay seems to be very generally looked to by the Whigs, and . . . by many of our opponents, for the Presidency — but to think that we must drag out more than two years and a half, in our present anomalous state, seems intolerable. . . .[63]

Finally, the session was over, and in September, 1842, he was back in Georgia mending political fences. But he was still a Whig, and spoke approvingly of the tariff, predicting it would cease to be a sectional matter as the South developed industries of its own.[64] He goaded Democratic Governor Charles J. McDonald into further action. The governor condemned Berrien's failure to follow instructions of the legislature in his annual message to that body in November. On December 6 it proceeded to pass new resolutions of censure which this time demanded the senator's resignation. But the large Whig minority in both houses of the legislature passed resolutions praising Berrien, and elsewhere Whigs bestirred themselves on his behalf.[65] In fact, resentment over the attempt of the legislature to instruct a United States senator undoubtedly helped bring the Whig party back to power in Georgia in 1843.

A great disappointment awaited the senator upon his return to Washington, however. Early in 1843 the Democrats mustered enough votes to repeal his uniform bankruptcy act.[66] During the same short session of Congress, moreover, the break with the President became complete. Berrien opposed the bill for the occupation and settlement of Oregon, a measure dear to the expansionist President.[67] Rumors began to circulate that Tyler would dismiss the appointees to federal jobs which had been filled on Berrien's recommendation back in 1841. When a friend of the threatened men approached the President, the latter remarked:

Ah Sir, you remind me that I appointed Col. Calhoun, Dr. Baber, and Col. Hunter at the request of Mr. Berrien. Does he think I will permit his friends to hold their important offices, when he is opposing me at every turn?[68]

Tyler was as good as his word, and Calhoun, Baber, and Hunter were shortly after relieved of their posts. In a letter dated May 1, Berrien raged:

A more bald, unblushing treason, than that committed by Mr. Tyler, is not recorded in history — and he is about to reap his merited reward. During the last session of Congress, the Whigs abstained from all communication with him. I did not see him even by accident in the course of it — and if I occasionally passed his house, I saw neither carriage nor footman. The locos too hold off. Their object was accomplished in severing him from the Whigs. Blair has just avowed it by declaring, in substance, that however pleased with his treason, they can have no connection with the traitor.[69]

But there was balm in the fall elections of 1843 in Georgia when the Whigs took the governorship and the legislature, and in the success of Whigs in Tennessee and Maryland, which assured their continued control of the United States Senate. But, as Berrien wrote on October 17,

. . . with this we must be content until we have an opportunity next year of shaking off the incumbrance which has pressed so heavily upon us since the death of Genl Harrison . . . latterly we have suffered from an influenza, which has come to be universally known in this country, as the "Tyler grippe."[70]

The long session of the 28th Congress (1843-44) marked Berrien's complete conversion to the position of the Whig party generally on the protective tariff. Senator George McDuffie of South Carolina started a move to revise downward the rates of the 1842 tariff, and Berrien promptly opposed it. He ardently defended the 1842 law, claiming that it had not only brought general prosperity, but had helped to start industrialization in the South, which development he favored.[71]

A new presidential election was now approaching, and Berrien lined up solidly behind Clay. The "Great Compromiser" had visited Georgia in the preceding winter and had been lodged in Berrien's Savannah home. When Clay was nominated at the Whig Convention in April, Berrien was chosen to notify him officially.[72]

Just as the campaign was getting under way, President Tyler threw in a bombshell — a treaty negotiated by Secretary of State Calhoun providing for the annexation of Texas, marking not only the beginning of the sweep to the Pacific, but also the sectional controversies which would end in civil war. Had Berrien been merely the spokesman for a slavocracy seeking to extend its boundaries, then here, surely, was an issue which must make him drop his Whig mask and rally behind Tyler and Calhoun! But he did not. Instead, he became a prime mover of the opposition in the Senate which ruined, for a few months, the plans of the President and his secretary of state. In his opposition to annexation, Berrien occasionally used some rather far-fetched arguments, but the gist of what he had to say was sound. Annexations, he declared, would stir up the slavery controversy between North and South, and this must be avoided at all costs. Moreover, once started on the road of annexations, there would be no stopping, and war with Mexico was sure to come. There can be no doubt that his influence helped mightily in delaying Tyler's plan until after the presidential election of 1844.[73]

Recognizing that there was considerable annexationist senti-

ment, the Democrats harped upon the themes of Oregon and
Texas during the campaign. For this reason Clay could not follow
Berrien completely on the question of Texas.[74] But the Georgia
senator held firmly to his position, and throughout the campaign,
sought to make the tariff, rather than Texas, the principal issue.
With other Georgia Whigs, he stumped the North during the
summer and fall of 1844. Free trade, he claimed, was "a fallacy
uttered but to deceive! A thing practically for the advantage of
foreign nations, ruinous to our holy brotherhood." He addressed
a mass meeting of Massachusetts Whigs on Boston Common
and was introduced by Webster. The protective tariff, he said,
would furnish home markets, give stability to currency, elevate
the national character, preserve public morals, and draw closer
the bonds of union.[75]

In a way it was the supreme moment for Berrien and the
Whiggism which he represented. But the forces against which he
was fighting were too powerful, and despite strenuous efforts he
made in Georgia during the closing months of the campaign, his
own state went for James K. Polk by a slender majority. And
what was worse, the younger Whigs in Georgia, most notably
Alexander H. Stephens and Robert Toombs, future leaders of
the Confederacy, began to question his leadership. Intelligent to
the last, he cannot but have understood that Polk's victory would
make it almost impossible to hold the Whigs together as a
national party.[76]

Nevertheless, he kept on trying for eight years longer, though
old age was now coming on. In the Senate from 1845 to 1849, he
was a constant thorn in the flesh to Polk. In February-March,
1845, he fought bitterly Tyler's successful effort to admit Texas
as a state, warning his fellow Southerners that the method used
involved a breach of the Constitution and would endanger slavery.[77] He did so in the face of desertion of his position by the
younger Georgia Whigs, including Stephens, and on leaving Washington in March, 1845, wrote that he went home "with a deep
sense of the downward tendency of our affairs."[78]

Criticism of his attitude toward Texas was bitter in Georgia
in the spring and summer of 1845,[79] but he wrote loftily to a
friend:

I understand the movements, and I think the motives of the Democratic presses. They have always honored me by special denunciation.
Vindictive it must always have been from the source from whence it

emanated, and it has more than once cheered me by the conviction that my course was right since they denounced it.[80]

He had, he said, faithfully carried out the principles of the Whig party, and had been gratified to find Georgia rising in the estimation of other states. He would not change his course, even if it meant the loss of his Senate seat in 1846. He still felt that the majority of the Georgia Whigs was behind him, though some two or three of them wanted his seat.[81] This was his mood in August.

In November, the Whigs having been again victorious in the state elections, he determined to seek a vote of confidence, and on November 8 resigned his Senate seat. Faced with this clear threat of a party split, the younger Whigs rallied around their patriarch, and had the legislature re-elect him; a year later, this mandate would be confirmed when he was chosen for a new term beginning in 1847, although he had not changed his basic position.[82] However, there was an effort to persuade him to take a seat on the newly-created Georgia Supreme Court, which offer he declined early in 1846.[83]

Meanwhile, in the long session of Congress in 1845-46, Berrien had begun attacking preparations for a war with Britain over Oregon. He did vote for the admission of Texas, saying that the issue had already been settled, but in March, 1846, he was again belaboring Polk's belligerence toward Great Britain.[84] In May he was denouncing the President's war message against Mexico, and accusing Polk of premeditated aggression. When the critical vote on war appropriations was taken in June, he was one of only three senators who abstained.[85] His position was not shaken by American victories over Mexico during the remainder of 1846, and when Congress met again in December, he returned to the attack. On February 2, 1847, he offered a no-annexations proviso to a bill appropriating $3,000,000 to be used in making peace with Mexico. In its defense, he vigorously denounced annexations, advancing the now familiar argument that they would cause the slavery issue to arise. His proviso was defeated by the close vote of 29 to 24, and the apologists for the Polk administration have universally denounced him.[86] But he was right about the slavery issue, for the Wilmot Proviso was considered by the Senate just after his own, though it was defeated by a somewhat wider margin. Polk was so angry that he urged Georgia Democrats to do all they could to oust Berrien.[87]

However, the senator now had more support in Georgia, and

Stephens agreed with him in opposing new annexations at Mexico's expense. Stephens went so far as to introduce resolutions in the House in December, 1847, condemning the war. Simultaneously, Berrien opposed making new army appropriations until it was determined whether the President intended to occupy all Mexico.[88] During debates on the ratification of the Treaty of Guadalupe Hidalgo, he told the Senate (March 17, 1848) that:

"We are now, for the first time, conquerors in a war of aggression; our bleeding foes lie prostrate beneath our sword, and humanity shudders at the desolation which we have spread through an adjoining republic."[89]

But now the question of slavery in the newly-acquired territories had to be faced, and in the debates over extension of civil government to Oregon in the summer of 1848, Berrien defended the rights of the slaveholder, though he supported an unsuccessful effort to extend the Missouri Compromise line to the Pacific.[90]

In the meantime, lines were being formed for a new presidential election. Though Berrien had spoken in warm terms of General Zachary Taylor on the floor of the Senate, he hoped very much that Clay would head the Whig ticket again.[91] Here was a new cause for disagreement with Stephens and Toombs, who thought that Clay had sold out to Northern anti-slavery men.[92] Toombs wrote back home to a Whig correspondent that:

Mr. Botts of the House and Mr. Berrien of the Senate, and Buckner of Kentucky are the only three men from the slave states who prefer Mr. Clay for our candidate, and there are not ten Southern representatives who would not support Genl. Taylor against him if he were nominated.[93]

In the end, there was a battle between Clay Whigs and Taylor Whigs in Georgia which was won by the latter, and Taylor was nominated by the Georgia Whig convention in June. Berrien acquiesced in the result, and urged that others do the same.[94] But what a contrast to 1840, when Berrien had succeeded in putting over Harrison!

In the meantime, the California gold rush was on, and by the time Congress met in December, 1848, a really serious sectional controversy was in progress. Early in 1849, Berrien was still numbered among those who believed a workable compromise, involving the extension of the Missouri Compromise line to the Pacific, could be found.[95] But as bitterness rose throughout 1849, he finally abandoned these hopes, and by early 1850 was reduced to a state of despair. He became convinced that the North was being led down the road of disaster by a radical band of fanatics, and was moved to pronounce on the Senate floor, after a recital of his record of opposition to territorial expansion, his complete loyalty to Georgia and her peculiar institution. And when Clay produced his compromise measures in 1850, he felt impelled, with many protestations of friendship for Clay, to oppose them as too unfavorable to the South. In the end, he refused to vote for the admission of California and the ending of the slave trade in the District of Columbia, though he voted for the features of Clay's plan which were favorable to the South. It may well have been that the sight of this aged Whig who had praised the protective tariff on Boston Common back in 1844, and who now could find no room for compromise, had much to do with causing Northern senators to accept the Compromise of 1850.[96]

Despite Berrien's seeming conversion to wholly pro-Southern views, he could not, characteristically, resist a return to a position of compromise. Normal party lines were down in Georgia in 1850, and the state was divided between a Union party, which favored acceptance of the Compromise of 1850, and a State Rights party, which advocated immediate secession. Berrien would not join either group. He advised Southerners to withdraw support of the tariff and advocated a policy of commercial non-intercourse with the North, but denounced secession as "impracticable" and "the worst of evils." When a state convention representing all groups was held, the Union party triumphed, but stated it would go no further in yielding to the North. It refused, moreover, to pass a resolution congratulating Berrien for opposing the admission of California.[97]

The Union party triumphed in the Georgia elections of 1851, when it chose Howell Cobb as governor. Cobb still held Berrien in high esteem, but the latter was now seventy, and his wavering course in 1848-50 convinced the Unionists that it was time to retire him from the Senate. At first he himself expressed a desire for retirement, but there can be no doubt of his disappointment when the legislature chose Toombs as his successor in the spring of 1852. Weighed down with grief following the death of his second wife, he resigned from the Senate in May, 1852, though his term still had some nine months to run.[98]

But his political career was not quite over, and he performed the role of elder statesman for four years longer. He managed to exert himself on behalf of Winfield Scott, Whig candidate for President in 1852,[99] and when the Whig party was finally shattered by the Kansas-Nebraska Bill two years later, he still could not make the transition to the Democratic party. Since he could not go over to the Republican party either, he had finally become, in 1855, the guiding spirit of an attempt to found a branch of the American or Know-Nothing party in Georgia, hoping still to prevent a return to one-party ascendancy. The exertions of presiding over a Know-Nothing convention in December, 1855, proved too much, and on the first day of 1856, he died. As was usual in such cases, the legislature named a Georgia county for him after his passing.[100]

The career of John McPherson Berrien leaves little doubt that the Hamiltonian idea had many sincere partisans in the antebellum South. In his case, Whiggery had a Southern champion who adopted it out of principle and not out of a desire merely to protect planter interests. On the crucial question of the Bank of the United States, and the hardly less crucial one of the uniform bankruptcy bill, Berrien was unquestionably a Whig. There is, admittedly, more than a touch of ambiguity and opportunism in his approach to the tariff; but support of it, within the frame of reference of a future industrialized South, represented his final, matured viewpoint. At all times, he was the upholder of stability, order, judicial process, and the interests of the propertied. That might still have left him a Democrat, but it certainly inclined him toward the Whigs. Finally, he was among the more vociferous opponents of precisely that territorial expansion, the support of which is supposed by some historians to prove that the Southern Whigs were mere agents of planter interests.

But it cannot be forgotten either that to Berrien, and ultimately to all Southern Whigs, there came times when the interests, real or assumed, of the South overrode differences with Southern Democrats on economic policies. If Berrien's position on the Creek question was less ardent than Troup's, there can be no doubt of his ultimate loyalty to Georgia and the South on the slavery issue. He resisted the tide longer than most, but in 1849-50 was swept away. Had he lived until 1861, he might very well have greeted even former President Tyler as a fellow member of the Confederate Congress.

Generalizing on the basis of Berrien's experience, we may say

then that while the battles of Democrat and Whig in the Old
South were real, there was always, in the sub-stratum, the common
bond of slavery. It could and did rise to the top in the 1850's.
Then, and only then, did the party battles of Dixie become "a
stage duel fought with wooden swords."

Generalizing still further, we may go on to recall that there
have been other genuine two-party manifestations in Southern
history — the battles of the Bourbons and Populists in the 1880's
and 1890's, and the presidential elections of 1928, 1948, 1952,
and 1956. But the twin pressures of the Negro from within and
the Yankee from without have invariably, in the long run, brought
a closing of ranks. Perhaps that situation is passing, but it would
take a rash prophet indeed to predict that, so long as the North
and the South remain basically divided on any major question,
the two-party system of the rest of the nation will take really firm
root in the South.

HOPKINS HOLSEY

BY HORACE MONTGOMERY

For three decades prior to the Civil War social and economic life in the United States was undergoing remarkable change. A significant aspect of this process was a reform activity representing a wide variety of causes and inspired by an abiding faith in the common man. Because this activity was to pose a serious threat to the South's institution of slavery, Southern reformers, though as sincere about many specific reforms as their Northern brethren, were to find themselves increasingly open to the charge of giving aid and comfort to abolitionists. While many of the causes were in time to lose their initial zeal, the campaign against slavery was to gain impetus. By 1848 it had sent its filaments through the nation's party system, threatening the union itself and bringing distress to Southern reformers and unionists alike. The career of Georgia's Hopkins Holsey, politician and journalist, reflects the agonies of a Southern Jacksonian who sought escape from the dilemma of these years by formulating a concept, whose temporary success deceived and finally discredited its author.

Born in Brunswick County, Virginia, in 1799, Holsey moved to Hancock County, Georgia, where during the 1820's he practiced law and assisted with the management of his deceased father's estate. In 1823 he barely missed election to one of Hancock's three seats in the state House of Representatives. Defeated again the next year, he won a close race in 1825.[1]

Holsey's single term in the state legislature must have been highly unsatisfactory to the voters of Hancock County, for in 1826 they decisively rejected his bid for re-election.[2] Brief though his career as a state legislator was, it showed him to be a man of considerable independence. At this time Georgia's enfevered

Horace Montgomery is a member of the history faculty at the University of Georgia.

Troup (State Rights) and Clark (Union) parties were acquiring the sinews of political warfare.[3] Why Holsey identified himself with the latter is not known. It was a risky venture in view of Governor George M. Troup's great popularity in Hancock County. He had beaten John Clark there in the gubernatorial contest of 1825 by a count of 859 to 170, though his state-wide majority was less than 700 votes.[4] In defense of Holsey's record as a legislator a correspondent of the Milledgeville *Georgia Journal* wrote that "his conduct in every instance was influenced by his own sense of propriety, and a strict regard to the general welfare."[5]

As a promising attorney with a keen interest in politics, young Holsey became acquainted with Hancock County's prominent citizens. Among them was General Henry Mitchell, a Revolutionary War veteran. He fell in love with the General's daughter Elizabeth and in June, 1826, they were married.[6] For a few years the couple remained in Hancock County, where Holsey pursued his political interests and continued to share in the management of his mother's property. Never a man to remain long in one place, Holsey decided soon after his bitter defeat of 1826 to move to neighboring Putnam County.[7] After a few years the Holseys moved again, this time to Harris County, on the Georgia frontier, where they remained during most of the 1830's. Meanwhile Hopkins gave up the practice of law, which apparently had neither rewarded nor challenged him. "Instead of narrowing his soul by the exclusive study of legal subtilties," wrote a friendly editor, "he has enriched his mind with ample stores of general knowledge."[8]

Practicing law was doubtless a "narrowing" experience for Holsey, whose curiosity aroused an abiding interest in political theory and history. An opportunity to reflect on matters about which he held strong convictions was provided by the challenge of South Carolina's attempted nullification in 1832-33. A resolute unionist, Holsey composed a series of four essays which were published during 1833-34 in the Milledgeville *Federal Union* over the signature "Americus."[9] Although turgid and at times pedantic, they presented a fairly well-reasoned case against nullification. They also reveal the author's familiarity with *The Federalist* and other writings of the Founding Fathers, as well as a knowledge of Emmrich de Vattel's classic work on the law of nations.

Writing before the dawn of what modern scholars call "legal realism," Holsey assumed the Constitution had fixed the bounds of the various types of federal power. In referring to these and the numerous state powers as "enumerated," "reserved," "exclusive," "concurrent," etc., he was employing accepted nomenclature.[10] By resting his argument on *The Federalist,* he was on solid union ground, though Alexander Hamilton and James Madison, the foremost contributors to this famous work, had long since exploded the assumption that powers remained fixed. For example, in 1815 while vetoing a bill to establish the Second Bank of the United States, Madison observed there was no longer a question about the Bank's constitutionality because Congress and the public had for a considerable time recognized it as such.[11] Whether Holsey was familiar with Madison's observation is unknown. He was, however, to become an unyielding adversary of banks and other contrivances of industrialism. As a member of Congress during the late 1830's and afterwards as editor of the Athens *Southern Banner* he was often to complain that industrialism was a constitutional savage armed with a weapon that resembled the prescriptive process Madison had extolled in 1815.

Drawing heavily from the standard arguments of the Founding Fathers, Holsey presented in his opening essay a strong case for the federal judiciary as the arbiter of disputes between the states and the general government. Using the same sources, he also argued the case for the supremacy of federal law, explaining that it operated upon individuals as distinguished from states. These views would seem to have clinched the case against nullification, but, he explained, only in the abstract sense. What would happen, he diffusely inquired, in case of an "unconstitutional" enactment by Congress which a single state decided to resist? The reply to his own query carried him into a discursive review of the nature of sanction and penalty. If a majority of a state's citizens refused obedience to such an enactment and the federal government attempted coercion by arms, the role of the latter would become so odious to the people generally as to reveal the absence of a sanction, in which case the enactment was not a law in the first place and the government had no right of execution.

Realizing this pretty theory was not an answer to the problem, the essayist contended in his first treatise that the crux of the matter was the determination of the locus of the power to judge what was constitutional. In tautological fashion he ascribed such authority to the federal judiciary, but conceded the ultimate remedy to be the "God of battles," rather than peaceful secession,

a right which did not exist by the very nature of the American
constitutional system. "Would not the right of withdrawal on
the part of a State," he asked in his second essay, " . . . carry with
it an *indefinite* supremacy over its citizens, and deprive the minority of the barrier erected by the fundamental laws against the
encroachments of the majority?" Holsey's preoccupation with the
doctrine of natural rights, emphasizing as it did the right of
revolution, would seem to offer a suitable explanation for his willingness to appeal to the "God of battles" when reason failed, while,
on the other hand, his adoration of the Founding Fathers and his
devotion to the federal union precluded acceptance of either
nullification or secession.

In his second essay Holsey returned to the question of the scope
and authority of federal acts for the purpose of clarifying his interpretation of the structure of the American system of federalism.
Although his terminology is at times somewhat confusing, the
sense seems clear enough. "When a government acts upon political
bodies or States," he contended, "it is considered as *federal*, when
upon the citizens of those States in their *private* capacities, it is
so far *national*." That the latter was the true *modus operandi* of
the American system was, he thought, plain enough to anyone who
would take the trouble to observe the Articles of Confederation,
to study the Constitution and the arguments in favor of its adoption, or to understand "the general sense of the American people."

General laws operated upon individuals, he believed, in the
same manner as acts of local governments. Since this was so, it
would be difficult "to prove that the minority have a stronger
claim to a negative in the former case, than in the latter."[12] The
contention here is plain enough, that is, that a minority of the
people of the United States could not be conceded the right to
set aside the will of a majority as expressed by an act of Congress.
In the case of a state's secession, it will be recalled, the offending
national minority became a ruthless state majority doing violence
to those inalienable rights expressed in the organic law of every
state and protected by such safeguards as bills of rights and checks
and balances. Throughout the first two essays the tricky problem
of majority and minority rights is belabored and finally dismissed
somewhat cavalierly with the claim that neither could be said to
have any rights over the other except such as were revolutionary
and belligerent. When the issue was thus remitted, the federal gov-

ernment was required to intercede under the constitutional provision guaranteeing every state a republican form of government,
a view sharply at variance with that expressed in the discussion
of penalty and sanction.

Although Holsey was more Jeffersonian than Hamiltonian, his
commentaries on sovereignty would have been highly pleasing to
the latter. In the first essay he asserted that the structure of the
American system was such as to "forever deprive the individual
members of the confederacy, of the high and boasted appellation
of 'A SOVEREIGN STATE.' " The essayist claimed in his third
effort that while the Constitution had been made by sovereigns,
they, by their ratification of that document, had "surrendered to
three-fourths of their number, every particle of sovereign power,
with the single exception of their equal suffrage in the Senate. . . ."

In the same essay the author finally aimed some resounding
blasts at South Carolina by asking whether a person "of common
discernment" could possibly "listen with composure to that kind
of argument, which tells us on the one hand, that the *sovereign*
State of *Massachusetts* has no right to abrogate the embargo laws,
and the government had the right of coercion, while on the other
hand, it affirms that the *sovereign* State of *South Carolina,* may
interpose her authority to arrest the operation of a tariff of protection, and the attempt to *coerce* her is usurpation." Because
South Carolina's leaders were either "stimulated by hopes of personal aggrandizement, or impelled by the stings of disappointed
ambition," they would "embroil the Confederacy in a perpetual
scene of anarchy and bloodshed." War against South Carolinians,
especially John C. Calhoun, was to become a normal indulgence
of Holsey.

In the final essay the difficult task of designating the residence
of sovereignty was undertaken. Having earlier denied state sovereignty, it was now affirmed that sovereignty resided in the states
"jointly," for the "people of every state constituted the State [the
United States], and consequently the *sovereignty* does not reside
in the 'People of the States severally,' but *collectively.*" Throughout that part of the fourth essay dealing with sovereignty's locus
Holsey used interchangeably the terms "jointly" and "collectively," neither of which, he cautioned, could be construed to mean
"majority." Finally it was pointed out that the *"constitution* is
the act of the United States, and to allow the people of one of

those states to be paramount . . . and consequently *supreme* over all the others, would be to reverse the natural order of society and make the *whole, [sic.]* subordinate to the parts."

On May 14, 1834, Holsey concluded his disquisition on the nature of the American political system in language that closely resembles the exhortations which Hamilton addressed to President Washington on the occasion of the so-called Whiskey Rebellion of 1794: "But when we reflect that in the *operation* of the powers vested in the Union, the system departs from the *federal* and maintains a *national* character — when we add to this, the constitutional provision, that 'Congress shall have power to call forth the militia of the Union to execute the law of the Union, to suppress insurrection, etc.' we may safely affirm, that the Constitution knows no individual or body of men short of the sovereign power it has established in three-fourths of the States [through the amending process], that may resist the laws of the federal government with impunity. . . ."

A little over a year after his fourth essay appeared in public print Holsey was in Milledgeville as a delegate from Harris County to the Union party's state convention.[13] Meeting to transact the party's business, the convention's most important work was the nomination of candidates for vacancies in the state's delegation to the 24th Congress. About one month after adjournment James C. Terrell, one of the nominees, resigned and the party's central committee named Holsey to the vacancy. The friendly *Federal Union* characterized the new nominee as "a man of strong natural talents, which have been highly improved by cultivation." As a speaker he was "most interesting, lucid, and graceful," as a reasoner "profound," and as a writer "accomplished."[14] The State Rights Macon *Georgia Messenger* dismissed him as "a stranger among us . . . isolated and unknown, even by his kindred."[15] Under the general ticket system then in use in Georgia, the voters chose the entire Union slate of congressional candidates. Holsey ran well behind his colleagues in the state-wide vote, but in Hancock and Putnam counties, where he had formerly lived, and in his home county of Harris he barely led the Union ticket.[16]

The new congressman's record in the 24th Congress revealed the predicament then confronting Southern politicians. Fresh from Georgia's frontier, he promptly defended the use of federal power against the Creek Indians. The white people of Georgia, as well as those of Alabama and Florida, must be protected and fed, argued Holsey and several of his Georgia colleagues, and only the federal government had the means for such an undertaking. On the other hand, he denied the federal government had any right to interfere with slavery either in the states or the District of Columbia.[17] His views on these and other issues before the 24th Congress involved him in sharp exchanges with some of his colleagues.

Most illustrious among his antagonists was former President John Quincy Adams, then a representative from Massachusetts. The New Englander's persistence in pressing the House to consider petitions in favor of the abolition of slavery, despite the understanding (Gag Rule) to table them, made him especially obnoxious to Southern members. When it was alleged that he had such a petition containing the names of slaves, which gave credence to the notion that they possessed the right of petition, Southerners were infuriated. Congressman Waddy Thompson, Jr., of South Carolina introduced a resolution calling for the "severest censure" of the former President.[18]

Speaking on this resolution, Holsey gave notice that the people he represented would deny the right of slaves to petition "with the sword in one hand and the Constitution in the other. . . ." He admonished Adams as a man "with a fixedness of purpose peculiar to fanaticism." Defiantly he continued: "It has devolved upon me, as a representative of a people whom he has deliberately and openly assailed in the recesses of their firesides, their altars, and their homes; and which, let me tell the gentleman and this House, they will defend at all and every hazard." The gratuitous wickedness of the former President had reached the point "at which the rights of others, and the peace and safety of your Union, requires he should be arrested."[19]

Holsey's outburst against Adams occurred early in 1837, over three months after his re-election to Congress. For Georgia voters the campaign of 1836 was much more spirited than that of the preceding year. They were now choosing a full congressional delegation as well as a slate of presidential electors. A greater stimulant was the persistence of both Union and State Rights leaders in thrusting personalities of national prominence into this campaign. In consequence Union leaders began to merge their organization with the national Democratic party, while the State Rights group moved perceptibly toward the rising Whig party.[20]

Of the Unionists, none was more forthright in declaring for the national Democratic party than Holsey. Early in his campaign for re-election he addressed the voters of Monticello a long letter which appeared in several of the state's leading political journals. ". . . I shall be presented to the people for re-election," he announced, "*as the political friend of Mr. Van Buren. . . . I never will unite with ultra Federalists, Nullifiers, Bankites, and revilers of Andrew Jackson. . . .*"[21] To this declaration the *Federal Union* responded: "We entertain high admiration for the firmness, and independence, and genius of our representative, the Hon. Hopkins Holsey. . . ."[22] Although the Union party's entire congressional ticket won in October, a month later Van Buren electors lost to those of Hugh White by 2,900 votes.[23] Beaten in Georgia, Van Buren was nonetheless elected to the nation's highest political office.

In March, 1837, the new President began what has sometimes been called the "third term of Jackson." A few months after his inauguration disaster began to settle over the nation's economy in the wake of the Panic of 1837. An immediate result of the panic was a disconcerted United States Treasury Department. In search of relief, President Van Buren summoned a special session of the 25th Congress to meet in September. To ease the treasury's embarrassment a bill was promptly introduced to postpone the fourth installment of federal money to the states as required by the Distribution Act of 1836.

As a member of the House Committee on Expenditures in the Department of the Treasury, Holsey was conversant with the new administration's problem. He presented a lengthy analysis of the treasury's report in support of the proposed relief measure, explaining that since the government no longer had a surplus, the distribution of which had been the purpose of the legislation of 1835, it was folly for the states to expect additional largess. With a reverend bow in the direction of Jacksonian Indian policy, he reminded the House that the costly Second Seminole War (1835-42) made it imperative that the federal government be released from further payments under the Distribution Act. The special session went along with the administration's request and by the time of its adjournment in October, Holsey had become an active spokesman for Van Buren on fiscal matters and a staunch defender of the Jacksonian policy of removing Indians to lands west of the Mississippi River.[24]

When the second session of the 25th Congress convened in December, 1837, Holsey was no longer a novice. His censorious outburst against Adams earlier in that year and his more recent defense of Van Buren's emergency legislation had won him favorable notice in the Georgia press. A characteristic defiance was thus fortified with a new-born confidence as he resumed action against Indians, loading his language, according to Adams, with "heavy, dull invective."[25] This time it was the Cherokees, whose removal from northern Georgia he urged Congress to assist by adopting such measures as were necessary to carry out the government's treaty obligations. Some charged the treaty in question had been improperly negotiated, Congressman Henry Wise of Virginia claiming the Cherokees to be "oppressed people." To Wise, Georgia's Indian baiter feverishly replied that his people "would never consent to have naturalized Indians among them, who, civilized as they were said to be, were not fit to associate with free-born citizens of the United States. Georgia would never submit to have a set of harpies forced upon her, to prey upon her substance."[26]

The Georgian's violent language disgusted Adams, the New Englander recording in his diary that "Holsey affects to be a systematic lawyer." A later entry suggests that Adams had detected what to him must have been an unforgiveable dichotomy in the Georgia congressman's moral code. "This same Holsey," he observed, "said on a former day that there were two kinds of justice —moral justice and political justice; that the people of Georgia were at all times willing to dispence political justice, but would never suffer that moral justice should be secured to them [Cherokees]."[27]

That Holsey possessed a generous endowment of Jacksonian prejudices is clear enough from the scoldings he gave nullifiers, Cherokees, and Adams. Equally convincing of his affinity for Old Hickory's views was the anti-bank sentiment he expressed during the second session of the 25th Congress. That the Second Bank of the United States had several years earlier been laid to rest by his hero mattered little to Holsey, for he was certain its spirit was still very much alive. The opportunity for an expression on banking was provided by Van Buren's state-of-the-union message. Presented early in the second session of the 25th Congress, it contained a recommendation for a sub-treasury plan as a means of divorcing public funds from private banks.[28] In

defending the President's proposal Holsey was especially critical
of the offspring of the Second Bank of the United States, then
operating as the United States Bank of Pennsylvania. Despite its
charter from that state, this institution was accused of improperly
exercising the power to issue paper money, a privilege which
the Georgian insisted had reverted to Congress with the expiration of the Second Bank. Congress was therefore urged to discharge its duty by ordering the Pennsylvania bank to stop issuing notes for public circulation.[29]

Holsey may not have known that a few months earlier the
Supreme Court had validated a Kentucky statute establishing a
state-owned and state-controlled bank empowered to issue notes
for public circulation.[30] His language strongly suggests that he
suspected the Pennsylvania institution of being a mere cloak for
the conduct of a function which he believed only Congress could
authorize.[31] Its misleading name and the fact that its management was in the hands of Nicholas Biddle, former president of
the Second Bank and *bete noire* of all true Jacksonians, may
have justified his suspicions.

Opposition to Van Buren's fiscal proposal was concentrated
in the Whig party. Perhaps it was their unpleasant memories of
Jackson's victory over Biddle five years earlier that caused Whig
leaders to rest much of their argument on purely political and
constitutional grounds. Whatever dictated their tactics, they were
able to postpone the adoption of the sub-treasury scheme until
1840, charging at the inception of the debate that President
Van Buren was advocating a plan that was contrary to the popular will and that he was trying to force the legislative branch into
acquiescence. Holsey shared in defending the administration
against these charges, responding in late 1837 with a tedious discourse in which he denied that a national voice was possible in
the American constitutional system. The source of a congressman's authority, he insisted, was "the people of a state, or district," not the "people of the United States."[32]

In answering the charge of executive dictatorship the Georgia
congressman cited the constitutional provision for the state-of-
the-union message. Its language, he asserted, authorized the President to propose a measure and specify all of its parts. Therefore
it was quite in order for a committee of the House of Representatives to receive drafts of bills from the chief executive. A

devoted Jacksonian, Holsey believed the President must be a positive force in the legislative process.[33]

Although Holsey was primarily concerned with Indians and banks during the second session of the 25th Congress, he also expressed an interest in other public issues. He spoke against a bill to prohibit American citizens from interfering in the Canadian Revolt of 1837, believing it an improper restraint on the right to trade. Always sensitive about anti-slavery utterances, he requested the entire Southern delegation to retire from the House Chamber after Representative William Slade of Vermont had spoken critically about the South's "peculiar institution." His position on the Indian question led him to oppose cuts in military appropriations, and a lengthy defense of a resolution to cede the Cumberland Road to the states through which it passed revealed his Jacksonian bias on internal improvements.[34]

As a legislator, Holsey was most active during the second session of the 25th Congress. With its adjournment in July, 1838, he retired from national politics. No reason has been found for his failure to attend the final session of this Congress. About midway in its second session he announced that he would not seek renomination. It is possible that his wife's death in April of the preceding year may have influenced his decision. A more likely explanation was the declining fortune of the Democratic party. Cursed by panic and hard times, it had lost the gubernatorial contest of 1837.[35] Whatever the reason for his retirement, some expressed regret, one editor registering astonishment that "our worthy representative should find himself anxious to retire from public life."[36]

Shortly after his return to private life Holsey moved to Athens. Why he left Harris County and moved to Athens, the seat of the state university, is not known, nor has it been possible to determine what business he engaged in during the half-dozen or so years after his arrival there. However, he quickly entered into the cultural and political life of the community, serving in 1843 on the Board of Visitors to examine the classes at the university and later in the same year acting as chairman of a Clarke County Democratic meeting. At this gathering he left the chair to deliver an address on the party's obligation to former President Van Buren. Never a modest man, he doubtless let it be known that Democrats were also indebted to him, a Van Buren spokesman in the 25th Congress.[37]

If Holsey entertained the hope of returning to Congress, and there is reason to believe he did, he was sure to encounter an obstacle in Congressman Howell Cobb of Athens. Still a young man, Cobb was already a skilled politician with a smoothly-running machine in Athens and Clarke County. Holsey had never had the benefit of the kind of a political organization he was observing in his new home. By temperment he was incapable of putting together such a machine. Ever the individualist, he had been accustomed to fighting his battles alone. Organized activity had always rankled him and by 1844 Cobb's methods had become so odious to him that he was determined to challenge his young rival.

The details of the ensuing effort are missing, but Cobb's private correspondence attests to its fierceness, one of the congressman's brothers writing that Holsey was "endeavoring to raise a prejudice against you all the time."[38] The challenger was especially formidable in open meetings, where he scorned Cobb's control of the local party and warned that he would never submit to such tyranny. Cobb was too clever to risk an intra-party fight with a fiery veteran like Holsey. The elder man must be put to work for the party. Thus it was arranged for Albon Chase, the congressman's friend and publisher of the Athens *Southern Banner,* to sell his newspaper to Holsey. Early in September, 1846, the transfer was completed and the new owner settled down to an editorial routine that was soon to please Cobb.[39]

From September, 1846, until May, 1853, Holsey published the *Southern Banner.* He once explained privately that a newspaperman's responsibility was "giving a proper direction to public opinion"; generally he acted as if he believed this could be accomplished simply by broadcasting his personal views on public questions. As a political analyst Holsey was probably the equal of most of his Georgia contemporaries. His editorials were often long, sometimes tedious, but rarely neutral. He had scarcely started his new career when Cobb began to receive complaints about the paper's management. There was criticism of the inadequate treatment of local news and the new editor was sometimes blistered for his insolent and egotistical style, one reader complaining that there "is not an article he writes but that he illustrates by some reference to himself and his career in Congress."[40]

That the new editor should at once presume to advise his

congressman on public policy was natural enough. He too had been in Congress, and besides he considered himself learned in law, political theory, and history. His early correspondence with Cobb thus often reveals him in the role of a patronizer, but always a zealous Democrat, he gave generously of his editorial space to his party's cause. For the latter Cobb expressed his appreciation, and if Holsey's private advice annoyed him, he succeeded in concealing his feelings.[41]

The habitually self-confident, independent, and often obstinate Holsey was nonetheless to become a captive of Cobb, for his relationship with Cobb soon began to give direction to his conduct as a journalist. Thus his newspaper career may be divided into three fairly distinct periods. The first comprised slightly over three years, ending in late 1849 with Cobb's election as speaker of the House of Representatives. The next two and one-half years were probably Holsey's happiest, for then he was the leading spokesman of that wing of the Georgia press which had joined Cobb and others in support of the Compromise of 1850. Because he could not dissociate himself from the effete Union party, which had been formed to sustain the compromise in Georgia, and because Cobb was determined to do so, the two men quarrelled, and in May, 1853, a beaten and disillusioned editor sold his paper to the Cobb interests.

From the start of his newspaper career Holsey found it hard to restrain his enthusiasm for sundry causes, and consequently he often espoused specific movements that were unpalatable to politicians because they threatened party harmony.[42] A strong agrarian, he was always distrustful of corporate wealth. Thus in his valedictory he could extol "the inherent moral beauty and philanthropy contained in the doctrine of Free Trade. . . ."[43] Later he exhorted every farmer and planter to advocate free trade. At another time he explained that England's repeal of her Corn Laws assured English laborers cheap bread and this in turn guaranteed her consumption of Southern cotton. This should "be crammed down the throats of Whig protectionists . . . every time they open their mouths in favor of the protective tariff."[44] His views on paper money were equally positive. Mindful of his experience with this problem while in Congress, he wrote soon after becoming editor that the system of paper money should be abolished and "we should have bankers lend us the real hard coin which will never lie, cheat, contract or expand."[45]

Holsey's extreme views on banking and currency were in part a result of the bank failures during the depression of 1837-44. It would be incorrect to ascribe similar views to all bank opponents in Georgia of the period after the depression. Yet many Georgians looked upon banking corporations with either suspicion or indifference, attitudes which affected markedly the course of corporation development in the state before the Civil War. Thus, in 1847, while the legislature was considering the so-called "liberal" charter bill, a spirited debate occurred. The sponsors of this measure were anxious to encourage manufacturing and they believed that by liberalizing corporate powers and privileges such a result would ensue. However, memories of corporate failures, especially in banking, endured and when the proponents of liberal charters sought to legalize the principle of limited liability, strong opposition quickly developed.[46]

Moving into this fight with characteristic abandon, Holsey charged that the proposed act would create "soulless corporations . . . divested . . . of the only principle (conscience) which holds individual wealth responsible."[47] The state, he warned, would quickly become infested with "moneyed giants" and promptly succumb to the fate of corporation-ridden Massachusetts.[48]

The *Southern Banner's* embittered attack on corporate wealth was subjected to considerable criticism, and even ridicule, by Whig newspapers generally and also by a portion of the Democratic press. The editor responded by explaining that he was really not opposed to manufacturing, but rather "to incorporating capital for that purpose." But he stubbornly clung to the view that shareholders should be liable in the same way as individual proprietors, whose entire assets might be confiscated to satisfy their business debts.[49] The Savannah *Republican,* a leading Whig journal, thought Holsey's views on the liberal charter measure were absurd and expressed regret that he "exercises sway over so many minds in Georgia."[50]

In the charter bill fight the *Southern Banner* was not without allies among the state's newspapers. Equally critical of corporate wealth was the Columbus *Times,* published in a city which the editor described as "Lowellized by the factories springing up" there. The mill owners were alleged to have brought with them a generous supply of Northern vices, including "ultra Whiggery" and a callous disregard for the civil rights of workers. Although unionization was not advocated as the answer, workers were urged to make their own terms with operators and especially to scorn all pressures aimed at influencing them to vote as Whigs. Northern owners were warned that Southern laborers were "free-born citizens, the peers of the richest man in the land."[51] Holsey thought the civil liberties of New England workers, though scandalously impaired, had survived complete extinction only because American labor could escape to the public lands of the West or to the agricultural states. Otherwise, he alleged, "the lordly capitalists . . . would soon show them whether they should have more . . . than the European pauper."[52]

As finally adopted, the incorporation act of 1847 required of manufacturing concerns sworn statements of paid-in capital, applying the rule of unlimited liability to stockholders only in cases of false statements and to officers and agents in cases where debts exceeded capital stock. Otherwise the rule that solvent stockholders were not responsible for proportionate shares of the insolvent ones was combined with a limit of double liability.[53]

Georgia's incorporation act of 1847 was part of a comprehensive movement to face the problem of the rising corporate empire's threat to the early nineteenth century idea of free enterprise. This movement was apparently widely shared throughout the nation, but unfortunately the slavery struggle and the Civil War smothered it. Yet such efforts to regulate corporate activity as were made in Georgia during the twelve or fifteen years before 1861 were not without significance. Whatever their shortcomings, they did reveal a willingness to face an important issue of the day in the only way apparently open to Americans of that age. It is also possible that they may have inspired a counteraction, which sought to discredit the idea of regulation and then to arrest it by means of legal obstacles. Recent scholarship advances the notion that during the Civil War certain groups interested in the regulation of business were brought under a cloud by the epithet "Copperhead."[54] This interpretation suggests that the "conspiracy theory" which was advanced years ago to explain the origin of the fourteenth amendment's due process clause, a legal device which for decades effectively restrained state regulation, needs to be reexamined in the light of such antebellum efforts as were made in Georgia to control corporate wealth.[55]

Such opponents of the rising industrial system as Holsey sincerely believed they were fighting the battle for popular rights, which, as they understood them, were meant only for the white man. When Thomas W. Dorr, the famous Rhode Island reformer, died in September, 1847, the *Southern Banner's* columns were shrouded in mourning and its editor offered an eloquent tribute to a man whose struggle for popular rights had caused his disfranchisement and imprisonment. His persecution "would dishonor the dark ages," wrote the aggrieved Holsey, but at last in the tomb this great man was free and one day his name would "arouse mankind to the vindication of their rights."[56] Here was a kindred spirit about whom the Athens editor could write with a great show of sentimentality. But the rights for which Dorr fought were by and large the very ones abolitionists insisted also belonged to slaves. Thus Southern Jacksonians like Holsey were to succumb to an inescapable ambivalence, whose frustrations could be only partially ameliorated by the solace of paternalism and the conviction that the South's "peculiar institution" was legal.

Holsey's devotion to popular rights, as he understood them, was made abundantly clear by his campaign to make Georgia's state and local governments more responsive to the people. Like Dorr, the Athens editor would carry on "the battles of *radical democracy*," and he so expressed himself privately soon after the Rhode Islander's death.[57] During 1848-49 he frequently found time to compose lengthy editorials outlining and defending a political reform program. Georgians were urged to reconstruct their government so as to preserve that "equality of rights" which was said to be disappearing and thus hurrying their state into a "practical aristocracy fostered by the law." They could arrest this unfortunate drift in public affairs by adopting two proposals, the most practical being a judiciary with a short term of service "dependent on no earthly power but the people themselves." Less likely of acceptance was the *Southern Banner's* plan to shift the emphasis from territory and property, particularly in the form of slaves, to population as a basis for representation in the state legislature.[58]

That Greene County's 900 voters had as much weight in the Lower House of the state legislature as Cass County's 2,400 was an example of how the federal ratio discriminated against the small farmers of the upcountry in favor of the big planters of the cotton belt. To correct this incongruity Holsey submitted numerous suggestions, the most interesting of which was to replace the bicameral legislature with a one-house body, a portion of whose members would be elected on a state-wide ticket. This was perfectly in order, he explained, because the Upper House of the state legislature was not really the counterpoise that had been intended.[59]

Like the movement to control corporate interests, political reforms were to be pushed aside by the slavery conflict. A few state administrative officers were made elective, but the popular election of judges, Holsey's most cherished project, failed, though the General Assembly did go so far as to provide a referendum on the election of superior court judges.[60]

As a professed spokesman of "radical democracy," Holsey found it necessary to present a rationale. Toward this end he constructed an interesting synthesis demonstrating the effect of freedom and truth. This he succinctly presented in 1849 when he wrote: "We live in an age in which the human mind cannot be fettered. Old political dogmas and preconceived opinions must bow to the spirit of inquiry which is abroad in the world, and crumble beneath the touch of reason and truth."[61]

Within a month after this announcement Holsey denied that liberty and Negro slavery were incompatible. Unlike Virginia's George Fitzhugh, who at this time believed slavery to be the normal condition of the laborer, whether white or black, the Athens editor explained that "slavery founded upon the antagonism of color and races is one thing, and the enslavement of one portion of the same race by another, a different thing."[62] To claim, however, as Holsey did, that the former was constitutional and the latter an inescapable product of industrial capitalism suggests that he was pretty close to admitting Fitzhugh's "slavery principle." Since the industrialist looked upon the slave-holder as a competitor of the North's labor system, he favored emancipation of Negro slaves. The destruction of the slave-owner would enable the managers of corporate wealth to record greater triumphs, resulting in an ever-increasing spread of "industrial slavery." The villian of all this treachery was the Whig party. Georgia Whigs were told they did not really understand the malignancy of the rising managerial class which had seized control of their party. They were urged to join with the Democrats, who, though committed to Negro slavery, stood for "a white man's chance."[63]

Although slavery must never be permitted to "crumble beneath the touch of reason and truth," or fall before an invading industrialism, yet "old political dogmas" were expected to "bow to the spirit of inquiry." Holsey had thus framed a concept precariously balanced on the dynamics of what he called "radical democracy" and the preservation of Negro slavery. He believed it contained the intellectual and emotional ingredients to sustain Southern Jacksonians. The Compromise of 1850 was to confirm this belief. Within less than two years thereafter the concept was to be discredited and Cobb was to be looking for a new editor.

When Holsey purchased the *Southern Banner,* the United States was at war with Mexico. As a good Democrat, he supported the war; as a loyal Southerner, he opposed the Wilmot Proviso, a proposal to prohibit slavery from such lands as would be acquired from Mexico; and as a unionist, he believed the issue of slavery in any territory ceded by Mexico should be compromised. Consistent adherence to these views compelled him to direct strong language at numerous editors and politicians. Among the most prominent of the latter group was Calhoun, who was accused of denouncing a war brought on by an act — the annexation of Texas — which he, as secretary of state under President John Tyler, had done so much to consummate. Scorned as a "soaptailed politician" and the "Lucifer of South Carolina," Calhoun was accused of ever operating upon the political principle of "rule or ruin." Repeated excoriations of this type came to be know as Holsey's "Calhouniacs."[64]

Equally critical was the *Southern Banner* of those who objected to compromising the issue of slavery in territory that Mexico was expected to cede to the United States after the war. Early in 1847 its editor warned that the hope of the union depended upon the application of the old Missouri Compromise line. Because James Buchanan, who was President James K. Polk's secretary of state, and Stephen A. Douglas of Illinois were reported to favor such a solution, Holsey believed most Northern Democrats could be relied upon to protect Southern rights. During 1847 he frequently wrote in defense of this treatment of slavery, usually contending that both the Wilmot Proviso and Calhoun's plan of nonintervention by Congress were impractical.[65]

Holsey's moderate view was the subject of some favorable editorial comment in the Northern press. When William Cullen Bryant's New York *Evening-Post,* a leading proponent of the Wilmot Proviso, commended him, some Georgia Whig editors pointed out that he was playing into the hands of abolitionists.[66] His moderation on slavery coupled with his constant ridicule of Calhoun placed him in somewhat the same position as his plea for "Dorrism." To extremists he was simply not going as far as he might in defense of Southern rights. Thus almost from the start of his editorial career he was to find himself in a highly vulnerable position. A sudden burst of unionist enthusiasm in 1850 was to afford him a short respite. While Holsey's case may not have been typical of those Georgians who professed moderation on the issue of slavery's expansion, yet Cobb, an astute politician, was to be similarly trapped. Although Cobb was able to extricate himself with considerable finesse, he was nevertheless a marked man from the day he chose to challenge the immoderate Southern rightists.

During the first three years of his editorship Holsey loyally supported the Democratic party's gubernatorial and presidential candidates. In 1847 his friend and former colleague in Congress, George W. Towns, was elected governor. Early the next year the *Southern Banner* expressed the view that Lewis Cass would make a suitable presidential candidate for the Democrats. Because Cass was already on record in favor of squatter sovereignty, by which territorial voters would decide for themselves the issue of slavery, the Athens journalist substituted this middle-of-the-road approach for the Missouri Compromise line. However, in the ensuing presidential canvass he was to generate less enthusiasm for squatter sovereignty than disapprobation for General Zachary Taylor, the Whig nominee for President. A Louisiana planter, Taylor was accused of favoring a restoration of the old tariff rates of 1842. His election would be followed by some clever logrolling by sugar planters, hemp growers, and Northern manufacturers. Equally ominous was Taylor's pledge not to use the veto power. Since all people of the more numerous nonslaveholding states were alleged to be "antislavery in the abstract," the only hope of averting the adoption of the Wilmot Proviso was the veto power. A Whig victory would indeed be a major catastrophe for the South.[87]

What acerbity the *Southern Banner's* editor had once borne toward Cobb was completely dissipated during the campaign of 1848. At the Democratic party's district convention he moved the congressman's renomination by acclamation. Of the efforts in behalf of Cobb's candidacy for re-election, none exceeded in adoration the editor's following description of one of the congressman's speeches: "For two hours did he enchain the auditory by one of his most brilliant and masterly efforts. . . . Never have we seen him more buoyant with hope — better prepared with facts and arguments — more felicitous in the use of them. . . ." His vigilance was "sleepless," his integrity "unshaken," and his ability to maintain them "acknowledged."[68]

A campaign which Holsey privately described as exciting and certain to result in a Democratic victory fell considerably short of his expectations. Although Cobb won easily enough in October, Taylor carried Georgia by a decisive margin in November.[69] Ironically, it was the editor's old hero, former President Van Buren, who as the Free Soil party's presidential candidate tipped the scales in enough nonslaveholding states to elect the general.

For months after Taylor's victory Holsey's editorials and private correspondence were heavily weighted with the most dire predictions. It was feared that Northern Democrats had fought their last battle for Southern rights. Turning the Southern political dilemma against Whiggery, he pointed out that because the slaveholder had foolishly joined that party, the Wilmot Proviso would soon be passed by Congress and Taylor would sign it. This ascendancy of slaveholders and abolitionists would soon break up the union.[70] In January, 1849, he wrote Cobb: "I love the Union for its justice — it is a beautiful idea in that dress; but I can not and will not bow down to a fanatical majority in Congress clothed with the garment of 'the Union.' "[71]

To these gloomy predictions an embittered editor joined a series of recommendations. The national Whig party must be dissolved; only then would Southerners be free to unite against their aggressor.[72] The South must now act like a "rough customer," he advised Southern Banner readers on January 11, 1849. The next month he wrote Cobb: "If we quail we are inevitably doomed. . . . I think we are forced by circumstances . . . to assume bold ground — say of defence or separation in the last resort."[73]

Despite his strong language, the apprehensive editor clung tenaciously to the belief that the South still had friends among Northern Democrats. But Southern disunity neutralized their efforts to help the South. The South must unite, but she must not sacrifice her alliance with Northern friends. Because Calhoun's Southern address of 1849 was believed to favor unity without such an alliance, Cobb, Robert Toombs, and others refused to sign it. Holsey agreed with them, though admitting privately, "we will not *follow* Calhoun, but must coöperate with him in resisting encroachment."[74]

The waning months of 1849 were to bring cheerful news to the

Athens editor. In October Governor Towns was re-elected and in December Cobb became speaker of the 31st Congress. A festive mood seized Athenians in the wake of Cobb's success. Holsey's dejection suddenly gave way to such jollity that one observer described him as "near deranged" on the occasion of a monstrous celebration in honor of the new speaker.[75] The editor probably captured the spirit of this event when he wrote Cobb as follows: "At 7 o'clock at night a band of music struck up in front of the *Banner* office, and the peoples assembled in large numbers considering the short notice — particularly the unconquerable and whole-souled democracy. The lights which had been put at the panes of the windows . . . bespoke . . . the occasion which had called us together. After the customary greetings, torches were lighted and a long and brilliant, and enthusiastic procession wound through the streets to your residence, preceded by the band and moving under the blazing rockets . . . which were continually thrown along the line. The procession was invited to march up to the dwelling and clustering around the front portico an address was demanded from your friend who writes this, which he accordingly gave to the best of his ability — certainly with a heart full of joy and enthusiasm for the occasion. It was, of course, responded to in the same spirit, and was followed by a collation and refreshments handsomely prepared and courteously tendered to the assemblage."[76]

Cobb's election was the prelude to an exciting debate in the 31st Congress on the issue of slavery. When Henry Clay's series of proposals known as the Compromise of 1850 was adopted, a political crisis ensued in Georgia. Acting on instructions from the legislature, Governor Towns ordered an election of delegates to a convention to decide whether the state would accept the compromise. Cobb and two of his Whig colleagues in Congress, Toombs and Alexander H. Stephens, hurried home to meet the crisis by taking the leadership in organizing a movement to defend the compromise.

Calling themselves Unionists, friends of the compromise were supported by a large segment of the Whig party and by those Democrats who were loyal to Cobb. Opposed to them was a Southern rights coalition composed of the main body of Democrats and a sprinkling of Whigs. In general, this political alignment was duplicated among the newspapers, with Whig editors supporting the rising Union party and those of Democratic affiliation becoming Southern Rightists. The notable exception was Holsey, most prominent of the Democratic editors in the new Union party.[77] His performance in the fight to elect convention delegates was loaded with invective and ridicule. An example of his lampoonery was the following:

PROCLAMATION OF ABSOLOM TRICKUM

Attention, Invincibles! To the rescue, Chivalry! Fire-eaters to your tents! Up with your new lights and down with the Union! You are ordered to muster at once in revolutionary style, and with your appearance touched off with a tint of the terrible, — your mustaches 18 inches long, your finger nails 3 inches long and pointed for gouging, knapsack of the shape and capacity of a coffin. . . . For regimental flag: 'United States we fall — Divided we stand'; and for company flags: 'Catspaws for South Carolina.' Col. Hydrogen Gass will take command with Rhettorical flourish, and lead you:

    Where hills and dales
        And Brooks that fail
    And Senator Hale so merrily sail
        On the ocean of wild disunion

Finally each man will kill twenty Yankees apiece, and capture New York . . . where they will seize Barnum and Jenny Lind — and then for the spoils of a real ridotto.[78]

By winning a decisive victory at the polls, the Unionists had little trouble in putting the state convention, meeting in late 1850, on record in favor of the Compromise of 1850. While the convention was in session Whigs and Democrats of unionists convictions formally organized their party, some hopefully looking forward to the launching of a "National Union Party" at the nation's capital on Washington's birthday in 1851.[79] A leading supporter of this project was the *Southern Banner,* which defiantly announced early in 1851 that only the "little insect [South Carolina] may be left to annoy a united South in support of a National Union Party." A short time later it urged: "We must know no distinction between Whigs and Democrats until the foul and dark spirits of disunion . . . shall be totally banished from among us. . . ."[80] Holsey's persistent clamor for a national Union party produced a serious difference with Cobb and presaged within a few months after its formal organization the ultimate collapse of Georgia's new Union party.[81]

The gubernatorial contest of 1851 was to be the first test of strength for the new parties. With Cobb as the Union candidate and former Democratic Governor Charles J. McDonald as his Southern Rights opponent, the campaign followed the pattern set in the first encounter between these two groups. Again the Union party won a decisive verdict, and again Holsey, with his battle cry "Cobb, the Compromise and the Union," was a key figure.[82]

Between Cobb's victory in 1851 and the close of the presidential contest of 1852, Holsey was in the thick of a bitter fight between Southern Rightists and Union Democrats for control of the state Democratic organization. By seizing the initiative the former convinced national party leaders that they were the true spokesmen of Georgia's Democracy. To this the *Southern Banner* responded with an assortment of claims and warnings. It boasted, for example, that Union Democrats of "the old iron-fisted, hard-handed, *Jackson* line" had saved the national party from "utter annihilation at the South" by taking "their position on the message of Gen. Jackson, against Nullification and Secession in 1833."[83]

Early in 1852, when House and Senate caucuses failed to affirm the finality of the Compromise of 1850, Holsey charged the national Democratic party had fallen to extremists of both sections. The country's only hope was a new party devoted to the settlement of 1850. With the contest for control of the state Democratic organization going to Southern Rightists, national party leaders were excoriated as a " . . . horde of corrupt, jiggling, and short-sighted politicians. . . ."[84]

As a Southern Jacksonian, Holsey was finding it increasingly difficult to accommodate himself to the growing threat of the abolitionists. Although his ardor for the union never abated, he temporarily gave up his plea for a national Union party and permanently abandoned the cause of dynamic "radical democracy." Instead, as the national conventions of 1852 approached, he undertook a campaign to interest planters in the Union Democrats. By assuming that planters were principally interested in protecting their property, it was easy to reduce their problem to one of containing Northern fanaticism. This could not be done by a permanent alliance between the South and Northern Whiggery, because such action would concentrate the nation's conservatism in a single party. Northern Democratic leaders would thus have no choice but to lead the crusade against slavery. In this role they would kindle a flame that would either destroy the planters' property or consume the union. Planters' best hopes lay in the South's alignment with the Democratic party. In language that contrasts sharply with that he used as the late champion of "radical democracy," Holsey declared: "The Masses are best restrained by the conservative portion of those who are enlisted with them under the same general banner, and who shall, at the same time, be in possession of the reins of government."[85] Here was a significant reversal of the Holsey of 1849. He would no longer support such causes as Jacksonian equalitarianism had once fostered; instead, he now exhorted the affluent planter class to join the party of Jackson and help check the dynamic Northern masses.

In defense of his revised position, Holsey operated from the premise that political parties sprang from what he called the "antagonism of interests." Northern society contained two great antagonistic forces: capital invested in manufacturing, banking, railroads, and other enterprises which yielded profitable returns; and labor with no capital to invest and "no wealth but in their bones and sinews." Northern Whiggery represented the former, Northern Democracy the latter. Because the South was almost totally agricultural, there existed no antagonism of interests. Hence Southern parties were unnatural. Even in the absence of slavery, Holsey believed the South could not maintain "natural parties."[86]

By Holsey's dialectics Southern Whiggery became anomalous. This was especially so, he pointed out, since the death of President Taylor in 1849, when it began to revert to the "Republican or anti-Federal" views that had originally inspired Georgia Whigs. The South must therefore become a "Solid South" and join the party which already contained powerful Northern allies who had always fought the "unjust exactions of Northern capital." Here was the basis for the only "natural and desirable" political coalition. Northern laboring and consuming classes could be counted on to respect Southern rights in return for Southern assistance in repelling the exactions of Northern business interests.[87]

Because it was "simply and wholly conservative" — politically so in the North and socially so in the South — Holsey contended that Whiggery was a potential threat to national stability. To combine all the conservative elements of society into one mass and all the progressive elements into another would soon end either in despotism or anarchy. The Democracy he was pleading for would escape such imbalance by blending Southern conservatism with Northern progressiveness. If that party's leaders would reaffirm, at their forthcoming convention, their faith in the finality of the Compromise of 1850, Holsey predicted the South was prepared "almost as one people" to co-operate with her "natural" allies on this basis. Failure to take such action would endanger not only the party but the union as well.[88] In short, the Athens editor was pleading for what he now believed to be the only kind of national party that could successfully manage both the drive of "radical democracy" and the determination to preserve slavery.

Stepping down from the Olympian heights, Holsey's well modulated prose gave way to violent charges. Although pleased with the Baltimore Convention's nomination of Franklin Pierce as the Democratic candidate for President and its endorsement of the Compromise of 1850, he immediately became the central figure in an untidy intra-party drama. With the fight for party control entering its last stage, Southern Rights and Union factions offered separate Pierce electoral tickets. Governor Cobb and other moderates of each group favored the withdrawal of both tickets in favor of a compromise slate of electors. For a time it seemed such an arrangement would be worked out. However, the *Southern Banner's* persistent denunciations of Southern Rights leaders as secessionists, bent on stealing the Democratic party and converting Georgia into a second South Carolina, helped destroy the possibility of a truce.[89]

With the effort to adjust differences over party mechanics ending in failure, one important leader who was close to Cobb privately expressed the view that it would be good strategy to withdraw the Union ticket, so that in case of Pierce's defeat the onus would "rest on the fire-eaters." Thus in mid-September the Unionists recalled their Pierce electors. Holsey branded the act as a surrender to the secessionists and twitted Union Democrats about the bondage their masters were preparing for them. But there was to be no bondage for him, for he and a few irreconcilable north Georgia Unionists raised another Pierce slate of electors, Holsey boasting they would "nobly peril everything in the attempt to maintain it."[90]

Known as the Tugalo faction, these uncompromising Unionists waged a hopeless campaign. It was natural that their leading editor should be subjected to extreme personal abuse, to which he responded in kind.[91] His habit of retreating into the misty area of lofty principles from which he was wont to admonish his readers, sometimes arrogantly, had always annoyed his newspaper colleagues. When the Savannah *Georgian* announced that the *Southern Banner* had at last been "shorn of its power," Holsey proudly countered: "It claims no power — it has no power — the power is in the hearts of our people, and the Banner understands full well it is but the organ which expresses it."[92] With the Tugalo slate attracting only about ten percent of the state's voting strength as against over fifty percent for the Regular Democrats, the *Southern Banner* had indeed been shorn of its power.[93]

The sound beating his Tugaloes received at the hands of the Regular Democrats produced no perceptible change in Holsey's mood. The victorious faction he continued to deride as the agent of the South Carolina doctrine of disunion, Unionists who joined them had become mere serfs, and no power on earth could make true Jacksonians the slaves of secessionists, especially the South Carolina breed.[94] When John Forsyth, Jr., of the Columbus *Times* announced that the *Southern Banner* must have no more pretexts for stabbing the party to which it professed to belong, the Columbus editor was reminded that he was the "son of the illustrious statesman who figured in the days of General Jackson in opposition to the doctrines now maintained by his descendant."[95] Recollecting that Jackson's equestrian statue was soon to be placed in the nation's capital, the Athens editor quipped: "It is intended to be a kind of democratic Avator, and who knows but that the old 'Brave' himself may descend, and take his seat in the saddle. If he should, woe be unto the secessionists."[96] Holsey also went after James Gardner of the Democratic Augusta *Constitutionalist.* The Augustan was reviled as a "he-goat," who "was lately seen heaving, like a ram at the gate post, against the strong and deep-laid pillars of the Union."[97]

Convinced that Georgia's Democratic machine had become the captive of secessionists, Holsey had no choice but to undertake a campaign to reconstruct the Union party in a desperate attempt to rescue his discredited formula. He was encouraged during the early months of 1853 as at least four journals joined him in his last effort to reshape the state's party system. But editorial support was not enough; the project needed the assistance of Governor Cobb. The governor, however, was now more interested in making peace with the men in command of the Democratic organization. He could therefore not afford to help those who were contemplating another diversion. Waiting until shortly after the inauguration of President Pierce, Cobb clarified his position with a temperate appeal for unity between the rival party factions. There had always been differences among Democrats, he explained, but they had never been, nor were they now, so great as to preclude adjustments within the family. He specifically urged his friends to discountenance the scheme that was so dear to the *Southern Banner's* editor.[98]

Holsey lost no time in going after Cobb's scalp. By renouncing the teachings of the idol Jackson and by bowing down in "humble submission to the Calhoun dynasty," the governor had become a slave. Although this was a grievous mistake which only a blunderer could make, lamented the distraught editor, the evil governor had compounded his folly by a sheer falsification of history. Meanwhile "Old Tugalo" offered his *Southern Banner* for sale, intimating that fire-eaters had made him some offers.[99] On May 12 his valedictory appeared.

Holsey's political views were rooted in the equalitarianism of the Jacksonian age. By the time he began his editorial career in 1846 this powerful dogma had become an article of faith among the opponents of slavery, who were already important enough to claim the attention of Northern politicians. As a Southern editor of Jacksonian persuasion it was inevitable that he should be caught between the great promise of Jacksonian Democracy and the defense of Southern rights. He had tried as early as 1849 to resolve this dilemma with a formula which he believed would provide a balance for antagonistic forces already in ominous conflict. He interpreted the successes of 1850-51 as a vindication of that formula. Yet Holsey was aware of the growing appeal of Southern rights, and he sought to meet it by surrendering his devotion to "radical democracy" and accepting the hard core of Southern rights. But when practical politicians like Cobb went farther and joined the old foes of 1850-51, Holsey went down charging his old friends with infidelity. A few days after his retirement the Milledgeville *Federal Union* combined eulogy with prophecy by observing that: "He dies with his armor on, firmly convinced that the old Democratic ship of state can never be righted until the present generation has passed away."[100]

Shortly after he sold his newspaper Holsey sought to assuage his humiliation by entering the congressional race. The *Southern Banner,* for which Governor Cobb was now writing an occasional editorial, accused the former editor of acting with the Whigs and, like General Taylor, hoping to achieve election "by spontaneous combustion."[101] Badly beaten in his bid for a seat in the 33rd Congress, the embittered veteran now carried his war against Cobb to Milledgeville, where, in November, 1853, the legislature was to elect a United States senator. A parlous campaign for control of the Democratic caucus had already begun when the unrelenting Holsey arrived. He now joined his old Southern Rights foes in a successful plan to block Cobb's nomination for the Senate.[102] This flourish of revenge ended his active political career.

By 1855 he had moved to Taylor County. Here with his second wife, the former Miss Mary J. Neisler whom he had married in 1850, he spent his last years on his farm "Brightwater."[103] Still distrustful of the Democratic party, he wrote a lengthy letter in 1855 defending the American party's gubernatorial candidate.[104] The next year he was reported as favoring the election of Buchanan, the Democratic presidential candidate. In poor health for some time, he died on March 31, 1859, and was buried on his Taylor County estate.[105]

In a lengthy obituary one of the state's leading newspapers characterized him as a "clear and forcible writer," but "too honest to be largely successful" as a politician.[106] At the time of his death the men he had successfully resisted in 1850-51 were intimately identified with those hopes and fears out of which secession and war were soon to be compounded. Because death denied him a chance to share in the Lost Cause, he was easily forgotten.

CHARLES JONES JENKINS, JR.

BY OLIVE H. SHADGETT

MUCH has been said and written about Georgia's great leaders of the Civil War era. Comparatively little is known, however, about one of the most outstanding of these men, Charles Jones Jenkins, Jr., the state's first elected governor after the war. His public career extended over a full half-century — from his election to the legislature in 1830 until shortly before his death in 1883 — but he has been overshadowed in history by the more colorful figures of the day.

Jenkins was not always on the side that won popular favor. He was a Whig at the time that party was crumbling away; he was a Unionist when the fires of secession were burning most brightly. Yet there were few men of his era in Georgia who enjoyed more fully the respect and confidence of the people of the state. In the declining years of his career, he was honored by the General Assembly with the award of a golden replica of the executive seal of Georgia. On the reverse side was the simple but significant legend, *In Arduis Fidelis.*

Jenkins was born on January 6, 1805, in the Beaufort District of South Carolina, where his father was the ordinary and the former clerk of the court of common pleas. The family home was known as the Grimball Hill Place. In 1816 the family moved to Jefferson County in Georgia, just to the southwest of Richmond County where Jenkins spent most of his adult life. Here the elder Jenkins purchased a tract of land and settled down to the quiet life of a planter.

Young Charles, an only child, was given the best educational advantages available. Even before the family moved to Georgia,

Olive H. Shadgett is a member of the political science faculty at the University of Georgia.

he had been sent to Savannah to school. After this he attended school in Bryan County and at Mount Zion in Hancock County, and finally was sent to Willington Academy in Abbeville District, South Carolina, the school headed by Dr. Moses Waddel. In 1819, when Dr. Waddel received the call to the presidency of the University of Georgia, Jenkins followed him to Athens. He completed his preparatory studies at the grammar school of that institution, and the following year matriculated as a "Freshman, half advanced."

Jenkins remained at the University only until February, 1822, when he transferred to Union College in Schenectady, New York. He graduated there in 1824, third in his class, winning membership in Phi Beta Kappa. Later he was honored by that college with the degree of LL.D.[1]

After his graduation Jenkins returned to Georgia, where he read law with a relative, John McPherson Berrien, who later became senator and attorney general of the United States. Berrien had recently retired from the bench of the superior court of the Eastern Judicial Circuit of Georgia and had a large and lucrative practice. The older man took a personal interest in his young student, and Jenkins spent most of his time in the private study and law office at Berrien's residence. In April, 1826, he was admitted to the bar in Screven County, where he was examined by Judge William Schley, afterwards governor. A month later Jenkins opened a law office in Sandersville, in Washington County, where he resided and practiced for the next three years.

Washington County was then a prosperous agricultural region with many wealthy planters. It afforded an excellent field for a young lawyer. Soon, according to Charles C. Jones, Jr., Jenkins had a "valuable clientage" and "honorable fame." This famous Georgia historian, who was a close friend of Jenkins, describes him at this period as a young man

much given to calm reflection, with a maturity of judgment beyond his years, . . . scrupulous in the discharge of the obligations devolving upon him, . . . bold and intelligent in the expression of his convictions, and yet tolerant of the opinions of others, . . . a ready and effective speaker, persuasive, logical and eloquent, — and with a character pure and decided in all the elements which unite in the formation of true Christian manhood.[2]

In 1829 Jenkins moved to Augusta and set up his law office there, but he continued to ride his old circuit and retained many

of his former clients. In 1830 he was elected as a member of the
Georgia House of Representatives from Richmond County. Jones
states that the nomination was wholly unsolicited on Jenkins's
part.[3] Thus began a career of public service which was to extend
over many years of Georgia history.

When Jenkins entered the legislature, the political scene of
Georgia was dominated more by factions and personalities than
by issues. While most Georgians considered themselves Republicans in the early years of the nineteenth century, they were split
into factions which fought each other as bitterly as if they had
been rival political parties. This growth of factions in Georgia
was based mainly upon personal antagonisms and was developed
in the beginning largely along economic lines. The well-to-do
planters tended to unite in one group and the small farmers in
another. These came under the leadership of George M. Troup
and John Clark respectively. Gradually the nature of the factions
became less personal, and the Troup party took the name of State
Rights, while the Clark followers called themselves the Union
party.[4] Later these local groups allied themselves, respectively, with
the national parties known as Whigs and Democrats, although
they were not completely identified as such until the election of
1840.

In 1830 Jenkins was a Troup man and a staunch member of
the State Rights party. His adherence to this faction was characteristic. He was always to be found allied with the prominent and
substantial people of the community. Stable, conservative, and
intellectual, he was consistently on the side of law and tradition,
of higher education, and of sound business. He was never a
rabble-rouser. In 1853, when he made his first bid for the governorship, the worst thing that his opponents could find to charge him
with was that he was "an aristocrat."

From the available records it would seem that Jenkins, then a
young man of twenty-five years, took a creditable but not an outstanding part in the proceedings of his first session of the legislature. He was appointed to the standing committee on Banks, and
his name appears often in the official record in the routine procedure of introducing and reporting bills. The first mention of
the young representative came on October 20, one day after he
took his seat in the House, when he introduced a bill to establish
election precincts in Richmond County and another "to separate
and divorce Cherry McRae and John McRae, her husband."[5] His

interest in legal matters can be seen in his frequent introduction of bills and resolutions pertaining to the judiciary.[6]

An important act of the 1830 legislature was that granting an annual appropriation to the University of Georgia. Jenkins voted for this measure, having consistently opposed the numerous efforts made to amend or strike out parts of the bill.[7]

Jenkins did not return to the General Assembly in 1831, but was elected by that body to serve as solicitor of the Middle Judicial Circuit and attorney general of Georgia. He resigned from these offices before the expiration of the term in order to run again for the legislature. This time he was defeated. It was not until 1836 that the political tide turned in Richmond County and swept Jenkins and other State Rights candidates back into the legislature.

During the six years that Jenkins was out of the General Assembly, he was strengthening himself in his profession and building a reputation for integrity and capability that was to remain with him all of his life. In 1836, when he returned to the House of Representatives, he was no longer a novice, either in politics or in the law. From this session on, he was increasingly influential in the legislature.

Beginning with the 1836 session Jenkins served for ten terms in the Lower House, until he retired voluntarily in 1850.[8] He was out of office only once during this period, in 1842, when he was defeated because of a local issue in Richmond County. In 1840, 1843, 1845, and 1847 — when the Whigs had majorities in the House of Representatives — Jenkins served as speaker. He was a member of the standing committee on the Judiciary and the standing committee on Finance, and for four terms he was chairman of the standing committee on Public Education and Free Schools. He was named to numerous special committees appointed in the House and had some part in almost every important measure which came before the body.

Jenkins was identified especially with the cause of education. In 1839, when the nationwide depression forced the General Assembly to repeal legislation passed in 1837 and 1838 to establish a common school system, a bill was introduced to repeal also the annual appropriation of $6,000 which had been granted in 1830 to the state university. As chairman of the Education Committee Jenkins reported this bill unfavorably, and put up a strong fight for the university. The committee was aware of the adverse conditions of the time, said he, but felt that the state should not withdraw support of the college. "Embarrassed she is," he declared, "but not poor enough to take back the patrimony she has already bestowed upon her first born and fairest daughter, the earliest offspring of her liberal legislation."[9]

In spite of his plea, the House rejected Jenkins's report and voted to repeal the appropriation. Fortunately the Senate tabled the measure on the closing day of the session. Two years later both houses voted to repeal the appropriation. Jenkins again opposed the move, failing to prevent the repeal but delaying its operation until March 1, 1842.[10]

He was more successful in his efforts to block the abandonment of another project, the construction of a state railroad from the Tennessee line to the southeastern bank of the Chattahoochee River. In 1836, when the plan was launched, Jenkins had been one of its strongest supporters, and in 1843 and 1847 he and a few others were given credit for saving the road and assuring its completion.[11]

While the representative from Richmond County was ready to appropriate state funds for such purposes as education and the state railroad, he consistently opposed attempts to use public money for ends that he considered unsound. On a number of occasions his conservatism in financial matters led him to oppose measures which would have granted state aid to various groups. These instances were later recalled and held against him when he ran for governor in 1853.

In 1842, after six successive terms in the General Assembly, Jenkins was defeated for re-election because of his support of the so-called "Algerine Law," a measure designed to protect the interest of property owners in Augusta. This law, introduced by the Richmond delegation and passed by the 1841 legislature, had amended the city charter to provide, in addition to the existing council, a board of aldermen with veto power over the city's financial affairs. The vulnerable spot in the act, and the point that made it unpopular with the masses, was the provision that the new board be composed of and elected by only those voters who were property owners and taxpayers. When asked in the 1842 election whether he would vote for the repeal of the law, Jenkins stated that he would if both the advocates and the opponents of the measure should request it. He declared, however, that he believed the law to be a wholesome one. "As an individual," said he, "I must frankly say that I am opposed to the repeal of the act. Nothing has occurred to change the opinion I entertained when I voted for it."[12] This issue not only defeated Jenkins in 1842 but rose again eleven years later to contribute to his defeat in his bid for the governorship.

During Jenkins's last two terms in the House, in 1847 and 1849, the members of the General Assembly were much concerned about national affairs. So great was the tension in 1849 that the legislature held a divided session, reconvening in January, 1850, in order to be in session as long as possible at the same time as the national Congress. Resolutions dealing with the grievances of the South and other related subjects poured into the legislative hopper. In order to secure concerted thought and action on these questions, Jenkins moved that the standing committees on the State of the Republic in both houses act jointly on all such measures. His resolution was adopted, and he himself was added to this important committee. A large part of the session was given over to consideration of the issues of slavery and the relations between the sections. In debating a series of resolutions on the subject, Jenkins tried unsuccessfully to modify the prevailing radical sentiment, but his amendments were voted down by the Democratic majority.

While the attention of the 1849 legislature was devoted primarily to national affairs, it was a local issue which furnished the chief sensation of the session and led to the resignation of Jenkins. In 1843 the Whigs had been accused of gerrymandering when setting up new state senatorial and congressional districts, and there had been a great deal of bitterness between the two parties. The Democrats, now in control of both houses, had their first opportunity to retaliate.

When a bill to reorganize the congressional districts was brought up in the House, every Whig member except Jenkins filed from the hall, leaving the House without a quorum. After three unsuccessful roll calls, the Democrats located enough of their absent members to provide a bare quorum and the bill was passed by a vote of 57 to 8. Jenkins, voting nay, was the only Whig who answered to his name.[13]

On the following morning, with the Whigs again present, Jenkins moved reconsideration of the act. When the question was put, all the Whigs except Jenkins again retired, leaving the House one short of a quorum. (One Democrat, believing the issue settled, had departed for his home.) This situation continued for a week. Jenkins was reported as in his seat for every roll call through Saturday, February 16, but at this point he submitted his resignation and left the Capitol, never again to serve as a member of the Georgia House of Representatives.[14]

Relating the proceedings with indignation, the Democratic *Federal Union* praised Jenkins's deportment as follows:

Undeniably the ablest Whig in the House and the acknowledged leader of that party, he has done all in his power to prevent its disorganization. Solitary and alone he retained his seat and answered to his name, rebuking by the moral grandeur of his course, his political associates.[15]

The praise heaped upon Jenkins by this rival paper was not echoed by the press of his own party.[16] In explaining his position Jenkins stated that he knew he had displeased many if not all of his own party by refusing to leave the hall, but that whenever the choice was between party behests and his duty to his country, "the latter had been, and always should be his rule of conduct."[17]

In the long-drawn-out session of the General Assembly in 1849-50, plans had been laid for a convention of protest to be called by the governor in the event of any one of five contingencies in the controversy between the North and the South. These included the admission of California as then constituted.[18] Before this session of the legislature came to an end, debate had already begun in Washington on the issues of the "Great Compromise" between the slaveholding and non-slaveholding states. In September, 1850, the compromise was completed. In most respects the five measures passed by Congress did not run counter to the resolutions of the Georgia Assembly. But California, extensive and sparsely populated, was admitted as a free state. In accordance with the mandate of the legislature, Governor George W. Towns issued a call for a convention to meet in Milledgeville on December 10.

People all over the state were aroused and alarmed at the turn of affairs, and the period before the election of delegates was filled with spirited campaigning. Party lines crumbled as extremists and moderates separated. This development had been foreshadowed months before in the legislature in the debate over the five contingencies, when conservative Democrats had joined Jenkins and James A. Nisbet in their attempts to modify the demands, while extremist Whigs, together with the more radical Democrats, had fought these attempts.[19]

Now the new alignments were crystallized in a Union party and a Southern Rights party, and in the election of delegates to the

Milledgeville convention the Unionists polled a large majority. In Richmond County there were eight candidates for the four places as delegates, and Jenkins led the field with 635 votes. The other three Union candidates trailed him closely, while the Southern Rights men were far behind.[20]

Among the first motions presented after the opening of the convention was a proposal by Jenkins that a committee of three from each judicial district be appointed by the chair to recommend action appropriate to the occasion.[21] This committee of thirty-three members was appointed, and Jenkins himself was named chairman.

Two days later Jenkins presented the report of the committee. Consisting of a lengthy preamble and five brief resolutions, the document declared that Georgia would recognize the Compromise of 1850 but would accept no further encroachments upon the rights of the South on the question of slavery. The committee remonstrated with the people of the North for the aggressive and unfriendly spirit shown by their representatives in Congress and by the agitators in their midst. On the whole, however, the tone of the report was conciliatory and designed to avoid the issue of immediate secession.[22]

Attempts were made by Southern Rights delegates to secure a stronger declaration from the convention. Amendments stressing the sovereignty of the states, the right of secession, the equality of rights in the territories, and the alleged violation of the constitutional rights of the South by the recent acts of Congress were rejected by an overwhelming vote.[23]

The report adopted by the Milledgeville convention became known as the "Georgia Platform." It was generally accepted through the state and, in turn, throughout the South. It has been credited by some with having saved the Union in 1850. Certainly it did much to stem the tide that might have led to immediate secession.

There is some difference of opinion regarding the importance of the part played by Jenkins in this matter. He is generally credited with being the author of the Georgia Platform.[24] In the official record of the convention, however, and in the detailed accounts of the proceedings that appeared contemporaneously in the *Federal Union,* there is nothing to indicate that he was the sole author. Later his political rivals denied that he was personally responsible for the famous document.[25]

Whether or not Jenkins actually drafted the Georgia Platform himself, the weight of evidence indicates that he was probably more responsible for it than any other one man. Certainly he seems to have been the outstanding figure in the convention itself, although Robert Toombs, Howell Cobb, and Alexander H. Stephens were the moving spirits in the pre-convention campaign and were no doubt more active behind the scenes at the convention than appears in the official reports. Herbert Fielder, a contemporary observer, writing shortly after the convention, said:

In this convention, Charles J. Jenkins was the Madison "come to judgment." He stood like a great, towering and impassable statue by the paths that seemed to lead to degradation and humility on the one side, or to disorder and strife on the other.[26]

In order to protect the work of the convention and to support the Georgia Platform in the coming state election, Union Democrats united with a majority of the Whigs in the new Constitutional Union party. Cobb, himself a Democrat but a strong Unionist, was elected governor by a large majority. After this victory and the general acceptance of the Georgia Platform, the immediate need for the coalition party seemed to have passed, and strenuous efforts were made to restore the old party alignments.

By the time of the presidential election in 1852 the Democratic party in Georgia had regained much of its strength, but the Whigs were never again able to present a united front. The main leadership of the Whig party came from the North and East, and on the national level it espoused causes and candidates that were not acceptable to the people of the South. The Georgia Whigs were hopelessly divided in the election of 1852. One segment — the *Tertium Quids,* they were called — went so far as to support a ticket on which Jenkins, as a candidate for the vice presidency, was teamed with Daniel Webster, nominated for the presidency. There was never any expectation that such a ticket could win a majority of votes in Georgia, but it was thought that Jenkins's personal popularity might draw enough votes away from the major candidates to throw the choice of electors into the Georgia legislature, where the Constitutional Union party still had a strong majority. But the Webster-Jenkins combination received only 5,324 votes throughout the state.[27]

The disintegration of the Whig party in the 1850's left Jenkins and other Georgia leaders in an unhappy position. Whigs in the North might become the nucleus for the emerging Republican party, but this was manifestly impossible in the South. To join the Democrats was almost equally unthinkable after the years of bitter rivalry in the state. Some Georgia Whigs found a temporary refuge in the so-called American, or Know Nothing, party. Others, like Jenkins and Stephens, floundered uncomfortably for a while in such movements as the *Tertium Quids* and in vain efforts to revive the Constitutional Union party. Most of them were forced eventually by circumstances into the ranks of the Democratic party, but they delayed the evil day as long as possible. "Whiggery died a slow death," says Ulrich Bonnell Phillips, "and no one can say when it breathed its last in Georgia."[28]

It was during this period of political uncertainty, in 1853, that Jenkins made his first bid for the governorship — and lost it by one of the narrowest margins recorded in a gubernatorial contest in Georgia. His opponent in this race was Herschel V. Johnson, the candidate of the reunited Democrats. One week after the nomination of Johnson, the opposing forces met in Milledgeville to choose their candidate. There were many in Georgia who were antagonistic to the Democratic party, but for the moment they had no effective party organization.

In the absence of regularly organized Whig or Union parties, the Milledgeville *Southern Recorder,* a leading Whig newspaper, took the initiative in calling "our Gubernatorial convention."[29] In issuing the call the *Recorder* had carefully avoided both the Whig and Union labels, and there was considerable speculation as to what the party would call itself. The Milledgeville *Federal Union* suggested beforehand that it be called the *"Conservative Union Whig* Party, with as slight an accent on the 'Whig' part as is compatible with policy and propriety."[30]

The term "Republicans" was adopted by some of the newspapers in sympathy with the movement. The Augusta *Chronicle and Sentinel,* one of its strongest supporters, consistently spoke of the party as the "Conservatives." The majority fell back on the old appellation, Union party. It seems clear that Jenkins's campaign was launched as a Union and not a Whig undertaking, but Phillips believes that he "committed a blunder by calling himself a Unionist rather than a Whig."[31] Many of Jenkins's contemporaries felt the same way, in spite of the earnest attempts of the party leaders to avoid a tie-up with the national Whig party.[32]

Attempts made by Jenkins's supporters to rally the old Constitutional Union party and to show that the issues were the same as in 1851 were not successful. True, Johnson had supported the Southern Rights cause in 1850 and 1851, opposing the Georgia Platform and fighting Cobb's election as governor, but in 1852 he had made his peace with the Union Democrats. Now, in 1853, a long list of prominent men who in 1851 were among the leaders and strong supporters of the Union party were aligned with the Johnson forces.[33]

At first Cobb took no part in the contest. As the summer wore on, however, it became evident that the race would be a close one, and increasing pressure was brought to bear upon the governor to enter the campaign in behalf of Johnson. Although Cobb had been elected governor on the Constitutional Union ticket with the aid of the Whigs, after the 1852 presidential election he had capitulated to the Southern Rights faction, which had gained the ascendancy in the Democratic party of Georgia. Now, in 1853, he had his eye upon the United States Senate and hoped for election when the legislature should meet in the fall. To ignore the urgent requests to aid the Democratic campaign against Jenkins put him in an extremely awkward position. Finally he yielded and agreed to enter the fight personally and to stump the Cherokee counties on behalf of Johnson.

This decision on the part of the governor may well have been the deciding factor in the election. There was no outstanding issue in the 1853 contest. The campaign was waged principally on the past records of the two candidates. Great stress had been placed by Jenkins's supporters on his role as "Father of the Georgia Platform," but, after Cobb entered the field in favor of Johnson, much of the force of this argument was lost. This was particularly true in the Cherokee counties, where Union sentiment was strong but where the governor had a great influence.

The nomination of Jenkins had brought forth a series of eulogies in the press all over the state. Even some of the opposition newspapers were lavish in their praise of the candidate. As the contest progressed, however, the editors took up the fight, and the Democratic *Federal Union,* ordinarily an admirer of Jenkins in spite of his politics, now led the campaign against him.

In spite of the general esteem in which the Augusta candidate was held, it would have been impossible for any man to have been in public office for so many years and to have been as active in party politics as he had been without incurring some enmity and opposition. Since there was no suspicion of scandal or corruption to be brought against him, and since his views on current issues were well known and generally accepted, the *Federal Union* and other Democratic papers reached far back into his political past for ammunition. The old matter of the "Algerine Law" was brought up, and Jenkins was dubbed the "thousand dollar candidate," a man who believed in two ballot boxes, one for the rich and one for the poor. He was said to be an aristocrat with no sympathy for the masses and no confidence in the common man. "There is an impassable gulf betwixt him and the common people. They have no principle, interest, or sympathies, in common to bring them together."[34]

The actual facts of the "Algerine Law" incident, when published, showed no discredit to Jenkins, but there is little doubt that his campaign was hurt by this attempt to picture him as "an aristocrat," separated from the interests of the common people. That this charge was not justified is indicated by newspaper accounts of the period which described Jenkins's public appearances. The Macon *Citizen*, a paper that had opposed his policies in the past, had this to say of the Union candidate:

Many persons have had an idea that Mr. Jenkins was an aristocrat in feeling and manner — that he was a "swelled-head" that looked down Pharisaically upon his fellow men. So far from seeing anything of this nature, we look upon him as one of the plainest and most republican citizens we have met with for many a day. There is no assumption of superiority, whatever, in his appearance or demeanor.[35]

"RAMBLER," frankly a Jenkins partisan, wrote in much the same vein in the Columbus *Enquirer*, a staunch Union paper. In describing the reaction of Jenkins's audiences, he said:

They see a plain, affable, unostentatious man, with an eye beaming with intelligence and kindliness of feeling, and a massive brow and forehead, that sure indication of great mental power, and finding him in every sense a proper man are ready and will vote for him.[36]

The comment was sometimes made that the campaign of 1853 was a dull one. The *Federal Union*, in spite of its hammer-and-tongs battle with the opposition press, complained on August 30 that the race was "not exciting enough to be pleasant." There was no vital current issue at stake, and it is probably true that neither Jenkins nor Johnson had the popular appeal of some others who might have been chosen.[37]

Although Jenkins was a leader in his party for many years, he was never the type for a rough-and-tumble political campaign. From all accounts, he was soft-spoken and courteous, a man whose words appealed to the intellect rather than to the emotions. Judging from his published letters and speeches, he was not lacking in eloquence, but his eloquence was more scholarly than exciting, and probably more effective in a court of law than on the hustings.

Despite the zeal of their promoters and the charges and counter-charges made by the newspapers, the two candidates were apparently on excellent terms throughout the campaign. Late in August they made a joint speaking tour into the Cherokee country, perhaps the most important battle ground of the campaign. It is related that they often traveled together, ate together, and sometimes even slept in the same room. Reports published at the time indicate that the joint debates were "conducted in the most gentlemanly and courteous manner."[38]

When the ballots were cast in October, the election was so close that the result could not be known definitely until all the returns were in. Then it was determined that Johnson was the victor by a margin of 510 votes. The official tally, as presented to the General Assembly in November, gave Johnson 47,638 votes and Jenkins 47,128.[39]

After the campaign of 1853 Jenkins was, for a few years, a man without a party. There were still many Whigs in Georgia, but the organization was dead, and the Constitutional Union party had also fallen to pieces. Jenkins could not endorse the doctrines of the Know Nothings, and he was not yet ready to become a Democrat. In 1855 he was again mentioned as a candidate for governor. The chief issue at this time was the existence of the Know Nothing party in Georgia, and Jenkins refused to join this organization. He was urged by some to come out as a candidate without a nomination by any party, but he declared, "I have concluded . . . that being neither a Democrat, nor a Know Nothing, there is no place for me in this contest."[40]

It was not until 1856 that Jenkins came out publicly in favor of the Democrats. By the end of the summer of that year there were three candidates in the field in the campaign for the presidency: James Buchanan for the Democrats; Millard Fillmore for the Know Nothings; and John C. Frémont for the newly-organized Republican party. When asked by a friend for his opinion of the three candidates, Jenkins replied in a long and carefully worded letter, which was published in the *Federal Union* on September 9 and widely publicized throughout the state.

It was no time, wrote Jenkins, to struggle for party ascendancy; men must now look to the country. Being assured that the contest was really between Buchanan and Frémont and that the election of the latter would bring ruin to the union, the old Whig solemnly announced his conclusion: "I say let every Southern electoral vote be cast for the Democratic nominee. — Let Georgia do so, laying all party prejudices and affinities, as an offering, on the altar of our common country."

Jenkins took no active part in politics for the next few years, but he remained in the public eye as one of the state's most prominent figures. In 1858 he was appointed by Governor Joseph E. Brown as one of nineteen delegates from the state at large to the Southern Commercial Convention held in Montgomery, Alabama. Isaac Avery, Georgia historian, cites the entire list as "showing who were the leading men of the State at this time."[41]

In 1860 Jenkins was appointed by the governor to a post which removed him from the political arena and made full use of his legal ability and his particular traits of disposition. He was made a justice of the Supreme Court of Georgia. He started his service on the court with the August term in 1860 and remained a member until December, 1865, resigning just before his inauguration as governor. His colleagues during his entire service on the supreme bench were Joseph Henry Lumpkin and Richard F. Lyon. Lumpkin, chief justice, was an original member of the court.

Georgia Reports record a total of 138 opinions written by Jenkins during his five-year period of service. Probably the actual figure was somewhat larger, as many records were lost or destroyed during the war, and some cases were necessarily omitted from the *Reports*.[42] Of the 138 opinions recorded, 74 affirmed and 62 reversed decisions of the lower courts. (In two instances, where several cases were heard together by the Supreme Court, there had been contradictory rulings in the trial courts.) A majority of the opinions written by Jenkins was delivered in the first two years of his term. Beginning with 1862, there was a marked decline in the number of cases heard by the Supreme Court. Witnesses, lawyers, court officials, and sometimes even the principals in cases were off at the war. Fewer suits than usual were filed in the lower courts, and still fewer reached the highest tribunal of the state.

Moreover, the type of cases considered during the period underwent a radical change. During Jenkins's first year on the court most of the cases had to do with property rights, such as contracts, notes, estates, the construction of wills, deeds, and land grants. Nearly a third of Jenkins's opinions dealt specifically with slave property. In 1862 the war issue first appeared in the adjudications, and by 1864 almost every case dealt either primarily or indirectly with questions brought on by the war. Conscription, in its various phases, was the issue most often argued, and on this question Jenkins handed down some of the most important decisions of the war.

Probably no other decision written by him was more far-reaching in its effects than that in the case of *Jeffers v. Fair,* in which the Supreme Court of Georgia upheld the constitutionality of the conscription acts passed by the Congress of the Confederacy.[43] This decision, handed down at the November, 1862, term at Milledgeville, aroused the wrath of Governor Brown and elicited some warm discussion in the General Assembly, then in session. Brown, opponent of conscription, declared that the ruling of the court had been "rendered under heavy outside pressure, and . . . under most peculiar circumstances."[44]

The case in issue had been started as a *habeas corpus* action brought by Asa O. Jeffers, conscript, against John Fair, enrolling officer, and had become a test case to determine the constitutionality of the conscription acts. Interest in the matter was high, and Jenkins read the decision of the court before a large audience in the Senate Chamber. His opinion was a long and able one. Not only did he analyze the conscription laws in relation to the Confederate Constitution, but he went back to the framing and adoption of the Federal Constitution to show that it was the intention of the Founding Fathers to grant such powers to Congress. Moreover, he quoted authorities to prove that the power to raise armies by conscription was essential to any government and inherent in its existence. Jenkins pointed out that the Confederate Constitution, with few exceptions, was "a liberal copy of the Constitution of the United States." Stating that "The experience that induced its adoption was our experience,"[45] he then launched into a long discussion of American history. The opinion is interesting as a dissertation on government, aside from its legal significance.

In the same manner, in others of the war cases, Jenkins took occasion to expound his theories on the philosophy of government.

The right to be exempt from conscription by providing a substitute, he explained, was not an absolute right nor a binding
contract, but was simply a "gratuitous privilege" extended by
Congress and subject to amendment at any time.[46] The legislature
could not divest itself or its successor of any power necessary to
the well-being of the state, he declared later. Exemptions must
always be revocable, and an act repealing the previous system
was valid and constitutional.[47]

The various exemptions provided in the conscription acts were
the source of much litigation. Occupational exemptions, exemptions by substitute, exemptions because of age and disability —
every possible loophole was seized by men trying desperately to
avoid conscription into the Confederate army. Many of these cases
reached the Supreme Court of Georgia. Judging from the opinions
written by Jenkins, that body was consistent in a strict construction
of the enrollment acts.

This attitude of the court in upholding the right of the general
government to compel service in the army was exercised also in
favor of the state in its power to enlist members in the state
militia. The court ruled that the exempting clause of the conscription act relieved only from service in the Confederate army,
and that persons exempted under that act were still subject to
military service exacted by the state of Georgia. Here Jenkins
summarized once again his conclusions regarding the power of
the government in such matters and added a dissertation on the
safeguards that had been provided in the Confederate Constitution against the abuse of such power.[48]

On another occasion Jenkins emphatically affirmed the right
of judges and other magistrates of the state to issue writs of *habeas
corpus* and to adjudicate cases arising under the enrolling acts of
the Confederate Congress.[49] This time he seized the occasion for
a scholarly discussion of the question of sovereignty. Again, in a
case involving the impressment of supplies, Jenkins declared that
while impressment in itself was constitutional, under the power
of eminent domain, the particular act in question was invalid in
that it failed to provide for just compensation. Here the jurist
moved into the field of economics to demonstrate why the system
of appraisement set up by Congress could not operate to insure
just compensation.[50]

The 138 decisions written by Jenkins attest to his learning. His
wide use of authorities, his evident grasp of the significance of

historical details, his smooth and expressive style all mark him as a scholar of the first rank. In analyzing the decisions handed down by the Augusta jurist, it seems apparent that he depended more upon logic than upon precedent in developing his opinions. While he aptly cited precedents on occasion, many of his opinions were based upon reasoning alone with no mention of specific cases. On the other hand, he frequently cited acts of the legislature or of Congress, and made extensive use of authorities. Evidently he was thoroughly familiar with the English common law. Where cases were cited, they were in many instances English cases, and he was very free in his reference to such figures as "Lord Eldon," "Lord Hardwick," and "Mr. Calvert, of the Inner Temple." In the war cases especially, he leaned heavily upon the lessons of history, integrating the Constitution of the Confederacy with that of the United States.

While Jenkins was removed from active participation in politics during his service on the Supreme Court, he was not removed entirely from public affairs. When it became apparent late in 1860 that Georgia must soon take some action on the question of secession, the Committee Upon the State of the Republic of the General Assembly requested a group of the leading men of the state to meet and recommend a line of policy for the legislature. Jenkins was named to this group, along with Brown, Toombs, the Stephens brothers, T. R. R. Cobb, Herschel V. Johnson, and a few others.[51]

When the secession convention met in January, 1861, Jenkins was not a delegate, but, along with the other justices of the Supreme Court, the judges of the superior courts, Governor Brown and Howell Cobb, he was invited to a seat on the floor.[52] Though Jenkins consistently maintained the right of secession for substantial cause, he was of the opinion that Georgia and the other Southern states, before withdrawing from the union, should wait for some overt act committed by the Lincoln administration. "When, however, Georgia passed her ordinance of secession, he recognized the fact that his supreme allegiance was due to her; and during the long and painful struggle which ensued, he wavered not in his devotion to State and Confederacy."[53]

The fact that Jenkins, as a justice of the Supreme Court, was not actively identified with the war effort in Georgia put him in position in 1865 to help the state when she most needed his help. At the close of the war many of the state's leaders were excluded from participation in public affairs. Georgia, with the rest of the South, had suffered losses which left her bruised and bleeding, and she had no alternative except to conform to the conditions set by President Andrew Johnson as requirements for restoration to the union.

The first steps toward such restoration were the appointment of a provisional governor, James Johnson of Columbus, and the setting of a date for a convention to draft a new constitution to comply with the President's requirements. In order to be eligible to vote for delegates to the convention, citizens must take the amnesty oath prescribed by the President. Between fifteen and twenty thousand Georgians were excepted from voluntary amnesty, either because of having held high civil or military office, or because of being worth more than $20,000. Jenkins was among those who were required to seek individual pardons from the President. He did so and urged others to qualify to take part in the election of delegates to the convention.[54]

The group of men who gathered in Milledgeville for the convention late in October had little resemblance to the famous convention of 1861, which has been described as "without doubt the most distinguished body of men which had ever assembled in Georgia."[55] Most of the state's outstanding prewar leaders were ineligible for membership, and the delegates were mainly "insignificant men who were not prominent either before or after 1865 . . . mostly old men, with a conspicuous lack of prominent men and rising politicians."[56] On the whole, the convention represented those who had opposed secession in 1861, but few of them had been thorough-going Unionists during the war.

Standing head and shoulders above the other delegates were Jenkins and Herschel V. Johnson, and between them they dominated the convention. Both men had opposed secession in 1861, but both had gone with the state and had served the cause during the war. Once more the old rivals of 1853 were brought together, as Johnson was elected president of the convention and Jenkins was named chairman of a committee of sixteen charged with the responsibility of reporting business for the convention.

In commenting on these developments, the editor of the Macon *Telegraph* wrote: "On the floor, Judge JENKINS will be of eminently more service, than he could possibly have been in the chair. Able, calm, dispassionate, energetic, his opinions and efforts will undoubtedly contribute largely to the harmony and wisdom of the convention, and consequently to the public good."[57]

Writing fifteen years later, Avery said: "The unquestioned leader of the convention was Judge Charles J. Jenkins, upon whose clear judgment and crystal honesty, the members reposed with an unreserved trust."[58]

Among the requirements set by the President for the restoration of a state to the union were the freeing of slaves, the repeal of the secession ordinance, and the repudiation of war debts. All of these were unpopular moves in Georgia, but the first two were already accomplished facts, and the convention had little difficulty in agreeing to conform. The repudiation of the war debt, however, was vigorously opposed, both in the convention and in the newspapers of the state. Jenkins refused to report the ordinance out of the committee and moved that the new constitution be adopted without this provision. This was done, but in the meanwhile the provisional governor appealed to high officials in Washington for instruction in the matter. The reply from Secretary of State William H. Seward left no doubt that the debts must be repudiated. Finally and reluctantly, on the last afternoon of the convention, the delegates passed the ordinance, 135 to 117, with Jenkins voting nay.[59]

On November 15, one week after the close of the convention, state officers were elected under the newly adopted constitution. There was no party organization and apparently no formal nomination, but Jenkins was elected governor with little opposition.[60] In 1853 there had been some question as to whether he was running as a Whig or a Constitutional Unionist. Now he was simply the people's candidate, with no party labels attached. He was safe and conservative, a tower of strength in a world that had fallen to pieces. Of his integrity and ability there could be no doubt, and his loyalty to the state had been proven many times over a period of thirty-five years in the public eye.

After some delay, while waiting upon recognition of his authority by officials in Washington, Jenkins was inaugurated on December 14. There was a thrill of joy throughout the state, in the mistaken belief that Reconstruction was over. "The cherished end seemed at last in sight, and the travail of a painful reconstruction gloriously ended."[61]

The people of Georgia were soon disillusioned, for Reconstruction was not over after all. The troops were not removed; the Freedmen's Bureau continued its control over the Negroes;

the senators and representatives elected in Georgia were rejected by Congress. But even with all these impediments, the state made great strides toward recovery in the year 1866.

Among the greatest problems facing the new administration were the impoverished condition of the state government, the destitution of thousands of individuals, especially in the areas that had been fought over, the many difficulties proceeding from the emancipation of the Negroes, and the lawlessness that had developed during the time when the state had no settled government.

When Jenkins took office the treasury was empty and there was a bonded indebtedness of more than half a million dollars and other debts amounting to another half million. No taxes had been collected for the preceding year, and there was literally no money. Fortunately Jenkins was thoroughly familiar with financial operations and was able not only to propose remedies but to take an active part in working them out. That he grappled personally with the problem is seen in a letter to a friend, where he made this comment: "I have by hard scuffling paid off the legislature."[62]

Jenkins was a man of means with influential contacts, and he worked continually to strengthen the credit of the state and to secure more favorable terms on loans than the market was at first inclined to grant. By the end of his administration the immediate crisis had passed, and there was money in the treasury. The state railroad, which had been almost unusable, had been renovated and put into successful operation, and other state properties had been repaired and refitted.

Economic and racial problems were being gradually resolved by his administration, and there seems every reason to believe that the state would have continued its march toward recovery had it been permitted to do so, free from political interference. But the Radical Republicans in Congress were determined to prolong the suffering of the Southern states, and their ideas were gaining the ascendancy over the plan of restoration advocated by President Johnson.

The first warning of the impending storm was the refusal of Congress to seat the state's representatives. Next came the demand that Georgia ratify the fourteenth amendment. The governor's message to the General Assembly when it convened on November 1, 1866, included an analysis of the proposed amendment and a recommendation that the legislature refuse to ratify it.[63] He pointed out the inconsistency of Congress in demanding that Georgia, as a state, should ratify the amendment as a condition to its recognition as a state. He showed also the effect that each section of the amendment would have, demonstrating that it would affect the North scarcely at all while it could ruin the South. Following his advice the General Assembly refused ratification, unanimously in the Senate and with only two dissenting votes in the House.

Up to this time Jenkins had consistently advised the people of Georgia to avoid conflict with federal authorities and to conform patiently to their demands, in the belief that a conciliatory attitude would speed the work of restoration. Apparently, however, he was outraged at the attempt to force the fourteenth amendment upon the people of the South. He defied the government in this instance, and thereafter his attitude stiffened noticeably.

A few months later, in March, 1867, when Congress passed the first of the Reconstruction Acts, placing the South under military rule and providing for Negro suffrage, Jenkins was convinced that the law was unconstitutional and hastened to Washington to file a suit in the Supreme Court. In Washington he secured some of the best legal talent in the country as counsel and initiated the case of *Georgia v. Stanton*.[64] The bill asked relief by a temporary injunction from all proceedings under the Reconstruction Acts, with a permanent injunction to follow final adjudication. The Supreme Court refused to take jurisdiction on the ground that the matter was a political one, involving neither interference nor threat of interference with property.[65]

While in Washington Governor Jenkins issued an address to the people of Georgia, counseling them to take no action under the military laws until their legality could be decided. On his return to Georgia he was reprimanded sharply by General John Pope, who had been placed in command of the military district of which Georgia was a part. Pope gave all civil officers of the state to understand that their authority was merely provisional, and that Georgia laws held only until overruled by military orders. Late in December, Pope, who had become extremely unpopular in the state, was replaced by General George Meade. Meade was a Democrat, and the people of Georgia hoped for better treatment at his hands. Before he took command, how-

ever, a situation had already developed which made inevitable
a clash of authority.

In accordance with the Reconstruction Acts, Pope had ordered
an election for a convention to draft a new constitution which
should incorporate the substance of the fourteenth amendment
and provide for Negro suffrage. The election, held late in October, was extended over five days to allow all the Negroes time
to vote. As might have been expected, the delegates chosen were
mainly scalawags, with a sprinkling of carpetbaggers and Negroes
and only about a dozen conservative whites.[66] Convening in
Atlanta in December, 1867, the delegates soon found themselves
without means of subsistence. Unable to secure credit, they
"turned their longing eyes upon the treasury of the state,"[67] and
passed an ordinance directing the state treasurer to pay $40,000
to defray the current costs of the convention. Treasurer John
Jones refused to do this without a warrant from the governor.
Such a warrant Jenkins would not issue. First, said he, the
Constitution of Georgia forbade him to issue an executive warrant for funds except when authorized to do so by an act of the
legislature. Second, it was not the responsibility of the state to
finance this convention called by the federal government.

General Meade tried to reason with Jenkins in the matter, but
the governor was adamant in his refusal to issue the warrant. After
his final and official refusal, he was removed from office on January 13, 1868, and was replaced by General Thomas H. Ruger,
who soon presented himself in Milledgeville to assume the duties
of office. Upon learning of Ruger's mission, Jenkins asked whether
he had been instructed, if necessary, to use force to dispossess him
of the office. Ruger replied that he had, and showed the governor
his orders to that effect. "Well, sir," responded Jenkins, "you have
the army of the United States at your back, and I can summon
not even a respectable police force. I therefore elect to bow out
to you, rather than to a file of soldiers with muskets and bayonets,
but I denounce this proceeding as an outrage upon the rights of
the State; and, had I adequate force, I would resist you to the
last extremity."[68]

At this time Governor Jenkins was confined to his house on
crutches as the result of a recent severe fall, and Ruger courteously
placed the executive mansion at his disposal. Jenkins remained
there, however, only long enough to arrange his affairs, and then
left for his home in Augusta. The night before his departure from

Milledgeville, the citizens, in torchlight procession, gathered at the mansion to express their respect and admiration for the staunch old statesman and their indignation at his ouster. He responded in a farewell address, "replete with dignity, emotion, affection, and eloquence."[69]

Before he left Milledgeville, Jenkins took the seal of the executive department of Georgia, executive records of his term of office, and some $400,000 of the state's money, to place them where they would not fall into the hands of the usurper. The money was deposited in a New York bank, and the seals and records were hidden until 1872 when the carpetbag regime was over in Georgia and the people regained control of their own government.[70]

After Jenkins was removed from office, he went again to Washington to seek redress from the Supreme Court. Since an actual seizure of property was now involved, he believed that the court could not refuse to take jurisdiction, in accordance with its own ruling of the preceding year. But a consideration of the case would involve the constitutionality of the entire congressional program of reconstruction, and the court was obviously reluctant to act. After a series of delays, Jenkins was informed that the term of the court was too near an end to permit it to hear and determine the motion for an injunction. Before the next term the damage had already been done in Georgia. The convention had finished its work; the new constitution had been adopted; Ruger and Meade were gone from the scene; and "Bullock and his hungry hordes" were in control. Jenkins had lost his last chance to fight the usurpers by constitutional means, and reluctantly he gave up the unequal contest.[71]

After his failure with the Supreme Court Jenkins spent the next few years away from Georgia, traveling in Europe for about half of the period. Late in 1870 he came home to stay.

At about this time the conservative whites were coming back into power in Georgia. The legislature that met in November, 1871, had a large Democratic majority in both houses, and in January, 1872, James M. Smith, a Democrat, became governor. Bullock, fearing impeachment, had resigned and left the state. Considering Smith the first legally elected governor since his own dismissal, Jenkins promptly turned over to him the executive documents, the seal, and a long and detailed report on his administration, especially on the events which had led up to his replacement. This report was in turn transmitted by Smith to the legislature. The General Assembly passed a resolution of gratitude for Jenkins's action and presented to him in the name of the people of Georgia a seal wrought in gold, a facsimile of the one preserved and restored by him. On the reverse side it had this inscription: "Presented to Charles J. Jenkins by the State of Georgia. *In Arduis Fidelis.*"[72]

Jenkins never held another elective office after his retirement from the governorship. He continued, however, to serve as a member of the Board of Trustees of the University of Georgia. Appointed to the board in 1839, he remained a member until shortly before his death in 1883.[73] He was unanimously elected president of the board at the annual meeting on July 28, 1871.[74] One of the first duties of the board under Jenkins was to effect the establishment of an agricultural and mechanical school under the terms of the land grant made by Congress in 1862. Jenkins called a meeting of the trustees on March 30, 1872, to adopt plans.[75]

Jenkins's last service in the political field was as president of the Constitutional Convention of 1877. Elected as a delegate from the eighteenth senatorial district, he was by acclamation named president of the body.[76]

After Jenkins's return to Augusta in 1870, he resumed his practice of law for a time. Twice in his later years he was persuaded to enter business for short periods, once as president of the Merchants' & Planters' Bank and again as temporary president of an Augusta factory. He spent his last years in retirement at Summerville, a little village near Augusta. His wife and only child had preceded him in death. After a long illness he died on June 14, 1883, acclaimed as the leading citizen of Augusta and one of the truly great men of Georgia. The funeral was held from St. Paul's Episcopal Church. An Augusta correspondent, writing for the Atlanta *Weekly Constitution,* predicted that it would "probably be the largest ever seen in the city, as the whole community entertained the most profound love and veneration for him."[77]

In evaluating any figure in history, it is necessary to remember that eulogies are sometimes misleading, and that a partisan press is not wholly to be trusted. In the case of Charles J. Jenkins, Jr., however, the reader cannot fail to be impressed with the tone of the praise accorded to him. This is particularly noticeable in the writings of the men who lived at the same time and who had personal contact with Jenkins. Several Georgia historians knew him well. Avery, who was not always kind to his contemporaries, referred to him as "the noble Jenkins." To Fielder, he was "the great good man." Jones termed him "the noblest Roman of them all." All of them stressed the purity of thought and action that characterized the man and the great affection and respect in which he was held. Similar comments appeared many times in contemporary newspapers, in those opposed to Jenkins politically as well as in those which supported his party.

In announcing the death of the Augusta statesman, the Atlanta *Weekly Constitution* gave four columns on its first page to his obituary and published it under this head:

CHARLES J. JENKINS

The Death of Georgia's Greatest Governor.[78]

Henry McDaniel, governor at the time, in issuing orders to close the executive offices for the day out of respect for Jenkins, said simply: "His long and useful public service was without a stain. . . . His memory is a priceless heritage of the state."[79]

CHARLES COLCOCK JONES, JR.
AND PAUL HAMILTON HAYNE

BY CLAUD B. GREEN

IN 1877 Charles Colcock Jones, Jr., after a residence of almost twelve years in New York City, returned to his native state of Georgia, settled in Augusta, and lived there until his death on July 19, 1893.[1] Born on October 28, 1831, in Savannah, where his father was pastor of the First Presbyterian Church, Jones was reared in Liberty County. Here the elder Jones, a wealthy planter, owned two separate plantations, one on the mainland called Montevideo and used for a winter home and another on Colonel's Island named Maybank, which was the family's summer residence.[2] Young Jones, the son of intellectual parents (his father and mother had read together Jonathan Edwards's *On the Will* during their honeymoon),[3] received his early education at home, attended South Carolina College for two years, and was graduated with the A. B. degree from the College of New Jersey at Princeton in 1852. Upon his graduation from the Harvard Law School in 1855, he was admitted to the bar in Savannah and became a partner in a law firm which included Henry Rootes Jackson.

Neither the law, however, nor any other single profession or hobby could circumscribe all of Jones's varied interests and versatile talents. In 1859 he was elected an alderman of Savannah, and the following year, without solicitation on his part, was nominated and elected mayor. He had found time, also in 1859, to prepare and deliver an address before the Georgia Historical Society published under the title *Indian Remains in Southern Georgia*. During this same period he was probably engaged in other historical research, for in 1861 he published *Monumental*

Claud Green is a member of the English faculty at Clemson College.

Remains of Georgia.[4] At about this time Jones also delivered one
of the first and most ardent pleas made for secession in Savannah.
By his thirtieth birthday, then, he had already established a
reputation as a lawyer, a politician, a historian, and an orator.
Soon he was to add that of a soldier, and after the Civil War he
would become known, also, as a collector, an archaeologist, an
anthropologist, and a defender of the philosophical views for
which the South had fought in the recent struggle between the
sections.[5] In all of these roles, Jones largely directed his energies
toward the study of his native state and the region of which it
was a part.

During the war he served with the Chatham Artillery, in the
beginning as senior first lieutenant and later as lieutenant
colonel. In December, 1865, after he had done perhaps all that
he could at the moment for the defeated Confederacy, Jones
moved to New York and set up a law practice.[6] Here the law was
no greater taskmaster than it had been in Savannah, and the
transplanted Georgian spent much of his time in historical research, making historical addresses, which were usually reprinted
as pamphlets, and sending copies of these reprints to friends and
literary acquaintances throughout the country. In 1870, for instance, Charles W. Eliot on behalf of the Harvard College Library,
O. W. Holmes, H. W. Longfellow, and G. W. J. DeRenne all had
occasion to thank Jones for copies of his *Reminiscences of the Last
Days of General Henry Lee.* It was in 1873, while he was still
residing in New York, that Jones published his *Antiquities of the
Southern Indians, Particularly of the Georgia Tribes.*

The choice of Augusta rather than his native city of Savannah
as his residence, when he returned to Georgia in 1877, was surely
influenced by the fact that the second Mrs. Jones, whom he had
married in 1863, was Eva Berrien Eve of Augusta. At Montrose
in the village of Summerville, situated in the Sand Hills just outside Augusta, the Jones family now made a permanent home. In
the mornings Jones would go to his law office in the city, and in
the evenings he would return to his books and his writing. He
immediately began to take an active part in the civic and social
life of Augusta, and he continued his flow of letters to correspondents all over the nation.

The first communication between Jones and Paul Hamilton
Hayne, who was then living at Copse Hill, Groveton, which was
near Augusta, was a brief letter which Jones addressed to Hayne

on July 20, 1877, asking for Hayne's autograph. The two-sentence letter reads: "I would be very glad to have your autograph for my Georgia portfolio. Will you pardon me for asking this favor of you?"[7] Thus was inaugurated a friendship which continued until Hayne's death in 1886. During their period of residence near Augusta, the two men were undoubtedly the outstanding literary figures of the vicinity. Their affection and esteem for each other deepened as they became better acquainted. Hayne sought advice from Jones about business matters, and on at least two occasions, the centennial of the Battle of King's Mountain and the sesquicentennial of the founding of Georgia, he asked Jones to recite the odes which he had especially composed for those celebrations. Of approximately the same age and disposed to see many matters in the same light, particularly the contrasting philosophies which seemed to animate the Old and the New South, Jones and Hayne enjoyed the exchange of ideas and opinions.

Not only ideas but publications and advice also were exchanged. On March 14, 1878, Jones thanked the author for the copy of his poem in aid of the Simms Memorial Fund. Two months later, on May 15, Jones mailed Hayne a copy of his *History of the Dead Towns of Georgia,* a publication printed at the expense of G. W. J. DeRenne and issued as the fourth volume in the *Collections of the Georgia Historical Society.* In mid-October Jones invited Hayne to visit him if the Haynes came into town on the thirty-first for the unveiling of the Confederate monument erected by the ladies of Augusta.[8]

Early in the new year (January 5) Jones replied to Hayne's letter of December 30 that he would inquire about Hayne's City of Augusta Bond, adding "My impression is it would not be wise for you at the moment to press for a sale." In November of the same year (1879), after a summer abroad, Jones again wrote Hayne about his finances: "In regard to the investment, I know of nothing at present more desirable than 6% bonds of the Georgia Rail Road and Banking Company. They can be purchased at about par, and I regard them as entirely safe. Should I hear of anything more advantageous I will advise you. Do not hesitate to command me at all times, and we are looking forward to a visit from Mrs. Hayne and yourself."[9]

Hayne not only relied upon Jones for financial advice, but he also called upon him to render a more personal service. The committee arranging for the observance on October 7, 1880, of the

centennial of the Battle of King's Mountain had invited Hayne
to write an ode for the occasion and to deliver it himself. Hayne
wrote the poem, but decided that his frail health would not permit
him to be present. In August he requested Jones to make the trip
to King's Mountain and recite the poem for him. Jones replied
that no one could read the poem so well as its author and that he
still hoped Hayne would "have strength for the occasion and
gladden the hearts of all by your presence and personal utterance.
Should it so chance, however, that you are unable to attend, and
I can comply with your request, it will afford me genuine pleasure
to do so."[10]

All through September the two men were in correspondence
about the poem, Jones's rendering of it, and the details of the
trip to King's Mountain. Late in the month Jones wrote Hayne
that he was more and more charmed with the ode, and believed
that he was prepared to render it with becoming effect. Two days
after the celebration at King's Mountain, Jones, who had been
accompanied on the trip by Hayne's son, William, wrote the
author that his poem had been complimented to the echo, and
enclosed a copy of the remarks introductory to the recitation in
which he had praised Hayne very highly and regretted that he
could not be present because of depressing illness. For the manuscript copy of the "King's Mountain Centennial Ode," Jones was
grateful and so expressed himself to the author within less than
a week after the North Carolina celebration.

The King's Mountain ceremony was one of numerous demonstrations of the early 1880's commemorating famous Revolutionary War battles. For the centennial celebration at Yorktown,
Hayne wrote another poem. On November 3, 1881, Jones complimented this ode, and asked Hayne's help in securing autographed letters of Arthur Middleton, Thomas Lynch, Jr., and
Thomas Heyward, Jr., for the collection of autographs of signers
of the Declaration of Independence which Jones was acquiring.

A week later Hayne replied:

I am gratified by what you say of *The Yorktown* lyric. It seems to
have suited the occasion; altho—*Entre nous*—, I would not give my
"King's Mt." ballad for 20 such odes! I had room and opportunity in
the former, you see, for *dramatic verve*, and vivid picturesque description.

You speak of everything being "dull and stupid in Augusta." Barring
the frequent *business* activity of the little town, (for which she deserves all credit), *don't* you think that the state of things you mention

is, (in any high *intellectual* sense), the normal condition of that "burgh"? "Speak it not in Gath, however, whisper it not in the streets of Askalon!"—or . . . I should be "stoned"; at least "tarred and feathered" upon my next visit to the Augustinian *locale.*

Hayne's preference for his King's Mountain poem and his frank opinion of Augusta were both shared by Jones and recorded in a prompt response:

Yes, excellent and appropriate as is your Yorktown Ode, I cannot resist the impression that it pales before your *King's Mountain Ballad.* The latter was an inspiration, and has the ring of immortality about it. Edgeworth, my son, declaimed it, before the Academy in Summerville on last Friday. It has taken firm possession of him, and I freely confess the oftener I read it the more thoroughly do its beauties and excellencies grow upon my appreciation. It will live long after you have ascended to the stars. We will not disagree about the intellectual lethargy of this little manufacturing and grocery-selling town. It is tedious and slow to the last degree. I turn with delight, each evening, to my little Home Circle and library on the Hill. Latterly too, the Authorities here have been daft upon the subject of racing after itinerant Yankees intent upon a free lunch and all at the public charge. This furnishing of free passes upon railways, free rides in hired carriages, free champagne, and free dinners, to a parcel of duffers, and all at the expense of the city treasury, is without warrant of law; and, as old Sconyers would say, *to all decent minded people natally disgustin'.*

During 1882 both Hayne and Jones were busy with their writing. An illustrated edition of Hayne's collected poems was issued under the Lothrop imprint, and Jones completed the two volumes of his general history of Georgia, which came from the press the following year.[11]

Toward the end of 1882 Georgians were preparing to observe in February, 1883, the one hundred and fiftieth anniversary of General Oglethorpe's landing at Savannah. A sesquicentennial general committee had been formed with Henry Rootes Jackson as its president and W. S. Bogart as one of its members. On December 20, 1882, Bogart invited Hayne to compose and read an ode for the occasion. At first Hayne declined, giving his poor health as a reason, and Bogart wrote him again on December 27 that Jackson expressed great regret at Hayne's declining.

Word of Hayne's refusal apparently drifted out to a few strategically placed individuals, for on December 28, 1882, Jones wrote Hayne urging that he reconsider his decision and adding that "we would all be delighted if you would attune your harp for this brave song." Then, on January 2, 1883, Governor Alexander H. Stephens added his voice to those entreating Hayne to compose the poem. Stephens wrote: "I trust you will reconsider the matter of the poem on the celebration of the birthday of Georgia, on the 12th of February. I undertook to deliver an address on that occasion with much misgivings. I do trust that my health and strength will enable me to meet the engagement — and be assured it will add much to my pleasure to meet you on that occasion, as one of the contributors, to the honor and fame of our beloved Commonwealth."

Even before Governor Stephens's entreaty reached him, Hayne had begun to reconsider. Writing Jones on December 29, he told him of the committee's invitation to write the poem, of his refusal because of chronic ill health, and of the committee's efforts to have him reconsider. He also revealed that he would probably write the poem after all, and asked for a copy of the historian's pamphlet on the settlement of Savannah. Expressing regret that Jones's history of Georgia was not yet in print, he blasted the Georgia legislature for refusing to subsidize its publication.[12]

A few days after confiding in Jones, Hayne informed the sesquicentennial committee that he would write the poem, and on January 4, 1883, he received a letter from Bogart expressing pleasure that the poet had reconsidered and notifying him that he was free to choose his subject, that his expenses to Savannah would be paid, and that there would be a fee for the ode. Bogart also mentioned that he was glad Jones would read the poem, for Jackson would have other duties that might conflict should he be asked to read it.

Hayne had probably communicated his decision to write the poem to Jones at the time he notified the committee, for on the day he heard from Bogart he also received a letter from Jones, who advised: "Duplicate your *King's Mountain Ode* and you will add to your immortality. In all matters of this sort, you are felicitous to the last degree. I have said to the gentlemen of the committee that I would entreat you to respond, no one can fill your place. There is enough in the event to enlist your earnest effort. Do not forget to let the aged Mico—*Tomo-chi-chi,*—the earliest and most potent friend the colonists had among the Red Men,—come in for a full share of the colouring in the picture you paint."

Hayne having finally been persuaded to write the poem for the occasion, the plans of the sesquicentennial committee seemed to be working out smoothly enough. There was only one other contingency that needed attention. Even though Governor Stephens had agreed to make the principal address, the committee well knew that the condition of the governor's health might prevent his being present. How could the committee insure that there would be an orator for the occasion if Stephens found it impossible to appear? Bogart, who apparently handled much of the committee's correspondence, attempted to meet this eventuality by inviting Jones to be the principal speaker if Stephens could not come. To this overture from Bogart, Jones replied rather coolly on January 10 that he thought it was "asking rather too much of me to undertake the preparation of the Sesqui-Centennial Address upon the bare chance that Mr. Stephens,—the selected orator of the occasion,—may possibly be prevented from keeping his appointment." Jones also suggested that if Hayne should be unable to recite his poem General Jackson might be asked to undertake the task.

Doubtless unaware of the correspondence between Jones and Bogart about the possibility of Jones substituting for Stephens as the principal orator, Hayne asked Jones in mid-January to recite his poem for him. (When Hayne had written Bogart some two weeks earlier that Jones would read the poem for him, he had at that time apparently not actually asked Jones whether he would do it.) To this request from Hayne, Jones promptly replied (January 18) that it would not be in his power to comply. Surprised by Jones's refusal, Hayne communicated his surprise to Jackson, who after conferring with Bogart replied on January 22:

I have again communicated with Mr. Bogart as to the recital of the Ode; & he gives a construction to the words used by Col. Jones in his note to yourself which I submit for consideration.

It appears that Mr. B. & the Col. have been in correspondence as to the possibility of Gov. Stephens being physically unable to make the Address; in which event the Committee will turn to Col. Jones. Upon comparing dates we ascertain that at the time the Col. wrote to you, he may have been under the impression that the "outlook" seemed to assign him to the position of the Orator of the day. This idea was probably dispelled by a later note from Mr. Bogart.

Suppose we enter into the following understanding. If Col. Jones be called upon to take the Gov.'s place as Orator, I will take his place

as reciter. If the uncertainty on his part arise from some other cause
&, he shall still hestitate, then I will accept.

In the absence of the complete correspondence of all those
involved, it is difficult to be sure why Jones refused Hayne's request to recite his "Sesqui-Cenntennial Ode." It may be that
Jones was displeased because he had not been asked in the first
place to make one of the principal addresses on the program.
And lacking a major role, he may have been determined not to
play a minor one by reading another's poem for him. It may be
that, in the early stages, Jones had really been deceived into
thinking that he would be called upon for a major address. In
the light of his letter to Bogart of January 10, it seems unlikely
that Jones was preparing, if not hoping, to take Stephens's place
if the governor failed to appear. In any event the cordial relationship between Jones and Hayne suffered little, if any, change.
On January 19, the historian wrote the poet that he was "entirely right in selecting Genl. Jackson to recite it in case you
find yourself too weak to attempt its utterance before a large
audience. That he should do so appears most appropriate, he
being not only the President of the Georgia Historical Society,
but a poet and orator of high repute." A few days later, on
January 25, Jones congratulated Hayne upon having secured
Jackson's service in reading the ode.

The Savannah *Weekly News* of February 17, 1883, described
the sesquicentennial celebration, which had taken place on the
previous Monday, February 12.[13] At the indoor exercises in the
morning Jackson presided and introduced Governor Stephens,
who "seated in his chair, was rolled to the front of the stage in
full view of the immense audience, amid cheers and enthusiastic
applause" and delivered his address. At the conclusion of Stephens's speech, Jackson, using the gracious oratory of his day,
prefaced his recitation of Hayne's poem with the following remarks:

By special request of the poet, himself too feeble in health to undertake the task, I will now undertake to recite his beautiful Ode. Sure
I am that the defects of the reader cannot wholly destroy the music
of his numbers; and that, as they shall fall upon the listening ear,
a heartborn inspiration will ascend to gracious Heaven that long may
be spared to the saddened South by far the sweetest of all her singers.
For, born in South Carolina, by Georgia adopted, Paul Hamilton
Hayne belongs, at last, to the South, Poet of the South, laureate by
royal power of his own genius.

Hayne was seated on the stage during the exercises, and that afternoon at the annual meeting of the Georgia Historical Society both he and Stephens were unanimously elected honorary members.

Both Stephens in his speech and Hayne in his poem spoke favorably about the role of Tomo-chi-chi in the settlement of Georgia. In his emphasis on the part which the Indian had played in the early history of the colony, Hayne was influenced by a pamphlet which Jones had published in 1868 entitled *Historical Sketch of Tomo-chi-chi, Mico of The Yamacraws*. In Hayne's personal copy of the sketch, sent to him by Jones, lines of poetry in Hayne's handwriting are scribbled on the front and back fly leaves.[14] Some of these lines were incorporated into the "Sesqui-Centennial Ode." Others were not used. Jones, of course, in his letter of January 4, 1883, had urged Hayne to give Tomo-chi-chi a prominent part in the poem.

Apart from its initial appearance in the newspaper reports of the sesquicentennial celebration, Hayne's ode was not published separately until 1885, when it was issued as a twelve-page pamphlet. On November 7, 1885, Jones thanked Hayne for the copy of the "Sesqui-Centennial Ode" which he had received. Jones might well have been especially pleased, for his friend had made a very flattering reference to him in the preface. The poet, thinking now more about Oglethorpe than of Tomo-chi-chi, wrote:

A special purpose of the Poem is to portray the life and character of Oglethorpe, an adventurer, hero, and Christian gentleman, who, in the loftiness of his nature and the philanthropic scope of his aims, has hardly been appreciated by the orthodox historians, excepting always that equally profound and brilliant annalist of Georgia, Col. Charles Colcock Jones.

Oglethorpe's combination of somewhat contradictory qualities, the courage of the soldier and ambition of the man of affairs, with the tenderness of the humanitarian, suggests a picture of heroism and purity as rare as it is fascinating.

The best part of Hayne's poem, however, is not his portrayal of the characters of Oglethorpe and Tomo-chi-chi or his account of the founding of the colony, but his tribute at the end of the poem to Georgia, his second mother. Here he achieves a lyric grace and sincerity which add considerably to the total effect of the ode. As the "Sesqui-Centennial Ode" is one of Hayne's uncollected poems it will not be amiss to quote in full the concluding section, which is the apostrophe to Hayne's adopted state:

GEORGIA! MY SECOND MOTHER! . . . vast the debt
Of deep, unsullied reverence that is thine;—
Hast thou not given me bread and balm and wine?—
The bread and balm of Comfort, and *that* wine,
Strong wine from mellowed grapes of *Eschol* wrought,
Grown on the sunniest hillside slopes of THOUGHT?

When my own Mother-Land, *first, last beloved,*
Writhing in shame and helpless anguish lay,—
Burdened by Hate, and ghastly with dismay,—
Struck down by hands of aliens, iron-gloved,—
And armored in the brazen mail of GREED,—
Robbed by the hireling Hound, and Traitor-knave,
Scourged by the Boor and throttled by the Slave,

When the marred grandeurs of her face august
Were darkened, and her fair locks trailed in dust,
While at her uttermost bitterness of need,—
Were none, it *seemed,* in earth or heaven to save;—
GEORGIA! MY SECOND MOTHER; on THY breast
The saddened exile found a couch of rest; —
I felt thy warm blood mount,—its pitying glow
In thy kind bosom thrill and throb below,—
And all thy heart's deep-tided overflow;—
So, by a smitten Life that thou did'st heal,—
A faltering will that slowly changed to steel,
Thro' some mysterious Charm that brooding fills
The stern recesses of thy lonely hills,
By fallen aims here buoyed and raised again,—
By weakness dowered with strength, joy born of pain;—
So, by unnumbered hours serene and high,
When thy grave sylvan Muses wandered nigh,—
So, by thy woods, thy waters, and thy skies,—
Thy winds that languish, and thy winds that rise,—
By all thy spring-tide ways that blush and bud,—
Thy summer splendours, purpling brain and blood,—
Lays of thy Pines, outbreathed in storm-swept might,—
Thy mock-bird's madness, and thine eagle's flight;—
So, by thy Dawns that flush, thine Eves that bloom,
By sacred ashes THOU hast given a tomb;
By wounded faiths, once more made hale and whole,—
By the strange quiet thou hast brought my soul;—
With all that Poet-tongue could sing or say,
Would I exalt thy loveliness to-day?—
But ah! this lyric fervor seems *so* pale!
The measure falters, and the numbers fail
That yearned to match FORDUSI'S nightingale;

> Thus, brave Protectress! at thy shining feet,
> Alas! alas! 'tis only mine to lay
> This simple wild-flower wreath of votive song!
> I know (how well) it does thy greatness wrong:—
> Still, oh Beloved! wilt Thou not lift it now,
> One moment to thy white, imperial brow?
> And if some glittering moisture here and there,
> The bay-leaf and the blossom chance to wear,—
> Pluck not the garland from thy stately head;—
> 'Tis but a few glad tears thy Poet shed,
> To keep his grateful offering pure and sweet!

Naturally Hayne was complimented by Georgians and other Southerners on his poem. From outside the South came one letter which delighted him. His friend, Professor Moses Coit Tyler of Cornell University, wrote on January 26, 1886, expressing his admiration of the poem, both for its intrinsic beauty and power and because Tyler admired Oglethorpe, to whom he directed the attention of his students every year as the one founder of an American colony who had a genius for blessing mankind and who had not yet been given his due place in history. Tyler assured Hayne that when he next came to the subject of Oglethorpe with his classes he would read to his students parts of Hayne's poem.

Writing to Jones on February 3, 1886, Hayne referred to Tyler's praise, and in the same letter expressed his opinion of Walt Whitman:

Are you acquainted with the work of this extraordinary creature. *"Walt Whitman,"* whom Stedman and other critics make such a fuss about? A nauseous maniac, *me judice,* fit only for the erotic ward of some lunatic asylum? He is the fellow who declares that the "sweat under his armpits is aroma sweeter than prayer."

Jones replied three days later:

Yes, I have seen some of the productions of *Walt Whitman,* and I freely confess I have no fancy either for the author or his effusions. In my judgement *he smells of the he goat,* and his utterances are uncivilized, misshapen, and often absolutely absurd. Heaven deliver us from such personal and poetical reputations. I think Mr. Stedman could be much better employed than in puffing such a specimen.

The discussion of Whitman was probably brought to a conclusion in Hayne's letter to Jones of February 14, 1886.[15] He wrote:

We agree concerning "Walt Whitman," I perceive!

To think that so colossal a "Humbug" should have "taken in" some of the genuine artists—*literary* artists—I mean, of G. Britain!!
What is the World coming to?

The following day, February 15, Jones acknowledged receipt of Hayne's letter, thanked him for the copy of Chancellor Andrew Adgate Lipscomb's tribute to the Savannah poem which he had sent, and discussed the Shakespeare-Bacon controversy to which Hayne had referred in a previous letter.[16] Jones wrote once again in 1886 to the Hayne family at Copse Hill, but this time, on July 25, the letter was addressed to Mrs. Paul H. Hayne and was a note sympathizing with her in the death of her husband. Four years later, on October 29, 1890, Jones expressed his appreciation to Mrs. Hayne for her note of sympathy upon the death of his wife.

One other activity of Jones, during his residence in Augusta, needs to be remembered. Beginning on Confederate Memorial Day, April 26, 1879, and continuing for the next fifteen years Jones addressed annually the Confederate Survivors' Association of Augusta. This group had been organized by some former Confederate soldiers on May 3, 1878.[17] At the meeting on Memorial Day in 1879, Jones made the address in the absence of the president; thereafter and until his death he served as both president and orator for the Memorial Day address.

For these speeches Jones chose a variety of topics — most of them dealing with battles and events of the Civil War. In all of them he sought to expound and defend the principles for which the South had fought. In two of them — "The Old South," delivered on April 26, 1887, and "Georgians During the War Between the States," given on April 26, 1889, — Jones compared and contrasted the South before 1860 with the South since the war, much to the disadvantage of the later period.[18] As a critique of the New South of the 1880's, which has some relevance to the South of today, and as an example of an old-fashioned type of Southern oratory at its best, excerpts from Jones's two addresses can be read with both profit and pleasure.

The address in 1887 followed one on the same topic, "The Old South," which Governor John B. Gordon delivered in the hall where the members had assembled. Gordon had said that he wanted to impress one thought upon his audience: "There is danger that the South may be inadequately represented, or wholly misrepresented in the future history of this country. Misrepresentation threatens the conquered always — the conqueror never."[19] The governor then went on to give a straightforward and rather able defence of the Old South. He pointed out that slavery was far from being an unmitigated evil and that its unfavorable aspects had been overemphasized and its beneficent results ignored. Gordon's entire address should be read again by those who feel, as some have seemed to feel, that he had completely surrendered to the charms of the "New Order."

Following the governor's address there was a parade to the Soldiers' Section in the city cemetery, and it was here that Jones gave his talk on "The Old South." He said in part:

We are saluted on every hand with eulogiums upon the New South, and with laudations of a new order of affairs. Far be it from me to undervalue or to gainsay this tide of prosperity, if such tide there be. Gladly would I behold this fair land blossoming as a garden of roses. Fain would I see each planter joyous and content beneath his own vine and fig tree. Fain would I have this native air vocal with the sounds of thrift and industry. Fain would I see prosperous railways dispersing the rich tributes of countless fields, the remunerative products of numberless manufactories. Fain would I see the bolts and bars withdrawn from the vaults of our rock-ribbed hills, and the treasures which they contain utilized for the general benefit. Fain would I see our rivers and harbors peopled with the sails of commerce. Gladly would I welcome every indication of genuine progress and substantial development. But, in the midst of such material growth, I would covet a remembrance and an observance of the patriotism, the purity, the manhood, the moderation, and the honesty of the days that are gone. I would still have this beloved South a peculiar people — peculiar in its conceptions and manifestations of propriety, of conservatism, of integrity, of honor towards God and man, of devotion to exalted womanhood. Heaven grant that this New South remain purged of all modern commercial methods. Heaven grant that it prove not the theatre of alien and demoralizing speculation — an arena wherein aggregated wealth may display its brazen power to the impairment of long-established values and the consummation of soulless, gainful consolidations.

Exalted in patriotism, brave in arms, wise in statesmanship, conservative in action, was that Old South which gave to the ages, as pledges of her principles and of her greatness, such men as Washington, and Jefferson, and Madison, and Henry, and Marshall, and Calhoun, and Jackson, and Lee. Alack the day when we fail to revere their memories, and to emulate the virtues inculcated by their lives and their acts. It was in the defense of home and principles dear to the hearts of these worthies that our fallen companions offered up their lives. In their names, my friends, and in the presence of their voiceful graves, do I exhort you, and those who have sprung and will descend from our loins, to a wholesome recognition and a becoming exhibition of the virtues which elevated their walk and conversation, and invested the true Southern character with the admirable elements of courtesy, hospitality, integrity, fair-mindedness, patriotism, and courage. Circumstances change, but the essentials of truth, justice, and manliness, are immutable. Upon the conservation of these distinguished traits of the Old South largely depend the honor of the present, and the hope of achieving for this land an enviable reputation in the sequent age.

In his address on "Georgians During the War Between the States," delivered before the Confederate Survivors' Association in 1889, Jones became even more specific in discussing the evils of the present:

In this epoch of commercial methods — of general and increasing poverty in the agricultural regions of the South — of absorption by foreign capital of favored localities, and of the creation in our midst of gigantic corporations intent upon self-aggrandizement, — in this era of manifest modification, if not actual obliteration of those sentiments and modes of thought and action which rendered us a peculiar people, — I call you to witness that there is a growing tendency to belittle the influences, the ways, the services, the lessons, and the characteristics of former years. I call you to witness that the moral and political standard of the present is not equal to that set up and zealously guarded by our fathers. I call you to witness that in the stern battle with poverty, — in the effort to retrieve lost fortunes, and in the attempt to amass large moneys by speculation, — in the commercial turn which the general thought and conduct have recently taken, — and in the struggle by shifts and questionable devices to outstrip the profits of legitimate ventures, there has occurred a lowering of the tone which marked our former manly, conservative, patriarchal civilization. I call you to witness that many have attempted and are now endeavouring by apologizing for the alleged short-comings of the past to stultify the record of the olden time, and by fawning upon the stranger to cast reproach upon the friend. I call you to witness that by false impressions and improper laudations of the new order of affairs, men in our midst have sought to minimize the capabilities of the past, and unduly to magnify the development of the present. I call you to witness that by adulation and fulsome entertainment of itinerant promoters and blatant schemers, seeking to inaugurate enterprises which are designed to benefit those only who are personally interested in them, the public has been sadly duped to its shame and loss. I call you to witness that the truest test of civilization lies not in the census, in the growth of cities, in railway combinations and the formation of Gargantuan trusts, in the expansion of manufactures, in the manipulation of land schemes and corporate securities, or in the aggregation of wealth, but in the mental, moral, political, and economic education and elevation of the population. I call you to witness that the present inclination to make one part of society inordinately affluent at the expense of the wretchedness and the unhappiness of the other, is in derogation of natural rights, impairing the equilibrium and disturbing the repose of the elements essential to the entity and the happiness of a great, honest, virtuous, and democratic nation. I call you to witness that a reign of plutocrats—a subjection of men, measures, and places to the will of millionaires and plethoric syndicates—is antagonistic to the liberty of the Republic and subversive of personal freedom. I call you to witness that this adoration of wealth —this bending the knee to the Golden Calf—this worship of mortals gifted with the Midas touch, savors of a sordid and debasing fetichism at variance with the spirit of true religion and emasculatory of all tokens of robust manhood. . . . Palsied be the Southern tongue which would speak disparagingly of a Confederate past, and withered be the Southern arm that refuses to lift itself in praise of the virtue and the valor which characterized the actors from the highest to the lowest, in a war not of "rebellion," but for the conservation of home, the maintenance of constitutional government and the supremacy of law, and the vindication of the natural rights of man.

Jones, like all of us at times, may have been propelled by his rhetoric and the occasion to overstate the case he was making in these two addresses, but there is no gainsaying that he was earnestly trying to say something that needed saying in his time and is not without its relevance to ours. In its efforts to regain some measure of economic well-being, the New South of the post-bellum period often seemed unduly and indiscriminately critical of anything identified with the old regime. It should be possible, Jones believed, to attract and utilize Northern wealth in rebuilding the shattered economy of the South without denying or being abjectly apologetic about the premises on which Southerners had fought the Civil War. Somewhere in the pursuit of capital there must be a point beyond which it would be impossible to go in the abandonment of principle and belief. Must the South in exchange for an economic assistance, which would certainly benefit those who gave as much as those who received it, confess that its previous philosophy and way of life had been in error and assume the entire guilt for bringing about a war which could have been avoided had the South been less stubbornly like itself and more wonderfully like the rest of the country? If this was to be the price, Jones, Paul Hamilton Hayne, and others felt that it was excessive and unthinkable. Surely, they reasoned, Southerners had a heritage which no amount of material aid should bring them to disavow. Even the mellifluous Henry Grady, who often seemed to be the chief spokesman for the opposing point of view, had not advocated that.

The views of those who were advocating the uncritical acceptance by the South of the materialistic standards of an industrial society were in the ascendency then, even as now. Jones, in proclaiming a contrary philosophy, was in a very real sense swimming upstream. He was opposing some of the most powerful currents in the development of nineteenth-century thought. Had he been less prominently identified with the "Lost Cause" and had his opinions been expressed before some group other than an assembly of Confederate veterans, Jones might have been listened to more respectfully and intelligently by outsiders. But, considering the indifferent success which Emerson had had in the North and Carlyle in England with the expression of somewhat similar views, that too is highly problematical.

HENRY BRADLEY PLANT

BY S. WALTER MARTIN

THE period between the Civil War and the end of the nineteenth century produced a number of railroad builders and developers in Georgia. Among the more prominent of these men was Henry Bradley Plant, a Connecticut Yankee, who came to Augusta, Georgia, in 1854 as a representative of the Adams Express Company, and by the time of his death in 1899 he had left his mark deeply imprinted on the economic life of Georgia and Florida.

Plant was born of Puritan stock in the little town of Branford, Connecticut, on October 27, 1819. The community in which he was born was as well known as the ancestry from which he came. Founded in 1644 as an offspring of the colony of New Haven, Branford was settled by some of the prominent followers of John Davenport. Plant's early ancestors left England about 1640, perhaps with the little company that came with John Davenport to America.[1]

Down through the years the Plants of Branford were a good lot of people. They were intelligent and industrious and in the main leaned toward farming for a livelihood. Henry's great grandfather on his father's side was a member of George Washington's Revolutionary Army, as was his great grandfather on his mother's side.[2] John Plant, the progenitor of the family, had been a faithful soldier in the war with the Narragansett Indians, and had received a grant of land from the Connecticut General Assembly as a reward for his services.[3] At various times during the colonial period other Plants helped to repel the Indians, and throughout these early years in America each generation of the family worked diligently for the interest of their new country.

S. Walter Martin, formerly Dean of the College of Arts and Sciences and member of the history faculty at the University of Georgia, is President of Emory University.

Henry Plant's father was Anderson Plant, son of Samuel and Lorana Beckwith Plant; and his mother was Betsey Bradley, daughter of Levi Bradley, all of Branford. Anderson Plant was a farmer of moderate circumstances but provided adequately for his family. He died of typhus fever when Henry was only six years old. The boy himself was stricken with the disease at the same time, and was not told of his father's death until he was well on the road to recovery. His sister too was claimed by the same disease and, like her father, did not survive. This double tragedy in the Plant family left Henry and his mother alone for a time. As a result, the mother and son became very close, and the influence she exerted on him endured throughout his lifetime. In time she was married to Philemon Hoadley of Martenburg, New York, and so Henry and his mother left their Branford home to be with her husband in New York. Shortly, however, Philemon Hoadley relocated in New Haven. Young Henry always considered Branford his home and visited his grandmother Plant there on numerous occasions. The boy became a favorite of his grandmother. She was a devout member of the Congregational Church, as were all the Plants. The story is told of how Henry liked to go to church with his grandmother on Sunday for she always carried a good lunch, which was eaten at the church house at the close of the morning services. After lunch the congregation would return to the church sanctuary, in the winter warmed only by the fervid sermons of the Puritan ministers, for another two hours of worship.[4]

The influence of the Congregational Church remained with young Plant throughout his lifetime. One minister in particular, Timothy P. Gillett, showed more than usual interest in the boy and his family and encouraged the youngster to prepare for Yale in hopes that he would eventually study for the ministry. Plant, however, was not the studious type and did not care for a college education even though his grandmother offered to pay his expenses at Yale.[5] His formal schooling was received in Branford and New Haven, and for a time he studied at a private academy. This was considered a fairly good education for that time. Restless and active, young Plant longed for the time when he could try his hand at some occupation. He made several unsuccessful attempts at one job and then another, but finally in 1837, at the age of 18, he found some employment much to his liking. It was with the New Haven Steamboat Company which ran an express line between New Haven and New York.[6] This was the beginning of a career that was eventually to bring the youth to Georgia.

Plant liked his job, and the captain of one of the boats, S. Bartlett Stone, took quite an interest in him. Henry was made captain's boy on the ship and for about five years traveled back and forth from New York to New Haven on a regular run. He often took his turn as a deck hand and also did other odd jobs. He was a thrifty fellow and usually turned most of his earnings over to his mother for safekeeping.[7] The company soon began to carry small packages from New Haven for delivery in New York. This small express venture quickly became a thriving business, and soon a large room on the boat was set aside to store and transport packages. Plant was placed in charge of the room, and the story goes that he was so conscientious about his work that he often slept there to protect the packages which had been placed in his care.[8]

During the time of his employment with the steamboat line, Plant met and courted Ellen Elizabeth Blackstone, a descendant of William Blackstone, an early settler of Boston. They were married in 1842. Two sons were born to this union, one who died in infancy, and Morton, who became a business associate of his father.[9]

Years of intense business activity ensued and Plant acquitted himself well of the mounting responsibilities with the express company. He was promoted and transferred to New York with the Adams Express Company, which had emerged from the old steamboat company to become a strong concern in its own right. The express business was now filling a much needed place in American life and its expansion was fast, especially in the South and West. Plant was in precisely the right spot at the right time. Here was a growing business, which offered a real challenge to a young man of his talents. Soon he was to become a key figure in the Adams Express Company's vigorous program of growth by consolidation of smaller companies.

The one stroke that made the Adams Express Company most widely known was its merger in 1854 with the Harnden Express Company. William F. Harnden, who was considered the father of the express business, had begun a modest express line in 1839 and by the time of the merger with Adams operated the most far-flung agency in the country. In the same year Adams also purchased three other concerns: Thompson, Livingston and Company; Kinsley and Company; and Hoey and Company. Following these transactions Adams reorganized over a million dollars' worth of stock into twelve thousand shares. The company was now prepared to dominate the express business in southeastern United States, and to this area was sent its youngest and brightest official, Henry B. Plant. He arrived in Augusta, Georgia, in 1854 to begin his duties as superintendent of the Southern territory.[10]

Plant welcomed the move to Augusta. Only the year before, Mrs. Plant had been seized with a lung ailment and advised by her physician that she must go to a warmer climate. On March 23, 1853, she and Plant left New York City on their first visit to the South. They went first to Charleston, South Carolina, on the steamer *Marion* and from there on the *Calhoun* to Savannah. The last leg of the journey from Savannah to Jacksonville was made on the *Welaka*. The entire journey took eight days. In the 1850's Jacksonville was a small village with one wharf extending into the St. Johns River. Though Florida was becoming widely known for its mild winters and ever-present sunshine, Jacksonville was not equipped to accommodate many visitors from the North. Hotel facilities were poor and inadequate. Consequently the Plants found a room in a private home several miles across the St. Johns River from Jacksonville at the setlement of Strawberry Mills. There on the banks of the St. Johns, Mrs. Plant's health gradually improved, the distressing cough soon leaving her completely. Early in May, Plant was able to return to his business in New York, his wife joining him two months later in apparent good health.[11]

Mrs. Plant's lung ailment was not one that could be cured so easily, however, and her husband knew it. For a short time she had no recurrence of her trouble, but in October, 1853, the cough returned and it was necessary for her to return to Florida, where again she improved in the warm climate. Meanwhile Plant became interested in his surroundings in Jacksonville and made a few trips down the St. Johns River. He even undertook a pleasure trip to St. Augustine, the oldest community in the United States.[12] The only road at that time between Jacksonville and St. Augustine was an old highway built during the days of Spanish occupation (1783-1819) and still known as the King's Highroad. Plant made the journey in a horse-drawn buggy accompanied by his wife and an Indian girl, who was a companion and nurse to Mrs. Plant.

The highway was almost impassable and there was considerable delay in their travel, especially on the homeward journey.

These days in Florida were happy ones for Plant and no doubt gave him some ideas as to the possibilities there, and in other undeveloped sections of the South. Therefore he welcomed the opportunity to come South as the Adams Express Company representative in 1854. First it meant a longer life for his wife, and second there were untold economic possibilities which a man of Plant's ability could make much of. This was the turning point in his career.[13]

Upon their arrival in Augusta in 1854, the Plant's boarded first at the Eagle Hotel and later at the Phoenix Hotel because Mrs. Plant was not physically able to care for a home. Her husband exercised every caution with regard to her health. His job in Augusta was a demanding one, and his duties carried him to many parts of the South. By this time the Adams Express Company was extending its routes over all the railroads and navigable rivers south of the Potomac River, and one of Plant's first tasks was to establish offices in all the principal towns of the South, including Nashville, Memphis, Vicksburg, Louisville, and New Orleans. By 1858 he had pushed the business into Texas by a consolidation with the New Orleans and Texas Express Company. It was also Plant's duty to see that efficient service was given at all offices in the South; to appoint officials to all jobs; and to gain the faith and confidence of the public.[14] He was the executive officer of the company, the public relations chief, and an efficiency expert all rolled into one. Though the business was still in its infancy in 1854, it developed rapidly under his guidance, and he is rightly considered the pioneer of the express business in the South.

Because of business reasons the Plants moved from Augusta to Atlanta in the Summer of 1858, but returned to Augusta in the fall of the same year. Though the climate in Georgia was milder than that of New York or Connecticut, his wife's health continued to fail. Occasional winter trips were made to Jacksonville, but nothing seemed to give her permanent relief from the lung ailment, and consequently she passed away on February 28, 1861.[15] She was buried in Augusta, but the body was some time later moved to the family burying plot in Branford, Connecticut. Her death, though a shock to her family and friends, was not unexpected. Her continued illness had not handicapped her husband in his business activities, because he had managed to give every phase of the work full attention. During her last days, however, changes of large proportions had to be made within the organization of the Adams Express Company because of the coming of the Civil War. By late 1860 war seemed inevitable and the question arose as to the future of a Northern concern operating in the South.

No one was more concerned over the approaching war than Plant, and hardly had the sound of Fort Sumter's guns died away before he began to carry out some well-conceived plans for the future of the express business in the South. The Adams Company feared confiscation by the South, so Plant was allowed to take control of all its Southern routes, doing business under the name of the Southern Express Company. For several months this arrangement prevailed, Plant meanwhile awaiting action by Georgia authorities on his application for a charter. On May 1, 1861 the transfer was formally made. The name, Southern Express Company, replaced Adams Express Company on signs above all offices in the South on that date.[16] Plant appointed Rufus B. Bullock, later a controversial character in Georgia history, as superintendent of the eastern division of the new company. He made Ed Hurlbert superintendent of the central division, and D. P. Ellwood superintendent of the western division. Though a new firm had been created and a separate charter secured, the Southern Express Company was still tied closely to the parent organization, the Adams Express Company. Newspapers throughout the South carried the anouncement of the division of the company and added that "business will continue without interruption."[17]

Apparently Plant was one Yankee who was in good standing in the South, because there was no demand that he leave as was the case with many Northerners who resided south of the Potomac. The express business was an enterprise greatly needed in the war, and Southern leaders realized it. Plant, wanting to help with the Southern cause though disapproving of the disruption of the nation, went to President Jefferson Davis in Montgomery and told him his story. He offered his services to the Confederate President and asked to remain in the South so that he could conduct his business without prejudice to political or military movements. By this time all Northern sympathizers had been asked to leave the South, but Plant assured Davis that his sympathy was with the Southern people.[18]

President Davis admired the frankness of the man and immediately saw that he could use the Southern Express Company to a very good advantage. He gave Plant permission to move about in the South at will, and to pass through army posts on business. This was an act of faith and confidence, but Plant's integrity justified all of the trust the President placed in him. It was strictly a matter of business with Plant. He had made money with the Adams Express Company, and he felt he could do so as president of the Southern Express Company, especially in time of war. His loyalty to the South was based on that assumption.

The Southern Express Company played an important role for the government during the Civil War. It transported mail and parcels throughout the South and in cooperation with the Adams Company delivered goods in the North as well. The United States post office did not handle mail from the South between 1861 and 1865. However, during the early phases of the war the Southern Express Company delivered mail at designated points to the Adams Express Company which in turn carried it to its destination.[19] An advertisement appeared in an Augusta, Georgia, paper in June, 1861, announcing that mail would be delivered in the North by the Southern and Adams companies provided the sender would pay delivery charges in advance. This relieved the post office department of any further trouble over mail service.[20]

Throughout the war the Southern Express Company continued to work through the military lines with Adams. During hostilities, as the federal forces moved into the South at various points, the Southern would abandon its offices and they would be taken over immediately by Adams. The armies' lines were constantly changing, railroads were being destroyed, and for a time employment of men for express service was a grave problem. The Southern Express Company, however, met each hardship with determination to give complete express service to the South. So impressed with Plant's service was President Davis that he made him collector of tariff upon all goods consigned by the express company. The Confederacy further showed its faith in him by asking that he transfer government funds from one place to another. This he did with efficiency and speed. He was given custody of all such funds while they were in the hands of his company. Confederate soldiers were often detailed for service with the express company when its own men were not available.[21]

The rates charged by the Southern Express Company ran to startlingly high figures when the value of Confederate paper

money sank to a low level. Newspapers often advertised rates of
a dollar a pound for only a short distance. Sometimes an agent
would refuse the worthless paper money and insist on barter instead. It was not uncommon for an express office to be filled with
articles of all sorts which were not being shipped but were being
tendered instead of money in payment of express charges. Clerks
were frequently busier selling bartered provisions than receiving
express articles. It is said that in Macon, Georgia, at one time the
Southern Express Wagon was pulled through the streets each day
with such items for sale as oats, corn, vegetables, corn meal, sides
of bacon, live chickens, pigs, ducks, kegs of sorghum, and the
like.[22] Such were the problems of the express people during the
Civil War.

As the war progressed the Southern Express Company came
under much criticism in some parts of the South, as did its president, Henry B. Plant. To many people Plant and the Southern
Express Company were representatives of the Northern cause.
Much was said about false Southern patriotism among former
Northerners now living in the South, and charges and counter-
charges were hurled back and forth. Though few were aimed
directly at him, Plant was made to feel uncomfortable at various
times. In the summer of 1863 he suffered an attack of gastric fever
and was advised to move to another climate. Receiving a pass
through the Confederate lines from the attorney general of the
Confederacy, he left Augusta for Wilmington, North Carolina,
and from there he went by boat to Bermuda. After a stay of a
month, he proceeded to Halifax, Nova Scotia, and then to New
Haven, Connecticut. In New Haven, he visited his mother and
son, Morton, before embarking in the fall for an extended trip
to Europe. An Augusta newspaper had the following to say about
Plant's departure: "We do not wish to be censorious. We do not
say that every man who leaves the Confederacy during the War
is of questionable patriotism. Inexorable necessity, business, [or]
health may make it imperative. But the requisition ought to be
so strong as to make the duty unquestionable."[23] Plant's leaving
was noted by J. B. Jones in his *A Rebel War Clerk's Diary* on
August 1, 1863. Said Jones, "I suppose his fortune is made."[24]

Regardless of Plant's motive for leaving the South during the
war, he had done a good job as president of the Southern Express
Company, and the company continued to serve the South in a
creditable manner throughout the conflict. Early in 1864 an At-

lanta newspaper had this to say about the Southern Express Company: "The company will merit all that has been said in its favor. It has become an indispensable institution. . . . Much censure has been bestowed upon the officers by those who are not acquainted with the immense and almost insurmountable difficulties they have to contend with. But it is both undeserved and unjust. Instead of being blamed and abused they should be praised for their untiring energy. There is no greater public convenience now existing than the Southern Express Co. Long may it flourish."[25]

Plant remained away from the South for nearly two years, returning during the spring of 1865. While abroad he spent some time in Liverpool, Paris, and Rome, and enjoyed a tour of Switzerland. He returned to America by way of Canada and remained in New York until the struggle between the North and South was over.

Plant got a taste of European travel which he liked, and said upon his return home that he would like some day to visit Europe again. And so he did. In 1873 he made his second European tour. This trip was in the form of a honeymoon, for only a few days before beginning the journey, he was married to Margaret Josephine Loughman, only daughter of Martin Loughman of New York. Since his first wife had been dead eleven years and since he had known Miss Loughman for quite some time, the marriage had the blessings of both families — so much so, in fact, that his mother and son, Morton Plant, accompanied him on the trip. The second marriage was a happy one in every respect.[26]

Plant made a third trip to Europe in 1889, on the occasion of the Paris Exposition, to which he carried a Florida exhibit at a personal cost to him of $15,000. Accompanying him was a decorator who made an attractive display of the Plant material at the fair.[27] He remained in Europe until November of that year.[28] His last visit abroad was a business trip to England in 1898. He went to discuss with British officials matters concerning certain steamship lines in the Caribbean and a proposed railroad in Cuba.[29] A visit to Japan was made in 1897 for business and pleasure. Governor William D. Bloxham of Florida gave him a letter of introduction which gained for him an audience with the Mikado.[30]

Plant's post-Civil War activities in Georgia and Florida were numerous and remunerative. After his two year absence (1863-65) he returned to Augusta and took up where he had left off. Interested in the rehabilitation of the South, he promptly undertook the reparation and expansion of Southern railroads and the restoration of the express business. Northern capital played a big part in these activities. By the early 1870's, the 10,000 miles built before the war in the South had been repaired or rebuilt, and 8,000 miles had been added.[31] Plant was in the thick of it all.

It is apparent that Plant kept in good standing with local groups in Georgia during the Reconstruction period. However, this is more than can be said of some of his associates in the Southern Express. When one of them, Rufus B. Bullock, became a much disputed governor of the state, Plant made it clear that he was not interested in becoming involved in political broils. Though a Republican, he was never linked with the radical wing of that party in the South.[32]

The Southern Express Company was reorganized after the war, and an eastern division was set up with headquarters in Augusta. A western division was also created with headquarters in Memphis. Plant was elected president of the reorganized company, including the Texas Express Company and remained in this position until his death in 1899. M. J. O'Brien was the long-time general superintendent under Plant. Principal offices were located in Augusta, Memphis, Richmond, Charleston, Atlanta, Montgomery, New Orleans, Savannah, and Vicksburg.[33] As the South continued to recover from the Civil War, so did the Southern Express Company. More railroads meant more express lines, and faster trains meant better express service. By 1875 nation-wide service by express was a reality. The Southern made connections with Adams Express, American Express, and United States Express, but it had no office east and north of Richmond. Plant and O'Brien had to spend more and more time in New York, so in December, 1875, eastern headquarters were established on Twenty-third Street in New York City, though the Southern office remained in Augusta. The stockholders were Southern men, and the company continued to be supported by the South.[34] After this time Plant spent less time in Augusta, but his base of operations was still in Georgia. He had now spread his interest from Texas to New York, and was to become further involved in the field of railroad activity. He was a man of unlimited energy and ambition, all of which came into play in the realization of his dreams for the New South.

The railroad business was closely associated with the express

business, and Plant had long been cognizant of that fact. Some of
the railroads in the nation had attempted to organize their own
express business, and it was not unprecedented for an express
magnate to become interested in railroads. So it was with Henry
B. Plant. He had Jay Gould before him as an example. Gould
had been interested in both railroads and express. He had obtained control of the Union Pacific, the Kansas Pacific, and the
Wabash railroads. Along with these railroads he had developed
an express business that ranked among the biggest and the best
in the nation for a quarter of a century.[35]

It was in 1879 that Plant ventured into the railroad field. A
modest move at first, it gave every indication of bigger things to
come. On November 4, 1879, he and a few associates purchased
the Atlantic and Gulf Railroad, then under the management and
direction of its receivers.[36] The sale was held in Savannah in the
form of a public auction and the price was $300,000; however,
mortgages in the amount of $4,410,000 were assumed by Plant,
which brought the total cost of the road to $4,710,000.[37] At the
time of the purchase the rolling stock of the road consisted of the
following: twenty-five engines, twenty-five passenger cars, ten baggage cars, and several hundred box and freight cars.[38]

Plant's railroad extended from Savannah to the southwestern
corner of Georgia. It had been the intention of the builders eventually to connect Savannah with the Gulf of Mexico. Originally
chartered in 1847 as the Savannah and Albany Railroad, it became
in 1854 the Savannah, Albany and Gulf, and soon thereafter actual
construction was completed to the site of the city of Waycross,
Georgia. A new charter was granted in 1856, and the road was
renamed Atlantic and Gulf. The tracks were extended to Thomasville in 1861, and to Bainbridge in 1867. A Florida branch, from
Dupont, Georgia, to Live Oak, Florida, was built in 1867-68, a
distance of 48 miles; and a branch from Thomasville to Albany
was purchased from the South Georgia and Florida Railroad in
1869. In all, the Atlantic and Gulf consisted of 350.18 miles in
1879 when it was purchased by Plant.[39]

After the purchase the road was rechartered by Plant under the
name Savannah, Florida and Western and was soon to become a
significant link in all east-west transportation in Georgia and the
Southern states. In 1880 the Waycross and Florida Railroad laid
a track from Waycross to the Florida border, the East Florida
Railroad building the road from that point to Jacksonville. This

line was soon acquired by Plant, thus shortening the distance from Savannah to Jacksonville by a number of hours. In the same year that the Waycross-Jacksonville road was built, Plant bought and rebuilt the Charleston and Savannah Railroad. This acquisition helped to perfect connections between Florida, Charleston, and the North. This road was under separate administration, and though at first it did not become a part of the Savannah, Florida and Western Railroad, it did become a part of the Plant system of railroads which was increasing in length and importance yearly.[40]

Plant's interests in railroads were growing so fast that it became necessary to form another company, comparable to Southern Express Company, to develop and control his railroad system. This resulted in the chartering in 1882 of the Plant Investment Company under the laws of the state of Connecticut. Plant was its president until his death. He owned most of the stock in the company, but other interested friends were invited to participate. When the company decided to make a purchase or build a railroad, each person paid his share of the expense. There were no bonds nor indebtedness; therefore there was no interest to pay. The policy of the company was to build and operate railroads; Plant and his associates were not in business for bond and stock speculation.[41]

Subsequent to the organization of the Plant Investment Company several more smaller roads were absorbed into the Savannah, Florida and Western Railroad; among them were the Live Oak (Florida) and Rowland's Bluff, the Chattahoochee (Florida) and East Pass, and the Live Oak, Tampa and Charlotte Harbor companies. These mergers added 99 miles to Plant's railroad, giving it a total of 479 miles.[42]

In contrast to the early purpose of the Atlantic and Gulf Railroad, which was to connect Savannah with the Gulf, Plant's aim after 1882 was to extend his business into central and south Florida with a terminus at Tampa. He had great dreams of tapping the rich South American trade with a steamboat line connection at Tampa. Working to this end, he extended the Dupont-Live Oak branch to Gainesville, Florida, in 1884 — a total of 118 miles. A branch line was completed from Fort White on the trunk line to Lake City, Florida, — 20 miles — in 1886, and a branch from Thomasville, Georgia, to Monticello, Florida, — a total of 24 miles — was opened in 1888.[43]

Though this Connecticut Yankee was primarily interested in extending his railroad to the frontier in central Florida, he did not ignore the possibilities in another east-west route. For some years Plant had been interested in the Brunswick and Western, a road that had been constructed from Brunswick to Albany, crossing the Savannah, Florida and Western at Waycross.[44] It fell into the hands of the Erlanger Syndicate, and on September 1, 1884, it was purchased by the Plant Investment Company.[45]

Chartered in 1835, the Brunswick and Western had a spotty history. It was never really a successful railroad, though many influential men, like Thomas P. King, wealthy St. Simons Island planter, were moving spirits back of it. The Panic of 1837 dealt it a heavy blow, and actual construction of the road was delayed for several years. It almost passed out of existence during the Civil War when it was seized under the Impressment Act by the Confederate government. Its rails were torn up and together with the rest of the company's properties were distributed among other railroads which the Confederate government considered to be principal military lines.[46]

Prior to 1863 the railroad extended some sixty miles from Brunswick to Waycross, connecting with the Atlantic and Gulf at a point 103 miles east of Thomasville and ninety miles west of Savannah. It was not until 1869 that the road was revived with a new charter. The proposed line of the new Brunswick and Albany Railroad was to run from Brunswick to Albany, and thence to Eufala, Alabama, to connect with the Chattahoochee River, a main artery of transportation.[47] Within a few years, after further setbacks and delays, the road was completed to Albany, and this was as far as it was to go. The road defaulted payment on the interest of its bonds and claims of creditors began to pour in on the company. The Georgia legislature added to the company's woes by repudiating an earlier endorsement of its bonds; in 1873 the road was sold under foreclosure.[48]

A new charter was granted nine years later, and it became the Brunswick and Western Railroad. Its new owners the Erlanger Syndicate failed to make it a paying concern. In fact, it did not pay more than running expenses as its trade was almost entirely local. The road was poorly equipped and could not stand the competition which was beginning to develop. Its bonds were largely held in Germany at the time Plant purchased it. The acquisition of the Brunswick and Western increased Plant's railroad system to about 900 miles of road in South Carolina, Georgia, and Florida.[49]

During the 1880's Plant was also engaged in acquiring and building portions of two railroads in Florida which helped to complete his railway system to Tampa and southern Florida. These were the South Florida Railroad and the Florida Southern Railroad. He first purchased controlling interest in the South Florida Railroad which was being built to connect Tampa with the great commercial highway, the St. Johns River. This road was to run from Sanford to Tampa by way of Orlando and Lakeland.[50] This entire section of Florida hummed with activity as the rails were laid mile by mile. Towns like Auburndale, Haines City, Lake Tracy, Plant City, and Lakeland grew into thriving little trading centers. By 1886 the road was completed to Tampa. This gave new life to the inactive little town which had been isolated from north Florida except by wagon or carriage line. In fact, in 1883 Plant had come to Tampa on a wagon line with some of his associates to look over the town, and to make preparations for the building of the railroad. At that time it was a seven-day journey from the junction on the St. Johns River, but by 1886 the trip could be made in three or four hours. The train in 1886 passed through towns and villages which were not in existence in 1883. This development meant much to Tampa.[51] Plant took a personal interest in the town and on many occasions showed his love for it and its people.

The Florida Southern Railroad from Palatka via Gainesville and Ocala to Charlotte Harbor, Plant's next venture, was virtually completed in the late 1880's. The charter was granted to a Boston enterprise in 1879, but work was not begun until March, 1882. Arrangements were made very early with the Savannah, Florida and Western for cooperation between the two roads. Plant steamers on the St. Johns River also connected with the road at Palatka by boat, and thence from Palatka via Gainesville to Tampa and the Bay area. The road south of Gainesville ran through Lakeland, crossing the South Florida Railroad at that point, and from there on to the Gulf coast. The route traversed some of the finest farm lands in the state.[52] The Florida Southern, like the South Florida Railroad, was not absorbed by the Savannah, Florida and Western all at one time but was gradually merged with the Plant interests to become a part of the Plant system.

By the 1890's Plant had a system of railroads covering 1,494 miles extending from Charleston on the north to Tampa and Punta Gorda on the south and from Savannah on the east to Montgomery on the west.[53] These roads serviced the best agricultural lands of four Southeastern states. Naval stores, lumber, cotton, watermelons, phosphorous, fruit, and other products were shipped daily from their places of production to the markets and shipping points at Savannah, Charleston, Jacksonville, or Tampa.

The last acquisition of the Plant Investment Company was the Jacksonville, Tampa and Key West Railway which connected Jacksonville with Sanford. It was begun in 1883, finished in 1886, and bought by Plant in 1899 to complete his system of railroads in Florida.[54] The Tampa *Daily Times* commented as follows on the purchase: "For more than twenty years he [Plant] has been engaged in perfecting his system, until today he has one of the largest in the country, comprising more than 2,000 miles of railway."[55]

Henry B. Plant felt that no system of transportation in Florida was complete without steamship lines. Early in 1886, after the railroad was completed to Tampa, he purchased the 200-foot steamer *Mascotte* and established a line connecting Tampa, Key West, and Havana. This line opened many new possibilities for trade with Key West and Cuba. In addition he established steamship lines on the St. Johns, the Chattahoochee, the Flint, and the Apalachicola rivers and a short line on the Manatee River in Florida.[56] All of his steamship lines made connections with his railroads for faster and more complete service.

Along with his railroads and steamship lines, Plant operated an extensive system of hotels for tourists, health seekers, and sportsmen. The largest and most elaborate was the Tampa Bay Hotel, completed in 1891 at a cost of two million dollars. Nearly $500,000 was spent for furnishings for the huge Moorish structure which sat in the center of a 16-acre plot of ground just north of the city bridge. Minarets and domes towered above the great five-story building, each one of which was surmounted with a crescent, and brilliantly lighted by electricity at night. Through the building ran a wide hall, on either side of which were bedrooms. The dining room was at the southern end of the building. The exterior walls were of darkened brick with buff and red brick arches. Three pairs of double doors flanked by sixteen polished granite columns formed the main entrance. There were beautiful staircases, luxuri-

ous drawing rooms, and expensive furnishings. All in all, the
Tampa Bay Hotel was a place of beauty and fine taste.[57]

Also among the Plant hotels was the comfortable and luxuriant
Hotel Belleview on the beach of Clearwater harbor. Hotel
Seminole at Winter Park was an ideal resort for pleasure, health,
and rest. The Ocala House offered many attractions, including
Silver Springs and the Ocklawaha River. The Inn at Port Tampa
was a resort for fishermen and a transient home for travelers who
came to and from Havana and other ports via the Plant steamship
line. At Kissimmee the Plant interests owned Hotel Kissimmee in
the center of Florida's fishing and hunting section.[58] These were
representative of the Plant hotels and were known widely throughout the North. Advertisements in Northern newspapers told of
the comfort and advantages of all the Plant hostelries.

Death on June 23, 1899, brought to an end a full life of activity
for Henry B. Plant. To his credit was a great network of railroads,[59] a well-developed express business, a growing system of
hotels, and an increasing and expanding steamship line, in addition to directorships in several other enterprises. One of the best-
known men in the South at the time of his death, he was loved
and honored by some and thoroughly despised by others. He was
a thrifty "Southern Yankee" who had made his fortune in the
South, unlike his contemporary Henry M. Flagler, who had made
the bulk of his fortune in the North and had come South to
spend it. There was neither a Standard Oil Company nor a John
D. Rockefeller back of Plant. Through his own efforts he founded
one successful enterprise after another. Though he never held a
political office, he had a strong following among those who were
elected to office in both Georgia and Florida.

The Augusta *Chronicle* believed he was a benefactor of the
South; but the Ocala *Banner* said if he were a benefactor it was
only in the narrow sense of the word. The Tampa *Morning Tribune* felt that he proved himself an unselfish friend to the people
of the South and won their love and admiration. And so it went.
Though Plant was a controversial figure, even those newspapers
most critical of his life found some things on which to commend
him.[60] It was fairly well agreed that Henry B. Plant was a pioneer
of the New South and a man who had faith in the future of Georgia and Florida. There were results to prove it.

REBECCA LATIMER FELTON

BY JOHN E. TALMADGE

AT THE close of her eventful life, which stretched from 1835 to 1930, Rebecca Latimer Felton was perhaps the best-known woman in Georgia. Moreover, she enjoyed something of a national reputation as an author, belligerent feminist, and shrewd politician. She has not been as well-remembered as she expected. Many Georgians will recall, vaguely and rather indifferently, that she was the first woman appointed to the United States Senate. A few, mostly older people, knew that she was a stormy figure in several decades of Georgia politics and a relentless fighter for prohibition, prison reform, and woman suffrage. In writing their own books, Southern historians consult, with caution, her two highly partisan books, *My Memoirs of Georgia Politics,* and *Early Country Life in Georgia.*

What was perhaps her most considerable achievement seems now completely forgotten. As a columnist on the Atlanta *Semi-Weekly Journal* from 1899 to 1920, she won and held the unshakable confidence of thousands of readers in the rural areas of Georgia and the Southeast. Rebecca Felton was singularly fitted, by life and temperament, for gaining loyalty and even response from these cautious, reticent people.

She was born near Decatur, Georgia, of sturdy, frontier-minded parents. Her mother, Eleanor Swift Latimer, was a person of great vitality; she loved the farm and was disposed to resent the dominance of man over so much of life. Rebecca was to have all of these traits. Her father, Charles Latimer, was an unusual man for his day. He gave to his first daughter that attention most fathers save for their sons. A man of liberal, decided views, he encouraged Rebecca's independent, competitive spirit, tom-boyish ways, and love of books and music.[1]

John E. Talmadge is a member of the English faculty at the University of Georgia.

Through him she came to know newspapers and was awed at first by their power and information. Latimer loved to entertain Whig editors and to read aloud their opinions to his less-literate neighbors gathered in his post office. He was quick to write letters to the press, usually attacking the latest Democratic iniquity. His style was hardly classical, but his delight in turning a homely, biting phrase was surely observed by his adoring young daughter.[2]

Antebellum Georgia might feel that a little education was enough for women, but Charles Latimer wanted the best the state could give for his daughter. He hired a good teacher for the local field-school and started Rebecca at the age of five. The desire to excel seemed to have stirred her as a tiny child. That first year she fought stubbornly to win the spelling prize and did share it with an older pupil. Later, at Miss Hayes School for Girls in Oxford, Georgia, and at Dr. John S. Wilson's school in Decatur she took other prizes. In 1852 she graduated from the Madison Female Academy in Madison, Georgia, sharing first honor with a classmate and delivering one of the commencement valedictories.

At the Madison Academy she evidently worked at her writing. One of her compositions, "The Spirit of Improvement," has been found in her papers. In it she praises earnestly the advancement of knowledge, especially among the Anglo-Saxon nations. As might be expected from a serious-minded girl of seventeen, the diction is flowery and artificial; but the composition is well-constructed and the sentences are grammatically correct.

In 1853 she married the commencement speaker at her graduation, Dr. William H. Felton of Cartersville, Georgia. Although a graduate of the Augusta Medical College and a licensed Methodist preacher, her husband, plagued by poor health, had turned to farming his large tract of land in the rich Etowah valley. Better educated and less worldly than Charles Latimer, Felton in many ways resembled his father-in-law. He, too, was a man of strong convictions who respected industry, learning, and religion. Although a Democrat, he was of the party's Union wing which usually stood with the Whigs against secession. But far more important for Rebecca, he believed that women should not be excluded from the world of ideas and public activities. He respected his young wife's intelligence and energy, and came to depend upon her help both in his personal affairs and later in his political campaigns.

Grief and danger brought them closer. Before the Civil War

they lost a son and a daughter and during its closing years they buried their two remaining boys from a refugee shack near Macon. The war years brought Mrs. Felton suffering, want, and fear, with no compensating glory. She worked with the mutilated men brought to Cartersville after Chickamauga; watched first Wheeler's Confederates and then Stoneman's blue-coated raiders take her horses and desperately-needed provisions; and listened fearfully in darkness while drunken Federals and Negroes roamed the Macon woods vowing vengeance for the assassination of Lincoln. She returned to Cartersville sick and childless, with an undying horror of war and a growing conviction that when governments passed into the hands of "stupid, cruel men," it was women, especially mothers, who suffered most.

She bore two more sons after the war, but only one survived babyhood. Injustice to women would always bring to her mind the sacredness and tragedy of motherhood. The ordeal of Reconstruction put a further strain upon her endurance, but she was finding her salvation from grief and fear through a variety of activities. Besides helping to manage the farm, she became active in the local temperance club and was elected first president of a woman's organization to aid the widows and orphans of those Confederates who had not come back to Cartersville. Then in 1874 Dr. Felton announced as an Independent candidate for Congress, and she joined eagerly in his fight against the powerful Democratic state machine.

She learned much about rural Georgia, where her husband got his chief support, during his three victorious campaigns and the defeats in 1880 and 1882. At first she worked in the background, keeping the doctor supplied with fresh linen, helping to write his speeches, and composing stinging letters for the press over the pseudonyms of "Bartow," "Etowah," and "Old Farmer." But after 1874 she began to startle conservative-minded Georgians by appearing more and more openly in all her husband's activities until she became his acknowledged press secretary and campaign manager.

At barbecues and in crowded courtrooms she shook hands and talked with the "wool-hat" Georgians, slow-speaking men deeply set in their inherited ways and capable of violence in defending them. She got to know their language, their distrust of the city business man, their instinctive hostility to unfamiliar ideas. Many probably did not approve of a woman at political rallies, but she was helping her husband in his fight against graft and corruption, and she was respected for her loyalty and courage.

She learned much also about journalism and the male sport of politics. In her letters to the newspapers she developed a racy, incisive style that penetrated more than once the skin of such Georgia celebrities as John B. Gordon, Joseph E. Brown, and Alfred Colquitt. In controversy she preferred the masculine give-and-take argument; but if hard pressed, she did not shame to reproach a man for his lack of respect for a woman, or even for his lack of reverence for a mother. She became a formidable opponent.[3]

Instead of trying again in 1884 to regain his old congressional seat, Dr. Felton stood for the state legislature, was elected and served for three terms. His wife helped mightily in his fights to get greater appropriations for the University of Georgia, to abolish the convict lease system, and to block the proposed sale of the state-owned Western and Atlantic Railroad. Her energy was abounding. In 1885 she and her husband started a weekly paper, the Cartersville *Courant,* to furnish the doctor political support and to give her a larger opportunity for her writing. With little help from the doctor, she edited a sprightly, readable weekly for over a year until the strain of her many activities persuaded her that they must sell the paper.

Dr. Felton ran unsuccessfully two more times for Congress: in 1890 as a regular Democrat and in 1894 as a Populist. His age and sickness were beginning to show; he retired to his farm — this time to stay.

Retirement was the furthest thing from Mrs. Felton's thoughts. She was kind and attentive to her husband in his last years, but the beginning of his decline marked also the opening of her period of greatest activities. In the 1880's she had joined the Woman's Christian Temperance Union to gain its support in the Feltons' crusade against convict leasing. Soon she was fighting just as lustily against the evils of strong drink. Heartened by the reception of her first temperance talks, she broadened her repertory and spoke on political, historical, and literary topics. Under the guidance of Tom Watson, fiery leader of the Georgian agrarians, she scheduled tours of lectures throughout the state, gaining many new friends and admirers — principally among women, but also among serious civic-minded men. She carried on many arguments through letters to the newspapers: with politicians, with bishops of her own Methodist Church, with anyone who dared to write ill of women. She had many things to say, and loved to say them.

In 1899 she was approaching her sixty-fifth birthday, the age when American men and women of today are eligible for social security benefits. But Rebecca Felton was looking for more, not less, to do. When Hoke Smith, publisher of the Atlanta *Journal*, offered her a position as a regular contributor to his *Semi-Weekly*, she accepted and set to work on her first column.[4]

Smith was seeking to increase the circulation of his paper and to gain friends for himself in Georgia's rural districts. His *Journal*, founded in 1883, had been the first Atlanta evening paper to weather the competition of the powerful morning *Constitution*. With the daily *Journal* now safeguarded by sufficient city circulation, Smith was adding new features to his *Semi-Weekly*, the paper's rural edition, in the hope of cutting into the huge number of readers still held by the *Weekly Constitution*. The *Journal's* publisher had political ambitions also, and with most of the Negroes driven from Georgia's polls, the vote of the independent-minded farmers and old Populists was going to decide future elections within the state. Even then Smith was undoubtedly moving in the direction of his alliance a few years later with his old enemy Tom Watson.[5]

The readers and supporters Smith sought would have to be handled with care. At the turn of the century rural Georgia had been troubled politically by the dissolution of their parties — first the Independent and then the Populist. Their beloved Watson had retired, so it seemed, to Hickory Hill and his literary work; and the state Democratic party was still dominated by their traditional enemies, the city business men and newspaper publishers. Economic and social troubles were also abroad on the land. Largely cotton growers, many farmers had lost their farms through the continuing low price of cotton and a grinding credit system manipulated by the merchant and the banker. By 1900 one third of the farms in the state were being tilled, often indifferently, by share-croppers. In contrast to agriculture, manufacturing in Georgia was thriving. Between 1870 and 1900 the number of factories doubled, and the value of their products trebled. The glare and opportunity of the city were drawing young people from the cotton fields, and the greater privileges and higher wages in the North were reducing the available Negro labor. The agrarian way of life, once the ideal of the Southerner, was now furnishing the "hicks and hayseeds" for the popular jokes. Many of those who still followed it had become embittered and shiftless.[6]

In introducing Mrs. Felton to these hard-pressed farm people, Smith tried to encourage them. The greatest need of rural life, he said, was "an enlargement of social pleasures and opportunities"; and Mrs. Felton, who had spent her life on a farm, desired "to be the means of brightening home life in the country." She would address herself "largely to an audience of farmers' wives and daughters," and the *Journal* believed she would "do a lot of good."[7]

Before she had written many of her columns Mrs. Felton made it clear she was not going to be bounded by the limits of her vague assignment. True, she offered many suggestions for making life in a farm house more pleasant and comfortable, and she did address many of her columns to wives and daughters. But she was too confirmed a feminist to stay out of the affairs of men, and she had been a social reformer too long to be content with writing food recipes and devising ways to entertain young people. Soon she was busy telling the farmer how to cultivate his acres and market his crops — and how to vote. Probably through sheer force of habit, she began to lecture her readers about the sins of strong drink, tobacco, and gambling. She discussed prevalent diseases and possible remedies, and she answered questions about the Bible and the Christian faith. On political questions she spoke with the authority of an elder statesman. The publisher of a modern newspaper hires a corps of specialized columnists to cover all these fields.

From her columns and letters much can be learned about the problems and ways of agrarian Georgia during the first two decades of the twentieth century.

Many of her strongly opinioned columns dealt with the problems and interests of each member of a farm family; the farmer, his wife, daughter, and son. More were addressed to the farmer than to his wife. By 1900 she owned and cultivated her own land, and undoubtly had largely taken over the management of the doctor's farm. She spoke therefore as one farmer to another.

Realistically she emphasized the risks and problems of farming. The merchant, banker, and cotton broker had joined in "a well-laid plan, if not a conspiracy, to keep down the price of cotton." Just as soon as the cotton crop was picked — if not before — the banker would call on the merchant for payment of his notes. The merchant would in turn demand that the farmer settle his bill for supplies. And the poor, cashless farmer would be forced to dump his cotton on the market and send its price downward. Then, the guano man would "loom up" with his "iron-clad" notes, perhaps followed by the mule seller. In the end the farmer would be left with his land — if that. But more conniving was ahead. About the time for buying guano, the cotton speculators would send the market up a bit to bait the guiless farmer. He would start planning for next year's crop and sign another batch of notes. As Mrs. Felton put it, "The bears and the guano man have the thoughtless farmer where the wool is long enough to hold him."[8]

She knew from experience that even greater variable in farming, the weather: the washing winter rains, the summer droughts, the unseasonable frosts. Anxiously she watched the skies and the signs and discussed frankly with her readers their suffering crops and gloomy prospects. Her columns frequently opened with a weather report: "The frost and freeze that succeeded the torrid spell . . ."; "I woke last night to hear the never-ceasing drip-drip . . ."; "The dry spell that afflicted Georgia this year. . . ." She would admit the damage done, warning that "unless all signs fail" next spring would be "a struggling time for everyone." Riding around Cartersville, she noticed that "drought and heat have been severe on cotton stalks." After an unusually hot May she warned her readers that the coming crop would probably not be "a bumper one."[9]

She admitted the growing labor shortage. Farmers' sons were moving to the cities, and the Negroes to the North. Within one six-months period over five hundred Negroes had bought tickets at Albany, Georgia, for Pittsburgh, Philadelphia, and New Jersey. Tenants were usually shiftless. She told of visiting a farm where the grass was as high as the cotton, yet the farmer, his wife, and several sons were sitting idly on the porch. There were other problems too. The boll weevil was ruining more cotton each year and the potato beetle was thriving. Finally if everything did seem to go right and there was a good crop, Congress was always likely to spoil prices by tinkering with the tariff. Farming was a hard way to make a living.[10]

In spite of all these uncertainties and problems, Mrs. Felton contended that farming could be made profitable if a farmer planned carefully and worked hard. "There was life," she was sure, "in the old land yet." She was glad there were "elements of a natural-born farmer" in her, and she loved the sight of plowing mules and the smell of freshly-plowed earth. True, it was not the occupation for a man who was afraid of steady labor and unable to meet new problems every day. But its stern routine developed character. She believed that the greatest men in America had come from its farms.[11]

She had no end of suggestions. When cotton crops were poor or the price low, the farm family should cut down on luxuries, wear old clothes, and make the farm as self-supporting as possible. In fact, the man who grew most of his own food and had enough grain and hay for his stock was better off during a depression than the city dweller. Credit was the ruin of most farmers. In good or bad years they should "charge" as little as possible. Those who bought mules, feed, and guano in the spring without paying for them were headed for trouble. They were "like the foolish virgins who had no oil in their lamps to show the way out." All they could do when the year was over was sign new notes at whatever interest rate asked, for the "man in debt must take what he can get."[12]

Two of the surest ways to avoid this predicament, she said, were to diversify crops and buy as little commercial fertilizer as possible. The Georgia farmer must learn that there were other money crops besides cotton. The sale of chickens, eggs, and butter could give "the farmer's wife a full pocket." Nothing was more salable than the goober pea, not even cotton. The consumption of sugar in the nation was increasing every year; the raising of sugar beets, so profitable in the West, should be tried in Georgia. There was money in sheep too, if the state would only pass the law against allowing "curs to run at large." Some crops should be varied according to the weather. In time of drought "rye should be planted for the feeding of stock . . . and turnips . . . for the table."[13]

The amount of commercial fertilizer sold in the state infuriated her. She wrote a sarcastic article against this wasteful expenditure under the caption "the smell of guano is loud in the land." Compost piles should be built, she said, and manure spread on poor land. When very rich land was needed for a certain crop, she advised fencing cows and sheep on it for awhile. Land should be "rested" from cotton and corn growing by sowing it first in grain and then in clover. An energetic farmer who used rainy days to collect barnyard manure would be the one with few bills and much grain and cotton at the end of the season.[14]

She hated to see the Negroes streaming North. They "knew more about cotton hoeing and picking than any other people in the United States." She had no notion of offering them those free-doms — said to be waiting in the North — but she did believe that as a practical, business move, the South should make them "more comfortable" so they would "be better satisfied." If the exodus continued, she favored encouraging Chinese to immigrate to Georgia; and she thought that good, hard-working Scandinavian families would be preferable to worthless tenants who had de-stroyed confidence "in the entire renting business."[15]

Although she maintained that "farm life well managed" offered "a fine opening for the young men of Georgia," she could under-stand why many boys were moving to the city. Many were finding life on the farm dull, and their fathers expected them to work for years at little more pay than their board and keep. There were things in the city exciting for young people, and they would be drawn there unless compensating pleasures were offered them. They should be taken to the city on week-ends, and they must be urged to invite friends to visit. As soon as he thinks it wise, the father should give the son a share in the farm that will yield a profit. There was nothing else, Mrs. Felton insisted, that would so "wake up interest in the disheartened and discouraged boy." Evidently Texas still had an appeal for restless Georgians, for she warned her young readers of the uncertain weather there and announced she had rather take "her chances among the old red hills than with the variable seasons in far-off Texas."[16]

Again and again she pointed out to farmers and to their sons that there was no substitute for hard work. Too many of them, she said, "expected the crop to make itself and the farm to run itself." She warned those hoping to find "easier times . . . better clothes . . . and more fun" in the city that only a few would find such things there. Success at any calling required industry, and she declared that "the fortunes of Georgia were made" by men who learned to rise early and labor till sunset. Few farmers be-came rich, but many enjoyed "the comforts that go with clean lives and pure thoughts."[17]

She continuously urged them not to be discouraged; to go about their hard tasks "as if everything was all right." But she knew and resented the predicament of an agrarian section ruled economically and politically by men committed wholeheartedly to a growing industrialism. The South was at the mercy of the manufacturing East. While Southern congressmen were fighting hopelessly to raise the import duty on cotton, she warned that "the tariff doctors in Washington" would "die in the last ditch before the duty on steel and iron is lowered."[18]

Though she wrote freely about state and national affairs, Mrs. Felton did not forget that her main concern as a columnist was to give advice on how the home could be made more comfortable. She had plenty of such advice. Modern conveniences, she said, should be installed. Some, however, were dangerous and must be handled with care. All should be bought only when they could be afforded. Electricity, she assured her readers, had given her many conveniences, but live wires, especially during lightning storms, could shock painfully and sometimes kill. Telephones were invaluable during emergencies, and could also keep the farmer in touch with market prices. Any decent husband would have water piped to his house as soon as he could afford it. If his hard-working wife was forced to get her household water from a well, she lifted, according to Mrs. Felton, 1,200 pounds every day.[19]

Mrs. Felton's first suggestion for a woman furnishing her house was "don't go beyond your means." It did not require "a gigantic spread of things" to make a home livable: a comfortable bed, a good set of chairs, an adequate fireplace or heater, and "a satis-factorily-arranged cooking place." Luxuries should only be added to these essentials when they could be afforded. If the modern housewife was as enterprising as her grandmother — and Mrs. Felton — she could make things, such as hooked rugs, for her home.[20]

Women and their daughters wanted to appear presentable, of course, but Mrs. Felton had some set opinions about female styles. A woman should buy the clothes that she could afford and never subject herself to the "care of dunning letters." By learning to sew, a mother could make many things and "stamp her person-ality" on the dresses worn by herself and daughters. A staunch isolationist, even in matters of dress, Mrs. Felton roundly con-demned those American women who "went to Paris for hobble skirts and hats as large as umbrellas." Current styles upset her, especially those skin-tight dresses which made the wearer's bosom "swell out like a pouter pigeon" and seemed always "about to pop around the lower limbs." Mrs. Felton reported that "even Chicago preachers" were condemning them. Knowing that most of her women readers wore corsets, she warned about an itinerant saleswoman traveling through Georgia selling "a fraudulent girdle for weakly women."[21]

To help with the eternal problem of planning tempting meals, Mrs. Felton furnished many recipes and encouraged her readers to send in theirs. She loved to recall the food on her mother's table and tell how it was prepared: cornmeal waffles, home-ground sausage, and her favorite dish, lye hominy. Stubbornly she refused to believe that a diet of corn products caused pellagra, offering as an example her long, healthy life.[22]

Little has been found in her columns about how mothers could make homes more attractive for their sons and daughters. She did advise that they be encouraged to entertain friends, and she even suggested a "spooning parlor" for the girls so that they would do their courting at home. She had much, however, to say about the rearing of children. They must be taught proper table manners, and she gave a stern set of rules, covering every step from sitting down quietly at the table to asking to be excused. Children should not be forced to eat, but tantrums were not to be tolerated, even if the culprit had to be tied in his chair until "he cried it out." They must answer their elders respectfully. If "yes sir" and "yes ma'm" seemed old-fashioned, they could be dropped and the older person's name added to the answer. Whipping she considered a risky punishment, but she admitted that recently her fingers had itched to slap the jaws of an impudent young girl.[23]

For the lesser problems that plagued the farm wife, Mrs. Felton furnished many helpful hints. Flaxseed should be used to get foreign matter out of the eye. Chloride of lime would remove mildew. In a sick room kerosene wicks should be sprinkled with salt to remove their oily odor. A girl wrote her how to get warts off a cow's teat: tie a silk thread around the wart and it would drop off in a few days. Mrs. Felton offered several remedies for bedbugs, but confessed she did not have great faith in any of them. However, the pests did always make her think of the story about a small child who had been taught that angels watched over her sleep. One night the mother heard her scream, "Mama, the angels are biting me."[24]

Mrs. Felton was sincerely concerned with those crises which many diseases can bring periodically into a home. She had lost three small sons and a daughter, and she understood that no greater sorrow can come to a mother. Having grown up in the days when doctors were not readily available and medicines were largely home-made, her opinions about the causes of certain diseases and her proposed remedies were not always reliable. Nervous prostration she considered an indication of weakness of character. It had become a "fashionable disease," and sufferers insisted on going to high-priced sanitariums instead of taking a rest at home. She was convinced that pellagra was caused by "some imported germ that has come across the water along with diseased immigrants." The increasing number of deaths from cancer worried her. Somewhere she had read that "mice are credited with carrying the virus to the ignorant and unsuspecting." But she could not offer this as a fact. She did, however, share the current belief that "severe bruises eventuate in cancer."[25]

She was puzzled by the fact that a troublesome appendix could be removed without any apparent loss to the body. The theory she advanced as an explanation had, at least, the merit of novelty:

It is a possible surmise that the rib taken from Adam may have left an unfinished organ that wanted to grow into something of value like the lungs, the heart, the liver and such like.[26]

Although she suggested many remedies and welcomed others sent in by her readers, she refused to publicize any that would cost the patient money. Her prescription that aroused the most interest was a cure for consumption by "the distinguished Dr. Hoff of Vienna." In recommending it to her readers, however, she merely supplied the formula, along with Dr. Hoff's rather modest account of its benefits. For historical interest she gave, with the help of Dr. Joe Jacobs of Atlanta, a detailed account of the drugs and remedies of antebellum Georgia. Always mindful of the injustice man was capable of doing to woman, she warned the farm wife to be careful in giving medicine to a sick husband. If he died later, from whatever cause, she might well be accused of having poisoned him.[27]

Mrs. Felton refused sharply to accept the idea that the wife alone was responsible for the comfort and operation of a home. She had no patience with Dorothy Dix's "extended" and "sometimes tiresome" advice that a woman should keep a smiling face before her husband, even when "she is greatly worried over the baby, or tired to death over a hot stove." Marriage was a contract, and the husband must live up to his part in it. Girls must help also. A daughter who has watched her mother cook and iron all day should, at least, be willing to do the dishes and keep the house in order.[28]

If her younger readers did not become good wives and mothers, it was not from Mrs. Felton's lack of effort. She had a column of "don'ts" for them too, which included such admonitions as "don't put off your good manners when you put off your good clothes," don't be disrespectful to older people, and don't listen to gossip and filthy stories.[29]

In a column under the caption "Dear Girls, Be Careful," she urged them to keep their thoughts and themselves innocent. There were dangers on all sides. No girl should be allowed to go on the city streets after dark, warned Mrs. Felton, "when lust and liquor have the right of way." Mothers should not permit daughters to ride to and from dances without chaperons. Even the innocent-looking soft-drink parlors could be a girl's downfall. Dope could easily be slipped into a harmless soda. She realized some girls would say, "Pshaw, Mrs. Felton is getting too old to understand that things have changed." Well, she had seen more than one girl whose reputation had been ruined by just such lack of watch-fullness.[30]

She insisted that the mother who wanted to be completely sure of her daughter's safety must curtail many accepted amusements. Mrs. Felton admitted dancing in her own youth, but now she saw the danger in it. If dancing aroused no sexual desire in men, why then, she asked triumphantly, did they not dance together? She had never watched the current "bunny-hug," but she suspected it was like "those oldtime waltz hugs, except a little more so." People of her generation had frowned on young girls who accepted presents from admirers, and she thought it still "an unwise thing to do." A girl could soon find herself under obligations to a man and be forced to suffer embarrassing humiliations. Mrs. Felton unearthed a more modern danger in the craze for "kodak like-nesses." Pictures of a girl could become a malicious instrument in the hands of a rejected suitor.[31]

The alarming increase in divorces Mrs. Felton blamed upon hasty and loveless marriages. When a man bought a piece of land, he examined the title carefully to make sure that there were no claims against it. A girl would do well to examine just as closely the history of a suitor she was inclined to accept. Marriages for social position or money were not likely to succeed. "The mixtures were wrong at the start, and the divisions will be troublesome at the end." Mrs. Felton refused to help young girls find husbands. Her capacity as a matchmaker, she said, was meagre, and she had "a distinct aversion to any sort of haphazard marriage." Nor would she try to persuade a girl not to marry some certain man. She had done so once, but the girl married the man, and he later "gave her a heap of worry." However, added Mrs. Felton philosophically, "I think she would have been just as unhappy if she had cast him off."[32]

Although Mrs. Felton undoubtedly believed that boys needed less protection than girls, she had pitfalls to point out to them. The cigarette habit, she said, was "destroying the physical and mental forces of the boys of our country." It was time Congress took action against this evil. She did not condemn theatre-going so roundly, but it should be done in moderation. She knew a "broken-hearted mother" whose son had stayed up so late at shows that he was unfit the following mornings for the alert work of a bank. Boys should not be allowed to drive automobiles, and she told of another mother who had died of grief when her son was killed in a speeding car. Profanity, especially in front of women, she denounced vigorously in one column, and the drink habit in many another. She warned her young readers that the first yielding to temptation might ruin their entire career.[33]

Probably the readers Mrs. Felton gave the greatest pleasure and help were the Confederate veterans. At the beginning of the new century the old soldiers had little to do but talk about their war experiences, as the younger generations were growing indifferent to what happened in the 'sixties. Her columns on the great battles and leaders reawakened the pride and interest of the men who had marched with Stonewall Jackson or ridden with Nathan Bedford Forrest. She knew what they had done and suffered, and she insisted that they must not be forgotten and neglected. Eagerly they read all that she wrote. The Atlanta *Journal* was elevated in their estimation to a place along side *The Confederate Veteran* and the *Wesleyan Christian Advocate.*[34]

Many of them had been too careless or proud to apply for the pension offered by their states. Now in their old age they needed this financial help, but could not furnish the proof of their war service required to get them on the pension rolls. Mrs. Felton gladly published their names and regiments, and urged their old comrades to send in the needed endorsements. She agitated for the state to extend a dead veteran's pension to any crippled children he might have. And she angrily attacked the Atlanta Soldiers' Home for turning out a troublesome old soldier.[35]

In her dictatorial way she became the champion of the men who had survived those days when she too had suffered greatly. She dared to tell them that the war had been a mistake, brought on by those hot-headed statesmen who had led for secession; but she hastened to point out that their great leader, Robert E. Lee, had stood for the union until his state left it. She did not absolve the Yankees of blame. Slavery had been the basic cause of the war, she said, and Northerners had brought in the first slaves and tried to work them. But when they could not stand a rigorous climate, they had been shipped South to be sold at a profit.[36]

Although she was older than some of the veterans, she worried about their taking those hard trips to reunions which she sometimes attended. The July sun would be hot again over Gettysburg, she warned. She was disturbed by their whiskey drinking. From one reunion she sadly reported that there was "some booze" in evidence. When General George P. Harrison, their commander, rallied his dwindling forces against national prohibition, she told him that such a sinful stand would injure the veterans' reputation. One old fellow who always got drunk when his pension money arrived exasperated her so that she thought his pension should be stopped.[37]

They understood, however, that her concern for them was sincere, and probably paid no more attention to her lectures than they did to those of their women folks at home. They respected her too highly to argue. One even kept his Georgia temper when she attacked his dead commander. Still bitter over the theft of needed horses forty years before, she wrote a column whose caption told plainly what was to follow: "Thieving Wheeler Raiders." A Veteran of that command, W. C. Dodson, composed a stout defense of his general, but added that he knew she would never "intentionally wound any worthy Confederate."[38]

Mrs. Felton's attitude towards whisky-drinking might be too strict for the veterans, and her code of conduct too stern for the younger people; but on those broader issues which concerned all of her readers, she undoubtedly expressed their views. Her religious beliefs, feelings about the Negro, and antagonism to alien ideas were basically those of agrarian Georgia.

By the turn of the century, Darwinism and a more liberal theology had won many converts in the urban North, but the

evangelical Protestents of the South, with their Bible schools and
revivals, were standing firm for traditional Christianity. Mrs. Felton was of their number. Since she joined the Methodist Church
as a young girl, she had apparently never questioned that faith.
Invited once to hear Robert Ingersoll, the vocal agnostic, she had
refused. Her religion, she said, was "too precious . . . and necessary
to take any chances with it." She fought with bishops about
woman's rights within and without her church, but she accepted
the literal interpretation of the Bible — and she was ready to
defend her orthodoxy.[39]

She knew that the higher criticism had weakened the faith of
many laymen and some preachers, but she saw no good resulting
from this rationalistic trend. If a Christian's belief was "wrenched
away" from the Bible, what could he "depend upon as a mainstay
for clean and upright living"? She brushed aside the theory of
evolution with the unoriginal conclusion that she "had rather
trace her descent from Adam than from a ring-tailed monkey at
any time." Her belief in a personal immortality was firm; she
expected to know again in heaven those small children she had
buried. Prayer accomplished much, she was sure, but she doubted
the advisability of praying for victory in war. God — like her —
must hate wars fought for whatever cause.[40]

Like her readers, she was suspicious of Roman Catholicism, and
she warned that its spread throughout the country, and especially
in New York, was endangering both religious and civil liberty in
America. Already, she declared, "the Pope dominates a large part
of the religious world on both continents." On the other hand,
she was substantially correct in informing the New York *Times*
that there was no "Jew-baiting" in Georgia. She deplored "the
harem features of Mormon life," but she was inclined to think
well of Mary Baker Eddy, the lady founder of Christian Science.[41]

The dynamic revivalism of Billy Sunday, Gipsy Smith, and
Cartersville's own Sam Jones did far more, she contended, to increase church membership than all the staid preaching of the
fashionable city churches. She was too nationalistic to approve
of foreign missions, and too old-fashioned to endorse cremation.
In attacking the movement towards national unity in her church,
she told how at a conference of the Northern Baptist Church, one
Reverend Alex Bealer had proudly announced that he was "part
Indian, part white and 'more nigger.' "[42]

Stoutly she maintained that the church should not only preach religion but should also fight for such needed reforms as national prohibition and woman's suffrage. She selected and published a long list of quotations from the Bible against the danger of strong drink. When the Southern Methodist Conference came out for prohibition, she announced that the church was now "allied to righteousness." She published, with evident delight, a quotation of Sam Jones sent her by a reader: "Liquor is all right in its place, and in hell is its place."[43]

Her fixed aversion to the male sex intensified her Southern antipathy for the Negro. The physical danger to white women from Negroes became an abiding obsession, and the retaliation she advocated was swift and primitive. In an address to the Georgia Agricultural Society in 1897, she demanded that the women of rural Georgia be protected from "black rapists." If the orderly processes of law could not put a stop to that crime, then she called for the lynching of a thousand Negroes a week — if necessary. Her intemperate words brought an angry reply from Negro editor A. L. Manley of Wilmington, North Carolina. His impudence to a white lady was publicized in the North Carolina press and not forgotten by the whites of Wilmington. A year later when they turned out their city's Republican administration, they paid a visit to Manley's newspaper office. Several Negroes were killed in the so-called "Manley Riots." The offending editor fled North to be welcomed warmly by his fellow-journalists of New York City.[44]

Rebecca Felton had lived close to such violent acts. She had listened one night in the ominous stillness of her farm house for the first sounds of a mob hunting the Negro charged with attacking a woman north of Cartersville. She also could feel the fear and anger that sent grim-faced men searching through the darkness. Bluntly she warned a New York newspaper that "as long as rape violence prevails in Georgia, then lynching is going to continue." She praised Governor Cole Blease of South Carolina when he announced that he would make no effort to identify anyone who had punished the ravisher of a white woman. However, she ridiculed the suggestion that farm wives should carry pistols. How, she asked, could a mother with a dangerous, cumbersome weapon in her apron pocket feed a child or cook a meal? No, let the men of Georgia find ways to protect the "child-bearing women of Georgia."[45]

Mrs. Felton stated flatly that the Anglo-Saxon and Celtic races

would always be superior to the Negro — and the Negro realized
his inferiority. Education and social equality only unfitted him to
live contentedly either among his own people or among those
whites who had unwisely advanced him. She told of a Haitian
Negro, educated at an English university, who finally came to
curse his black skin. When she lived in Washington she had
strongly disapproved of the attention showered upon Frederick
Douglass, the American Negro consul general to Haiti. Years later
in her *Journal* column, she repeated the rumor that Douglass,
before he died, claimed to have been born of white parents.[46]

Ironically, Mrs. Felton took up her first reform cause, the
abolition of convict leasing, because of injustice done to a member of the Negro race. A young colored girl had been sentenced,
for a trivial misdemeanor, to a prison camp. Mrs. Felton's racial
feeling, however, was stronger than her concern for her own sex.
She persistently attacked Northern philanthropists for donating
money to give Southern Negro girls an education "far beyond
that of the untrained white girls of the mountains and wiregrass."[47]

With evident satisfaction she pointed out that other sections
of the country were now learning the facts about racial problems.
In California the continuous Japanese immigration had "put the
shoe . . . on the other foot." Bloody race riots were disturbing
Illinois, and in several Eastern cities a steady influx of Negroes
was depressing real estate values. More problems and disorders,
she warned, were in store for those who had been so free in
criticizing the South's treatment of its Negroes.[48]

From the Southern viewpoint her only radicalism was her
advocacy of wider rights for women. In pushing this reform, however, she appealed to deeper prejudices in the Southern male.
Never would she let Georgia men forget that the fourteenth and
fifteenth amendments extended suffrage to Negro men but not to
white women. She quoted Senator George Hoar of Massachusetts
who asked if any man, however wealthy, had a greater stake in
the country's welfare than did a mother. Women voting now in
certain Western states were, she insisted, as good wives and mothers as the women of the South. Besides, their votes had helped
keep political control out of the hands of racial groups. A Georgia
male might not accept such arguments, but he would not have
cared to debate them.[49]

She was determined that white women must be safeguarded
against the brutality not only of Negroes but of white men, and

she recommended the same violent punishment for offenders from both races. Hearing that an Atlanta white man had whipped his wife, she urged that "the two-legged brute . . . be made to feel the lash." A south Georgia woman wrote that a neighboring farmer had unjustly accused his daughter of immorality and shot her. "If I had my way," replied Mrs. Felton, "I'd lynch him." On the other hand, her extreme feminism led her to beg that a proved murderess be spared execution because she was a woman and could have had "the privilege, or maybe only the pain, of motherhood."[50]

On almost all other issues she was rigidly conservative. She believed that the spread of wars and revolutions in Europe had been caused by socialism. Property rights to her were sacred. Many Americans were using socialism "as a cloak to rob people who by thrift and industry have accumulated fortunes." Socialists were already disturbing politics in the North, and she predicted, with some vision, that in the future many office-seekers would get votes by promising legislation to help the poor.[51]

Anarchists, she said, had caused the rift between capital and labor. Unless both sides regained mutual "respect and consideration, the difficulty might end in civil strife." She urged that labor be allowed "the enjoyment of its rights," but opposed both the Eight Hour Labor Law and the Child Labor Law. Paying the same wages for less work was going to disturb the nation's economy, she protested; and refusing to allow the children of widows to work in cotton factories would work a hardship on many families.[52]

Mrs. Felton's conservative temperament persuaded her that isolationism was the nation's only safe foreign policy. If the Monroe Doctrine was the country's "established doctrine," then it should be applied "at all points and be maintained at all hazards." Disliking the British heartily, she insisted that in annexing Hawaii and the Philippines, the United States was adopting "the policy of England in South Africa." She admired Theodore Roosevelt and supported his Bull Moose Party in 1912, but she considered his mania for a great navy a "crazy" idea. Never enthusiastic about Woodrow Wilson, she became a bitter opponent of his League of Nations.[53]

August, 1914, reawakened and intensified her horror of war. She recalled an article in *Scribner's Magazine* of 1894 forecasting the destruction of the next European war, but found "the reality so far exceeds the prophecy that it sounds like cheap talk." The deadly new weapons appalled her, and she kept her readers informed of their grisly efficiency. After a zeppelin raid over London women were found "dying from absolute terror with not a scratch on their dead bodies." The submarine was as dangerous as a "mad dog," and liquid fire destroyed soldiers "like rats." Fervently she prayed that her country could stay out of the holocaust, and use its great powers to bring peace. She berated people who jeered at Henry Ford's Peace Ship, promising that if she were twenty years younger she would be among the passengers.[54]

She refused to cheer the Russian Revolution, seeing it rather as a triumph of anarchy. "When the mob rules," she warned, "the issue is more than uncertain." Her gloomy prediction, she felt, was more than confirmed when she read that the Bolsheviki had ordered all women of child-bearing age to select a man and produce children for the state. She prayed that the poor women might be "taken out of the world by a plague."[55]

When America entered the war, she admitted that it had no other choice. She was glad the fighting would be done on foreign soil, but she refused to "shout over the opportunity to go to France and fight the Germans." She worried over the comfort and safety of the American soldiers and thanked God devoutly when peace came to all.[56]

When the isolationists of Georgia made the League of Nations a political issue, she gave them loud support. William Randolph Hearst's Atlanta *Georgian* welcomed her fiery articles demanding that no more American boys be sent to Europe's wars. She gave valuable aid in re-electing Watson to the Senate and electing Thomas Hardwick governor. In 1922 Hardwick repaid her with an interim appointment to Georgia's Senate seat made vacant by Watson's death. Rebecca Felton could never retire from public affairs, but after her high honor, she relaxed a little and became something of a grandmother to the nation.[57]

It is impossible to say exactly when she gave up her column in the *Journal*. Few clippings of articles written after 1918 are found in her scrapbooks. The copy of a letter from her to James Gray, editor of the *Journal,* reveals that by February, 1919, she had become unhappy on that pro-League paper. An article of hers had been left out of the *Journal,* and she was furious. She did not "pet poodle dogs or paint china plates or embroider table mats," but she knew that the paper's readers had always been pleased with what she wrote. No reply from Gray has been located, but a date on one of her clippings indicates that she was still working for the *Journal* in the fall of 1921. At least it can be assumed that when she returned from Washington in 1922 as a former senator she had given up her position with the paper.[58] She lived until 1930, full of her memories and of forebodings about the changing world around her.

It is difficult to estimate the influence of most journalists. Mrs. Felton could, however, offer proof that her columns in the *Journal* were read by many with interest and considerable approval. As she once wrote her publisher, "hundreds of private letters" assured her "that the readers were pleased with my ideas and comments." She published many of these letters in her columns, sometimes adding comments, sometimes discussing them in later columns. Frequently a published letter would impel other readers to comment upon it, send in needed information, or tell of similar experiences.[59]

In one mail she received letters from the following people: a widow trying to sell some short stories; a widower seeking a second wife and giving specifications; a young girl asking for comfort in the loss of a mother; a school boy needing information for a debate; and a needy man requesting the name of a kind philanthropist.[60]

Both men and women brought their problems to her. A farmer wanted her suggestions for cleaning cotton just before ginning. Another asked what to do about his turkeys that were "dying suddenly with their heads drawn back." A wife did not know what to do about her husband who "was a great hand at dancing," and a mother needed advice on safe books for her children to read. An unusual request came from an old veteran who could "get along all right with preserves and jellies," but wanted a recipe for tomato catsup and spiced tomatoes.[61]

A request from Mrs. Felton for information always seemed to bring replies. A woman in Round Oak sent in three remedies for killing chinch bugs, and three men hastened to tell her how to break a sow from eating its litter. When she announced in her column that she wished to buy some pigs — possibly the sow could not be cured of her infanticide — a farmer in Quitman wrote that he would "do his best" to get her the kind she wanted. When the ever-troublesome animals began to die with hog cholera, a lady in Cairo offered a remedy. A farmer in Senoia modestly tried to solve her problem of a portable fence. He was sure she would receive "many letters and drawings much better written," but he would "show a willingness" by doing the best he could.[62]

She reported her accidents and ailments to her readers, and they were quick to offer sympathy and cures. When she stuck a nail in her foot, she received a variety of remedies. A man in Rome seemed most confident that saltpeter sealed in the wound would heal it immediately. He had tried the remedy most successfully on "man and beast." Her inflamed eye worried an anonymous reader so much that he wrote advising steam and the white of an egg. A South Carolina lady was most sympathetic when Mrs. Felton mashed a finger, and after her injury in a railroad wreck near Atlanta, she received so many letters that she could not answer them individually.[63]

Like Mrs. Felton, many of her women readers were intensely interested in the prevalent diseases of the day. There was evidently a widespread dread of consumption. Several wrote for Dr. Hoff's medicine, but others had homemade remedies to suggest. A woman in Ruffin, North Carolina, believed that warm cow's milk could start a recovery, and "a friend" sent in a hot-lemonade cure that became popular with the readers. Meningitis could be relieved, wrote a farmer's wife from Maddox, by rubbing with turpentine and giving "a quick dose of salts." A lady who signed her letter "Winnie" advised for teething babies the milk recipe in *Annie Dennis Cook Book*. Although Mrs. Felton insisted she would not recommend medicines that cost money, she did allow a man from Greer, South Carolina, to offer a cure for nasal catarrh "for anything they wish to give me in return."[64]

Men praised her views on current issues. From Waxhaw, North Carolina, one encouraged her to keep up her fight against high taxation, and a veteran in Mena, Alabama, hoped she would go on "puncturing the ulcers of Corruption." A man in Dallas, Georgia, made a scrapbook of her articles, and a citizen of Cartersville was so impressed with her piece on profanity that he promised "if he cussed, he would stay out of the presence of ladies."[65]

Women brought their personal, as well as their practical, problems to her. One wanted to know what to do about a husband who was "carrying on illicit relations with a fast woman." Should one leave a husband who "sits down and waits for his wife to support him"? A farm wife wondered if she should persuade her husband to take a job in an Augusta factory. When the husband seemed set in his sinful or careless ways, Mrs. Felton's advice was brief and to the point: leave him. One woman mourning the death of her mother begged her to "write occasionally" on any subject.[66]

Even young girls wrote the stern old grandmother for advice. Should they marry a jealous man? Should they be honest and tell everything to their husbands? One young lady asked, rather coyly, if it was all right to be engaged to two men. She got a blunt answer: it was all right if she was willing to risk a "shooting scrape." Strict moralist that she was, Mrs. Felton helped one fallen girl to find another home.[67]

Men and women brought their religious doubts and questions to her. Yes, she believed in a personal immortality. No, Woodrow Wilson was not a Catholic. All foreigners were not Jews. When a man in Blaine, Georgia, sent her "a newspaper reprint of what is said to be a letter written by Christ," she warned him to "go a trifle slow on things of this kind." As World War I drew to a close a man in Culberson, North Carolina, advised her that "we are nearing the end of the world."[68]

Her columns were thrown open to those seeking lost relatives. A girl in Stockbridge had not heard from her brother since he left for Mississippi. A needy widow in Dalton was trying to communicate with her grandfather. Mrs. Felton urged that anyone knowing the whereabouts of a Milledgeville man inform his wife who was left with five small children. At least one of the lost was found through her efforts: a boy who had escaped from an Alabama orphanage. It could be that he was not as jubilant over Mrs. Felton's success as she was.[69]

Evidently her readers were quick to send her news that might bring forth her fiery comments. A man in Cartersville wrote about a prison guard who had unmercifully beaten a white woman prisoner. A woman heard a Yankee say that the murder of Mary Phagan in an Atlanta pencil factory did not matter greatly since she was "nothing but a poor work girl." Reading in the *Saturday Evening Post* a slur on the late Mrs. Jefferson Davis, a "Mrs. B.S.W." wanted Mrs. Felton to write "a protest." Usually she responded in the way her readers expected. In discussing the evil ways of men, however, one letter writer, signing herself "A Georgia Grandmother," outdid Grandma Felton in the severity of the punishment suggested. A white man who slept with Negro women,

she said, should be branded "with a proper letter or mark on
his face."[70]

Some must have believed she ran the state legislature. They
wanted bills passed prohibiting the buying of a Negro "out of jail
or off the chaingang," "limiting the time of a rural mail carrier
to four years," and forbidding the driving of automobiles in the
city on Wednesdays, Saturdays, and Sundays so that country people could walk there in safety. A man, obviously believing that her
influence extended to the national legislature, urged her to get a
congressional bill passed making it illegal to use the Virgin Mary's
picture in tobacco and whisky advertising. She did lead two rousing campaigns to raise the age of consent in the state and to tax
dogs. Her readers helped with heavily-endorsed petitions.[71]

She prized her letters from the Confederate veterans and published many of them in her column. "Send on your letters, Veterans," she begged, "I'll shape them up for you." Their experiences, she assured them, were needed for a true understanding of
the war, and their comrades would love to hear from them through
her articles. They hastened to oblige the lady in their "stammer-
ing way," as one veteran put it.[72]

Some were still full of fight and resentment. One boasted that
"we always whipped them," and another said that for three years
he fought in every battle of the Army of Northern Virginia until
he lost his leg. A Georgia veteran wrote that the only roll call
before battle he missed was when he went home to marry his
present wife. They told how the earth shook from the Fredericks-
burg cannonade; how the Yankees charged six deep at Second
Manassas; how men in the grey columns marched asleep as they
came into Spotsylvania. There were angry comments about the
Negro guards at Point Lookout and against the Reconstruction
governors who had disfranchised former Confederates. A Georgian
was proud of a comrade who had never asked for pardon, and a
North Carolinian reported a peacetime achievement: he could
count seventy-eight grandchildren.[73]

Other letters, however, told of age and loneliness — harder to
bear than the trenches around Petersburg and the blazing breast-
works at Franklin. They wrote, also, of their ailments: "I have
been down with rhumatism for eight years"; "I am now unable to
do much but talk"; and "I have been on crutches for twenty-five
years." They had little to look forward to now but death. As an
Alabama veteran put it, there were only "a few old stragglers . . .

still on this side of the river." He was surely speaking for those remaining comrades when he thanked her for "the efforts" she was making "to honor and comfort them."[74]

The veterans were not her only readers to send their fulsome thanks and admiration. Men wrote that she was "the smartest woman in Georgia"; that she spoke the truth "on every subject"; that they had admired "her letters" from the day she wrote the first one. A Florida lady considered her "a wonderfully good, broad-minded, thinking woman," and from Texas another sent wishes that she would "be spared many years to continue her good work." A father prayed that young girls would "read carefully" all she wrote and "heed her timely advice," and an Atlanta woman wrote that if she was "so fortunate as to get to heaven" she knew she would see Mrs. Felton there.[75]

They found many ways to express their affection. One man compared her to "a faithful clock," and a rather unusual son-in-law thought her picture in the *Journal* looked "so much like his wife's sainted mother." At least two poems were written in her honor and three children named for her. Gifts came steadily to the Bartow County farmhouse: oranges, goobers, and seeds said to grow plants that would keep away house flies. When she told in her column how her Christmas turkey had been stolen from its pen, a Lavonia farmer sent her a dressed one so as to "overcome the turkey thief this time." Perhaps the most unique compliment received was the request from a man in Florida to christen with her name "a fast boat for running iced fish."[76]

They greeted her on her birthdays and worried about her health and advancing age. They wrote her, sometimes anonymously, of their secret thoughts and most urgent problems. Letters came from Dickey, Warwick, Brown's Crossing, and Chauncy in Georgia; from Gaylesville in Alabama, Ruffin in North Carolina, and Slidell in Louisiana. They came from Georgians in distant states: Texas, Arkansas, even Montana and Iowa. Two Baptist missionaries in Guadalajara, Mexico, sent a New Year's card. She loved their letters and promised that she would always try to reply "especially when a stamp" was enclosed "for the return letter."[77]

When her column appeared no more in the *Journal,* many must have felt a real loss. For over two decades she had spoken for them, said the things they wanted to say, attacked what they hated, defended what they cherished. Perhaps a story of hers best illustrates their feeling for her. As she was getting off the train at

Ashburn, Georgia, a young conductor looked at her closely and asked: "Aren't you the Mrs. Felton who writes for us?" She could hardly have asked for greater praise.[78]

HOKE SMITH

BY JOHN CHALMERS VINSON

FEW MEN in Georgia's history have contributed more to the advancement of the state and the nation than Hoke Smith. One of the first Southerners to hold cabinet rank in the years after the Civil War, he served as secretary of the interior during Grover Cleveland's second administration. Later he was twice chosen to be governor of the state and twice elected to the United States Senate. He concluded his career with an unsuccessful campaign for the Senate in 1920. In each of these important phases of his public service he discharged his duties with distinction.

A native of North Carolina, he was born at Chapel Hill in 1855. His father, Hosea Smith, was at the time professor of Greek and Latin at the University of North Carolina. After the Civil War the elder Smith was forced to resign when the university fell under the control of the carpetbag government.[1] Little is known of Hoke Smith's boyhood, but family adversities during the Reconstruction days could not have failed to impress him deeply. No doubt his deep and unwavering devotion to the Democratic party was rooted in the harsh and bitter experiences of those blighted years. His father, who had once been president of Catawba College, operated a private school in Lincolnton, North Carolina, after leaving Chapel Hill. Some years later he moved to Atlanta, Georgia, where he was in the public school system for the rest of his life. It must have been a great disappointment to one so learned to be unable to bestow upon his son the opportunities of a formal education. As best he could, the father sought to make up for this deficiency by tutoring the son who acquired a very well-rounded education for the times in which he lived.

At the age of seventeen, the year he arrived in Atlanta, Hoke

John Chalmers Vinson is a member of the history faculty at the University of Georgia.

decided on a career in law. As was the custom, he read law in an office, in his case that of Collier, Mynatt, and Collier, to prepare himself for his profession. The devotion of the father, the ability of the son, and possibly to some extent the laxness of the requirements were demonstrated when he was able to pass the bar examination the next year at the age of eighteen.[2]

Beginning the practice of law the same year and renting an office in the same building with Smith was another ambitious young man, Woodrow Wilson. Smith met with immediate success; Wilson did not. This circumstance was supposed to have fostered a rivalry forty years later when the former was a senator and the latter the President.

Smith brought to his profession in addition to native intelligence and a comparatively good education a fine speaking voice and a talent for oratory. Although not handsome, his appearance was impressive, for he was more than six feet in height and proportioned along broad lines. Probably through necessity rather than choice the young lawyer built his practice upon service to the general public rather than to the corporations. A large number of his early cases were suits against the railroads, a fact that was an asset in his later career as a politician. So industrious and determined was Smith in his work, so keen was his business acumen, and so polished his legal skill that he amassed a fortune estimated at not less than $300,000 by the time he had reached the age of thirty-five.[3]

From the beginning of his career, Smith took a keen interest in politics. He became actively engaged in the work of the Democratic party as soon as he entered the practice of law, and served as chairman of the Democratic Executive Board for Fulton County before he was old enough to vote.[4] This early promise of a public career was not immediately realized. He did not hold another party office until 1882, when he served as a delegate to the state Democratic convention. From that time on, he was an important figure in party circles, but did not seek public office for another decade. His interest was concentrated on the organization of the party and the promotion of his favorites. It was as king-maker rather than king that Smith applied his political energies in the 1880's.

His growing political influence was augmented in 1887 when he purchased the Atlanta *Journal*. At this time Henry Grady was at the height of his powers as a journalist and sideline statesman.

Many thought Smith was seeking to emulate his famous fellow Georgian by entering the field of journalism.[5] The $10,000 paid for what was then a second-rate paper became a profitable investment, as Smith with unbounded energy and sagacious direction rapidly improved the *Journal,* making financial and political capital from its rivalry with the *Constitution.*

Thus equipped by professional success, party influence, and journalistic power, Smith was ready to assume an important role in Georgia politics. Opportunity presented itself in 1890 with the race for the Senate. Grady had died the year before, leaving the role of leadership in the Democratic party in Georgia open to a new champion. Smith was drawn into the campaign because an old friend, General John B. Gordon, was a candidate. The old hero faced a more difficult race than usual. The Democratic party and its conservative leaders were being challenged by the newly-organized Farmer's Alliance, later to be known as the Populist party. The appeal of the Alliance lay in its advocacy of a definite plan of reform which offered the first ray of hope in years to the poverty-stricken Southern farmer. Although growing rapidly, the Alliance did not in 1890 have the strength to defeat the Democratic party. It was able, however, to offer the first challenge to the Democrats in twenty years by exploiting the factional nature of the dominant party. The Alliance, holding the balance of power between warring Democrats, could force candidates to espouse its principles in order to win its support.

"Bring out the yard stick and let the candidate be measured," was the slogan of the hour. General Gordon's affinity for railroad finance and big business rendered his stature small as measured by the Alliance yard stick. To Hoke Smith was given the difficult task of presenting a former railroad president as the farmers' friend.

Smith handled this crucial issue superbly, making good use of the *Journal* as a forum for informing the electorate.[6] Aiding him in this task of reconciliation was his own record as a determined legal foe of the railroads. The candidate's qualifications were shown to fit the Alliance's requirements. Before the campaign was over Gordon had embraced the entire Alliance platform except the sub-treasury plank. With Smith leading the way the general and the Alliance marched to victory.[7]

An unusual opportunity for further use of his rapidly growing influence came to Smith with the pre-convention contest for the Democratic presidential nomination in 1892. Former President

Grover Cleveland, the only successful standard bearer of his party in a generation, was the leading candidate. Conservative in view and callous to the trend of the times, Cleveland had alienated many Georgians with his outspoken opposition to the "free silver" panacea which was beginning to fire the imagination of the frustrated farm population. The "ugly honest man" dismayed even his closest friends by refusing to modify his stand or to remain silent on this issue.

Other Democrats, including Governor David B. Hill of New York, sought to exploit Cleveland's indiscretion as a means of blocking his nomination. Hill hoped by snap conventions in Georgia and New York to win the support which would make him the choice of the party. This situation gave young Hoke Smith an inordinately large voice in national politics in 1892. The Georgian threw his support behind Cleveland and was largely responsible for thwarting Hill's hopes. As a delegate-at-large to the Democratic National Convention, Smith continued his effective support of Cleveland's candidacy. When the nomination had been secured for his favorite, no effort in canvassing the state in the interest of a Democratic victory was spared by Smith.[8]

After the election a number of Smith's friends began insisting that the President not overlook the talent and service of Hoke Smith when selecting his cabinet. Many wrote Senator Gordon, who was a close friend of Cleveland, to use his influence in Smith's behalf. The senator, mindful of his own debt, needed little encouragement to present his friend's case. The President, not personally acquainted with Smith, requested proof of the young man's ability. The senator began his plea by citing the fact that Smith had made $150,000 as a lawyer in the poverty-stricken state of Georgia in the preceding ten years. While Gordon had many other evidences of his client's ability, Cleveland felt no further proof was needed.[9] Shortly afterwards Smith was called into conference with Cleveland. The President first offered him the position of secretary of agriculture. Apparently confident of his claims, Smith declined this office and was given the post of secretary of the interior.[10]

The announcement, made in April, 1893, represented an unusual honor. Only five men from the South had held such offices since the Civil War. Three of these — Secretary of the Navy Hilary A. Herbert, Secretary of the Treasury John G. Carlisle, and Smith himself — were members of Cleveland's second cabinet. The state of Georgia had not been so honored since before the Civil War, when Howell Cobb, an uncle of Smith's wife, served in President Buchanan's cabinet.[11]

Smith's success was a source of much gratification to the state. Shortly after his appointment he was honored, along with Vice President Adlai Stevenson and Secretary of the Navy Herbert, at an exposition held in Augusta, Georgia. Each of the distinguished visitors spoke at some length on the theme of the day — the reuniting of the North and the South.[12]

Although the least well-known of Cleveland's cabinet members, Smith had a much broader background in politics and business than his lack of national reputation and youthful appearance might have indicated. This was well, for the interior department at the time Smith took charge was said to be the biggest business office in the world. This one office had charge of the census, pensions, public lands, general welfare of the Indians, Indian land, Indian schools, and preservation of the forests and other public resources.[13] Smith, having had no previous experience in this work, had a very short time to familiarize himself thoroughly with these diverse problems in order to make suitable appointments and properly supervise the department. He went to work immediately upon receiving his appointment, and averaged fourteen hours a day in his office for the first few months.

This strenuous schedule was necessary in order to cope with the demands of the position. The Pension Bureau in the first year handled more than forty thousand applications. Each of these had to be examined closely. The fraudulent claims rejected during Smith's first year represented a saving to the government of $25,000,000.[14] The land office was nearly four years behind in the processing of claims when Smith took charge. This operation was complicated when the depression that followed the Panic of 1893 increased the demand for the rapidly dwindling supply of free land.

The Indian problem was no more muddled than usual, but no nearer final solution. The increasing white population in the West intensified the problem of relations between the two races. The future of the Indian as well as his current welfare was likewise a concern of the thoughtful and conscientious administrator. Little had been done before Smith's time toward the conservation of natural resources. Why should we save resources for posterity? What has posterity done for us? This was the widespread attitude of the time. Exploitation was rampant on the part of railroads, timber companies, and mining outfits. Resources seemed limitless. The apathy of the people aided the exploiter and made more difficult the work of the reformer.

In meeting the numerous and varied problems of the administration the department labored almost from the start under the cloud of economic depression. This forced the most stringent economies into all departments, a sharp contrast to the generous spending of the Harrison administration with its "billion dollar Congress." Regardless of necessity, the administration that effected economy was bound to become unpopular with many people.

The position of secretary of the interior was difficult at best. When Smith took office, a combination of circumstances made official duties even more arduous than usual. However, it was said of Smith that his most marked characteristic was a very strong will and a determination to succeed in any task he undertook.[15] This he did in the judgment of his contemporaries. His term in office was said to be representative of the ideals of a man of high character who believed in good government. He was described as being bold in his denunciation of the wrong, as he saw and understood it, and possessed of moral courage, the greatest attribute of a statesman.[16]

Other commentators praised Smith for putting his department on a current basis by the end of his term. When he took the office, all divisions of the department of the interior were at least six months behind in their work, and in some cases as much as four years in arrears. Only by the best of organization and the utmost efficiency in each division had this improvement been possible.[17] This alone afforded proof that the secretary of the interior had done his work extremely well and in a manner far superior to many of his predecessors.

Smith's economies in office were added evidence of his success. The most striking achievement had been in the pension office where he had saved an estimated $25,000,000 during his first year. Economy was introduced wherever possible, and included saving $80,000 by opening bids on the census printing, reduction of the number of clerks in the land office, and many savings in the Indian service.[18] In each case the economy was the result of greater efficiency rather than an illogical program of cutting expenses simply for the sake of saving.

As another of his accomplishments, Smith was instrumental in bringing to an end a shameful state of affairs in the patent office, where it was then possible to delay indefinitely the issuance of a patent. A typical instance concerned the Berlinger Telephone Company, which held a monopoly on the business in the East. To protect this position, the office was delaying the issuing of certain patents. In rendering a decision on this case, Smith made such a fraudulent delay on a patent impossible in the future.[19]

One achievement praised by Smith's partisans was his work in providing for the conservation of forest lands. Although President Harrison had created, under the terms of the General Revision Act of 1891, six forest reserves, real conservation demanded much more. To this end Smith obtained an appropriation from Congress of $25,000 a year to defray the cost of a survey of the forest conservation problem by a group of experts from the National Academy of Science. A recommendation that thirteen new forest reserves be established grew out of this survey. Smith left the cabinet before the recommendation was enacted into law by Cleveland just before leaving office in 1897. This pioneer work in forest conservation was carried on by Theodore Roosevelt who created in 1907 twenty-one additional reserves.[20]

Probably even more indicative of the success with which Smith discharged his office was the suggestion, frequently made, that he seek even more important political positions in the future. Early in 1896 he was mentioned prominently as a presidential candidate. At the time there was a movement on foot to choose the Democratic nominee from the South. Smith was acclaimed as the most outstanding man in public life from the South and eminently available for the post.[21] While this movement never reached the proportions of a boom, the fact that he was mentioned at all indicates that he had made the most of his three years of public service. Further proof was to be found in the mention he received for a place on the Supreme Court bench, and in the persistent rumors that he would become a senator from Georgia at the conclusion of his term as secretary of the interior.[22]

The manner in which he carried out his duty to the party during his tenure in office dispelled what little doubt there might have been as to his intention of making a career in politics. Beginning early in 1894, and continuing with increasing vigor throughout 1895 and 1896, Smith conducted a campaign which was ostensibly for the purpose of strengthening the Cleveland wing of the Democratic party. He did not go about this duty in

a perfunctory manner. Indeed, so whole-hearted was his elec-
tioneering that he was even accused of neglecting his duty in
Washington in order to be in Georgia on speaking tours. The
facts, however, do not substantiate this charge. He could not have
succeeded as he did had he given only part of his time to official
duties. Time for stumping the state he took from his vacation
periods.[23]

The Cleveland Democrats stood for the gold standard. That
gospel Hoke took to every voter in Georgia he could get to listen
to him. It was freely predicted that the secretary had in mind the
Senate race of 1896. When Smith began his campaign in earnest
early in 1895, the chances of a victory for the "gold" Democrats
seemed good, and a Senate seat appeared to be his for the asking.
The balance, however, soon shifted to the "silver" wing. Smith
did not slacken his pace, but he worked against ever-mounting
odds. The fact that in all of his speeches he pledged his support
to the Democratic party, its candidate, and its platform was to
cause him trouble. Despite Smith's labors the Democratic party,
in its national convention, repudiated Cleveland and endorsed
"free silver."

This confronted Smith with an impossible dilemma — Cleveland and gold, or the Democratic party and silver. Smith bowed
to the decisions of the Democratic National Convention and the
need for party unity. There was no sympathy from the President
he had been forced to repudiate. In September, 1896, Smith resigned from the cabinet. His statement that he would support
the party during the presidential campaign but not accept the
platform did nothing to refurbish his fading political prestige.[24]
Both "gold" and "silver" Democrats attacked him. He was vilified
as a man who had forsaken both his President and his conscience.[25]
Party politician, traitor, inconsistent turncoat, and other less mild
epithets were hurled at him.[26] Politically, Smith was in eclipse.
This, added to the disappointment and disillusionment of a disastrous campaign, removed him from public life for the next
ten years.

True to the conviction which had cost him his cabinet seat,
Smith supported William Jennings Bryan in the campaign but
with the reservation that he would never support the "Great
Commoner" again. At the moment this did not seem to be a
dire threat in view of the low ebb of Smith's political prestige.
It appeared that the promising political career of the forty-one

year old Southerner had fallen victim of an early blight. Even
Smith seemed to accept this theory. He made no move to seek
public office for years. The Atlanta *Journal,* which had played
so important a role in his rise to political preeminence, he sold
in 1900, giving further support to the idea that he had given
up political ambition. The sale price of $300,000 and the fact
that it was in the hands of a close friend, James Gray, may have
afforded him considerable consolation for the loss of the paper.[27]
When he returned to politics at a later date, the *Journal* was to
play an important role.

It was not in Smith's nature to be idle and the depletion of
his wealth as a result of tenure in the cabinet gave him added
incentive for activity. Returning to the full-time practice of law,
his success, particularly in damage suits, was greater than ever
before. This work he thoroughly enjoyed. In later years he declared that a Senate seat was the only position that he would
prefer to that of lawyer. Friends remarked that he found "the
joy in a legal contest that the Viking found in battle."[28]

Another interest of this period was real estate. It was said
that Smith had a golden touch; land which he purchased at a
bargain invariably rose rapidly in value.[29] Broadening his financial and business interests he and some associates built in
1903 the Piedmont Hotel in downtown Atlanta, which proved
to be one of his most important ventures. He also took a prominent role in the establishment of the Fulton National Bank,
which he served as a director for the remainder of his life.[30]

The busy lawyer and financier found time in these years to
give leadership to many local and national organizations dedicated
to the improvement of the community. Among these were the
International Sunday School Association, which he served as
president in 1899,[31] and the Peabody Educational Fund of which
he was a trustee.[32]

Education became his greatest interest in the field of public
service. He personally provided funds for the expansion of Girls'
High School in Atlanta when the city was unable to do so. A
great deal of the wealth he accumulated he distributed to schools
and libraries over the state.[33] Not only his money but his time
was devoted to this cause. Tirelessly Smith toured the state
speaking in favor of the development of more agricultural high
schools and common schools. Education, he felt, should be the
practical tool for the development of the resources of the state.[34]

In great demand as a commencement speaker, he inspired count-less classes of young graduates with his vision of the future greatness of the South and of Georgia.

Such activity aroused the suspicions of those who did not feel any man would serve the public so slavishly without hoping to gain more in return than the knowledge that he had improved the community and the state. It was whispered that the Atlanta lawyer was actually paving the way for a return to the political arena.[35]

This theory was strengthened by Smith's great concern for the numerous farmers of the state. He devoted a great deal of time to study and speaking on the recurring problem of low farm prices. A measure of his insight into the problem was his suggestion that a reduction of acreage was the surest method to bring about an increase in price. Possible political connotations were read into another of his humanitarian activities — support of a child-labor law. He was a strong advocate of this reform, so active indeed as to be appointed to the National Child Labor Committee. When a national child-labor law was passed in 1906, Smith found satisfaction in the knowledge that his unceasing work was in a measure responsible for the victory.

Rumors continued to herald Smith's return to politics. Prob-ably it was not choice but necessity that had accounted for his retirement. Smith's position on the monetary issue during the unhappy days of 1896 had caused him to lose the confidence of both wings of the Democratic party. When the Democratic Con-vention of 1900 endorsed Bryan and "free silver" once again, Smith bent his back declaring that he would support the Democratic ticket regardless of the nominee.[36] At the same time he advised the party to look to a new candidate and a new platform for 1904. The election of 1900 and the prosperity which the country en-joyed thereafter tended to obliterate "free silver" as an issue. As it sank into oblivion, Smith's political star began to rise.

The position most frequently linked with Smith's name was that of governor. This honor he steadfastly refused, but his resurging interest in politics was indicated by the statement in 1902 that he would like to seek a Senate seat at some future date.[37] The Democratic state convention of 1902 demonstrated the grow-ing power of Smith when it refused to approve the party's national platform adopted at Kansas City in 1900. This was a clear indica-tion that the opponents of "free silver" who had lost in 1896 were back in power.[38] The national party reached a position very pleasing to Smith when it nominated Alton B. Parker in 1904. The Georgian conferred with several members of the platform committee at the national convention that year. The Democratic candidate and platform of 1904 were the first that he could endorse out of more than a sense of duty since 1892. Late in the campaign he delivered in Augusta an attack on President Theodore Roosevelt and his administration. This diatribe ranked with the most famous speeches Smith had ever made.[39] Nationally it was hailed as signalizing "The Revival of Hoke."[40]

This view was not mistaken. The tide of progressivism was sweeping the land, providing a new political future for a career that had almost been wrecked by the "free silver" craze. Railroad regulation, a national aim of the progressives, became a burning issue in Georgia. More adequate support for public education and curbs on child labor were other issues that excited the liberals of the state. No man in public life had a better record on these issues than Hoke Smith. His law practice had been built on damage suits against the railroads. He had been most active in advocating educational and labor reforms. However, the state government in Atlanta was not favorably disposed toward any of these objectives.

The Atlanta *Journal* now began a campaign to draft Smith as a candidate for the governorship.[41] These efforts at first were rebuffed, but Smith pledged an active effort to defeat "railroad and ring rule." An open debate with Clark Howell, candidate of the leading opposing faction and editor of the Atlanta *Constitution,* led Smith to declare himself in the race as of June 3, 1905.[42]

The campaign that followed was one of epic proportions even in Georgia. To win a term of two years in office, Smith campaigned for fourteen months, from June, 1905 to August, 1906. Nor was this effort confined to a front porch and poster appeal. The candidate covered 25,000 miles within the borders of the state and spoke as frequently as six times a day.

In addition to Howell and Smith, four other candidates entered the race including Richard B. Russell, former judge of the superior court and father of Senator Richard B. Russell, Jr., and G. A. Nunnally, a Newnan preacher. The latter did not remain in the race until the end, but made sensational news by attacking Smith's Piedmont Hotel as a cesspool of sin. The minister was angered by the fact that a nude statue of a woman adorned the bar of the hostelry. He denounced this work of art as "an insult to Georgia womanhood."[43]

In fact, all of the other candidates devoted most of their time to attacking Smith. There were supporters as well. Chief of these was that faction in the state which was determined to bring about reform. In the Atlanta *Journal* it found leadership and was effective in sponsoring Smith. Another camp in the atomized political picture in Georgia was that led by the redoubtable Tom Watson, now a staunch champion of white supremacy. The fire had gone out of the old Populist movement, and the Sage of Hickory Hill needed a new conflict to warm his spirit. As early as 1904, Watson, who controlled a large personal following, promised to lend his support to any Democrat who would en- dorse disfranchisement of the Negro by writing the white prima- ry into the law of the state.[44] Neither this program nor Watson himself had appealed to Smith in the past. The two men had been bitter critics of one another in the 1890's. Smith had not openly championed the disfranchisement of the Negro. He had always preached and practiced support of the Democratic party as the safeguard of white home rule. However, it may be that he was "yielding to expediency in using the issue as a stalking horse for political preferment."[45]

Negro disfranchisement was part of the platform Smith an- nounced in June, 1905. In September, Watson, keeping his pledge, added his forces to those of Smith. This, in the opinion of many, assured the success of the ticket. Smith presented disfranchise- ment to the voters as nothing more than a step to carry out legally and openly an objective accomplished by violence and subterfuge. The Negro voter was ignorant and easily corrupted in the discharge of his civic duty. Good government and reform would be promoted by withholding from him a duty he was incapable of performing. In developing this issue Smith reiter- ated his belief that "the wise course is to plant ourselves squarely upon the proposition in Georgia that the Negro is in no respect the equal of the white man, and that he cannot in the future in this state occupy a position of equality."[46]

Howell, the principal opponent of the Smith faction, devoted most of his attack to the failure of his rival to maintain a con- sistent record. He made much of the fact that while Smith was now proposing to disfranchise the Negro, he had once sought

the favor of that race. During his term as secretary of the interior
Smith had appointed Negroes to office. These positions were in
many cases desired by deserving and destitute white Georgians.[47]
Smith's real purpose in emphasizing white supremacy was to create an emotional appeal which would divert the voters from the
real issues of the day.

In many speeches, including three or four joint debates, Howell questioned Smith's sincerity as a foe of the corporations.
When he retired from the cabinet, he had borrowed $50,000
from Wall Street. Now the opponent of the railroads, Smith
had received a fee of $5,000 from the Southern Railroad for his
services as a lawyer in defending the road.[48]

In his extensive countercampaign Smith announced his determination to ruin the railroad ring and break the grip of machine
politics. Later in the campaign, after Watson's entry, he turned
to the Negro issue in earnest. Few men could rival Smith as a
public speaker. His refutations of Howell's charges give some
key to his effectiveness. It was true, Smith explained, that he
had borrowed money from Wall Street. The amount was $40,-
000 rather than $50,000, and the only reason he got it from
Wall Street was that the interest rate was the lowest he could
find. He needed money because of the financial sacrifices entailed
by serving the nation as a cabinet officer. More important than
these negative steps was the former secretary's success in convincing the voters that Howell was the champion of all of the abuses
of government which beset Georgia.

When the votes were counted after the August 22 election,
a resounding victory was recorded for Smith. With little newspaper support, the opposition of four candidates, and the determination of the Democratic machine to defeat him, he
managed to win 104,796 votes to 79,477 for all of his opponents.
Not in twenty-five years had the political machine within the
state suffered defeat. In part, the success was attributed to the
nationwide progressive movement for reform exemplified in the
work of governors, like Robert LaFollette of Wisconsin, and the
President, the irrepressible Theodore Roosevelt. The support of
Watson could not be discounted as a factor, but most important
was the political acumen and platform appeal of the apparently
indefatigable Hoke Smith.

The program of reform on which Smith had campaigned was
not simply a device to draw votes and win an election. As soon

as the votes had been counted, he set to work immediately to draft his program into legislative measures which could be placed before the General Assembly when it met.[49] In this matter he had the aid of Watson and Hardwick. Such an approach was necessary, for the Assembly which would meet was in no way pledged to the new governor and represented the outgoing regime more completely than the new order. To overcome the opposition which he anticipated, Smith planned to present his complete program as soon as the legislature convened and to push it through before legislative committees and parliamentary devices of delay could become effective.

In his inaugural address he listed the objectives which he hoped would be accomplished during the session. These included laws to prohibit lobbying, stop the issuing of free passes to legislators by the railroads, insure honest elections, regulate primaries by state law, strengthen the railroad commission, regulate the practices of railroads, determine the percentage of profit for transportation and public service companies, and others.[50] This was an ambitious program. At the outset it appeared that Smith's work and planning would go for naught.

Prohibition, long agitated for Georgia, became a major issue in 1907. It had not been a part of the Smith program of reform. But the prohibitionists felt it should have been and they were determined to capitalize on the zeal for moral improvement which seemed to have gripped the state. Circumstances aided their cause. In developing the race issue during the campaign Smith and his newspaper following had made much of the high rate of crime among the Negroes. These dry statistics were confirmed in blood, so it seemed to many, when the race riot of 1906 shook Atlanta. The prohibitionist had little difficulty in convincing the public that liquor was responsible for much of this crime. Under the leadership of Fred Loring Seely and Mrs. Sam Jones the militant advocates of prohibition dominated the legislative scene.[51] No doubt the opponents of reform welcomed this unexpected reprieve. Governor Smith was now unable to promote his carefully developed program. Its future was jeopardized as he sought to act on the prohibition issue without offending any faction of legislators. This was most difficult to do. If he favored state-wide prohibition, he would lose the support of the local option faction. If he endorsed local option, which in fact he did, he would earn the disfavor of those promoting state-wide prohibition. If he did nothing, he would yield to the Assembly the initiative he had hoped to gain as the means of driving his program through to success. Equally critical was the matter of time. Each day devoted to the question of controling liquor meant one day less which would be spent in fashioning legislation on other reforms. There was little he could do, and Smith left the issue up to the legislature. At length a state-wide prohibition law was adopted on August 2, 1907.

In the short time remaining in the session Smith was not able to get all parts of his program adopted. A good beginning was made, however. The Railroad Commission was reorganized.[52] So sweeping were the changes authorized by this measure that it was described as the most powerful public utilities law ever enacted by a state.[53] A constitutional amendment providing for the disfranchisement of the Negro was adopted after considerable debate.[54] The Atlanta *Journal* hailed this event, rejoicing that the issue had been boldly faced and that the ignorant and venal Negro would no longer vote in Georgia.[55]

Smith complained that the legislature was not with him and that only through the most intense effort on his part had anything been accomplished. His advisers were not as discouraged, feeling that a good beginning had been made. Part of Smith's impatience seemed to arise from a desire to complete his entire program before leaving office. A second term was almost customary for governors, but Smith was thinking of the Senate race which would come up in 1908.[56]

With the second session of the legislature Smith returned to his work with a will. Probably the most important accomplishment was the adoption of a law providing for primary elections. This law, Smith felt, would go far toward guaranteeing honest elections and freeing the state of machine politics. His work in this respect was outstanding and contributed much to his stature as a progressive leader.[57] Another notable achievement of this session was the authorization of the largest appropriations for public schools in the state's history. The increase for the common schools was almost thirty per cent, and it was recorded that the state "came nearer to paying the salaries of rural school teachers than ever before."

Despite these accomplishments a special session of the legislature had to be called in 1908 to deal with the convict lease system. The leases ran out in 1908, and there was a strong public demand that the system be abolished. For some unexplained reason Smith had not made this issue one of his planks in the platform of reform. Indeed, he had taken no position even though the expiration of the leases made some action necessary. He was not slow to recognize the public's will, and recommended to the special session the abolition of the lease system. He urged that criminals be used to build public highways and other internal improvements. These recommendations and his further suggestions for juvenile courts and a parole system were all incorporated in an act adopted in 1908.[58]

The first administration was now complete in so far as its legislative work was concerned. Not all of Smith's program of reform had become law. However, two measures of reform he had not emphasized had been added and enough of the original program adopted to justify the appraisal "that Smith's administration witnessed the passage of more constructive reform legislation than any previous one in Georgia's history."[59]

Early in 1908 Smith had decided not to make the race for the Senate, but to seek a second term as governor. With the record of accomplishment which he had fashioned, re-election would appear to be a foregone conclusion. The actions of the Georgia political populace had never been easy to predetermine. In this case Smith, hailed as the most popular and most politically powerful man in Georgia in 1906, could not win renomination which in the past had been almost automatic.

This startling reversal of the electorate stemmed from several factors. Most important of these was the opposing candidate and the circumstances surrounding his decision to run. He was, Joseph M. Brown, the son of the famous Civil War governor of Georgia. Apparently none of the sire's superabundance of political sagacity had been inherited by his son. Over fifty years of age, he had never held elective office. These were years when chance quite as much as prearrangement entered into the success of a politician in Georgia. Circumstances were to bring Brown before the public in a favorable light in 1907. At the time he was serving on the Railroad Commission. Governor Smith supervised the work of this body closely and pushed it to do his will with the zeal of a man who had just won the governorship by a resounding majority.

A long period of disagreement between Smith and Brown reached a climax when in June, 1907, Brown refused to favor reclassifying and reducing railroad passenger rates as the governor wished. Nothing was done until August 21, a few days after the legislature adjourned. Then Smith fired the railroad commissioner. No full explanation for the action was given at the time, and the public felt that the governor had taken unfair advantage of his position to punish one who disagreed with him. This idea Brown sedulously cultivated through the distribution of pamphlets stating his side of the controversy. These earned for him the title of "the card writing commissioner," as bestowed by the governor, but the public continued to side with Brown.

Another factor contributing to Smith's failure in this second bid for the governorship was the defection of Tom Watson. In part this came about as the culmination of many small disagreements. Watson was miffed when Smith did not ask him to make speeches in the 1906 campaign. Failure to oppose the Democratic machine in Augusta was in Watson's eyes another unpardonable act on the part of Smith. Also working to break the coalition were the old Populists on the one hand and the conservative Democrats on the other. They spared no efforts to end the alliance that had spelled defeat for them in 1906.[60]

More spectacular and probably more important in speeding the rift between the two leaders was the Glover case. Arthur Price Glover, convicted for the murder of a mill worker, was to be executed in 1908. His case came before Governor Smith for clemency. This seemingly unrelated event became of greatest significance to the political fortunes of Smith. So strange was the connection that if recounted in fiction, it would be passed off as improbable. Glover, it developed, had been a loyal supporter of Watson in the Populist campaigns of the 1890's. Boykin Wright, the lawyer who had secured Glover's conviction, was an old foe of the Populist movement and a personal enemy of Glover. Further to complicate the issue, Wright was thought to have great influence with Smith. In Watson's mind the issue became a simple case of an innocent man being persecuted for political and personal beliefs. Watson presented his case to Smith in person in forceful fashion and warned that Glover must not be executed. At the conclusion of the interview Watson felt that he had gained Smith's assent to his plea. However, Smith after careful study of the case could find no valid reason for freeing Glover. Watson's first reaction was to remove from his library the set of Voltaire's works given him by Smith.[61]

Fate which had thus cast two favors to Joseph M. Brown had for him one more gift. In 1907 Georgia and the nation suffered a financial panic. Those forces opposing change had always warned that financial disaster might follow in the wake of reform. Brown was able to make good use of the syllogism that Smith had brought reforms; a panic had followed; therefore the reforms had brought ruin. "Brown and Bread; Hoke and Hunger" became the slogan of the campaign.[62]

This combination of misfortunes put Smith on the defensive for the entire campaign. He campaigned vigorously and sought to stir the issue of Negro disfranchisement, then being voted upon by the people of the state, but it aroused little interest. Brown, the governor charged, was supported by the liquor interests and the railroad tycoons, but still the people were unmoved. Even the type of campaign which Brown waged was difficult for Smith to combat. Few if any public speakers were the superiors of the governor, but Brown refused to take the stump at all. Telling the voters that his inability to make a public speech placed him in the company of Moses and Thomas Jefferson, Brown confined his personal campaigning to circulating some fifteen messages on his "cards."[63]

Fate and the resurgent political machine of the conservatives were too much for Smith. When the votes were tallied, Brown had a popular count of 109,806 to 98,949 for Smith. It is interesting to note that the defeated candidate's total was only some 6,000 less than his landslide victory two years earlier. However, the opposition had narrowed from four candidates to one and had increased by almost 30,000 votes.

Yet Smith's political future was far from dark. The former governor returned to his law practice, but it was generally felt that this was a temporary expedient. He continued to speak over the state in behalf of educational and agricultural reforms, a good groundwork for a future campaign. His office in Atlanta was accessible to members of the legislature, many of whom called and urged him to enter the race for the governorship in 1910. The final event influencing him on such a course was Brown's annual message in 1910. In Smith's eyes this document was nothing more than a challenge to all that he had attempted to do. On June 23, 1910, Smith announced: "I will be in the race for governor."[64]

In marked contrast to his Herculean efforts of 1905-06 was

Smith's campaign of 1910. It also differed from the disastrous 1908 race in which he felt that he had tried too hard. In 1910 he made only about a dozen speeches, all during the last days of the campaign. In these he defined the issue to be a clear choice between "progressive democracy" and "reactionary democrats."[65] Taking a leaf from his opponent's political handbook, Smith issued a pamphlet of his own. Entitled "The Records of Two Administrations: What They Did," the first half was devoted to the numerous accomplishments of the Smith administration. The last half of the document which dealt with Brown's achievements consisted of twelve blank pages.[66]

For his part, Brown, too, was content to leave the work of campaigning to grass-roots organizations inspired by campaign literature and supporting speakers. The relatively quiet campaign closed with victory for Smith by the count of 96,638 to 92,469.[67] Curiously enough, this represented a decline of 2,000 as compared to the vote Smith had polled as the losing candidate in 1908.

Possibly Brown's failure was due to the fact that Watson had not opposed Smith. However, the old Populist leader was to be heard from before the campaign was concluded. Supporting an independent ticket, he challenged Smith in the general election in the fall of the year. With Brown agreeing to a second race against Smith in the same year, Watson may have hoped to reverse the primary election result. At any rate, he devoted several weeks and much newspaper space to a sensational attack on Smith's character. Other than providing grist for the gossip's mill, this maneuver had no effect. Smith won the general election easily, and the Atlanta *Georgian* exonerated him of all charges in a front-page story.

Another event in the fall of 1910 was to prove far more significant in the career of Hoke Smith. This was the death of Alexander S. Clay, who had been elected to the Senate in 1908. Governor Brown had appointed Joseph M. Terrell to serve until the legislature could convene and elect a successor. There was much speculation that Smith would be a candidate. A number of aspirants entered the field, including Terrell, Tom Watson, and W. A. Covington. Smith refused to announce his intentions until June 28, only a few days before the election, when he stated that he would accept the position if elected. Even then, he made no campaign for the office. Those forces opposing Smith made a loud demand that the issue be settled in a popular election by means of a primary. The Smith government ruled out this method, and in the elections in the legislature on July 11-12 Smith won. All agreed that he was gratified by the outcome; none could charge that he had made any effort to gain the office.[68]

If his conduct before the election was blameless, his action afterwards was the subject of great controversy. As soon as the legislature voted, Terrell resigned, expecting Smith to give up the governorship and move to Washington. This was not to be the case, however. Announcing that there was much important business to be completed in Georgia, Smith continued to serve as governor until the end of the legislative session. His opponents were beside themselves with rage, but there was nothing they could do.

Smith went to work with great zest. An anti-lobbying measure, one of the uncompleted aims of his first administration, was enacted. Further legislation created a department of commerce and labor headed by an elected commissioner. The public school system, always an object of interest with Smith, was reorganized along more efficient lines. A state superintendent of schools, advised by a Board of Education, headed the new system. Smith insisted that the latter group be made up of men with practical experience in teaching. Another important improvement was the provision for the licensing of teachers. A series of extensive reforms in the financial methods of the state completed the governor's program for the session. Not all of his objectives had been met. Progressive bills such as the initiative and referendum, preferential primary, and women's suffrage did not even come up for voting. Nevertheless, the session represented solid accomplishment in the cause of reform.[69]

When Smith became a senator on December 4, 1911, having resigned as governor in the middle of November, a lifelong ambition was at last realized.[70] He had long felt that his talents could be utilized to best advantage in Washington. His early years in the Senate seemed to confirm this view, but the latter witnessed less and less activity. In part this development could be attributed to advancing years, in part to the catastrophe of World War I, shifting emphasis from the domestic issues he knew so well to the unfamiliar problems of world affairs.

In the Democratic National Convention of 1912, Smith supported Wilson.[71] With the Democratic victory of that year the new

President came to Washington with the progressive program he styled the New Freedom. In his demand that the nation "cleanse, reconsider, and reform," Wilson had the enthusiastic support of the junior senator from Georgia. As these ideals were written into legislation, Hoke Smith was described as a sturdy fighter for advanced views.[72] "Indeed he was in the vanguard of the able southern leaders who led in the enactment of the 'New Freedom' legislation during the years 1913 to 1917."[73] The measure of influence which Smith achieved was demonstrated by his appointment to the Senate Steering Committee in 1913, just two years after entering that body.

In the Wilson program Smith's work was particularly effective in support of the Underwood-Simmons Tariff and in getting the Federal Reserve System accepted. After the new banking program was adopted, Smith worked hard and successfully to have one of the district banks located in Atlanta. Always sympathetic with the farmer, the Georgia senator was very active in advocating the passage of the Federal Farm Loan Bill.[74]

Smith's service was not limited to these administration measures. He served as chairman of the Commission on National Aid to Vocational Education, and as chairman of the Senate Committee on Education and Labor. The Cotton Warehouse Bill of 1914 he strongly supported and used his influence to gain the establishment of a division of markets in the department of agriculture to aid the farmer in the sale of his crops.

Most notable of his achievements in the Senate were his contributions in the field of agricultural and vocational education. In each case a bill bearing his name set the basic laws for federal participation in these activities for many years. The Smith-Lever Bill provided for agricultural extension work, and the Smith-Hughes Act for vocational education below the college level in agricultural, industrial, and domestic arts.[75]

With the advent of the war in 1914, Smith's relationship with President Wilson began to become strained. The President proclaimed a policy of neutrality in word and in deed along with the protection of American rights. In practice the German violation of neutral rights through the deadly submarine aroused more severe reprimand than the less spectacular seizure of American goods by the British. Such a policy was satisfactory to the majority of the public, but it did not meet with Smith's approval. The British consistently seized American cotton which was being shipped to Germany, clearly an infraction of neutral rights. Angered by what appeared to him to be the administration's ineffective efforts to protect Americans, Smith protested so vehemently as to be classified an anglophobe.[76]

The Senate election of 1914 saw two old foes pitted against each other for the last time when Joseph M. Brown opposed Smith. The latter did no campaigning, being content to stand on his record. Apparently, the people of Georgia were pleased with his accomplishment, for they gave him 120,355 votes to 61,644 for his old foe.[77]

Smith's second term was not marked by great activity. He viewed with alarm the increasing power of the President. The drift toward intervention in the war he could not favor. However, when the declaration of war was made in 1917 he voted for it, and supported most of the war measures brought before Congress. Wilson's program for peace as exemplified in the League of Nations was the last straw for Smith. With the majority of the Senate he favored reservations which would make certain the preservation of American rights. Not entirely satisfied with the efforts of Henry Cabot Lodge along that line, Smith presented seven reservations of his own in October, 1919. Article X, the real dividing line on the League issue, was in Smith's opinion a pledge of "lead and sabers" in its guarantee to protect the territorial integrity of member states.[78] In the tense atmosphere of the Senate Chamber in November of 1919, those Democrats loyal to Wilson, ill since September, voted against the motion to adopt the League of Nations with the Lodge reservations. Voting for the treaty with reservations were two Southern senators. One of them was Hoke Smith. On this occasion and when the treaty was debated again in 1920, Smith voted for eleven of the Lodge reservations.[79]

Back in Georgia the redoubtable Tom Watson was campaigning once again. This time he sought Smith's Senate seat and the leading issue was the League. The campaign was well summed up by Watson who told voters that if they were against the League, they should vote for him. If they were for the League, they should vote for Dorsey. "If you don't know where in the Hell you are, vote for Hoke Smith."[80] Most Georgians seemed to be against the League or for Watson.

Apparently Smith was not unhappy at the termination of his public career. Well off financially, he practiced law in Washington until 1924, returning to Atlanta that year. Although his name was frequently connected with public office, he remained firm in his decision to retire from public life. He continued to have a keen interest in the civic life of his community and served along with other duties on the Atlanta school board. Much in demand as a speaker, he addressed many public gatherings.

In 1931, at the age of seventy-six, he died leaving behind him, as the Atlanta *Constitution,* his most acute critic conceded, "an indelible imprint on the state he served so long and well."[81]

APPENDIX

THE PUBLICATIONS OF E. M. COULTER TO
JANUARY 1, 1958

Books

History of Kentucky. Chicago: American Historical Society, 1922. 2 vols. William E. Connelley, co-author.

The Cincinnati Southern Railroad and the Struggle for Southern Commerce, 1865-1872. Chicago: American Historical Society, 1922.

The Civil War and Readjustment in Kentucky. Chapel Hill: University of North Carolina Press, 1926.

College Life in the Old South. New York: Macmillan Company, 1928. (Reprinted by University of Georgia Press, 1951.)

A Short History of Georgia. Chapel Hill: University of North Carolina Press, 1933.

Georgia's Disputed Ruins. Chapel Hill: University of North Carolina Press, 1937. Editor.

William G. Brownlow, Fighting Parson of the Southern Highlands. Chapel Hill: University of North Carolina Press, 1937.

The United States in the Making. Boston: Houghton Mifflin Company, 1937. L. H. Canfield, H. B. Wilder, F. L. Paxson, and N. P. Mead, co-authors.

First Lessons in Georgia History. New York: American Book Company, 1938. Lawton B. Evans, co-author.

The Other Half of Old New Orleans. Baton Rouge: Louisiana State University Press, 1939. Editor.

The Course of the South to Secession . . . An Interpretation by Ulrich Bonnell Phillips. New York: D. Appleton-Century Company, 1939. Editor.

Thomas Spalding of Sapelo. Baton Rouge: Louisiana State University Press, 1940.

John Jacobus Flournoy. Champion of the Common Man in the Antebellum South. Savannah: Georgia Historical Society, 1942.

Georgia: A Short History (Revision of *A Short History of Georgia*). Chapel Hill: University of North Carolina Press, 1947.

The South During Reconstruction, 1865-1877. Baton Rouge: Louisiana State University Press, 1947.

Travels in the Confederate States. A Bibliography. Norman: University of Oklahoma Press, 1948.

A List of the Early Settlers of Georgia. Athens: University of Georgia Press, 1949. Albert B. Saye, co-editor.

The Confederate States of America, 1861-1865. Baton Rouge: Louisiana State University Press; The Littlefield Fund for Southern History of the University of Texas, 1950.

College Life in the Old South. Reprint, Second Edition. Athens: University of Georgia Press, 1951.

Wormsloe: Two Centuries of a Georgia Family. Wormsloe Foundation Publications, Number 1. Athens: University of Georgia Press, 1955.

Lost Generation: The Life and Death of James Barrow, C. S. A. Confederate Centennial Studies, Number 1. Tuscaloosa: Confederate Publishing Company, 1956.

Auraria: The Story of a Georgia Gold-Mining Town. Athens: University of Georgia Press, 1956.

ARTICLES

"Early Life and Regulations at the University of North Carolina," in *Universilty of North Carolina Magazine*, Old Series, vol. 42, New Series, vol. 29, No. 4 (February, 1912).

"The Granville District," in *James Sprunt Historical Publications*, XIII, 1 (1913).

"Effects of Secession upon the Commerce of the Mississippi Valley," in *Mississippi Valley Historical Review*, III, 3 (December, 1916).

"Commercial Intercourse with the Confederacy in the Mississippi Valley, 1861-1865," in *Mississippi Valley Historical Review*, V, 4 (March, 1919).

"The Nullification Movement in Georgia," in *Georgia Historical Quarterly*, V, 1 (March, 1921).

"Elijah Clarke's Foreign Intrigues and the 'Trans-Oconee Republic,'" in *Mississippi Valley Historical Review* (Proceedings of the Mississippi Valley Historical Association, 1919-1920), extra number (November, 1921). Reprinted as *Bulletin of the University of Georgia*, XXIII, 4 (December, 1922).

"The Ante-Bellum Academy Movement in Georgia," in *Georgia Historical Quarterly*, V, 4 (December, 1921).

"Historical Activities of the South, 1917-1921," in *Mississippi Valley Historical Review* (Proceedings of the Mississippi Valley Historical Association, 1921-1922 and 1922-1923, extra number, April, 1924).

"Early Frontier Democracy in the First Kentucky Constitution," in *Political Science Quarterly*, XXXIX, 4 (December, 1924).

"The Efforts of the Democratic Societies of the West to Open the Navigation of the Mississippi," in *Mississippi Valley Historical Review*, XI, 3 (December, 1924).

"A Georgia Educational Movement during the Eighteen Hundred Fifties," in *Georgia Historical Quarterly*, IX, 1 (March, 1925). Reprinted in *Bulletin of the University of Georgia*, XXV, 4b (April, 1925).

"The Downfall of the Whig Party in Kentucky," in *Register of the Kentucky States Historical Society*, vol. 23, no. 68 (May, 1925).

"When John Wesley Preached in Georgia," in *Georgia Historical Quarterly*, IX, 4 (December, 1925).

"The Genesis of Henry Clay's American System," in *South Atlantic Quarterly*, XXV, 1 (January, 1926).

"The Movement for Agricultural Reorganization in the Cotton South during the Civil War," in *North Carolina Historical Review*, IV, 1 (January, 1927). Reprinted in *Agricultural History*, I, 1 (January, 1927).

"Mary Musgrove, 'Queen of the Creeks': A Chapter of Early Georgia Troubles," in *Georgia Historical Quarterly*, XI, 1 (March, 1927). Reprinted as a separate pamphlet.

"Planters' Wants in the Days of the Confederacy," in *Georgia Historical Quarterly*, XII, 1 (March, 1928). Reprinted as a separate pamphlet.

"A Century of a Georgia Plantation," in *Mississippi Valley Historical Review*, XVI, 3 (December, 1929). Reprinted in *Agricultural History*, III, 4 (October, 1929).

"Southern Agriculture and Southern Nationalism before the Civil War," in *Agricultural History*, IV, 3 (July, 1930).

"Sherman and the South," in *North Carolina Historical Review*, VIII, 1 (January, 1931). Reprinted in *Georgia Historical Quarterly*, XV, 1 (March, 1931).

"The Attempt of William Howard Taft to Break the Solid South," in *Georgia Historical Quarterly*, XIX, 2 (June, 1935).

"Edward Telfair," in *Georgia Historical Quarterly*, XX, 2 (June, 1936).

"What the South has done about its History," in *Journal of Southern History*, II, 1 (February, 1936).

Georgia and the Constitution — Georgia in the Making and Ratification of the Constitution of the United States. Issued by the United States Constitution Sesquicentennial Commission, Sol Bloom, Director General. Washington, D. C., 1937.

"The Great Savannah Fire of 1820," in *Georgia Historical Quarterly*, XXIII, 1 (March, 1939).

"Boating as a Sport in the Old South," in *Georgia Historical Quarterly*, XXVII, 3 (September, 1943).

"Wanderings of a Painting: The Alonzo Church Portrait," in *Georgia Historical Quarterly*, XXX, 2 (June, 1946).

"The Early Historians of Georgia," in *Georgia Historical Quarterly*, XXXI, 3 (September, 1947).

"A List of the First Shipload of Georgia Settlers," in *Georgia Historical Quarterly*, XXXI, 4 (December, 1947).

"Georgia — Empire State of the South," in *Think* (New York City), XIV, 11 (November, 1948).

"William Bacon Stevens: Physician, Historian, Teacher, Preacher," in *Georgia Review*, II, 2 (Summer, 1948). Reprinted in *Georgia Historical Quarterly*, XXXIII, 2 (June, 1949).

"Franklin College as a Name for the University of Georgia," in *Georgia Historical Quarterly*, XXXIV, 3 (September, 1950).

"The University of Georgia — Old and New," in *Georgia Review*, V, 1 (Spring, 1951).

"A Name for the American War of 1861-1865," in *Georgia Review*, V, 3 (Fall, 1951). Reprinted in *Georgia Historical Quarterly*, XXXVI, 2 (June, 1952).

"The Georgia-Tennessee Boundary Line," in *Georgia Historical Quarterly*, XXXV, 4 (December, 1951).

"The Flags of the Confederacy," in *Georgia Review*, VI, 1 (Spring, 1952). Reprinted in *United Daughters of the Confederacy Magazine*, XV, 5 (May, 1952) and in *Georgia Historical Quarterly*, XXXVII, 3 (September, 1953).

"The Beginnings of Georgia," in *American Heritage*, Winter, 1953.

"The Founding of Two Nations: Israel and the United States," in *Georgia Review*, VIII, 2 (Summer, 1954).

"Cudjo Fye's Insurrection," in *Georgia Historical Quarterly*, XXXVIII, 3 (September, 1954). Reprinted in pamphlet form.

"Nancy Hart, Georgia Heroine of the Revolution: The Story of the Growth of a Tradition," Part I, in *Georgia Review*, VIII, 3 (Fall, 1954).

"Nancy Hart: Georgia Heroine of the Revolution: The Story of the Growth of a Tradition," Part II, in *Georgia Review*, VIII, 4 (Winter, 1954).

"The Confederate States of America," in *American Story*, prepared by Broadcast Music, Inc., in association with the Society of American Historians. Copyright 1955, Broadcast Music, Inc. Reprinted in *Georgia Historical Quarterly*, XL, 3 (September, 1956).

"Father Sherman's 'March to the Sea,'" in *Georgia Review*, X, 4 (Winter, 1956).

"From Spotsylvania Courthouse to Andersonville: A Diary of Darius Starr," in *Georgia Historical Quarterly*, XLI, 2 (June, 1957).

"Four Slave Trials in Elbert County, Georgia," *Georgia Historical Quarterly*, XLI, 3 (September, 1957).

NOTES

CHAPTER ONE

1. Among the better ones are Amos Aschbach Ettinger, *James Edward Oglethorpe: Imperial Idealist* (Oxford: The Clarendon Press, 1936), Leslie F. Church, *Oglethorpe: A Study of Philanthropy in England and Georgia* (London: The Epworth Press, 1932), and Henry Bruce, *Life of General Oglethorpe* (New York: Dodd, Mead & Company, 1890).

2. *A Genealogical History of the House of Yvery in its Different Branches of Yvery, Luvel, Perceval, and Gournay* (London: H. Woodfall, Jr., 1742. 2 vols.). Cited hereafter as *House of Ivery*. James Anderson appears to have collected the material for both volumes and to have been the author of Volume I. He died before the work was completed, and the author of Volume II is not indicated.

3. *House of Ivery*, I, 27.

4. *Ibid.*, I, 21-22.

5. *Ibid.*, II, 389.

6. *Ibid.*, I, 92.

7. *Ibid.*, II, 395-396.

8. *Ibid.*, II, 187.

9. *Ibid.*, II, 404.

10. Sir John Percival to Sir Robert Southwell, May 3, 1698, in Historical Manuscripts Commission's *Report on the Manuscripts of the Earl of Egmont* (Dublin: His Majesty's Stationery Office, 1909), II, 190. Hereinafter cited *Report on Manuscripts.*

11. *Ibid.*

12. *Id.* to *id.*, November 18, 1699, *ibid.*, 191.

13. *Id.* to *id.*, November 20, 1699, *ibid.*, 191.

14. Smallbrook to Southwell, February 4, 1701, *ibid.*, 193.

15. Percival to Digby Cotes, September 18, 1701, *ibid.*, 206.

16. Southwell to Percival, September, 1702, *ibid.*, 209.

17. *House of Ivery*, II, 405.

18. Percival to Reverend Dr. Perceval, December 27, 1707, in *Report on Manuscripts*, II, 219-221.

19. *Id.* to Elizabeth Southwell, September 20, 1709, *ibid.*, 241.

20. See Benjamin Rand, *Berkeley and Percival, the Correspondence of . . .* (Cambridge: The University Press, 1914).

21. *Ibid.*, 34.

22. Percival to Helena Le Grand, December 7, 1708, quoted in Rand, *Berkeley and Percival*, 4-5.

23. *House of Ivery*, II, 406, 453-454.

24. *Ibid.*, 407. The head of the Percival family from his great-grandfather, Sir Philip Percivalle, had been a privy councillor.

25. *Ibid.*, 454.

26. Historical Manuscripts Commission, *Seventh Report*, Appendix (London: His Majesty's Stationery Office, 1879), 247.

27. Percival to Berkeley, October 8, 1728, quoted in Rand, *Berkeley and Percival*, 213.

28. Percival to Berkeley, December 29, 1725 and June 6, 1726, quoted in Rand, *Berkeley and Percival*, 227, 233.

29. *House of Ivery*, II, 431.

30. Historical Manuscripts Commission, *Diary of John Percival, First Earl*

of Egmont, (London: His Majesty's Stationery Office, 1920-23. 3 vols.), I, 293. Cited hereinafter as *Diary*.

31. *Diary*, I, 162.
32. *Diary*, I, 409.
33. *Diary*, II, 60.
34. *House of Ivery*, II, 443.
35. *Diary*, I, 196.
36. *Diary*, I, 101-102, 364.
37. *Diary*, 1, 231.
38. *Diary*, I, 297.
39. *Diary*, I, 399.
40. For example, see *Diary*, I, 294, 444.
41. *Diary*, I, 191.
42. See note above. The published *Diary* covers the period 1729-47. He kept a diary at an earlier period in his life (see letter to Sir Robert Southwell, June 2, 1698, in *Report on Manuscripts*, II, 190), but its present location is unknown. The diary of Percival's father from October, 1685 to April, 1686, is included as an appendix in Volume III of the published *Diary*.
43. "This day [December 28, 1730] I finished my 'Treatise of the Duty of Obedience to Government in general, and to the present Government in England in particular,' in three sections," in *Diary*, I, 121. "This day [January 3, 1731] I writ a small discourse entitled, 'Some Thoughts concerning Religion, and the Reformation from Popery,' " in *Diary*, I, 122. Today [December 23, 1732] "my servant Hassack brought me down three copies of my printed pamphlet against taking off the Test, but the publisher took the liberty to alter the title and gave it not only too pompous a one, but in part a false one, for in it I say nothing for or against the Corporation Act. The title I gave it was, *A Diologue between a Church of England man affectionate to the Government and a Dissenter concerning taking off the Test;* but the publisher has given it the following one: *The Controversy in relation to the Test and Corporation Acts clearly disputed, in a Dialogue between a Dissenter and a member of*

the Established Church.... Printed for John Roberts in Warwick Lane, 1733. Price, six-pence," in *Diary*, I, 303-304. Saturday, January 27, 1733: "After this I went to Court, where the Queen talked a great deal to me of my Collection of Heads ... and asked how far I had proceeded in them this year. I answered I had only time to make up three volumes. She said she heard I placed them chronologically, which she said the best way. I cannot imagine who tells her such minuteness," in *Diary*, I, 311. June 19, 1733: "I visited Mr. Clerke, and left with him four more books of my printed heads to shew the Queen, who now has eight of them," in *Diary*, I, 364. June 7, 1733: "I sent my small treatise upon *Idolatry of the Papists* to Mr. Read, publisher of the *Weekly Journal or British Gazetteer,* and the Saturday following saw it in print," in *Diary*, I, 385. July 28, 1733: "In this day's weekly journal, my discourse of the 'Rise and Progress of Idolatry from the Flood to the birth of Jesus Christ' is printed. This is my first section," in *Diary*, I, 397. November 25, 1733: "This week my pamphlet entitled, *The Thoughts of an Impartial Man upon the present temper of the Nation offered to the consideration of the Freeholders of Great Britain,* printed at London for J. Roberts, was sent me up enclosed by Mr. Leak, from Bath, who took upon him the printing it," in *Diary*, I, 448. For references to other pamphlets, see *Diary* I, 34, 92, 125, 293, 299, 448, 450; II, 14 (a letter to the *Craftsman*), 39, 122.
44. *Diary*, II, 19, 399; III, 264, 267.
45. *Diary*, I, 151.
46. *Diary*, I, 342.
47. For example, see *ibid.*, 291-292.
48. *Diary*, I, 190; II, 145, 217.
49. *Diary*, I, 263.
50. *Diary*, I, 390. See also Vol. III, 270.
51. *Diary*, I, 259-260.
52. *Diary*, I, 264.

53. *Diary*, I, 250.

54. *Diary*, I, 101.

55. *Diary*, I, 301.

56. *Diary*, I, 380-477, passim.

57. *Calendar of State Papers, Colonial Series, America and the West Indies, 1732* (London: His Majesty's Stationery Office, 1939), x.

58. *Diary*, I, 283.

59. *Diary*, I, 295.

60. Albert B. Saye, *New Viewpoints in Georgia History* (Athens: University of Georgia Press, 1943), 31-42.

61. See E. Merton Coulter and Albert B. Saye, eds., *A List of the Early Settlers of Georgia* (Athens: University of Georgia Press, 1949).

62. *Diary*, I, 109, 272 273, 274, 276, 370, 373; II, 168; III, 103, 104, 107, 109, 112, 113, 184, 185, 195, 200, 310, 315.

63. *Diary* II, 237, 242.

64. See *Diary*, III, 428, for an index to the parliamentary debates recorded in Egmont's *Diary*.

65. *Diary*, II, 121. John Musgrove accompanied the Indians as interpreter.

66. *Diary*, II, 122.

67. *Diary*, II, 41.

68. *Diary*, II, 335.

69. Allen D. Candler, ed., *The Colonial Records of Georgia* (Atlanta: Franklin Printing and Publishing Company, 1904-1916. 26 vols.), IV and its Supplement. Hereinafter cited as Candler, ed., *Colonial Records*.

70. *Diary*, III, 209, 222-223.

71. "Please to present my Duty to My Good Lord Egmont: his kind remembrance, and Notice of an Old depressed Man, gives me fresh Vigour when I read it: I wish I were capable of serving him in any thing. The Potter has the Model from his Lordship of the Flower Pot, & the Coffee cup from his Countess, both before him; wch he has been chewing upon some days; but has not yet fully told me what can be done in it; I hope in my next to acquaint you how far he is capable of performing." Stephens to Harnan Verelst, November 22, 1738, in Candler, ed.,

Colonial Records, XXII, Part I, 331.

"Please to allow me a few Words in a separate letter from my other of this date: begging the favour of you to present my best Respects to my Good Lord Egmont, with my most gratefull acknowledgment of his unmerited Present to me, of three casks of fine English Beer, wch I lately receiv'd with little Damage; only one of 'em sustaining a little Leakidge, occasioned (as the Sailors term it) by a small Worm hole, which gave room for tasting it; but more sparingly yn I have often known; and there is Plenty sufficient of it, come safe & well, to put me frequently in mind of the Generous and honourable Donor." *Id.* to *id.*, April 8, 1741, *ibid.*, Part II, 474-475.

72. *Diary*, III, 265. See also Candler, ed., *Colonial Records*, V, 643.

73. *Diary*, III, 55, 265. Protest against a law prohibiting Negro slavery, adopted in 1735, ran throughout the records. But neither the Salzburgers nor Scotch Highlanders wanted slaves, and the settlers at Darien, basing their objection to slavery upon moral grounds, went so far as to present a counter petition in 1739 against the petition for slavery from Savannah, the seat from which the loudest protest to the Trustees' policy was always raised. Thomas Stephens' action brought much grief to his father. The latter declared that of the twenty-six malcontents present on October 14, 1741, when his son was chosen as their agent, "two only voted for another." See Candler, ed., *Colonial Records*, IV, Supplement, 263.

74. A letter from John Dobell to the Trustees in 1742 stated that Thomas Stephens in one of his letters "made the good Earl of Egmont (if not the cause of all the evil) the obstructor of all Good: For after he had mentioned his Lordships illness, and that he was given over by

the physicians for death, as a consequent hereupon says to his clients, that, now they might soon expect glorious times. A suggestion and inferrence, so impudently wicked, that not many who know ought of his Lordship but will forever despise and abhor Stephens." See *ibid.*, XXIII, 441.

75. James Ross McCain, *Georgia as a Proprietary Colony* (Boston: R. G. Badger, 1917) , 244, 249.

76. *Diary*, II, 184.
77. *Diary*, I, 54, 70, 103, 221; III, 153, 159; Candler, ed., *Colonial Records*, II, 7; IV, 11.
78. McCain, *Georgia as a Proprietary Colony*, 241.
79. *Diary*, III, 275.
80. *Diary*, I, 180, 188, 190, 224, 235, 287, 290, 302, 309; II, 135; III, 263.
81. *Diary*, I, 452.
82. *Diary*, II, 98.
83. *House of Ivery*, II, 460-463.

CHAPTER TWO

1. Henry Ellis, "An Account of the Heat of the Weather in Georgia...," *The London Magazine* (1759) , 371-372.
2. John Nichols, *Literary Anecdotes of the Eighteenth Century* (London: Printed for the author by Nichols, Son, and Bentley, 1812-15. 9 vols.) , IX, 533.
3. Ellis, "An Account of the Heat of the Weather in Georgia...," *loc. cit.*
4. John Nichols, *Illustrations of the Literary History of the Eighteenth Century* (London: Printed for the author by Nichols, Son, and Bentley, 1817-1858. 8 vols.) , I, 477.
5. Henry Ellis, *A Voyage to Hudson's-Bay, by the Dobbs Galley and California, in the Years 1746-1747, for Discovering a North West Passage* (Dublin: George and Alexander Ewing, 1749) , 48-50.
6. Henry Ellis to William Pitt, June 26, 1761, in Chatham Papers, Vol. 31, Public Record Office, London.
7. *Savannah Georgia Gazette*, September 11, 1763.
8. Ellis to Lord Hawkesbury, March 27, 1788, in Add. MSS. 38416, folio 65, in Liverpool Papers, British Museum.
9. Nichols, *Literary Anecdotes*, IX, 534.
10. *Ibid.*, 533.
11. Ellis to Richard Twining, September 21, 1798, in Add. MSS. 39930, folio 298, in Twining Papers, British Museum; *id.* to *id.*, January 7, 1799, *ibid.*, folio 308.

12. Nichols, *Illustrations*, I, 477.
13. Ellis to Board of Trade, Savannah, March 11, 1757, in unpublished Colonial Records of the State of Georgia, XXVIII, Part I, 4-15. The unpublished Colonial Records comprise vols. 27-39 and may be found in the Library of the Georgia Historical Society, Savannah, and in the Georgia Department of Archives and History, Atlanta. Hereinafter cited unpublished Colonial Records.
14. Charleston *South Carolina Gazette*, April 28, 1757.
15. John Reynolds to Board of Trade, December 5, 1754, in unpublished Colonial Records, XXVII, 69-72.
16. "An Exemplification of the Proceedings of the Court between our Sovereign Lord the King and Thomas Goldsmith at Savannay [*sic.*] 28 Jany. 1754," in Raymond Demere Papers, Manuscript Department, Duke University, Durham, North Carolina. Only five freeholders could be found at Frederica in 1754.
17. Reynolds to Board of Trade, January 5, 1756, in unpublished Colonial Records, XXVII, 237-243.
18. *Ibid.*
19. Ellis to Board of Trade, March 11, 1757, in unpublished Colonial Records, XXVIII, Part I, 4-15.
20. Charleston *South Carolina Gazette*, April 28, 1757.

21. Minutes of Governor and Council, February 16-17, 1757, in Candler, ed., *Colonial Records*, VII, 485-491.
22. Ellis to Board of Trade, March 11, 1757, in unpublished Colonial Records, XXVIII, Part I, 6.
23. *Ibid.*, 4.
24. *Ibid.*, 5.
25. *Ibid.*, 10.
26. *Id.* to *id.*, February 10, 1759, *ibid.*, 260-264.
27. Minutes of Governor and Council, in Candler, ed., *Colonial Records*, VII, 498-499, 500, 539, 542, 544-545, 546, 610.
28. Ellis to Board of Trade, January 1, 1758, in unpublished Colonial Records, XXVIII, Part I, 144-147.
29. *Id.* to *id.*, May 5, 1757, *ibid.*, 18-31.
30. Minutes of Governor and Council, April 4, 20, 1757, in Candler, ed., *Colonial Records*, VII, 507, 545.
31. Ellis to Board of Trade, August 1, 1757, in unpublished Colonial Records, XXVIII, Part I, 50-55.
32. *Id.* to *id.*, March 11, 1757, *ibid.*, 4-15; Journal of the Commons House of Assembly, February 1, 1757, in Candler, ed., *Colonial Records*, XIII, 145-146. Cited hereinafter as Commons House Journal; and Journal of Upper House of Assembly as Upper House Journal.
33. Minutes of Governor and Council, March 29, 1757, in Candler, ed., *Colonial Records*, VII, 504-505.
34. Ellis to Board of Trade, May 5, 1757, in unpublished Colonial Records, XXVIII, Part I, 18-31.
35. *Id.* to *id.*, March 11, 1757, *ibid.*, 4-15.
36. *Id.* to *id.*, May 5, 1757, *ibid.*, 29.
37. *Id.* to *id.*, March 11, 1757, *ibid.*, 4-15.
38. Minutes of Governor and Council, March 29, 1757, in Candler, ed., *Colonial Records*, VII, 504.
39. Ellis to Board of Trade, March 11, 1757, in unpublished Colonial Records, XXVIII, Part I, 4-15.
40. Ellis's notation on William Little to The House of Assembly, May 25, 1757, *ibid.*, 46-48.
41. Ellis to Board of Trade, March 11, 1757, *ibid.*, 6.
42. *Ibid.*, 14.
43. *Ibid.*, 4-15.
44. *Id.* to *id.*, May 5, 1757, *ibid.*, 23-24.
45. William Little to The House of Assembly, May 25, 1757, *ibid.*, 46-48.
46. Ellis to Board of Trade, July 8, 1757, *ibid.*, 42-45; *id.* to *id.*, February 10, 1759, *ibid.*, 260-264.
47. *Id.* to *id.*, July 8, 1757, *ibid.*, 42-45.
48. *Ibid.*, 42.
49. *Id.* to *id.*, March 11, 1757, *ibid.*, 14.
50. *Id.* to *id.*, February 18, 1758, *ibid.*, 171-173; *id.* to *id.*, August 25, 1760, *ibid.*, 456-459; Minutes of Governor and Council, November 17, 1758, in Candler, ed., *Colonial Records*, VII, 842.
51. Ellis to Board of Trade, March 11, 1757, in unpublished Colonial Records, XXVIII, Part I, 10.
52. *Id.* to *id.*, May 5, 1757, *ibid.*, 18-31; Minutes of Governor and Council, March 14, 1757, in Candler, ed., *Colonial Records*, VII, 498-499; Commons House Journal, June 16, 1757, *ibid.*, XIII, 171.
53. Reynolds to Board of Trade, January 5, 1756, in unpublished Colonial Records, XXVII, 237-243.
54. Ellis to Board of Trade, August 1, 1757, *ibid.*, 50-55; *id.* to *id.*, September 20, 1757, *ibid.*, 92-94.
55. *Id.* to *id.*, March 11, 1757, *ibid.*, 4-15.
56. Minutes of Governor and Council, March 25, 1757, November 17, 21, 1758, in Candler, ed., *Colonial Records*, VII, 503, 842, 845-846.
57. Ellis to Pitt, August 1, 1757, in unpublished Colonial Records, XXVIII, Part I, 57-60; *id.* to Board of Trade, May 5, 25, 1757, *ibid.*, 18-31, 36-39; Minutes of Governor and Council, July 4, 1757, in Candler, ed., *Colonial Records*, VI, 600.
58. Commons House Journal, July 19, 1757, *ibid.*, XIII, 220-221; Ellis to Board of Trade, September 20, 1757, in unpublished Colonial Records, XXVIII, Part I, 92-94.
59. *Id.* to *id.*, March 11, August 1, 1757, April 24, 1759, August 25,

1760, *ibid.*, 4-15, 50-55, 291-303, 456-459.

60. *Id.* to *id.*, July 8, 1757, *ibid.*, 42-45.

61. Ellis to Pitt, August 1, 1757, *ibid.*, 57.

62. Ellis to Board of Trade, April 24, 1759, *ibid.*, 291-303.

63. Board of Trade to Ellis, April 21, 1758, *ibid.*, XXXIV, 220-236.

64. Ellis to Board of Trade, April 24, 1759, *ibid.*, XXVIII, Part I, 293.

65. *Id.* to *id.*, May 5, 1757, *ibid.*, 18-31; Commons House Journal, in Candler, ed., *Colonial Records*, XIII, 171.

66. Ellis to Board of Trade, March 20, May 5, 1757, April 24, 1759, in unpublished Colonial Records XXVIII, Part I, 16-17, 18-31, 291-303.

67. Board of Trade to Ellis, April 21, 1758, *ibid.*, XXXIV, 220-236.

68. Ellis to Board of Trade, April 24, 1759, *ibid.*, XXVIII, Part I, 301.

69. *Id.* to *id.*, November 25, 1757, *ibid.*, 114-117.

70. *Id.* to *id.*, May 5, October 22, 1757, July 26, 1759, *ibid.*, 18-31, 100, 306-310; Minutes of Governor and Council, September 13, 1757, in Candler, ed., *Colonial Records*, VII, 626.

71. Charleston *South Carolina Gazette*, June 21, July 12, 1760; Minutes of Governor and Council, May 26, 1768, in Candler, ed., *Colonial Records*, VII, 763-765; Ellis to Board of Trade, March 31, 1758, in unpublished Colonial Records, XXVIII, Part I, 184-186.

72. *Id.* to *id.*, May 25, 1757, *ibid.*, 36-39.

73. *Id.* to *id.*, July 8, 1757, *ibid.*, 42-45; Minutes of Governor and Council, June 28, 1757, in Candler, ed., *Colonial Records*, VII, 597.

74. Commons House Journal, July 20, 1757, *ibid.*, XIII, 225-226.

75. Ellis to Board of Trade, November 25, 1757, in unpublished Colonial Records, XXVIII, Part I, 114-117; Charleston *South Carolina Gazette*, June 19, 1757.

76. Minutes of Governor and Council, October 25, 1757, in Candler, ed.,

Colonial Records, VII, 643-648; Ellis to Board of Trade, November 25, 1757, in unpublished Colonial Records, XXVIII, Part I, 114-117.

77. Minutes of Governor and Council, November 3, 1757, in Candler, ed., *Colonial Records*, VII, 657-667.

78. Minutes of Governor and Council, November 3, 7, 1757, *ibid.*, 657-668.

79. Ellis to Board of Trade, November 25, 1757, in unpublished Colonial Records, XXVIII, Part I, 114-117.

80. *Id.* to *id.*, June 28, 1758, July 26, 1759, *ibid.*, 220-222, 306-310.

81. *Id.* to *id.*, October 25, 1758, *ibid.*, 231-233.

82. Commons House Journal, January 11, 1758, in Candler, ed., *Colonial Records*, XIII, 239; Minutes of Governor and Council, December 6, 1759, January 31, 1760, *ibid.*, VIII, 214-215; Upper House Journal, October 25, 1759, *ibid.*, XVI, 388.

83. Commons House Journal, February 15, 1758, *ibid.*, XIII, 282.

84. Ellis to Board of Trade, October 25, 1758, July 10, 1760, in unpublished Colonial Records, XXVIII, Part I, 231-233, 384-386; Minutes of Governor and Council, June 30, 1760, in Candler, ed., *Colonial Records*, VIII, 325-334.

85. Ellis to Board of Trade, November 9, 1758, in unpublished Colonial Records, XXVIII, Part I, 242-243.

86. *Id.* to *id.*, September 6, 1759, *ibid.*, 313-314.

87. *Id.* to *id.*, January 6, February 15, 1760, *ibid.*, 329-331, 333-335; Minutes of Governor and Council, February 3, 1760, in Candler, ed., *Colonial Records*, VIII, 328.

88. Upper House Journal, February 12, 1760, *ibid.*, XVI, 435-436.

89. *Ibid.*; Minutes of Governor and Council, February 18, March 26, June 17, 1760, *ibid.*, VIII, 250-251, 266, 324; Ellis to Board of Trade, August 25, 1760, in unpublished Colonial Records, XXVIII, Part I, 456-459.

90. *Id.* to *id.*, March 5, 1760, *ibid.*, 341-342.

91. Charleston *South Carolina Gazette,* April 12, May 10, 1760; Minutes of Governor and Council, February 9, 21, April 14, May 2, 20, 1760, in Candler, ed., *Colonial Records,* VIII, 248, 253, 284-285, 295-297, 308-313.

92. Upper House Journal, February 12, 1760, *ibid.,* XVI, 435-436.

93. Ellis to Board of Trade, June 7, 1760, in unpublished Colonial Records, XXVIII, Part I, 384-386.

94. Upper House Journal, June 2, 1760, in Candler, ed., *Colonial Records,* XVI, 498-500.

95. Ellis to Board of Trade, June 7, July 10, 1760, in unpublished Colonial Records, XXVIII, Part I, 384-386, 453; Minutes of Governor and Council, May 26, June 5, 1760, in Candler, ed., *Colonial Records,* VIII, 314-317, 319-323.

96. Ellis to Pitt, July 10, 1760, in unpublished Colonial Records, XXVIII, Part I, 453.

97. Ellis to Board of Trade, October 20, 1760, *ibid.,* 468.

98. *Id.* to *id.,* November 25, 1759, *ibid.,* 318.

CHAPTER THREE

1. Henry Ellis to Board of Trade, October 20, 1760, in unpublished Colonial Records, XXVIII, Part I, 468; James Wright to Board of Trade, October 23, December 23, 1760, *ibid.,* 472-473, 477-488.

2. E. Irving Carlyle, "Sir James Wright," in Leslie Stephens and Sidney Lee, eds., *Dictionary of National Biography* (New York: The MacMillan Company, 1888-1900. 63 vols.), LXIII, 107-109.

3. Order in Council, March 20, 1761, in unpublished Colonial Records, XXVIII, Part I, 507.

4. February 20, 1762.

5. Wright to Duke of Hillsborough, May 31, 1768, in unpublished Colonial Records, XXXVII, 311.

6. For information on Wright's property see *Collections of the Georgia Historical Society* (Savannah, 1840-1955. 11 vols.), VI, 102. Hereinafter cited as *Collections.*

7. For an account of this congress with a copy of the treaty of cession see Charles C. Jones, Jr., *History of Georgia* (Boston: Houghton, Mifflin and Company, 1883. 2 vols.), II, 43-46; John R. Alden, *John Stuart and the Southern Colonial Frontier* (Ann Arbor: University of Michigan Press, 1944), *passim.* A complete journal is in William L. Sanders, ed., *The Colonial Records of North Carolina* (Raleigh: P. M.

Hale and Josephus Daniels, 1886-1890. 10 vols.), X, 156-207.

8. For this law about the control of slaves in Georgia see Candler, ed., *Colonial Records,* XVIII, 649-688, XIX, Part I, 209-249; unpublished Colonial Records, XXXVII, 363-367, 395, XXXIX, 79-81; *Acts of the Privy Council, Colonial Series, 1613-1783* (Hereford: His Majesty's Stationery Office, 1911-1912. 6 vols.), V, 177.

9. Wright to Hillsborough, May 23, 1768, in unpublished Colonial Records, XXXVII, 284-285.

10. Candler, ed., *Colonial Records,* XV, 295-296, XI, 253-257.

11. *Ibid.,* XIV, 518.

12. *Ibid.,* XVII, 689-691, X, 945-946, XV, 46-49, 86-87, 123-124, 127-128, 159-160, XIX, Part I, 170; Percy Scott Flippin, "Royal Government in Georgia, 1752-1776," *Georgia Historical Quarterly,* VIII (1924), 245; unpublished Colonial Records, XXXVII, 450-451, 453-457.

13. Candler, ed., *Colonial Records,* XV, 202, 206-207, 298-299; Hillsborough to Wright, December 11, 1770, in unpublished Colonial Records, XXXVII, 489.

14. Wright to Earl of Dartmouth, August 10, 1773, *ibid.,* 83-84; Dartmouth to Wright, October 28, 1773, *ibid.,* 92-93.

15. Records of lands granted are in Candler, ed., *Colonial Records,* VII-

338 *Georgians in Profile*

XII. See also Wright to Earl of Shelburne, May 18, 1767, in unpublished Colonial Records, XXXVII, 210-211; Wright to Hillsborough, March 8, 1769, *ibid.*, 400-410; Wright to Board of Trade, December 27, 1771, in *Journal of the Commissioners for Trade and Plantations, 1768-75* (London: His Majesty's Stationery Office, 1937), 294.

16. Jones, *History of Georgia*, II, 28-40; Wright to Board of Trade, April 20, May 6, 1763, in unpublished Colonial Records, XXVIII, Part I, 731-744, 763-765; *id.* to *id.*, April 4, July 5, 1765, *ibid.*, Part II, 82-84, 180-184; Candler, ed., *Colonial Records*, XVII, 426, XVIII, 627-636; *Acts of the Privy Council, Colonial Series*, V, 113-114.

17. Recommendations of Board of Trade, November 9, 1772, in unpublished Colonial Records, XXXIV, 628-638, XXXVIII, Part I, 15-26; Dartmouth to Wright, December 12, 1772, January 6, 1773, *ibid.*, 31-37; John Stuart to Thomas Gage, February 15, 1773, in Gage Papers, American Series, Clements Library, University of Michigan; Wright to Dartmouth, August 10, 1773, in unpublished Colonial Records, XXXVII, Part I, 83; Alden, *John Stuart*, 301-308.

18. Wright to Board of Trade, August 27, 1764, in unpublished Colonial Records, XXVIII, Part II, 114-116.

19. Alden, *John Stuart*, 209-214, 234-235, 250-254; Wright to Shelburne, November 29, 1766, January 5, 1767 in unpublished Colonial Records, XXXVII, 146-149, 154-155; Wright to Hillsborough, August 8, 1768, *ibid.*, 254; Stuart to Wright, December 17, 1767, *ibid.*, 162-164; Wright to Stuart, January 5, 1767, *ibid.*, 165-166.

20. *Dictionary of National Biography*, LXIII, 107-109.

21. Candler, ed., *Colonial Records*, XIV, 142-144, 252-253, XVII, 199-200; *Collections*, VI, 30-33.

22. Wright to Earl of Halifax, September 20, 1765, quoted in William B.

Stevens, *A History of Georgia* (Philadelphia: D. Appleton and Company, 1847-59. 2 vols.), II, 41; Candler, ed., *Colonial Records*, XIV, 270-274.

23. Wright to Henry S. Conway, January 31, 1766, quoted in Jones, *History of Georgia*, II, 60-65; Savannah *Georgia Gazette*, October 31, November 7, 14, 1765; Candler, ed., *Colonial Records*, IX, 438-439.

24. *Ibid.*, XIV, 300-301, 304-306, 315-317.

25. *Ibid.*, IX, 454-458, 460.

26. Wright to Board of Trade, January 15, 1766, quoted in Flippin, "Royal Government in Georgia, 1752-1776," *loc. cit.*, 91-92; Wright to Conway, January 31, 1766, quoted in Jones, *History of Georgia*, II, 62; *The Newport Mercury*, February 10, 1766; extract of a letter from Georgia, January 6, 1766, quoted in Charleston *South Carolina Gazette and Country Journal*, January 21, 1766.

27. James Habersham to George Whitefield, January 27, 1766, in *Collections*, VI, 54-55; Charleston *South Carolina Gazette*, February 25, 1766; unpublished Colonial Records, XXXVII, 112, 121-122; Wright to Conway, February 7, 1766, quoted in Jones, *History of Georgia*, II, 64-65; see sources cited in footnote No. 26.

28. Wright to Conway, March 10, 1766, in unpublished Colonial Records, XXXVII, 116-117.

29. Candler, ed., *Colonial Records*, XIV, 370-372, 374, 377-381.

30. *Ibid.*, 293-294, 317-319, 335-336, XVII, 224, 269; *Collections*, VI, 40-41, 44-49, 59.

31. Candler, ed., *Colonial Records*, XIV, 327, 337, 387, 458, 474, 527, XVII, 356, 363-368, 372-375, 392, X, 433; *Collections*, VI, 58-60.

32. In 1774 this argument between the two houses was repeated about Franklin's work as agent. See Savannah *Georgia Gazette*, January 26, March 9, 1774; Candler, ed., *Colonial Records*, XVII, 774-786;

Alfred Owen Aldridge, "Benjamin Franklin as Georgia Agent," *Georgia Review,* VI (1952), 161-173.

33. Savannah *Georgia Gazette,* October 14, 1767, December, 1767-April, 1768; Candler, ed., *Colonial Records,* XIV, 584; Wright to Hillsborough, in unpublished Colonial Records, XXXVII, 282-283.

34. Candler, ed., *Colonial Records,* XIV, 592-593, 595-596, XVII, 454.

35. *Ibid.,* XIV, 643-659; Savannah *Georgia Gazette,* December 28, 1768; Wright to Hillsborough, December 24, 1768, in unpublished Colonial Records, XXXVII, 380.

36. Savannah *Georgia Gazette,* September 6, 13, 20, 1769; Wright to Hillsborough, August 15, September 20, 1769, in unpublished Colonial Records, XXXVII, 417-418; Flippin, "Royal Government in Georgia, 1752-1776," *loc. cit.,* 100.

37. Candler, ed., *Colonial Records,* XV, 305-306, 311-312, 313-314, XI, 335-336; Wright to Hillsborough, April 30, 1771, in unpublished Colonial Records, XXXVII, 535-538.

38. *Ibid.*

39. Hillsborough to James Habersham, December 4, 1771, *ibid.,* 552-553; Candler, ed., *Colonial Records,* XI, 429.

40. *Ibid.,* XV, 320-323, 324-325, 329-334, XVII, 655-658; Habersham to Hillsborough, April 30, 1772, in *Collections,* VI, 174-180.

41. Wright to Dartmouth, July 25, 1774, in unpublished Colonial Records, XXXVIII, Part I, 293-294; Savannah *Georgia Gazette,* August 3, 1774; George White, *Historical Collections of Georgia* (New York: Pudney and Russell, 1854), 46; Allen D. Candler, ed., *The Revolutionary Records of the State of Georgia* (Atlanta: The Franklin-Turner Company, 1908. 3 vols.), I, 11-17.

42. Wright to Dartmouth, August 18, 24, 1774, in unpublished Colonial Records, XXXVIII, Part I, 298, 302-311; Wright to Thomas Gage, August 19, 1774, in Gage Papers,

American Series; Candler, ed., *Revolutionary Records,* I, 17-34; Savannah *Georgia Gazette,* September 7, 21, 28, October 12, 1774; Stevens, *History of Georgia,* II, 81-82.

43. Wright to Gage, November 4, December 24, 1774, in Gage Papers, American Series; Savannah *Georgia Gazette,* November 16, 1774.

44. *Ibid.,* January 25, 1775.

45. Candler, ed., *Revolutionary Records,* I, 34-37.

46. *Ibid.,* 63-66.

47. *Collections,* X, 11-12.

48. *Ibid.,* 13-16, 24-25; Wright to Dartmouth, February 24, July 8, 10, 1775, in unpublished Colonial Records, XXXVIII, Part I, 395-417, 480-495, 606-616, 631-634.

49. *Collections,* X, 21-22.

50. Savannah *Georgia Gazette,* June 7, 1775.

51. Wright to Dartmouth, June 9, 1775, in unpublished Colonial Records, XXXVIII, Part I, 446-449; *id.* to *id.,* June 17, July 10, 1775, in *Collections,* III, 183-186, 195; Patrick Tonyn to Gage, July 17, 1775, in Gage Papers, American Series; Lord William Campbell to Gage, July 29, 1775, *ibid.;* Noble W. Jones to Boston Relief Committee, June 1, 1775, quoted in White, *Historical Collections of Georgia,* 63-64; letter from Charleston, June 29, 1775, in *American Archives: Fourth Series* (Washington: M. St. Clair Clarke and Peter Force, 1837-1846. 6 vols.), II, 1120; circular from Committee of South Carolina, June 30, 1775, in Sanders, ed., *Colonial Records of North Carolina,* X, 57.

52. Gage to Wright, April 16, 1775, in *Collections, III,* 188; Wright to Gage, June 7, 1775, in Gage Papers, American Series; Council Minutes, July 25, 1775, *Collections,* X, 34.

53. Wright to Dartmouth, June 17, July 10, 1775, in *Collections,* III, 185, 195.

54. *Id.* to *id.,* July 8, 1775, *ibid.,* 192-193.

55. The records of the Congress are in Candler, ed., *Revolutionary Records,* I, 229-259.

56. Savannah *Georgia Gazette*, November 1, 15, December 6, 1775; Wright to Dartmouth, October 14, December 9, 1775, in *Collections*, III, 216-217, 223-224; Anthony Stokes, *A Narrative of the Official Conduct of Anthony Stokes* (London: privately printed, 1784.), 10, 12-22, 26.

57. Information from Savannah, Georgia, January 18, 1776, in *American Archives, Fourth Series*, IV, 799; Candler, ed., *Revolutionary Records*, I, 101-104.

58. Wright to Sir Henry Clinton, February 21, 1776, in Henry Clinton Papers, Clements Library; Candler, ed., *Revolutionary Records*, I, 106-107.

59. Wright to Clinton, February 21, 1776, in Henry Clinton Papers; Candler, ed., *Revolutionary Records*, I, 106-107, 269-272.

60. Memorials of August 29, 1777, July 17, 1778, in unpublished Colonial Records, XXXIV, 4-9, 10-15.

61. George Germain to Clinton, March 8, August 5, 1778, in Historical Manuscripts Commission, *Report on the Manuscripts of Mrs. Stopford-Sackville* (London: His Majesty's Stationery Office, 1904-1910. 2 vols.), II, 94-99, 151.

62. Alexander A. Lawrence, "General Robert Howe and the British capture of Savannah in 1778," *Georgia Historical Quarterly*, XXXVI (1952), 303-327; Campbell to Clinton, March 4, 1779, in Public Record Office, Colonial Office 5, Vol. 182, 151-155.

63. Unpublished Colonial Records, XXXVIII, Part II, 153-154, XXXIX, 101-102.

64. *Ibid.*, XXXVIII, Part II, 176-179.

65. Wright to Germain, July 31, 1779, in *Collections*, III, 254-255; eighteen questions answered by Wright, in undated papers, in Germain Papers, Clements Library.

66. Augustine Prevost to Clinton, August 7, 1779, in Historical Manuscripts Commission, *Report on American Manuscripts in the Royal Institution* (London: His Majesty's

Stationery Office, 1904-1909. 4 vols.), II, 5-6; Wright to Clinton, August 7, 1779, *ibid.*

67. Alexander A. Lawrence, *Storm Over Savannah: The Story of Count d'Estaing and the Siege of the Town in 1779* (Athens: University of Georgia Press, 1951).

68. Council Minutes, September 6, 1779, in *Collections*, X, 49-50.

69. Clinton to Germain, November 10, 1779, in Henry Clinton Papers.

70. Wright to Germain, November 4, 6, 1779, January 20, February 20, 1780, in unpublished Colonial Records, XXXVIII, Part II, 244; *Collections*, III, 269-270, 272-273, 276; Council Minutes, November and December, 1779, *ibid.*, X, 54-77; Savannah *Royal Georgia Gazette*, December 14, 23, 1779.

71. Council Minutes, February 16, March 8, 1780, in *Collections*, X, 89-91.

72. Council Minutes, March 24, 1780, *ibid.*, 95-96; Wright to Germain, March 24, 1780, *ibid.*, III, 279-281.

73. Candler, ed., *Colonial Records*, XV, 548-552, 556-558; unpublished Colonial Records, XXXVIII, Part II, 349-352.

74. The journal of the Commons House is in Candler, ed., *Colonial Records*, XV, 547-624. The acts passed are in Public Record Office, Colonial Office 5, vol. 685, 1-24. Wright to Germain, July 19, 1780, in *Collections*, III, 310.

75. Wright to Germain, July 19, 1780, *ibid.*, 310; Council Minutes, June 29, August 1-September 8, 1780, *ibid.*, X, 111-112, 115-121.

76. Wright to Germain, December 20, 1780, *ibid.*, III, 328.

77. Board of Trade to Wright, June 12, 1781, in unpublished Colonial Records, XXXIV, 658-659; Germain to Wright, June 4, 1781, *ibid.*, XXXVIII, Part II, 492-493.

78. *Collections*, III, 254-375, *passim*.

79. Wright to William Knox, February 16, 1782, *ibid.*, 371; Lieutenant Colonel Nisbit Balfour to Lord Cornwallis, November 5, 1780, in Public

Record Office, Cornwallis Papers, Bundle 4, No. 15, 13.

80. *Collections,* X, 67-68, 74, 88-89, 97-98; Wright to Clinton, May 10, June 2, 1780, in Historical Manuscripts Commission, *Royal Institution,* II, 120-135; Wright to Cornwallis, July 3, 1780, in Cornwallis Papers, Bundle 2, No. 169; Balfour to Cornwallis, June 27, 1780, *ibid.,* No. 97.

81. Wayne to Greene, January 25, 1782, Greene Papers, Clements Library.

82. Wright to Germain, January 18, 1782, in *Collections,* III, 362-363; Wright to Board of Trade, January 23, 1782, *ibid.,* 364; Wright's February correspondence, *ibid., passim.*

83. Wright to Germain, December 21, 1780, January 18, 1782, *ibid.,* 329, 362.

84. Sir Guy Carleton to General Alexander Leslie, May 23, 27, 1782, in Historical Manuscripts Commission, *Royal Institution,* II, 494-495, 500.

85. Candler, ed., *Colonial Records,* XV, 662-665.

CHAPTER FOUR

1. The works will hereinafter be cited respectively as *View of the Constitution of the British Colonies, Narrative,* and *Desultory Observations.*

2. The year of Chief Justice Stokes's birth is based on Lorenzo Sabine, *Biographical Sketches of Loyaltists of the American Revolution* (Boston: Little Brown and Company, 1864. 2 vols.), II, 336. It is corroborated by Stokes's marriage license, dated July 13, 1759, which gives his age as twenty-three. See Records, Faculty Office, London. Reverend George White states in his *Historical Collections of Georgia,* 366, that Chief Justice Stokes was a native of Wales. Anthony's parentage, which was not previously known, was established through references in the last will and testament of his mother, Florence Stokes, of Pill, in the County of Pembroke. The will was probated in 1775.

3. Anthony Stokes's bookplate is No. 28, 251 in the Franks Collection of Bookplates, Print Room, British Museum. Reference to the coat of arms of the Stokes line said to have descended from Peter de Stok is found in John Burke and John Bernard Burke, *A General Armory of England, Scotland, and Ireland* (London: Edward Churston, 1842).

4. *Desultory Observations,* 30. While Anthony left Wales in 1758, he al-ways prided himself upon his Welsh background, a fact evidenced by the prominent role "Tony Stokes" took in a celebration at Savannah of the festival of St. David, patron saint of Wales. See the verse by James Herriott printed in the Savannah *Gazette of the State of Georgia,* May 29, 1783.

5. Bench Table Minutes, Easter Term, 1760, Records of the Inner Temple, London. An utter barrister was one recently admitted and who was accustomed to plead outside the bar as distinguished from the benchers who were permitted to plead within the bar.

6. *Narrative,* 2.

7. Parish Registers of St. Andrews Holborn, London. The marriage took place on July 14.

8. Earl of Hillsborough to Governor Wright, January 4, 1769, in Public Record Office, Colonial Office 5, vol. 660, 1.

9. Stokes to William Pitt, first Lord Commissioner of his Majesty's Treasury, January 10, 1785. A copy of this letter is in Public Record Office, Stokes's Claim, Georgia Loyalist Papers AO, Bundle 13-36 A. Microfilm of the Loyalists Papers is in the Department of Archives and History of Georgia, Atlanta, and in the Georgia Historical Society, Savannah. These voluminous files consist of the claims submitted

to the commissioners appointed to examine into the losses and services of the American Loyalists. They are an unexploited and indispensable source of information concerning the Loyalists of the province of Georgia.

10. Hillsborough to Wright, March 23, 1769, *ibid.*, Colonial Office 5, vol. 660, 61. This letter is in the unpublished Colonial Records, XXXVII, 397.

11. Wright to Hillsborough, June 26, 1769, in Public Record Office, Colonial Office 5, vol. 650, 247f.

12. Stokes's commission is printed in unpublished Colonial Records, XXXVIII, Part II, 145f. The oath of Allegiance and Supremacy which he took is in White, *Historical Collections of Georgia,* 38f. In it he renounced the Jacobite line; affirmed his disbelief in the "Transubstantiation in the Sacrament of the Lord's Supper," and abjured the "damnable doctrine" that Princes ex-communicated by the Pope could be deposed or murdered by their subjects.

13. James Habersham to Hillsborough, April 30, 1772, in Public Record Office, Colonial Office 5, vol. 651, 372f. Acting Governor Habersham was paraphrasing a report he had received a short time before from Chief Justice Stokes.

14. Records of the prothonotaries of the General Court presented in support of Stokes's Claim before the Commissioners of American Claims, in Public Record Office, Georgia Loyalist Papers, AO, Bundle 13-36 A.

15. *View of the Constitution of the British Colonies,* 269.

16. *Ibid.,* 270.

17. Charles C. Jones, Jr., *Memorial History of Augusta, Georgia* (Syracuse, New York: D. Mason & Company, 1890), 211.

18. Remarks of Chief Justice Stokes, January 10, 1776, quoted in *Narrative,* 23; Public Record Office,

Stokes's Claim, Georgia Loyalist Papers, AO, Bundle 13-37.

19. Jones, *Memorial History of Augusta,* 201.

20. Savannah, 1771, James Johnston, printer. It was once thought that this pamphlet was lost. See Joseph Rucker Lamar, "The Bench and Bar of Georgia during the Eighteenth Century," in *Report of the Thirtieth Annual Session of the Georgia Bar Association* (Macon: J. W. Burke Company, 1913), 69. The only known copy is in the Library of the Harvard Law School, Cambridge, Massachusetts.

21. *View of the Constitution of the British Colonies,* 132.

22. Letters that Stokes wrote in 1776, while he was staying in the country, were date lined "Pembroke." See *Narrative,* 35, 39. Apparently his plantation was located next to Harrock Hall on Roche Creek, now called Herb River. "Pembroke" was described in *The Royal Georgia Gazette,* January 4, 1781, as a 200 acre tract situated on Roche Creek. Stokes was not its owner at that time and the identity of the "Pembroke" mentioned there and his property is not definite.

23. "A List of the Landed and personal property in Georgia; of Anthony Stokes, Barrister at Law, Chief Justice of that Province . . .," in unpublished Colonial Records, XXXIX, 51.

24. *View of the Constitution of the British Colonies,* 415.

25. *Desultory Observations,* 54. For other animadversions by Stokes on slavery in Georgia see *Desultory Observations,* 53f.

26. Stokes to Edward Langworthy, May 2, 1776, quoted in *Narrative,* 40.

27. *View of the Constitution of the British Colonies,* 415.

28. Statement of Stokes, October 29, 1774, quoted in Savannah *Georgia Gazette,* November 2, 1774.

29. *View of the Constitution of the British Colonies,* 140.

30. *Desultory Observations,* 18.
31. *View of the Constitution of the British Colonies,* 137.
32. *Ibid.,* 139.
33. *Narrative,* 5.
34. *View of the Constitution of the British Colonies,* 139.
35. Charles Nephew West, "The Bench and Bar of Georgia," in *Memoirs of Georgia, Historical and Biographical* (Atlanta: Southern Historical Association, 1895. 2 vols.), II, 256.
36. Stokes to Edward Langworthy, May 2, 1776, quoted in *Narrative,* 40; Stokes to Lachlan McIntosh, March 6, 1776, *ibid.,* 28. See also *ibid.,* 36 and unpublished Colonial Records, XXXIX, 59. The similarities and the contrasts between the viewpoints of Stokes and the theories of two other royal chief justices, William Smith, of New York, and Thomas Hutchinson, of Massachusetts, afford a rather interesting comparison. See William H. W. Sabine, ed., *Historical Memoirs from 16 March 1763 to 9 July 1776 of William Smith, Historian of the Province of New York, Member of the Governor's Council and Last Chief Justice of that Province Under the Crown, Chief Justice of Quebec* (New York: Colburn & Tegg, 1856), 239, 250, 272, 274; Peter Orlando Hutchinson, ed., *The Diary and Letters of his Excellency Thomas Hutchinson, Esq.* (London: Sampson Low, Marston, Searle & Rivington, 1883, 1886. 2 vols.), I, 14, 15, 233, 285f., 388.
37. *Desultory Observations,* 57-58.
38. *View of the Constitution of the British Colonies,* 138, v.
39. Savannah *Georgia Gazette,* November 16, 1774. The writer, who signed himself "Veritas," went on to criticize Stokes for expressing what was termed a precipitate opinion concerning a lease to Jonathan Bryan made by Indians of a vast tract of land. The chief justice had written a letter to the *Gazette* stating his impressions of what had occurred on that subject at the congress with the Creeks held at Savannah in 1774. See *ibid.,* November 2, 1774.
40. Robertson's testimonial, March 17, 1787, in Public Record Office, Stokes's Claim, Georgia Loyalist Papers, AO, Bundle 13-36 A. Robertson, who was attorney general of Georgia, 1779-82, became chief justice of the Virgin Islands after the Revolution.
41. This endorsement, dated December 2, 1784, and signed by leading Loyalists, including John Graham, *ibid.*
42. Wright to Hillsborough, July 20, 1770, in Public Record Office, Colonial Office 5, vol. 678, 194; unpublished Colonial Records, XXXVII, 467. For his part, Stokes paid tribute to Governor Wright for his "whole fidelity to the Crown, and unwearied attention to the welfare of the Colony." See *View of the Constitution of the British Colonies,* iii, iv.
43. *View of the Constitution of the British Colonies,* 137.
44. *Ibid.,* 138. Governor Francis Bernard of Massachusetts once proposed a plan which included the creation of an American nobility.
45. *Desultory Observations,* 49.
46. *View of the Constitution of the British Colonies,* 264.
47. "A List of the landed and personal property in Georgia; of Anthony Stokes, Barrister at Law, Chief Justice of that Province . . .," in unpublished Colonial Records, XXXIX, 55.
48. Minutes of the General Court, January 17, 1772, May 3, 1773, quoted in *Narrative,* 5-7.
49. R. Carter Pittman, "Admissions to and Disbarments from the Bar of Justice," *Georgia Bar Journal* XVII, (1954), 173.
50. *Desultory Observations,* 48.
51. Stokes to the Lords Commissioners of the Treasury, January 13,

1779, in Public Record Office, Stokes's Claim, Georgia Loyalist Papers, AO, Bundle 13-17.

52. Endorsement of Stokes by James Hume and William Jones, July 28, 1786, *ibid.*, Bundle 13-36 A. It is possible that the chief justice was one of the writers who in 1774 and 1775, under various pen names, waged a lively war of polemics in the Savannah *Georgia Gazette.* Stokes's failure, however, to mention that fact in any of his writings militates against the possibility.

53. *Desultory Observations,* 55f.

54. *Narrative,* 9.

55. Wright to Earl of Dartmouth, June 17, 1775, in unpublished Colonial Records, XXXVIII, Part I, 466.

56. Opinion of Stokes to the Council, August 15, 1775, in *Collections,* X, 40-42. See also Candler, ed., *Colonial Records,* XII, 430-433.

57. Memorial of Stokes addressed to the Lords Commissioners of his Majesty's Treasury, January 5, 1778, in unpublished Colonial Records, XXXIX, 36. This lengthy account of the chief justice's record in Georgia was not sent to the Treasury. A copy was delivered by Stokes to Lord George Germain; see *ibid.,* 47, 49. The original copy is in Public Record Office, Colonial Office 5, vol. 116. 335ff.

58. Opinion of Chief Justice Stokes to the Council, August 15, 1775, in *Collections,* X, 41. This was a common Loyalist attitude concerning the social effects of the upheaval in America. *Cf.* Governor Wright's letter in *Collections,* III, 228, and Elizabeth Lichtenstein Johnston, *Memoirs of a Georgia Loyalist* (New York and London: M. F. Mansfield & Company, 1901), 45.

59. *Collections,* X, 41.

60. Information of Isaac Roberts, September 12, 1775, in unpublished Colonial Records, XXXVIII, Part I, 625. Stokes says that he "had a vast deal of Trouble in taking the Informations of a great number of people," using their own words "as nearly as possible." See *ibid.,* XXXIX, 58; *Narrative,* 59.

61. Affidavit of Reverend Hadden Smith, August 7, 1775, in unpublished Colonial Records, XXXVIII, Part I, 545ff.

62. *Ibid.,* XXXIX, 41, 55; see also *Narrative,* 26. Butler was at this time an active member of the Council of Safety. Deveaux was the father-in-law of the rebel leader, Archibald Bulloch.

63. Unpublished Colonial Records, XXXIX, 38. Stokes reported that he said "many severe Things agt. the unconstitutional proceedings, that have been carried on in this Province." See *ibid.,* XXXVIII, Part 2, 50. The reference to his "amiable and inoffensive manners" is from *The European Magazine and London Review,* IV (1783), 135.

64. Wright to Dartmouth, October 14, 1775, in Public Record Office, Colonial Office 5, vol. 655, 4; unpublished Colonial Records, XXXVIII, Part II, 4.

65. *Narrative,* 10. Stokes fined the recalcitrant jurors £4 each, the fine being dischargeable on presenting excuse. The citation to the defaulting jurors is quoted in Savannah *Georgia Gazette,* October 18, 1775. See also *ibid.,* December 27, 1775.

66. Joseph Farley to Stokes, October 13, 1775, in unpublished Colonial Records, XXXVIII, Part II, 6.

67. Stokes to Wright, December 7, 1775, *ibid.,* XXXVIII, Part II, 45f; see also *ibid.,* XXXIX, 38f.

68. James Johnston to Stokes, December 15, 1775, in unpublished Colonial Records, XXXVIII, Part II, 47; Stokes to Johnston, December 16, 1775, *ibid.,* 48. Apparently Stokes's rule, which was dated December 12, was not filed in the prothonotary's office. See minutes of the Council of Safety, December 20,

1775, in Candler, ed., *Revolutionary Records,* I, 79.

69. *Narrative,* 20-22.

70. *Desultory Observations,* 61. Among the lawyers espousing the American cause were John Houstoun, George Walton, John Glen, William Stephens, Edward Jones, Thomas Ross, William Young, Robert Hamilton, and Joseph Wood, Jr. On the King's side were numbered James Hume, James Robertson, Henry Yonge, Samuel Farley, and William Jones. Hume, the attorney general, was the governor's nephew. Farley initially supported the American cause but soon departed for England. Returning to Georgia in 1779, he took a prominent part in the restored royal government. See Certificate of Anthony Stokes and John Graham, July 26, 1787, in Public Record Office, Farley Claim, Georgia Loyalist Papers, AO, Bundle 13-35. Glen and Stephens, who would serve as rebel chief justices, returned to British allegiance before the end of the Revolution.

71. *Narrative,* 25; Stokes's Claim, in Public Record Office, Georgia Loyalist Papers, AO, Bundle 13-37; unpublished Colonial Records, XXXIX, 40.

72. *Narrative,* 26f. The liberties allowed Governor Wright under his original parole were curtailed by the Provincial Congress as a result of "a hint being dropt by Mr. Stokes one of ye council, that should a Party from the British Vessells then lying at Cox spur come & by force carry him away, he [Stokes] should consider himself released and his Parole not infringed upon." Subsequently, the royal governor escaped to the vessels at Tybee although he had given his word "upon his honor as a Gentleman that he should consider himself a prisoner who could not exceed the Town in his excursions." See Francis Henry Harris to General Benjamin Lincoln, November 1, 1779, in Miscellaneous Manuscripts, Thomas Addis Emmet Collection, in the New York Public Library, New York City.

73. "The Narrative of Henry Preston," January 25, 1776, MS. in Miscellaneous Papers of the Georgia Historical Society, Savannah.

74. Stokes to William Knox, February 11, 1779, in Public Record Office, Colonial Office 5, vol. 655, 221; unpublished Colonial Records XXXVIII, Part II, 140. The loss of the provincial legal records is a regrettable one, destroying the means of adequate knowledge of the character and volume of litigation in the royal courts during Stokes's tenure of office.

75. Stokes to McIntosh, March 6, 1776, quoted in *Narrative,* 28f.

76. *Desultory Observations,* 52. Stokes gave credit to Thomas Young, a Loyalist, for his exchange. Young carried a letter from the chief justice to the British commander at Tybee as a result of which negotiations for his exchange were commenced. Otherwise, he said that he would have been taken to Philadelphia by the rebels. See Thomas Young Claim, in Public Record Office, Georgia Loyalist Papers, AO, Bundles 13-38, 13-83.

77. *Narrative,* 38f. Stokes's statement as to his refusal to have any communication with the rebels was made on a copy of his permit to leave the province, dated May 6, 1776, in Public Record Office, Colonial Office 5, vol. 655, 182; unpublished Colonial Records, XXXVIII, Part II, 114f.

78. Stokes to Langworthy, May 2, 1776, quoted in *Narrative,* 40.

79. Stokes to Captain Stanhope of the *Raven,* April 15, 1776, *ibid.,* 37.

80. Synopsis of his letter to Mackay, April 15, 1776, and of Mackay's reply, dated April 23, 1776, in

unpublished Colonial Records, XXXIX, 43-44.

81. *Narrative,* 43.

82. John Wereat to Stokes, May 16, 1776, quoted in *Narrative,* 44f. Wereat wished Stokes "health, peace, and freedom; for the last of which," he added, "America is contending, and will contend at every hazard." Stokes declared that in 1782 a man named Howley (Richard Howly?) opposed the confiscation of his property, remarking that " 'if there was an honest man among them' (meaning the friends of government) 'it was me.' " See *Narrative,* 106.

83. *View of the Constitution of the British Colonies,* vi, 141f.

84. This will was probated in 1799 in the Prerogative Court, Canterbury. The original is in the Probate Registry, Somerset House, London.

85. Germain to Stokes, January 19, 1779, in unpublished Colonial Records, XXXIX, 427.

86. Memorial of Stokes and Assistant Justice Martin Jollie to Governor Wright, January 10, 1780, in *Collections,* X, 84.

87. *The Royal Georgia Gazette,* November 25, 1779.

88. Stokes to Mrs. Stokes, November 5, 1779, quoted in Frank Moore, ed., *Diary of the American Revolution* (New York: Charles T. Evans, 1863. 2 vols.), II, 228. The original clipping is from an unidentified English gazette in The New York Historical Society's Upcott Collection of Newspaper Extracts, Vol. 5, 335. The text of the original article rather than that found in *Diary of the American Revolution* has been used in quoting from Stokes's letter.

89. Stokes to Mrs. Stokes, November 5, 1779, *ibid.,* II, 227.

90. *Narrative,* 50; *Collections,* X, 62; *View of the Constitution of the British Colonies,* iii.

91. Stokes to Mrs. Stokes, November 5, 1779, quoted in Moore, ed., *Diary*

of the American Revolution, II, 230.

92. *Narrative,* 70ff.; *The Royal Georgia Gazette,* December 23, 1779. The charge was published in the *Gazette* under a notation by the chief justice that it was "drawn up in a Hurry" and was "too inaccurate for the Publick Eye" but was "inserted out of Respect to the Gentlemen of the Grand Jury, who were pleased to think too favourably of it."

93. *Narrative,* 88f. Stokes also mentions this diary in a certificate, dated May 22, 1787, which he furnished to the Commissioners of American Claims on behalf of James Martin. He refers to "my Diary, which I have kept for several years." See Martin's Claim, in Public Record Office, Georgia Loyalist Papers, AO, Bundle 13-36. It is unfortunate that this journal, which would be of much historical value, has not been located.

94. This opinion, dated November 11, 1779, is incorporated in the Minutes of the Governor and Council, November 15, 1779, in *Collections,* X, 62.

95. Stokes to the commanding officer of his Majesty's forces, November 15, 1779, quoted in *Narrative,* 55.

96. *Collections,* X, 86.

97. *Ibid.*

98. E. Merton Coulter, *Georgia, A Short History* (Chapel Hill: University of North Carolina Press, 1947), 155.

99. *Narrative,* 90-91. In 1778 the Georgia House of Assembly had attainted Stokes and other leading Loyalists of high treason, declaring them subject to arrest, trial, and to death upon conviction, if they returned. See Candler, ed., *Revolutionary Records,* I, 330.

100. *Narrative,* 2, 99.

101. *View of the Constitution of the British Colonies,* ii, iii; *Narrative,* 2, 99.

102. Review of *View of the Constitution of the British Colonies* in *The European Magazine and London Review,* IV (1783), 135.

103. Stokes to William Pitt, first Lord Commissioner of his Majesty's Treasury, January 10, 1785, in Public Record Office, Stokes's Claim, Georgia Loyalist Papers, AO, Bundle 13-36 A.

104. Petition of Anthony Stokes, James Robertson and James Kitching to the Rt. Hon. the Earl of Shelburne, September 12, 1782, in unpublished Colonial Records, XXXVIII, Part II, 635.

105. Stokes to Commissioners of Claims, March 22, 1787, in Public Record Office, Stokes's Claim, Georgia Loyalist Papers, AO, Bundle 13-36 A. Stokes's law clerk furnished a certificate on his behalf explaining his position as to taking an oath and particularly in reference to the application of the required oath to the compensation he was receiving from the Bahama Islands as agent in London. See Certificate of Edward Harraden, August 29, 1788, *ibid.,* Georgia Loyalist Papers, AO, Bundle 13-83.

106. Stokes to Commissioners of Claims, October 15, 1785, *ibid.,* Stokes's Claim, Georgia Loyalist Papers, AO, Bundle 13-37.

107. *Id.* to *id.,* February 23, 1789, *ibid.*

108. The American Loyalists who had settled in the Bahamas apparently objected to British trade restrictions and duties. Upon the information of John Mulryne Tattnall, formerly of Georgia, Stokes was presented by a grand jury there for falsely and maliciously representing to his Majesty's secretary of state, as justification for the suspension of the courts there, that a state of actual rebellion existed in the Islands. See Savannah *Georgia Gazette,* March 26, 1789.

109. Clay to Stokes, March [?], 1793, in *Letters of Joseph Clay, Merchant of Savannah, 1776-1793,* in *Collections,* VIII, 254ff.

110. *The European Magazine and London Review,* IV (1783), 134. Another reviewer described it as a useful volume, "compiled with judgment and accuracy." See *The Critical Review* (London), Vol. 56, 313.

111. George Wymberley Jones De Renne quoted in E. Merton Coulter, *Wormsloe, Two Centuries of a Georgia Family* (Athens: University of Georgia Press, 1955), 227, 228, 285.

112. *Gentleman's Magazine,* LXIX, Part I (1799), 349. He was buried, as shown by the burial record of the Church, at St. Mary Abbotts, the Parish Church of Kensington, London. His grave was not located there and no compilation of the epitaphs on the tombstones in the old graveyard exists.

113. *Columbian Museum & Savannah Advertiser,* June 14, 1799. In reporting Stokes's death this paper followed verbatim the language of *Gentleman's Magazine* down to the point of the passage quoted above. Since the latter did not appear in that magazine and as none of the contemporary London newspapers seems to have carried a death notice of Stokes, it is quite possible that the tribute was added when the item was printed in the *Columbian Museum & Savannah Advertiser.*

CHAPTER FIVE

1. Much of the information contained in this article has been published by the author as "Colonel Benjamin Hawkins—North Carolinian—Benefactor of the Southern Indians," *North Carolina Historical Review,* XIX (1942). See also Merritt B. Pound, *Benjamin Hawkins —Indian Agent* (Athens: The University of Georgia Press, 1950). It

is the purpose of this sketch to relate Hawkins's career to the history of Georgia.

2. William E. Dodd, *The Life of Nathaniel Macon* (Raleigh: Edwards and Broughton Printers, 1903), 10.

3. Max Farrand, "The Indian Boundary Line," *American Historical Review*, X (1905), 4.

4. Walter P. Clark, ed., *The State Records of North Carolina* (Winston: M. I. and J. C. Steward, 1896. 20 vols.), XVII, 431; Worthington C. Ford, ed., *Journals of Continental Congress, Edited from Original Records in Library of Congress* (Washington: Government Printing Office, 1904. 32 vols.), XXVIII, 183.

5. *American State Papers* (Washington: Gales and Seaton, 1832-1861. 38 vols.), *Indian Affairs*, I, 19-20.

6. *Ibid.*, 16.

7. *Ibid.*

8. *Ibid.*, 44; Clark, ed., *The State Records of North Carolina*, XVII, 580.

9. Neither Carroll of Maryland nor William Perry of Delaware attended the conferences and Lachlan McIntosh from Georgia served with Hawkins, Martin, and Pickens.

10. *American State Papers, Indian Affairs*, I, 14.

11. Lucian Lamar Knight, *Georgia and Georgians* (Chicago: The Lewis Publishing Company, 1917. 6 vols.), I, 338.

12. Frank Landon Humphreys, *Life and Times of David Humphreys* (New York: G. P. Putnam & Sons, 1917. 2 vols.), II, 3. Rock Landing was near where Milledgeville is now located.

13. *Ibid.*, 9-13.

14. John C. Fitzpatrick, ed., *The Diaries of George Washington* (Boston: Houghton Mifflin Company, 1925. 4 vols.), IV, 90; Washington Letter Books, Correspondence with the War Department.

15. Coulter, *Georgia, A Short History*, 183.

16. *American State Papers, Indian Affairs*, I, 560.

17. Of the three Georgia commissioners James Jackson was the only one of prominence and with whom Hawkins had future relations. He had been a Revolutionary officer, had recently resigned from the United States Senate to aid in rescinding the Yazoo Act, and was soon to become governor of the state. As governor he had much correspondence with Hawkins which, on the whole, was cordial and indicates that despite decided differences of opinion each developed considerable respect for the other.

18. *American State Papers, Indian Affairs*, I, 586-587, 609-610.

19. *American State Papers, Foreign Relations*, I, 30.

20. *Ibid.*, 19.

21. R. S. Cotterill, "Federal Indian Management in the South, 1789-1825," *Mississippi Valley Historical Review*, XX (1933), 335.

22. September 15, 1812.

23. Fortunately nine manuscript volumes of this journal have been preserved in the Library of the Georgia Historical Society and have been published by that organization under the title, *The Letters of Benjamin Hawkins* (Savannah: Collections of the Georgia Historical Society, IX, 1918).

24. James Byers from Tellico to Edward Price at Coleraine, in Indian Office Files, The National Archives, Washington, D. C.

25. *Letters of Benjamin Hawkins*, 287.

26. Andrew Ellicott, *The Journal of Andrew Ellicott* (Philadelphia: Thomas Dobson, 1803), 199.

27. *Ibid.*, 209.

28. *Ibid.*, 217-223.

29. Quoted in Caroline Mays Brevard, *A History of Florida from the Treaty of 1763 to Our Own Times* (Deland: Florida State Historical Society, 1924. 2 vols.), I, 14. The location of this letter is not given, neither is the date, nor the person to whom it was written.

30. Hawkins Papers, Georgia Department of Archives and History, Atlanta.

31. *Letters of Benjamin Hawkins*, 299.

32. *American State Papers, Indian Affairs*, I, 647.

33. *American State Papers, Foreign Relations*, I, 70.

34. *Republican and Savannah Evening Ledger*, August 27, 1808.

35. *Ibid.*, August 30, 1808.

36. *Letters of Benjamin Hawkins*, 256.

37. Lewis Lawshe & Others vs. Francis Bacon & Wife, suit in the Crawford County Superior Court, 1834, papers in the Georgia Department of Archives and History. Hawkins's will was filed for probate in the Jones County Courthouse. A copy is in the Georgia Department of Archives and History.

38. *Republican and Savannah Evening Ledger*, April 26, 1808.

39. Madison Papers, XXV, 93, Library of Congress.

40. Quoted in Dunbar Rowland, ed., *Executive Journals of Governor Winthrop Sargent and Governor William Charles Cole Claiborne*, Vol. I of *The Mississippi Territorial Archives 1798-1803* (Nashville, 1905), 107-108.

41. *American State Papers, Indian Affairs*, I, 647.

42. *Columbian Museum & Savannah Advertiser*, November 17, 1807.

43. Tustunnuggee to Hawkins, December 21, 1801, in Hawkins Papers, Georgia Department of Archives and History.

44. Ellicott, *Journal*, 226-227.

45. "Journal of the Occurences in the Creek Agency from January to the Conclusion of Conference and Treaty at Fort Wilkinson . . . 1802," manuscript in collection of the American Philosophical Society, Philadelphia. Microfilm copy in University of Georgia Library.

46. Augusta *Chronicle*, July 25, 1803.

47. Hawkins to Governor John Milledge of Georgia, May 30, 1803, in Hawkins Papers, Georgia Department of Archives and History.

48. Augusta *Chronicle*, June 7, 1806.

49. Hawkins to Milledge, June 8, 1803, in Hawkins Papers, Georgia Department of Archives and History.

50. Hawkins Papers, Georgia Department of Archives and History.

51. Milledgeville *Georgia Journal*, March 25, 1812.

52. Edward Eggleston, and Lillie Eggleston Seelye, *Tecumseh and the Shawnee Prophet* (New York: Dodd, Mead & Company, 1878), 208-209. According to this account the term "redsticks" as applied to hostile Creek Indians during the war dates from this incident.

53. *Ibid.*, 208-210.

54. Hawkins to Governor Mitchell, September 20, 1812, October 12, 1812, February 13, 1813, in Hawkins Papers, Georgia Department of Archives and History.

55. *Id.* to *id.*, June 21, 1813, *ibid.*

56. Alexander Cornells to Hawkins, June 22, 23, 1813, *ibid.*

57. *American State Papers, Indian Affairs*, I, 848.

58. *Ibid.*, 847.

59. Indian Office Files, Secretary of War Letter Book C, 161, The National Archives.

60. Milledgeville *Georgia Journal*, July 29, 1813.

61. Hawkins to Mitchell, August 9, 1813, in Hawkins Papers, Georgia Department of Archives and History.

62. Quoted in *American State Papers, Indian Affairs*, I, 851.

63. Augusta *Chronicle*, August 27, 1813

64. Peter J. Hamilton, *Colonial Mobile* (Boston and New York: Houghton Mifflin Company, 1898), 370.

65. Hawkins to Floyd, October 8, 1813, in Hawkins Papers, Georgia Department of Archives and History

66. Augusta *Chronicle*, November 19 1813.

67. Hawkins to Floyd, November 19, 1813, in Hawkins Papers, Georgia Department of Archives and History.

68. Floyd to Pinckney, January 27,

1814, quoted in Raleigh *Register,*
February 11, 1814.

69. *American State Papers, Indian Affairs,* I, 836-837.
70. *Ibid.*
71. *Ibid.,* 857-858.
72. Hawkins to Pinckney, April 25, 1814, quoted *ibid.,* 858.
73. Quoted in John Spencer Bassett, ed., *Correspondence of Andrew Jackson* (Washington: The Carnegie Institution of Washington, 1926-35. 7 vols.) , II, 3.
74. *Ibid.,* II, 14-15.
75. Jackson to Blount, quoted *ibid.,* II, 24.
76. Jackson to Armstrong, quoted *ibid.,* II, 26.
77. Chiefs to Hawkins, in Indian Office Files, The National Archives.
78. Hawkins to Governor Early, November 1, 1814, in Telamon Cuyler Collection, University of Georgia Library.
79. *Id.* to *id.,* January 22, 1815, *ibid.*
80. Hawkins to Nicholls, June 10, 1815, quoted in *Niles Weekly Register,* VIII, 285. As the witnesses re-

ferred to were Colonel Nicholls, Captain Woodbine, Lieutenant Hamby, and Captain Henry (the commandant and three of his officers) , this statement was bitter sarcasm.
81. July 30, 1813.
82. Quoted in *American State Papers, Indian Affairs,* I, 852-853.
83. Woodward to Edward Hamrick, May 12, 1857, quoted in *Publications of the Alabama Historical Society, Miscellaneous Collections* (Montgomery, 1901) , I, 175.
84. Madison to Washington, March 18, 1787, quoted in Jared Sparks, ed., *Correspondence of the American Revolution; Being the Letters of Eminent Men to George Washington from the Time of His Taking Command of the Army to the End of His Presidency* (Boston: Little, Brown & Company, 1853. 4 vols.) , IV, 165.
85. Marquis James, *Andrew Jackson, Border Captain* (New York: The Literary Guild, 1933) , 166.

CHAPTER SIX

1. Milledgeville *Southern Recorder,* May 3, 1825; *Niles Weekly Register,* May 21, 1825, 178.
2. John Crowell to Secretary of War, May 2, 1825, in *United States Congress, Report on Messages of the President, Select Committee. House Reports, No. 98, 19 Cong., 2 Sess., Vol. III. The Georgia Indian Controversy,* March 3, 1827 (Government Printing Office) , 148. Hereinafter cited as *House Reports, No. 98.*
3. *Ibid.,* 449.
4. *Ibid.,* 89, 336, 571; Thomas S. Woodward, *Woodward's Reminiscences of the Creek, or Muscogee Indians* (Tuscaloosa: Weatherford Printing Company, 1939) , 35.
5. Joseph Gaston Baillie Bulloch, *A History and Genealogy of the Family of Baillie of Dunain* (Green Bay: The Gazette Company, 1898) ,

8-9, 70-71; Edward Jenkins Harden, *The Life of George M. Troup* (Savannah: E. J. Purse, 1859) , 8; John Richard Alden, *John Stuart and the Southern Colonial Frontier* (Ann Arbor: The University of Michigan Press, 1944) , 203-204, 212, 318.
6. Thomas Gamble, *Savannah Duels and Duellists, 1733-1877* (Savannah: Review Publishing and Printing Company, 1923) , 318; Woodward, *Reminiscences,* 114. Woodward is in error concerning the genealogy of the McIntosh family as is Albert James Picket in *History of Alabama* (Sheffield: R. C. Randolph, 1896) , 477.
7. John R. Swanton, *The Indians of the Southeastern United States* (Washington: Government Printing Office, 1946) , 703-704; Carolyn Thomas Foreman, "A Creek Pio-

neer," *Chronicles of Oklahoma,* XXI (1943), 271; Woodward, *Reminiscences,* 114; *House Reports, No. 98,* 339.

8. *Ibid.,* 47, 283, 336, 339; Carolyn Thomas Foreman, "North Fork Town," *Chronicles of Oklahoma,* XXIX (1951), 99; John Bartlett Meserve, "The McIntoshes," *Chronicles of Oklahoma,* X (1932), 320-323.

9. *Ibid.,* 313. Coweta town was on the west bank of the Chattahoochee River. The exact date of McIntosh's birth is obscured by conflicting data. He was between forty and fifty years of age at the time of his death in 1825.

10. *Letters of Benjamin Hawkins,* 342.

11. Harden, *Life of George M. Troup,* 170. It was estimated that the value of plunder taken from Lockchau Talofau was $40,000, of which $20,000 was in bonds or specie. McIntosh owned a considerable number of slaves and a quantity of livestock. He operated a trading house and at least two taverns. See *House Reports, No. 98,* 560-574.

12. Charles J. Kappler, *Indian Affairs, Laws and Treaties* (Washington: Government Printing Office, 1892-1913. 3 vols.), II, 85-86; Robert S. Cotterill, *The Southern Indians* (Norman: University of Oklahoma Press, 1953), 149, 152.

13. Pound, *Benjamin Hawkins,* 186; Augusta *Chronicle,* October 10, 1805.

14. Arthur P. Whitaker, *Spanish American Frontier, 1783-1795* (Boston: Houghton Mifflin Company, 1927), 24. The Federal Road ran from Fort Wilkinson on the Oconee through what is today Macon, Roberta, Talbotton, Columbus, and thence southwestward.

15. Quoted from a Milledgeville newspaper of July, 1811, in George White, *Historical Collections of Georgia,* 268.

16. Cotterill, *Southern Indians,* 178.

17. Woodward, *Reminiscences,* 84. Tuckabatchee was on the west bank of the Tallapoosa River. Tallasee and Autassee were in the same vicinity but on the east side of the river (*ibid.,* 31). These towns were at the great bend of the Tallapoosa where its course changes from a southerly to a westerly direction.

18. Pound, *Benjamin Hawkins,* 212; Cotterill, *Southern Indians,* 172, 178.

19. *American State Papers, Indian Affairs,* I, 809; Arthur H. Hall, "The Red Stick War: Creek Indian Affairs During the War of 1812," *Chronicles of Oklahoma,* XII (1934), 272.

20. Woodward, *Reminiscences,* 35.

21. *American State Papers, Indian Affairs,* I, 829, 843, 847.

22. *Ibid.,* 845.

23. Woodward, *Reminiscences,* 38.

24. *Ibid.,* 97-98; Cotterill, *Southern Indians,* 180; *American State Papers, Indian Affairs,* I, 851.

25. Pound, *Benjamin Hawkins,* 233.

26. Hall, "The Red Stick War . . .," *loc. cit.,* 283.

27. Cotterill, *Southern Indians,* 185; Woodward, *Reminiscences,* 101.

28. James Parton, *Life of Andrew Jackson* (New York: Mason Brothers, 1860. 3 vols.), II, 446.

29. Ulrich B. Phillips, *Georgia and State Rights* (Washington: Government Printing Office, 1902), 52.

30. [United States] Commissioner of Indian Affairs, *Treaties Between the United States of America and the General Indian Tribes from 1778 to 1837* (Washington: Langtree and O'Sullivan, 1837), 162. Hereinafter cited as *Indian Treaties.*

31. Cotterill, *Southern Indians,* 188; Parton, *Life of Andrew Jackson,* II, 552.

32. Bassett, ed., *Correspondence of Andrew Jackson,* II, 36, 73, 83; Cotterill, *Southern Indians,* 188.

33. Sydney Walter Martin, *Florida During the Territorial Days* (Athens: The University of Georgia Press, 1944), 42.

34. Grant Foreman, *Indian Removal* (Norman: University of Oklahoma Press, 1932), 316.
35. Parton, *Life of Andrew Jackson*, III, 342.
36. Benjamin Hawkins, *A Sketch of the Creek Country* (Americus: Americus Book Company, 1938), Appendix, iv.
37. *House Reports, No. 98*, 449; Parton, *Life of Andrew Jackson*, II, 442, 445, 446; Woodward, *Reminiscences*, 53.
38. Bassett, *Correspondence of Andrew Jackson*, II, 358.
39. Parton, *Life of Andrew Jackson*, II, 459.
40. Bassett, *Correspondence of Andrew Jackson*, II, 361.
41. Parton, *Life of Andrew Jackson*, II, 459; Woodward, *Reminiscences*, 45, 55.
42. Parton, *Life of Andrew Jackson*, II, 457.
43. *American State Papers, Indian Affairs*, I, 860; Woodward, *Reminiscences*, 44.
44. *House Reports, No. 98*, 337.
45. Parton, *Life of Andrew Jackson*, II, 463; J. E. D. Shipp, *The Last Night of a Nation* (Americus: Americus Book Company, 1938), Appendix, vii-xi; *American State Papers, Military Affairs*, I, 774-78; Richard Peters, *The Private Statutes . . . of the United States of America* (Boston: Charles C. Little and James Brown, 1846), 191.
46. Woodward, *Reminiscences*, 43, 117.
47. Absolom H. Chappell, *Miscellanies of Georgia, Historical, Biographical, Descriptive, Etc.* (Atlanta: James F. Meegan, 1874), 72; Woodward, *Reminiscences*, 116.
48. *House Reports, No. 98*, 47; Cotterill, *Southern Indians*, 220.
49. Bassett, *Correspondence of Andrew Jackson*, II, 214.
50. *Ibid.;* Cotterill, *Southern Indians*, 193.
51. *Ibid.,* 213; *House Reports, No. 98*, 835.
52. *Indian Treaties*, 160.
53. Cotterill, *Southern Indians*, 193.

54. *American State Papers, Indian Affairs*, II, 153.
55. Augustin S. Clayton, *A Compilation of the Laws of the State of Georgia . . .* (Augusta: Adams and Duyckinck, 1813), 48.
56. *House Reports, No. 98*, 415; Cotterill, *Southern Indians*, 213.
57. *American State Papers, Indian Affairs*, II, 294-255; Kappler, *Indian Affairs*, II, 195-196; *Indian Treaties*, 293.
58. *House Reports, No. 98*, 90, 275-278; Swanton, *Indians of Southeastern United States*, 127.
59. *House Reports, No. 98*, 258; Thomas L. McKenney and James Hall, *The Indian Tribes of North America* (Edinburgh: J. Grant, 1933. 3 vols.), II, 18.
60. *American State Papers, Indian Affairs*, II, 784-787.
61. Swanton, *Indians of Southeastern United States*, 652.
62. Annie Heloise Abel, *The History of Events Resulting in Indian Consolidation West of the Mississippi* (Washington: Government Printing Office, 1906), 335; Cotterill, *Southern Indians*, 209.
63. *House Reports, No. 98*, 813.
64. *Ibid.,* 397, 490.
65. Abel, *Indian Consolidation*, 335.
66. Harden, *Life of George M. Troup*, 249; *House Reports, No. 98*, 123.
67. Abel, *Indian Consolidation*, 335; *House Reports, No. 98*, 124, 415.
68. *Ibid.,* 373, 420.
69. *Ibid.,* 290, 334, 388, 420, 813; Milledgeville *Georgia Journal*, May 17, 1825.
70. Mount Zion *Missionary*, February 14, 1825; *House Reports, No. 98*, 72.
71. *Ibid.,* 24-25, 43, 48.
72. *Ibid.,* 24, 35, 47, 50.
73. *Ibid.,* 117; Harden, *Life of George M. Troup*, 250.
74. *House Reports, No. 98*, 638-639.
75. *Ibid.,* 451.
76. *American State Papers, Indian Affairs*, II, 547; Cotterill, *Southern Indians*, 220.
77. *House Reports, No. 98*, 412, 470.

78. *Ibid.*, 546, 815, 819; Foreman, *Indian Removal*, 325.
79. *House Reports, No. 98*, 117.
80. *Ibid.*, 428, 432, 546.
81. *American State Papers, Indian Affairs*, II, 508, 568-584.
82. Abel, *Indian Consolidation*, 336.
83. *American State Papers, Indian Affairs*, II, 567, 573.
84. *House Reports, No. 98*, 408, 447.
85. *Ibid.*, 261, 305, 418, 447.
86. *Ibid.*, 332, 394-395; Abel, *Indian Consolidation*, 338; *Journal of the House of Representatives of the State of Georgia, 1825* (Milledgeville, 1825), 102. Hereinafter cited as *Georgia House Journal*, with appropriate year, etc.
87. *House Reports, No. 98*, 332.
88. *Ibid.*, 261, 408, 415, 418, 447, 632.
89. *American State Papers, Indian Affairs*, II, 579-580.
90. *House Reports, No. 98*, 440, 632.
91. *American State Papers, Indian Affairs*, II, 579.
92. *House Reports, No. 98*, 440, 632.
93. *American State Papers, Indian Affairs*, II, 579.
94. *House Reports, No. 98*, 405, 440, 775.
95. Abel, *Indian Consolidation*, 339; *American State Papers, Indian Affairs*, II, 578.
96. *House Reports, No. 98*, 817.
97. *Ibid.*, 802-826.
98. *Ibid.*, 439, 707-826; Abel, *Indian Consolidation*, 340.
99. *House Reports, No. 98*, 442.
100. *Ibid.*, 751.
101. *Ibid.*, 261, 534-535; Abel, *Indian Consolidation*, 340.
102. *Indian Treaties*, 323-325.
103. *American State Papers, Indian Affairs*, II, 582.

104. *House Reports, No. 98*, 534-536.
105. *Ibid.*, 543-45; Abel, *Indian Consolidation*, 340; *Indian Treaties*, 323-325.
106. *House Reports, No. 98*, 277.
107. *Indian Treaties*, 323-325.
108. *Ibid.*, 233; *House Reports, No. 98*, 75, 305, 828.
109. *Indian Treaties*, 32-25; Abel, *Indian Consolidation*, 340.
110. *House Reports, No. 98*, 254-255, 534-535, 825.
111. *Ibid.*, 7; Harden, *Life of George M. Troup*, 265, 266.
112. *Ibid.*, 263-268.
113. *Ibid.*, 269; *House Reports, No. 98*, 327. Chilly McIntosh later returned to the Nation after the promise of immunity by Little Prince. *Ibid.*, 484.
114. *Ibid.*, 142, 540, 527; Harden, *Life of George M. Troup*, 276.
115. *House Reports, No. 98*, 404, 561, 563, 595.
116. *Ibid.*, 143.
117. *Ibid.*, 140-141.
118. The 1825 election of a governor was the first in Georgia to be determined by popular vote. The acreage involved in the forthcoming land lottery was almost 5,000,000. *Ibid.*, 214, *et passim*; Harden, *Life of George M. Troup*, 399.
119. Cotterill, *Southern Indians*, 222; *House Reports, No. 98*, 414, 472.
120. *Ibid.*, 352.
121. *House Reports, No. 98*, 572, 705, 717; Milledgeville *Georgia Journal*, May 17, 1825; Albert James Picket, "General William McIntosh" in White, *Historical Collections of Georgia*, 170-173; *American State Papers, Indian Affairs*, II, 869.

CHAPTER SEVEN

1. MS "phrenological analysis" of Lumpkin by O. S. Fowler, Washington, May 30, 1830. All sources are located in the University of Georgia library unless otherwise noted.
2. *Ibid.*

3. Wilson Lumpkin, *The Removal of the Cherokee Indians from Georgia* (New York: Dodd, Mead and Company, 1907. 2 vols.), I, 9-11. Privately printed by Wymberley Jones DeRenne from two MS volumes written by Lumpkin, entitled "Inci-

dents Connected with the Life of Wilson Lumpkin, Illustrated by Selections from his Speeches and Official Writings. Written and Compiled by Himself in the Seventieth Year of his Age, 1852." The MS volumes contain some materials omitted from the printed version, and hereinafter are cited as Lumpkin, "Incidents."

4. Miscellaneous letters from Lumpkin to his children, in Lumpkin, "Incidents," II, _passim._

5. The son adopted the more plebeian spelling of his last name in the democratic political interest.

6. Lumpkin, _Removal of the Cherokees,_ I, 13, 15-17.

7. _Ibid.,_ 15.

8. _Ibid.,_ 20-22, 30.

9. _Ibid.,_ 24-25.

10. _Ibid.,_ 27-29.

11. _Ibid.,_ 31.

12. Lumpkin to Governor William Rabun, February 11, April 2, 1819, in Georgia Department of Archives and History, Atlanta. This collection of MS letters of Lumpkin hereinafter cited as Wilson Lumpkin Papers.

13. Lumpkin, _Removal of the Cherokees,_ I, 34; MS "phrenological analysis" by O. S. Fowler.

14. Lumpkin, _Removal of the Cherokees,_ I, 32-33.

15. _Ibid.,_ 33.

16. _Ibid.,_ 36-37.

17. _Ibid.,_ 37-38.

18. _Ibid.,_ 38; Lumpkin to Troup, June 20, 1826, in Wilson Lumpkin Papers.

19. Lumpkin, _Removal of the Cherokees,_ I, 40; Lumpkin to Troup, June 6, 1826, in Wilson Lumpkin Papers.

20. Ulrich Bonnell Phillips, _A History of Transportation in the Eastern Cotton Belt to 1860_ (New York: Columbia University Press, 1908), 113, 304.

21. Lumpkin, _Removal of the Cherokees,_ I, 40.

22. _Ibid.,_ 54; also _Register of Debates in Congress,_ 20 Cong., 1 Sess., 926.

23. Samuel G. Drake, _The Aboriginal Races of North America_ . . . (New York: Hurst and Company, 1880), 437; Lumpkin, _Removal of the Cherokees,_ I, 61, 70.

24. Edwin Williams, ed., _Statesman's Manual. The Addresses and Messages of the Presidents of the United States_ . . . _from 1789 to 1849_ . . . (New York: Edward Walker, 1849. 3 vols.), II, 709.

25. Coulter, _Georgia, a Short History,_ 230; Edward Everett Dale and Gaston Litton, _Cherokee Cavaliers, Forty Years of Cherokee History as Told in the Correspondence of the Ridge-Watie-Boudinot Family_ (Norman: University of Oklahoma Press, 1940), xv.

26. _Acts of the General Assembly of the State of Georgia, 1827_ (Milledgeville: Prince and Ragland, 1828), 236-350.

27. Lumpkin, _Removal of the Cherokees,_ I, 44-45.

28. _Ibid.,_ 46-48.

29. _Acts of the General Assembly, 1828,_ 88-89.

30. John Spencer Bassett, _The Life of Andrew Jackson_ (New York: Macmillan Company, 1931), 686.

31. Williams, ed., _Statesman's Manual,_ II, 709-711.

32. Lumpkin, _Removal of the Cherokees,_ I, 49; Lumpkin to Annis Lumpkin, January 27, 1830.

33. Lumpkin, _Removal of the Cherokees,_ I, 64.

34. _Register of Debates in Congress,_ 21 Cong., 1 Sess., 456, 1133.

35. Lumpkin, _Removal of the Cherokees,_ I, 90.

36. Milledgeville _Federal Union,_ February 22, April 28, June 2, 16, 1831.

37. See Lumpkin's defense in Milledgeville _Federal Union,_ June 23, 1831.

38. Phillips, _Georgia and State Rights,_ 126-127.

39. Milledgeville _Federal Union,_ June 16, 23, 1831.

40. _Ibid.,_ November 10, 1831.

41. Phillips, _Georgia and State Rights,_ 72.

42. _Niles' Weekly Register,_ XXXXI,

227; Coulter, *Georgia, a Short History*, 234; Milledgeville *Federal Union*, September 15, 20, 1831.

43. Phillips, *Georgia and State Rights*, 75-78, 83-84.

44. Quoted in Lumpkin, *Removal of the Cherokees*, I, 93-94; Milledgeville *Federal Union*, December 15, 1831.

45. *Ibid.*, January 10, 1833.

46. Lumpkin, *Removal of the Cherokees*, I, 202.

47. Milledgeville *Federal Union*, September 15, October 27, 1831.

48. *Acts of the General Assembly*, 1831, 126-143.

49. Lumpkin to Jackson, November 1, 1831, in Lumpkin, *Removal of the Cherokees*, I, 193-194; 194-195.

50. *Acts of the General Assembly*, 1831, 141-142; Lumpkin to Daniel Newnan, May 12, 1832, in "Letter Books of the Governors, 1832," 207-209, in Georgia Department of Archives and History.

51. Lumpkin to Coffee, April 5, 1832, in Lumpkin, "Incidents," I, 325-327.

52. Brown to Lumpkin, September 15, 1832, in "Georgia Military Affairs," VI (1830-35), 163-172. Typescript copies of letters to the governors on military and Indian matters. Originals in Georgia Department of Archives and History.

53. Coffee to Lumpkin, June 30, 1832, in Wilson Lumpkin Papers; Lumpkin to Coffee, July 10, 1832, *ibid.*

54. Lumpkin, *Removal of the Cherokees*, I, 119.

55. *Acts of the General Assembly, 1830*, 128; *ibid., 1831*, 316.

56. Lumpkin, *Removal of the Cherokees*, I, 128.

57. Lumpkin, "Incidents," I, 294-295; *Acts of the General Assembly, 1830*, 145-146; *ibid., 1831*, 144-145.

58. Dale and Litton, *Cherokee Cavaliers*, xvi-xvii.

59. Thomas Valentine Parker, *The Cherokee Indians, with Special Reference to their Relations with the United States Government* (New York: Grafton Press, 1907),

30-31; Milledgeville *Federal Union*, October 31, 1835.

60. Journal of the proceedings at New Echota in *Senate Document No. 120*, 25 Cong., 2 Sess., 513 *et seq.*

61. *Ibid.*, 526; full reproduction of the treaty in Lumpkin, *Removal of the Cherokees*, II, 15-31; Milledgeville *Federal Union*, January 15, 1836.

62. Schermerhorn to Secretary of War Lewis Cass, March 3, 1836, in *Senate Document No. 120*, 25 Cong., 2 Sess., 532-539.

63. Lumpkin, *Removal of the Cherokees*, II, 8-10.

64. *Senate Document No. 120*, 25 Cong., 2 Sess., 672.

65. *Ibid.*, 675-677.

66. *Executive Document No. 286*, 24 Cong., 1 Sess., 160-161.

67. Articles 9 and 10 of Treaty of 1835, in Lumpkin, *Removal of the Cherokees*, II, 21-22.

68. *Ibid.*, 8-9.

69. *Ibid.*, 10-11; Lumpkin to Annis Lumpkin, February 13, 1837.

70. Lumpkin, *Removal of the Cherokees*, II, 159.

71. *Ibid.*, 149.

72. *Ibid.*, I, 183.

73. State Executive Order, November 23, 1837, in Wilson Lumpkin Papers.

74. Lumpkin, *Removal of the Cherokees*, II, 13-14.

75. *Ibid.*, 11-12.

76. Quoted *ibid.*, 21.

77. *Ibid.*, 226.

78. *Ibid.*, 231.

79. *Ibid.*, 193.

80. *Ibid.*, 32-33.

81. Lumpkin to Annis Lumpkin, May 2, 1838.

82. Lumpkin, *Removal of the Cherokees*, II, 226-230.

83. *Ibid.*, 224.

84. *Ibid.*, 224-225.

85. *Ibid.*, I, 89.

86. E. Merton Coulter, "The Nullification Movement in Georgia," *Georgia Historical Quarterly*, V (1921), 3-39.

87. Annual Message to the Legislature, November 6, 1832, in Lumpkin

Removal of the Cherokees, I, 120-125.

88. Annual Message to the Legislature, November 5, 1833, *ibid.,* 127.

89. Second Inaugural Address, November 6, 1833, *ibid.,* 142.

90. Annual Message to the Legislature, November 5, 1833, *ibid.,* 133.

91. George H. Slappey, "Early Foundations of Georgia's System of Common School Education," *Georgia Historical Quarterly,* XIV (1930), 139-140.

92. Lumpkin, *Removal of the Cherokees,* I, 112-113, 133.

93. *Ibid.,* 114-115.

94. *Ibid.,* 133-134, 154.

95. *Ibid.,* 155.

96. *Ibid.,* 153.

97. *Ibid.,* 110-111, 172.

98. Milledgeville *Federal Union,* December 15, 1831; *Acts of the General Assembly, 1831,* 169-170.

99. Lumpkin, *Removal of the Cherokees,* I, 109.

100. Milledgeville *Federal Union,* January 10, 1832.

101. Lumpkin, *Removal of the Cherokees,* I, 135-136.

102. *Ibid.,* 158-159.

103. *Ibid.,* 130; Coulter, *Georgia, a Short History,* 279.

104. Lumpkin, *Removal of the Cherokees,* I, 117-119; *Acts of the General Assembly, 1832,* 20-31; Lumpkin to Editor of the Milledgeville *Georgia Courier,* April 18, 1833, in Lumpkin, *Removal of the Cherokees,* I, 214-216.

105. *Ibid.,* 132, 155-156; *Journal of the Senate of the State of Georgia, 1834* (Milledgeville: John A. Cuthbert, 1835), 76-77.

106. Lumpkin, *Removal of the Cherokees,* I, 137-139.

107. Lumpkin to General E. P. Gaines, March 3, 1834, *ibid.,* 245-247; *cf.* also *ibid.,* 152-153.

108. *Ibid.,* 176-177.

109. Coulter, *Georgia, a Short History,* 257-258; Phillips, *History of Transportation,* 226-227, 252; Lumpkin, *Removal of the Cherokees,* I, 137.

110. James Houstoun Johnston, *Western and Atlantic Railroad of the State of Georgia* (Atlanta: Stein Printing Company, 1931), 19-20, 24-25.

111. William S. Irvine, "Ex-governor Wilson Lumpkin, and the Naming of Marthasville," *Atlanta Historical Bulletin,* II (1937), 2.

112. Phillips, *History of Transportation,* 312-316.

113. *Ibid.,* 318; Lumpkin, *Removal of the Cherokees,* II, 268-269, 273-274; Lumpkin to Colonel Jesse C. Farrar, May 28, 1842, in Georgia Department of Archives and History.

114. Lumpkin, *Removal of the Cherokees,* II, 274-280; Phillips, *History of Transportation,* 318.

115. Lumpkin, *Removal of the Cherokees,* I, 40.

116. *Ibid.,* 163.

117. *Ibid.*

118. *Ibid.,* 164.

119. Lumpkin to Annis Lumpkin and children, February 1, 1840; Milledgeville *Federal Union,* April 29, 1856, December 14, 1860.

CHAPTER EIGHT

1. For example, see C. G. Sellers, Jr., "Who Were the Southern Whigs?" *American Historical Review,* LIX (1954), 335-346; Thomas P. Govan, "Was the Old South Different?" *Journal of Southern History,* XXI (1955), 447-455. On the other hand, there is the view of the late Professor Charles S. Sydnor, who evidently thought that both the Southern Democrats and the Southern Whigs of the antebellum period were primarily planter parties, interested only in advancing state rights. Sydnor claimed that the Southern political battle of 1833-53 "had the hollow sound of a stage duel with tin swords." See Charles S. Sydnor, *The Development of Southern Sec-*

tionalism, 1819-1848 (Baton Rouge: Louisiana State University Press, 1948) , 316.

2. Sellers, "Who Were the Southern Whigs?" *loc. cit.;* Govan, "Was the Old South Different?" *loc. cit.*

3. The background of Berrien's political career can be traced in Paul Murray, *The Whig Party in Georgia, 1825-1853* (Chapel Hill: University of North Carolina Press, 1948) . See also Ulrich B. Phillips, *Georgia and States Rights.*

4. Stephen F. Miller, *Bench and Bar of Georgia: Memoirs and Sketches* (Philadelphia: J. B. Lippincott and Company, 1858. 2 vols.) , I, 44-45; Charles C. Jones, Jr., *John McPherson Berrien, Address Delivered Before the Georgia Bar Association at its Eighth Annual Meeting Held at Columbus, Georgia, May 20 and 21, 1891* (Atlanta: James P. Harrison and Company, Printers, 1891) . Hereinafter cited as Jones, *Berrien Address.*

5. Miller, *Bench and Bar,* I, 44-45; Major John Berrien to General Anthony Wayne, May 31, 1792, in *American Historical Record* (Philadelphia: Chase and Town, 1872-74. 5 vols.) , III.

6. Savannah *Republican,* August 6, 1831.

7. Miller, *Bench and Bar,* I, 45-46; Jones, *Berrien Address;* E. Merton Coulter, *Georgia, A Short History* (Chapel Hill: University of North Carolina Press, 1947) , 295.

8. Coulter, *Georgia, A Short History,* 238-244; Miller, *Bench and Bar,* I, 46; Milledgeville *Georgia Journal,* May 11, November 9, 1824, October 4, 1825; Savannah *Republican,* July 7, 1825; Harden, *Life of George M. Troup,* 159-193.

9. Savannah *Republican,* October 22, 1831; Marquis James, *The Life of Andrew Jackson* (New York: Garden City Publishing Company, 1940) , 491, 492, 511, 574; Arthur M. Schlesinger, Jr., *The Age of Jackson* (Boston: Little, Brown & Company, 1945) , 54; Claude G.

Bowers, *The Party Battles of the Jackson Period* (Cambridge: Houghton, Mifflin Company, 1922) , 44.

10. Coulter, *Georgia, A Short History,* 204-215; Harden, *Life of Troup,* 194-493.

11. William Harden, *A History of Savannah and South Georgia* (Chicago and New York: Lewis Publishing Company, 1913. 2 vols.) , I, 306.

12. Charles Francis Adams ed., *Memoirs of John Quincy Adams* (Philadelphia: J. B. Lippincott and Company, 1876. 12 vols.) , VIII, 128-129.

13. Milledgeville *Georgia Journal,* October 4, 5, 1825; Joseph Henry Lumpkin to Berrien, May 27, 1825, in Telamon Cuyler Collection, University of Georgia Library, Athens, Georgia.

14. James Barbour to the Georgia Delegation in Congress, Washington, December 24, 1825, in Telamon Cuyler Collection; Berrien to Troup, April 22, 1826, *ibid.;* Savannah *Republican,* March 11, 1826; Milledgeville *Georgia Journal,* June 13, 1826; *Journal of the Senate of the United States of America,* 19 Cong., 1 Sess., 134.

15. Berrien to Troup, April 22, May 7, May 18, 1826, in Telamon Cuyler Collection; Milledgeville *Georgia Journal,* June 13, 1826; Savannah *Republican,* March 22, April 19, 20, 21, 1826; *Register of Debates in Congress, Comprising the Leading Debates and Incidents,* 19 Cong., 1 Sess., 620-623, 775-780; *Senate Journal,* 19 Cong., 1 Sess., 287, 319, 358, 372.

16. *Register of Debates in Congress,* 19 Cong. 1 Sess., 527.

17. *Ibid.,* 672-682.

18. *Ibid.,* 19 Cong., 2 Sess., 270, 498; *Senate Journal,* 19 Cong., 2 Sess., 150.

19. *Register of Debates in Congress,* 19 Cong., 2 Sess., 83-88, 153, 194, 289, 462-468.

20. Adams, ed., *Memoirs of John Quincy Adams,* VII, 247, 259, 260, 264, 265.

21. *Register of Debates in Congress,* 20 Cong., 1 Sess., 19, 20, 33, 34, 48, 49, 76-80, 205-214, 399-400; *ibid.,* 2 Sess., 22, 23, 40, 41; Miller, *Bench and Bar,* I, 49. During the summer of 1828, Berrien had taken part in anti-tariff demonstrations in Georgia. See Murray, *Whig Party in Georgia,* 10-11.

22. James, *Life of Jackson,* 491-492, 511, 574; Schlesinger, *Age of Jackson,* 54; Bowers, *Party Battles,* 44.

23. Milledgeville *Georgia Journal,* August 18, 1831.

24. New York *Morning Courier* quoted in the Milledgeville *Georgia Journal,* January 4, 1829; Bowers, *Party Battles,* 44.

25. Miller, *Bench and Bar,* I, 47; Washington *Chronicle,* April 4, 1829, quoted in the Milledgeville *Georgia Journal,* April 20, 1829; *Niles Weekly Register,* XXXVII, 121; Bowers, *Party Battles,* 60-61.

26. Milledgeville *Georgia Journal,* August 18, 1831.

27. *Ibid.*

28. Littleton W. Tazewell to Jackson, Washington, March 30, 1829, in Bassett, ed., *Correspondence of Andrew Jackson,* IV, 16-17; Berrien to Jackson, April 9, 1829, *ibid.,* 22.

29. *Id.* to *Id.,* November 27, 1829, *ibid.,* IV, 76.

30. James, *Life of Jackson,* 533, 535, 563, 574, 576; Schlesinger, *Age of Jackson,* 54, 54n Bowers, *Party Battles,* 121-130.

31. Milledgeville *Georgia Journal,* August 18, 1831; Bassett, ed., *Correspondence of Jackson,* IV, 123-124, 183; Adams, ed., *Memoirs of John Quincy Adams,* VIII, 203.

32. Milledgeville *Georgia Journal,* August 18, 1831; Bassett, ed., *Correspondence of Jackson,* VIII, 235, 236; Thomas Hart Benton, *Thirty Years View, or, A History of the Working of the American Government for Thirty Years, from 1820 to 1850* (New York: Appleton and Company, 1857. 2 vols.), I, 181.

33. *Niles Weekly Register,* L, 260-261; Miller, *Bench and Bar,* I, 48-49.

34. Miller, *Bench and Bar,* I, 48-49; Bassett, ed., *Correspondence of Jackson,* IV, 303, 313; Adams, ed., *Memoirs of John Quincy Adams,* VIII, 373.

35. Milledgeville *Georgia Journal,* August 14, 18, October 20, 1831; Bassett, *Correspondence of Jackson,* IV, 316, 321, 329-330; Savannah *Republican,* July 2, August 6, 11, 1831.

36. Milledgeville *Georgia Journal,* September 15, 1831.

37. *Niles Weekly Register,* L, 260.

38. *Ibid.,* XLI, 105; Murray, *Whig Party in Georgia,* 23-24; Milledgeville *Georgia Journal,* October 18, 1831; New York *Courier and Enquirer,* October 8, 1831, quoted in Milledgeville *Georgia Journal,* November 3, 1831.

39. Milledgeville *Southern Recorder,* November 18, 1831, quoted in the Savannah *Republican,* November 21, 1831; Miller, *Bench and Bar,* I, 51-52; Savannah *Republican,* November 21, 1831; Milledgeville *Georgia Journal,* January 19, 1832; Phillips, *Georgia and States Rights,* 120. Berrien had declined the nomination of the Troup Party for a seat in Congress in 1831, because the pro-Jackson atmosphere in Georgia caused him to fear defeat. See Murray, *Whig Party in Georgia,* 25.

40. Macon *Advertiser* and Augusta *Constitutionalist,* quoted in Milledgeville *Georgia Journal,* August 23, October 18, 1832; Coulter, "The Nullification Movement in Georgia", *loc. cit.,* 3-39; Phillips, *Georgia and States Rights,* 129, 143-147; Murray, *Whig Party in Georgia,* 30-32, 42, 44-48.

41. Miller, *Bench and Bar,* I, 59-63; Milledgeville *Georgia Journal,* November 15, 19, December 17, 1832; Phillips, *Georgia and States Rights,* 130, 133-134.

42. Miller, *Bench and Bar,* I, 50-59, 99; Murray, *Whig Party in Georgia,* 52-53, 58, 70, 74, 84.

43. Phillips, *Georgia and States Rights,* 143-147; Murray, *Whig Party in Georgia,* 30-32, 42, 44-48.

44. Adams, ed., *Memoirs of John Quincy Adams,* IX, 308.

45. Berrien to Dr. Ambrose Baber, November 24, 1836, in the Baber-Blackshear Collection, University of Georgia Library, Athens, Georgia.

46. Miller, *Bench and Bar,* I, 54-57. In 1837 Berrien unsuccessfully sought to obtain from the legislature election to his old seat in the United States Senate. See Murray, *Whig Party in Georgia,* 74.

47. Richard H. Shryock, *Georgia and the Union in 1850* (Durham: Duke University Press, 1926), 102; Berrien to Baber, April 20, May 26, 1840 in Baber-Blackshear Collection; Milledgeville *Weekly Georgian,* June 6, 1840; Murray, *Whig Party in Georgia,* 92.

48. Milledgeville *Weekly Georgian,* February 27, 1841.

49. Berrien to Baber, October 30, November 25, 1840, in Baber-Blackshear Collection; Milledgeville *Weekly Georgian,* December 12, 1840; Murray, *Whig Party in Georgia,* 95.

50. *The Congressional Globe: Containing the Debates and Proceedings of . . . Congress,* 26 Cong., 2 Sess., IX, 255. Hereinafter cited *Cong. Globe with appropriate Congress, Session, etc.*

51. *Ibid.,* 27 Cong., 1 Sess., X.

52. *Ibid.,* X, 30, 152, 240.

53. Berrien to Baber, August 15, 1841, in Baber-Blackshear Collection.

54. *Cong. Globe,* 27 Cong., 1 Sess., X, 337-338, 346, 347-350; Benton, *Thirty Years View,* II, 347, 357; George R. Poage, *Henry Clay and the Whig Party* (Chapel Hill: University of North Carolina Press, 1936), 79-91.

55. Milledgeville *Weekly Georgian,* September 13, 27, October 1, 1841.

56. Chauncey S. Boucher and R. P. Brooks, eds., *Correspondence Addressed to John C. Calhoun, 1837-1849,* in the *Annual Report of the American Historical Association for 1929: Sixteenth Report of the Historical Manuscripts Commission* (Washington: Government Printing Office, 1931), 167.

57. Harrisburg *Telegraph* quoted in Milledgeville *Southern Recorder,* January 4, 1842; Murray, *Whig Party in Georgia,* 100-101.

58. *Cong. Globe,* 27 Cong., 2 Sess., XI, 101, 105, 120, 173.

59. *Ibid.,* XI, 415, 417.

60. Fletcher Webster, ed., *The Private Correspondence of Daniel Webster* (Boston: Little, Brown and Company, 1857. 2 vols.), II, 112-113; *Cong. Globe,* 27 Cong., 2 Sess., XI, 443, 444, 729, 730; XII, 556-558.

61. Arthur C. Cole, *The Whig Party in the South* (Washington: American Historical Association, 1913), 101.

62. Berrien to Baber, June 11, 1842, in Baber-Blackshear Collection.

63. *Id.* to *id.,* July 2, 1842, *ibid.*

64. Milledgeville *Southern Recorder,* September 27, October 18, 1842; Murray, *Whig Party in Georgia,* 103-104.

65. Milledgeville *Southern Recorder,* November 8, December 6, 13, 20, 1842, January 3, 10, 1843; Murray, *Whig Party in Georgia,* 113-114.

66. *Cong. Globe,* 27 Cong., 3 Sess., XII, 51, 84, 341, 342, 349.

67. *Ibid.,* 212.

68. Berrien to Baber, May 1, 1843, in Baber-Blackshear Collection.

69. *Ibid.*

70. *Id.* to *id.,* October 17, 1843, *ibid.*

71. *Cong. Globe,* 28 Cong., 1 Sess., XIII, 215, 492-494; Phillips, *Georgia and States Rights,* 149-150; Murray, *Whig Party in Georgia,* 104-107.

72. Miller, *Bench and Bar,* I, 67-68; Poage, *Henry Clay and the Whig Party,* 121; Murray, *Whig Party in Georgia,* 104-107. The Georgia delegation to the convention intended at first to nominate Berrien for Vice President, but later changed its mind.

73. *Cong. Globe,* 28 Cong., 1 Sess., XIII, 492-494, 701, 702, 704; Myrta L. Avary, ed., *Recollections of Alexander H. Stephens* (New York: Doubleday and Company, 1910), 17.

74. Avary, *Recollections of Alexander H. Stephens,* 17.

75. Cole, *Whig Party in the South,* 101n.; Miller, *Bench and Bar,* I, 68-72; Murray, *Whig Party in Georgia,* 109.

76. Richard H. Shryock, ed., *Letters of Richard D. Arnold, M.D., 1808-1876* (Durham: Duke University Press, 1929), 24.

77. *Cong. Globe,* 28 Cong., 2 Sess., XIV, 378, 383, 384, 387.

78. Berrien to Baber, March 12, 1845, in Baber-Blackshear Collection.

79. J. W. Burney to Howell Cobb, January 31, 1845, in Ulrich B. Phillips, ed., *The Correspondence of Robert Toombs, Alexander H. Stephens, and Howell Cobb,* in *Annual Report of the American Historical Association for the Year 1911* (Washington, 1913, 2 vols.), II, 62; Junius Hillyer to Howell Cobb, *ibid.,* 63; Berrien to Baber, April 15, 1845, in Baber-Blackshear Collection.

80. *Id.* to *id.,* August 12, 1845, *ibid.*

81. *Ibid.*

82. *Id.* to *id.,* August 29, 1845, *ibid.;* Berrien to Governor George W. Crawford, November 8, 1845, in Telamon Cuyler Collection; Miller, *Bench and Bar,* I, 72-75; Murray, *Whig Party in Georgia,* 123-124.

83. Miller, *Bench and Bar,* I, 75-77; Murray, *Whig Party in Georgia,* 129.

84. Miller, *Bench and Bar,* I, 76; *Cong. Globe,* 29 Cong., 1 Sess., XV, 505, 506, 510.

85. *Cong. Globe,* 29 Cong., 1 Sess., XV, 801, 808.

86. *Ibid.,* 2 Sess., XVII, 309-310, 399, 400; Justin H. Smith, *The War With Mexico* (New York: The Macmillan Company, 1919), 287-288.

87. Eugene Irving McCormac, *James K. Polk, A Political Biography* (Berkeley: University of California Press, 1922), 622; Edward J. Harden to Howell Cobb, May 3, 1847, in Phillips, ed., *Correspondence of Toombs, Stephens, and Cobb,* 87; Shryock, *Georgia and the Union in 1850,* 136n.

88. Cole, *Whig Party in the South,* 122; Shryock, *Georgia and the Union in 1850,* 138; *Cong. Globe,* 30 Cong., 1 Sess., XVIII, 79.

89. *Cong. Globe,* 30 Cong., 1 Sess., XVIII, 483.

90. *Ibid.,* 879-880, 928, 1061, 1074, 1078; Shryock, *Georgia and the Union in 1850,* 155-157; Murray, *Whig Party in Georgia,* 133-134.

91. Miller, *Bench and Bar,* I, 77-78.

92. Cole, *Whig Party in the South,* 128.

93. Toombs to James Thomas, April 16, 1848, in Phillips, *Correspondence of Toombs, Stephens, and Cobb,* 103-104.

94. Shryock, *Georgia and the Union in 1850,* 162, 163; Miller, *Bench and Bar,* I, 136-137.

95. At a caucus of Southern Congressmen and Senators in December, 1848-January, 1849, Berrien led an unsuccessful Whig movement to restrain Calhoun and other uncompromising Southerners. See Murray, *Whig Party in Georgia,* 140-141 and Cole, *Whig Party in the South,* 140.

96. Shryock, *Georgia and the Union in 1850,* 184, 185, 199, 205, 208, 267, 268; Poage, *Henry Clay and the Whig Party,* 264; *Cong. Globe,* 30 Cong., 2 Sess., XX, 46, 48, 195, 196, 313, 314, 629, 632, 31 Cong., 1 Sess., XXI, 202, 203, 210, 267, 268, 502, 503, 949, 950; Horace Montgomery, *Cracker Parties* (Baton Rouge: Louisiana State University Press, 1950), 2, 6, 12-13, 18.

97. Shryock, *Georgia and the Union in 1850,* 292, 306, 315-317, 327.

98. Berrien to Howell Cobb, December 17, 1851, in Telamon Cuyler Collection; *Cong. Globe,* 32 Cong., 1 Sess., XXIV, 1493; Shryock, *Georgia and the Union in 1850,* 358, 358n.; Miller, *Bench and Bar,* I, 99; Phillips, *Georgia and State Rights,*

166-167; Murray, *Whig Party in Georgia*, 160-161.

99. Cole, *Whig Party in the South*, 269; Montgomery, *Cracker Parties*, 65-66. In 1853 there were unconfirmed newspaper reports that Berrien wanted to be elected governor or

to return to his old seat in the Senate. See Montgomery, *Cracker Parties*, 112-116.

100. Miller, *Bench and Bar*, I, 87-88, 91; Phillips, *Georgia and States Rights*, 179; Murray, *Whig Party in Georgia*, 160-161.

CHAPTER NINE

1. Athens *Southern Banner*, June 22, 1847; Mount Zion *Missionary*, May 27, 1822, March 3, October 13, 1823, December 22, 29, 1823, October 11, 1824, October 10, 1825. The newspapers quoted in this essay are on file in the University of Georgia Library.

2. Sparta *Reporter and Christian Gazette*, October 2, 1826.

3. Murray, *Whig Party in Georgia*, 4-5.

4. Milledgeville *Georgia Journal*, October 11, 1825; Augusta *Constitutionalist*, December 23, 1825; *Georgia House Journal, 1825*, 188-189.

5. January 31, 1826.

6. Sparta *Reporter and Christian Gazette*, July 3, 1826.

7. *Ibid.*, July 31, August 9, September 11, 18, October 2, 1826; Mount Zion *Hancock Advertiser*, December 15, 22, 29, 1828, October 19, 26, December 7, 14, 21, 28, 1829; *1830 Census Population: Georgia*, microfilm copy, University of Georgia Library.

8. Milledgeville *Federal Union*, July 4, 1835.

9. *Ibid.*, September 19, 1835. The essays appeared in the following issues of the Milledgeville *Federal Union:* February 28, May 9, October 3, 1833, and May 14, 1834. It will usually be clear from the text which of the four is under discussion. Where this is not the case, the essay will be cited hereinafter by reference to the appropriate issue of the *Federal Union*.

10. *Ibid.*, February 28, 1833.

11. Alfred H. Kelley and Winfred A. Harbison, *The American Constitution: Its Origin and Development*

(New York: W. W. Norton and Company, 1955), 255.

12. Milledgeville *Federal Union*, February 28, 1833.

13. Proceedings quoted *ibid.*, July 4, 1835.

14. *Ibid.*, August 29, 1835.

15. September 24, 1835.

16. Official returns quoted in Augusta *Georgia Constitutionalist*, October 24, November 3, 1835.

17. *Cong. Globe*, 24 Cong., 1 Sess., 122, 144, 391, 402, 2 Sess., Appendix, 306; Augusta *Georgia Constitutionalist*, June 7, 1836.

18. *Cong. Globe*, 24 Cong., 2 Sess., 164-165, Appendix, 162.

19. *Ibid.*; Milledgeville *Federal Union*, April 18, 1837.

20. Murray, *Whig Party in Georgia*, 65-66; Milledgeville *Southern Recorder*, September 27, 1836; Paul Murray, "Party Organization in Georgia Politics, 1825-1853," *Georgia Historical Quarterly*, XXIX (1945), 202.

21. Quoted in Milledgeville *Southern Recorder*, September 27, 1836, Milledgeville *Federal Union*, September 27, 1836, and Augusta *Georgia Constitutionalist*, September 20, 1836.

22. October 3, 1836.

23. Official returns quoted in Columbus *Enquirer*, November 24, 1836.

24. *Cong. Globe*, 25 Cong., 1 Sess., 18, 46, Appendix, 18; Milledgeville *Federal Union*, October 3, 1837.

25. Adams, ed., *Memoirs of John Quincy Adams*, IX, 548-549.

26. *Cong. Globe*, 25 Cong., 2 Sess., 68, 247.

27. Adams, ed., *Memoirs of John Quincy Adams*, IX, 548-549.

28. James D. Richardson, ed., *A Compilation of the Messages and Papers of the Presidents, 1789-1899* (Washington: Published by Authority of Congress, 1899. 10 vols.), III, 380ff.

29. *Cong. Globe,* 25 Cong., 2 Sess., Appendix, 12.

30. *Briscoe v. Bank of Kentucky,* 11 Peters 257 (1837).

31. *Cong. Globe,* 25 Cong., 2 Sess., Appendix, 12.

32. *Ibid.;* Milledgeville *Federal Union,* May 14, 1834.

33. *Cong. Globe,* 25 Cong., 2 Sess., Appendix, 12.

34. *Ibid.,* 54, 185-186, 193, 268, 302.

35. Letter of declination quoted in Milledgeville *Federal Union,* March 12, 1838; Athens *Southern Banner,* April 8, 1837, October 14, 1837; Murray, *Whig Party in Georgia,* 66-72.

36. Columbus *Sentinel and Herald,* March 22, 1838.

37. *1840 Census Population: Georgia,* microfilm copy, University of Georgia Library; Athens *Southern Banner,* June 11, December 7, 1843.

38. T. R. R. Cobb to Howell Cobb, December 14, 18, 1844, in Cobb MSS., in private possession, Athens, Georgia.

39. *Ibid.;* Athens *Southern Banner,* January 16, 1845, September 1, 8, 1846; Cobb to wife, February 4, 1847, in Cobb MSS.

40. Holsey to Cobb, September 1, 1847, *ibid.;* Mrs. Cobb to husband, December 15, 1846, *ibid.;* Cobb to wife, February 4, 1847, *ibid.;* [?] to Cobb, January 16, 1847, *ibid.;* Cobb to wife, January 25, 1847, *ibid.; id.* to *id.,* February 4, 1847, *ibid.;* Athens *Southern Banner,* January 5, April 8, 1847.

41. Holsey to Cobb, January 9, 1847, in Cobb MSS.; *id.* to *id.,* February 3, 1847, *ibid.;* Cobb to wife, February 4, 1847, *ibid.*

42. John B. Lamar to Cobb, October 28, 1847, *ibid.*

43. Athens *Southern Banner,* September 8, 1846.

44. *Ibid.,* August 5, 1847, June 21, 1849.

45. *Ibid.,* April 20, 1848.

46. Milton Sidney Heath, *Constructive Liberalism: The Role of the State in Economic Development in Georgia to 1860* (Cambridge: Harvard University Press, 1954), 208, 225-226, 326; *Georgia House Journal, 1847,* 191; *Georgia Senate Journal, 1847,* 367; Savannah *Republican* quoted in Athens *Southern Banner,* May 4, 1848.

47. *Ibid.,* November 27, 1847.

48. *Ibid.,* March 20, May 4, 1848.

49. Holsey to Cobb, December 3, 1847, in Phillips, ed., *Correspondence of Toombs, Stephens, and Cobb,* 89-91; Athens *Southern Banner,* May 4, 1848.

50. Quoted in *Southern Banner,* May 4, 1848.

51. Quoted *ibid.,* November 9, 1848.

52. *Ibid.,* April 20, 1848.

53. *Acts of the General Assembly, 1847,* 219-221; Heath, *Constructive Liberalism,* 318.

54. See Eugene H. Roseboom, "Southern Ohio and the Union in 1863," *Mississippi Valley Historical Review,* XXXIX (1952), 29-44.

55. Heath, *Constructive Liberalism,* 318; See James F. S. Russell, "The Railroads in the 'Conspiracy Theory' of the Fourteenth Amendment," *Mississippi Valley Historical Review,* XLI (1955), 601-622, for an exoneration of the railroads. Until other business interests are exonerated, as Professor Russell points out, the "conspiracy theory" cannot be dismissed.

56. Athens *Southern Banner,* September 9, 1847.

57. Holsey to Cobb, December 3, 1847, in Phillips, ed., *Correspondence of Toombs, Stephens, and Cobb,* 90.

58. Athens *Southern Banner,* April 27, December 6, 1848.

59. *Ibid.,* December 6, 1848, May 24, 1849.

60. *Ibid.,* December 6, 1849, February 7, 1850; *Acts of the State of Georgia, 1849-50,* 418; see Fletcher M. Green, *Constitutional Development in the South Atlantic States, 1776-*

1860 (Chapel Hill: University of North Carolina Press, 1930), 260-261.

61. Athens *Southern Banner,* May 24, 1849.

62. *Ibid.,* June 21, 1849. See Harvey Wish, *George Fitzhugh: Propagandist of the Old South* (Baton Rouge: Louisiana State University Press, 1943).

63. Athens *Southern Banner,* June 21, 1849.

64. *Ibid.,* March 9, 1847, May 18, 1848; Augusta *Constitutionalist,* September 1, 1849.

65. Athens *Southern Banner,* February 2, April 6, June 22, September 9, 1847.

66. *Ibid.,* July 6, 20, August 4, 1847.

67. *Ibid.,* July 6, 1847, January 13, May 25, August 17, October 19, 1848.

68. *Ibid.,* June 15, August 31, 1848.

69. Holsey to Cobb, June 29, 1848, in Cobb MSS.; official returns quoted in Athens *Southern Banner,* November 16, 1848.

70. *Ibid.,* November 16, 30, 1848; Holsey to Cobb, February 13, 24, 1849, in Phillips, ed., *Correspondence of Toombs, Stephens, and Cobb,* 148, 152.

71. *Id.* to *id.,* January 29, 1849, *ibid.,* 142.

72. *Id.* to *id.,* February 13, 1849, *ibid.,* 148; Athens *Southern Banner,* January 11, February 8, 1849.

73. Holsey to Cobb, February 24, 1849, in Phillips, ed., *Correspondence of Toombs, Stephens, and Cobb,* 152.

74. *Ibid.;* Athens *Southern Banner,* March 1, 8, 1849.

75. William Hope Hull to Cobb, January 9, 1850, in Cobb MSS.

76. Holsey to Cobb, December 29, 1849, *ibid.*

77. Montgomery, *Cracker Parties,* 27-30, 50.

78. Quoted in Shryock, *Georgia and the Union in 1850,* 318-319.

79. Augusta *Chronicle and Sentinel,* December 18, 24, 31, 1850.

80. January 16, 23, 30, 1851.

81. Cobb to Absolom Chappell and others, February 7, in Cobb MSS.

82. Athens *Southern Banner,* September 25, 1851; see Montgomery, *Cracker Parties* for a discussion of this and other campaigns of the early 1850s.

83. Athens *Southern Banner,* January 8, 1852.

84. *Ibid.,* January 8, 15, February 26, 1852.

85. *Ibid.,* April 8, 1852.

86. *Ibid.,* May 27, 1852.

87. *Ibid*

88. *Ibid.,* May 27, June 24, 1852.

89. *Ibid.,* June 17, July 1, 22, 29, August 5, 12, 19, 1852; Alex B. Morton to Cobb, July 19, 1852, in Cobb MSS.

90. William H. Hull to *id.,* August 23, 1852, *ibid.;* Cobb to John B. Lamar, September 18, 1852, in Phillips, ed., *Correspondence of Toombs, Stephens, and Cobb,* 320; Athens *Southern Banner,* September 23, 1852.

91. *Ibid.,* October 7, 1852; John Talmadge, "The Origin of the Tugalo Party's Name," *Georgia Historical Quarterly,* XXXVI (1952); Savannah *Georgian,* October 8, 1852.

92. Athens *Southern Banner,* October 7, 1852.

93. Montgomery, *Cracker Parties,* 90.

94. Athens *Southern Banner,* November 11, 18, 25, December 23, 1852, March 24, April 14, 1853; James Jackson to Cobb, February 14, 1853, in Cobb MSS.

95. Athens *Southern Banner,* December 9, 1852.

96. *Ibid.,* December 2, 1852.

97. *Ibid.,* March 31, 1853.

98. *Ibid.,* March 17, April 28, 1853; Cobb to Thomas Morris, March 21, quoted *ibid.,* April 7, 1853.

99. *Ibid.,* April 28, May 5, 1853; William H. Hull to Cobb, April 9, 1853, in Cobb MSS.; John B. Lamar to *id.,* May 7, 1853, *ibid.*

100. May 17, 1853.

101. James Sledge to Cobb, June 10, 1853, in Cobb MSS.; Athens *Southern Banner,* August 18, 1853.

102. *Ibid.,* October 13, 1853; John B. Cobb to Cobb, November 3, 1853, in Cobb MSS.; William H. Hull to *id.,* November 2, 1853, *ibid.*

103. *Biographical Dictionary of the American Congress, 1774-1949* (Washington: Government Printing Office, 1950), 1326.

104. Quoted in Athens *Southern Watch man,* August 5, 1855.

105. Griffin *Empire State,* July 9, 1855; Columbus *Daily Enquirer,* April 6, 1859.

106. Augusta *Weekly Chronicle and Sentinel,* April 13, 1859.

CHAPTER TEN

1. Facts relating to the early life of Jenkins have been taken mainly from Dumas Malone and Allan Johnson, eds., *Dictionary of American Biography* (New York: Charles Scribner's Sons, 1928-46. 22 vols.), X, 44; William J. Northen, ed., *Men of Mark in Georgia* (Atlanta: A. B. Caldwell, 1907-12. 6 vols.), III, 281-293; and Charles C. Jones, Jr., *The Life and Services of Ex-Governor Charles Jones Jenkins, A Memorial Address* (Atlanta: James P. Harrison & Company, 1884), *passim.* Jones's memorial address approaches more nearly a biography than anything else written about Jenkins, but it is highly eulogistic in tone and probably does not give an objective picture.

2. Jones, *Life and Services of Jenkins,* 8-9.

3. *Ibid.,* 9.

4. Phillips, *Georgia and State Rights.* 90-112.

5. *Georgia House Journal, 1830,* 38.

6. *Ibid.,* 46, 127, 194.

7. *Ibid.,* 300.

8. From 1836 through 1842 the General Assembly was elected annually. Beginning with 1843 the sessions were biennial.

9. *Georgia House Journal, 1839,* 277, 160-163.

10. *Ibid., 1841,* 72-73.

11. Milledgeville *Federal Union,* December 13, 1836, December 26, 1843, December 14, 1847, January 4, 1848. Probably the best contemporary source regarding the work of the General Assembly during this period was the Milledgeville *Federal Union.* While the legislature was in session the paper carried a day-by-day account of its proceedings, and, at the end of the term, published a complete list of bills passed. Many of Jenkins's speeches in the House were either quoted verbatim or summarized. Editorial matter and letters from the paper's readers furnish a commentary on public sentiment not found in the official journals.

12. Augusta *Weekly Chronicle and Sentinel,* July 13, 1853.

13. Milledgeville *Federal Union,* February 19, 1850; *Georgia House Journal, 1849-50,* 816.

14. *Ibid.,* 842-846; Milledgeville *Federal Union,* February 19, 1850. In 1856 Jenkins was elected to fill an unexpired term as state senator from Richmond County. The election, however, took place at the end of the session and Jenkins apparently (so far as can be learned from the records) never took his seat.

15. *Ibid.* Through the years the *Federal Union* consistently praised Jenkins even while attacking other Whig leaders and their policies. The only marked departure from this practice occurred during the gubernatorial campaign of 1853. Even then the paper first turned its fire on Robert Toombs and other Whigs backing Jenkins's candidacy and expressed admiration for Jenkins himself.

16. For comments from the Whig point of view see Athens *Southern Whig,* February 21, 1850. Excerpts from a number of other papers are reproduced there.

17. Augusta *Chronicle and Sentinel*

quoted in Athens *Southern Whig,*
February 21, 1850.

18. *Ibid.,* February 7, 1850.

19. Shryock, *Georgia and the Union in
    1850,* 236.

20. Milledgeville *Federal Union,* December 3, 1850.

21. *Journal of the State Convention
    Held in Milledgeville, in December,
    1850* (Milledgeville, 1850) , 6.

22. *Ibid.,* 11-19.

23. *Ibid,* 31-33.

24. Coulter, *Georgia, A Short History,*
    309; Herbert Fielder, *A Sketch of
    the Life and Times and Speeches
    of Joseph E. Brown* (Springfield,
    Mass.: Press of Springfield Printing
    Company, 1883) , 75; Amanda Johnson, *Georgia as Colony and State*
    Atlanta: Walter W. Brown Publishing Company, 1938) , 331; Jones,
    Life and Services of Jenkins, 13;
    Phillips, ed., *Correspondence of
    Toombs, Stephens, and Cobb,*
    212, 2n.

25. Milledgeville *Federal Union,* August 16, September 13, 1953; Shryock, *Georgia and the Union in
    1850,* 329.

26. Fielder, *Life and Times of Joseph
    E. Brown,* 72.

27. Edward Stanwood, *A History of the
    Presidency from 1788 to 1897* (Boston: Houghton Mifflin Company,
    1898) , 257.

28. Phillips, *Georgia and State Rights,*
    169.

29. Helen Ione Greene, "Politics in
    Georgia, 1853-54: The Ordeal of
    Howell Cobb," *Georgia Historical
    Quarterly,* XXX (1946) , 195.

30. June 21, 1853.

31. Ulrich Bonnell Phillips, *The Life
    of Robert Toombs* (New York: The
    Macmillan Company, 1913) , 167.

32. The Milledgeville *Federal Union,*
    June 28, 1853, reported that at the
    nominating convention "they all
    avoided their old name of *Whig,*
    as a murderer would shun the
    ghastly corpse of his victim." William Hope Hull, after hearing
    Jenkins speak, wrote to Howell
    Cobb: "He took the Union line

very distinctly repudiating for himself and party all alliances with
national parties as at present organized, but striking out for a
national Union organization — a
false move in my humble judgment.
He would have run better under
the name of Whig." See Phillips,
ed., *Correspondence of Toombs,
Stephens, and Cobb,* 334.

33. Milledgeville *Federal Union,* September 13, 1853.

34. Milledgeville *Federal Union,* July
    19, 26, 1853.

35. Quoted in Augusta *Weekly Chronicle and Sentinel,* September 21,
    1853.

36. Quoted *Ibid.*

37. Nevertheless, almost as many votes
    were cast as in the turbulent election of 1851. Judging from this
    widespread participation and the
    extremely small margin between
    the two candidates, the election
    could not have been wholly lacking
    in interest. An account of the campaign and of the Georgia political
    scene is found in Montgomery,
    Cracker Parties, 92-122.

38. Rome *Southerner* quoted in Augusta *Weekly Chronicle and Sentinel,*
    August 24, 1853.

39. *Georgia House Journal, 1853-54,* 34.
    Some other sources give slightly
    different totals, with a margin of
    540 votes in favor of Johnson.

40. Letter to a friend, June 15, 1855,
    quoted in Augusta *Chronicle and
    Sentinel,* June 27, 1855.

41. Isaac W. Avery, *The History of
    the State of Georgia from 1850 to
    1881* (New York: Brown & Derby,
    1881) , 72.

42. *Reports of Cases in Law and
    Equity . . . Supreme Court of
    Georgia . . .* XXXI, XXXII,
    XXXIII, *Supplement* to XXXIII
    (Macon: J. W. Burke & Company,
    1871, 1869, 1870, 1876) ; *Reports of
    Cases in Law and Equity . . . Supreme court of Georgia . . .* XXXIV
    (Atlanta: Intelligencer Book and
    Job Office, 1866) . The cases omitted were mainly cases tried in 1863

and 1864, according to notes by the court reporter. Several hundred pages of Volume XXXII, already in print, were destroyed while the reporter was absent in military service. The original manuscripts of scores of cases were scattered or destroyed, but most of these could be reconstructed. Painstaking work on the part of George N. Lester, reporter for the first four volumes, was responsible for their being as nearly complete as they are. The material in the Supplement to Volume XXXIII, prepared originally by Greenlee Butler, was completely lost, and was later reassembled and pieced together by Lester, not being published until 1876. Volume XXXIV, beginning with the last year of the war and prepared by Logan E. Bleckley, was the only volume of the period to be published at the normal time.

43. 33 *Georgia Reports* (1862), 347.
44. *The Confederate Union,* November 18, 1862. For several issues this paper (the former Milledgeville *Federal Union*) published accounts of debates in the legislature, letters from correspondents, and various messages from the governor.
45. 33 *Georgia Reports* (1862), 354.
46. *Weems v. Farrell and Williams, ibid.,* 413, 420.
47. *Daly v. Harris, Supplement to 33 Georgia Reports* (1864), 38.
48. *Barber v. Irwin,* 34 *Georgia Reports* (1864), 27.
49. *Mims and Burdett v. Wimberly,* 33 *Georgia Reports* (1863), 587.
50. *Cunningham v. Campbell et al., ibid.,* 625.
51. Avery, *History of Georgia,* 131.
52. Allen D. Candler, ed., *The Confederate Records of the State of Georgia* (Atlanta: C. P. Byrd, 1909. 6 vols.), I, 227. Volume V of this series was never published.
53. Jones, *Life and Services of Jenkins,* 19.
54. Jenkins had not received his pardon up to the time of the election, and was permitted to serve as a

delegate only by a last-minute dispensation from President Johnson. See Macon *Telegraph,* October 20, 1865.
55. Phillips, *Georgia and State Rights,* 202.
56. C. Mildred Thompson, *Reconstruction in Georgia, Economic, Social, Political, 1865-1872* (New York: The Columbia University Press, 1915), 149. There were, however, some able men in the group, including future Governor Henry McDaniel.
57. October 26, 1865.
58. *History of Georgia,* 348.
59. Candler, ed., *Confederate Records,* IV, 282-284, 304-305, 335-339.
60. *Georgia House Journal, 1865-66,* 17-18.
61. Avery, *History of Georgia,* 352-354.
62. Jenkins to George B. Carhart, March 23, 1866, in the Georgia Department of Archives and History.
63. Candler, ed., *Confederate Records,* IV, 544-548.
64. 6 *Wallace* (1867), 50.
65. *Georgia House Journal, 1872,* 413. Probably the most authentic account of Jenkins's administration is the report written by the governor himself and published in the *House Journal, 1872,* 405-419. The most complete accounts found in secondary works are in: Avery, *History of Georgia;* Jones, *Life and Services of Jenkins;* and Thompson, *Reconstruction in Georgia.* Jenkins's obituary in the Atlanta *Weekly Constitution,* June 19, 1883, gives a good over-all picture.
66. Albert B. Saye, *A Constitutional History of Georgia* (Athens: The University of Georgia Press, 1948), 263-264.
67. *Georgia House Journal, 1872,* 414.
68. For an account purporting to be in Jenkins's own words see Jones, *Life and Services of Jenkins,* 41-46. Substantially the same details are given in Jenkins's 1872 report to Governor Smith. Here he comments, "[T]he *argument* was with me; but the *power* was with the

General." See *Georgia House Journal, 1872*, 415.

69. Jones, *Life and Services of Jenkins*, 47.

70. There is considerable disagreement among historians regarding the details of this incident of Jenkins's removal of the state seal. Some say that it was the great seal of Georgia, some the executive seal, some that he carried it with him to Canada, others that he left it hidden in Georgia. Candler, ed., *Confederate Records*, VI, 15, contains an account which may explain these discrepancies. According to Candler, Jenkins carried with him the *executive* seal, while Colonel Nathan Barnett, deposed secretary of state, kept hidden the *great* seal until he was restored to office. "[T]hus neither one of these seals was ever desecrated by the hands of an enemy of Georgia." In Lucian Lamar Knight, *Reminiscences of Famous Georgians* (Atlanta: Franklin-Turner Company, 1907-08. 2 vols.), II, 291, it is recorded that Jenkins took the great seal with him to the highlands of Nova Scotia. Later Knight corrected this, stating that it was the executive seal which Jenkins carried into exile and that the great seal never left the state. Colonel Barnett, he said, removed the great seal to his home in Milledgeville, "where he buried it under the house at dead of night," sharing the secret with

no one except his wife. For the corrected version see Lucian Lamar Knight, *Georgia Landmarks, Memories and Legends* (Atlanta: Byrd Printing Company, 1913-14. 2 vols.), II, 96. In Jenkins's report transmitted to the legislature in 1872, he says specifically that when he left office he took with him "the seal of the Executive Department," a statement that would seem to settle the matter. See *Georgia House Journal, 1872*, 418.

71. *Ibid.*, 416.

72. Northern, ed., *Men of Mark*, III, 291-292.

73. A. L. Hull, *A Historical Sketch of the University of Georgia* (Athens: Foote & Davies Company, 1894), in his Catalogue of Trustees, gives the date of Jenkins's resignation as 1884, an obvious but unexplained discrepancy.

74. Minutes of the Proceedings of the Board of Trustees of the University of Georgia, 1858-77, a MS book in the Rare Book Room, University of Georgia Library, 357.

75. *Ibid.*, 397.

76. Samuel W. Small, *A Stenographic Report of the Proceedings of the Constitutional Convention Held in Atlanta, Ga., 1877* (Atlanta: Constitution Publishing Company, 1877), 2.

77. June 19, 1883.

78. *Ibid.*

79. *Ibid.*

CHAPTER ELEVEN

1. Jones had moved to New York in December, 1865. The principal events in his life are given in various biographical sketches. See, for example, the one by John D. Wade in Malone and Johnson, eds., *Dictionary of American Biography*, X, 165, and others in Northen, ed., *Men of Mark in Georgia*, III, 457-463, *Lamb's Biographical Dictionary of the United States* (Boston: H. Lamb Company, c. 1899-1903.

7 vols.), IV, 429-430, and *The American Anthropologist*, VI (1893), 457-458. For an incomplete bibliography of Jones, see Paul Leicester Ford, "Partial Bibliography of The Writings of Charles Colcock Jones," *Annual Report of The American Historical Association for the Year 1889* (Washington: Government Printing Office, 1890), 287-293.

The Manuscript Room of the Duke University Library has the largest and best collection of Jones manuscripts, letterbooks, portfolios, and other materials. The DeRenne Collection of the University of Georgia Library has a complete file of the fifteen addresses, in pamphlet form, which Jones delivered before the Confederate Survivors' Association in Augusta, Georgia, 1879-93. Forty-six letters exchanged between Jones and Paul Hamilton Hayne (thirty-six from Jones to Hayne and ten from Hayne to Jones) were found in the Jones and Hayne Collections at Duke University. The Library of Duke University has kindly granted permission to use the Jones-Hayne correspondence in this essay. For permission to use the Jones pamphlets in the DeRenne Collection the author is grateful to the University of Georgia Library.

2. For an account of the home life of the Jones family, see R. Q. Mallard, *Montevideo-Maybank: Some Memoirs of a Southern Christian Household in the Olden Time: or, The Family Life of the Rev. Charles Colcock Jones, D. D., of Library County, Ga.* (Richmond: Presbyterian Committee of Publication, 1898). Mallard married the only daughter of C. C. Jones, Sr.

3. *Ibid.,* 13.

4. (Savannah: J. M. Cooper and Company).

5. There is no full-length biography of Jones. His philosophic defense of the Old South has been discussed in John D. Wade, "Old Wine in a New Bottle," *Virginia Quarterly Review,* XI (1935), 239-252. Jones, the historian, has been treated in James Calvin Bonner, "Charles Colcock Jones: The Macaulay of the South," *Georgia Historical Quarterly,* XXII (1943), 324-338.

6. On August 10, 1872, Jones wrote General Albert Pike on stationery listing himself, John E. Ward, and Charles E. Whitehead as members of his law firm and giving its location as 61 Wall Street. This letter and all others mentioned hereafter, unless otherwise noted, are in the Jones and Hayne Collections of the Duke University Library.

7. Some, perhaps all, of the Jones portfolios containing autographs, autographed letters, and portraits illustrative of American history are now in the Duke University Library. These volumes are handsomely bound and beautifully decorated.

8. Jones to Hayne, October 18, 1878. Jones made the principal address at the unveiling and according to custom sent Hayne a reprint of it.

9. Jones to Hayne, November 8, 1879. Jones signed himself "Your Friend and Kinsman." No attempt has been made to work out the precise degree of kinship between Jones and Hayne. Northen, *Men of Mark in Georgia,* III, 457, notes that the Jones family had originally settled in South Carolina, where it had intermarried with the Pinckneys, Haynes, Swintons, and Legares.

Almost two years later, in July, 1881, Hayne was still seeking advice from Jones about the best investment for $4,000, which Mrs. Hayne had inherited from her father. Hayne, in his letter of July 8, wrote Jones that the money was currently invested in a first mortgage upon the house and lot of a Mr. Cox, but that some man for whom Cox had stood security had up to then prevented sale of the property and the payment of the note. On the following day, July 9, Hayne wrote a second letter to Jones giving additional details and making it clear that the advice he had sought from Jones in November, 1879, was how to invest most advantageously the money Mrs. Hayne had in the Cox property, if and when she was able to get it.

On July 12, 1881, Jones wrote Hayne that the whole matter of the Cox investment should be left in the hands of the trustee of the estate of Mrs. Hayne's father.

10. Jones's letter was written from New York, August 21, 1880.

11. Jones to Hayne, November 4, 1882.

12. Hayne may have been thinking of Jones's pamphlet, *The Siege of Savannah*. On January 4, 1883, Jones wrote Hayne: "I really cannot recall any tract of mine relating to the settlement of Savannah."

13. A single file of the *Weekly News* for this date is in the Duke University Library.

14. This copy is in the Rare Book Room of the Duke University Library.

15. This is the last letter from Hayne to Jones which the author has been able to locate. It may well be the final one, as Hayne died on July 6, 1886.

16. This seems to be the last Jones letter to Hayne. No other letter to Hayne appears in the Jones letter-books.

17. Jones in his first address before the Confederate Survivors' Association, April 26, 1879, gave the details of its organization in Augusta.

18. C. Vann Woodward, *Origins of the New South* (Baton Rouge: Louisiana State University Press, 1951), 173, has observed that "In the dustbins of the eighties . . . are the remains of an elaborately resoned critique of the Brave New South. The critique was identified with the Lost Cause, since the men who proclaimed it, men like Robert L. Dabney, of Virginia and Charles Colcock Jones of Georgia, wore the uniform of the Confederacy and spoke in its name and memory."

19. The addresses of both Gordon and Jones are reprinted in the same pamphlet of the Confederate Survivors' Association.

CHAPTER TWELVE

1. G. H. Smythe, *The Life of Henry Bradley Plant* (New York: G. P. Putnam's Sons, 1898), 15, 117. This is a life of Plant written by a friend at the time of the former's death. It is very biased, but many of the facts are accurate, especially those dealing with the background and early life of Plant.

2. "Henry B. Plant, The King of Florida," *Success* (November, 1898), 5-6. This article in a contemporary magazine cited hereinafter as *Success*.

3. Smythe, *Henry B. Plant*, 309.

4. *Ibid.*, 18, 40.

5. *Ibid.*, 41.

6. *Success*, 6.

7. Franklin Q. Brown to Alfred J. Hanna, January 24, 1938, in the P. K. Yonge Collection, University of Florida Library, Gainesville, Florida. Brown was a contemporary of Henry B. Plant.

8. *Ibid.*

9. Karl H. Grismer, *A History of the City of Tampa and the Tampa Bay Region of Florida* (St. Petersburg: St. Petersburg Printing Company, 1950), 337. Factual account of Tampa's history.

10. A. F. Harlow, *Old Waybills* (New York: D. Appleton-Century Company, 1937), 65. An interesting story of the romance of the early express companies.

11. Smythe, *Henry B. Plant*, 46.

12. Founded in 1565 by the Spaniard Menendez.

13. Brown to Hanna, January 24, 1938 in Yonge Collection, University of Florida Library.

14. Harlow, *Old Waybills*, 67.

15. Smythe, *Henry B. Plant*, 63.

16. A. L. Stimson, *History of the Express Business* (New York: Baker & Godwin Printers, 1881), 160. Hereinafter cited as *Express Business*. This is a good story of the express business in America, including the origin of the railway system

in America, and the relation of
both to the increase of new settlements and the prosperity of the
cities in the United States.

17. Savannah *Daily Morning News,*
    May 16, 1861; Augusta *Weekly
    Chronicle and Sentinel,* May 22,
    1861.

18. Tampa *Daily Times,* December 29,
    1897.

19. E. Menton Coulter, *The Confede-
    rate States of America, 1861-1865*
    (Baton Rouge: Louisiana State
    University Press and the Little-
    field Fund for Southern History,
    1950) , 127.

20. Augusta *Chronicle and Sentinel,*
    June 5, 1861.

21. Smythe, *Henry B. Plant,* 56.

22. Harlow, *Old Waybills,* 298.

23. Augusta *Chronicle and Sentinel,*
    September 2, 1863.

24. J. B. Jones, *A Rebel War Clerk's
    Diary* (New York: Old Hickory
    Bookshop, 1935. 2 vols.) , II, 4. An
    interesting account of happenings
    during the war years as seen by an
    official at the Confederate States
    Capital.

25. Atlanta *Appeal* quoted in ·Augusta
    Chronicle and Sentinel, January 13,
    1864.

26. Smythe, *Henry B. Plant,* 59-66.

27. Tampa *Journal,* May 30, 1889.

28. Florida *Times-Union,* November 24,
    1889. This was the leading Florida
    newspaper during the Plant era.
    The name was changed several
    times.

29. Tampa *Daily Times,* August 26,
    1898.

30. Florida *Times-Union,* June 9, 1897.

31. Francis B. Simkins, *The South, Old
    and New A History, 1820-1947*
    (New York: Alfred A. Knopf,
    1947) , 238.

32. Augusta *Chronicle and Sentinel,*
    May 3, 1870.

33. *Office Directory and Way-Billing
    Guide* (Southern Express Com-
    pany) , 1874. An annual publica-
    tion by the company for use of the
    employees.

34. Stimson, *Express Business,* 127.

35. Harlow, *Old Waybills,* 317.

36. Savannah *Morning News,* Septem-
    ber 3, 1887. This paper is especi-
    ally good on railroad development
    during the late nineteenth century.

37. Atlanta *Constitution,* November 7,
    1879.

38. Henry V. Poor, *Manual of the
    Railroads of the United States for
    1880* (New York: H. V. & H. W.
    Poor, 1880) , 532. Hereinafter cited
    as *Railroad Manual.* A summary
    of railroad history and activities.

39. *Ibid.,* 531.

40. Savannah *Morning News,* Septem-
    ber 3, 1887.

41. Florida *Times-Union,* January 11,
    1884.

42. Poor, *Railroad Manual, 1884,* 457-
    459.

43. *Ibid., 1888,* **644.**

44. Waycross got its name when the
    tracks of the two roads crossed
    there. The last syllable of railway
    (way) was added to the first sylla-
    ble of the word crossing (cross) ,
    making the word Waycross which
    was chosen as the name of the
    town.

45. Savannah *Morning News,* August
    27, 1884.

46. Poor, *Railroad Manual, 1868-1869,*
    337.

47. Atlanta *Constitution,* July 10, 1869.

48. Avery, *History of Georgia,* 459.

49. Savannah *Morning News,* August
    27, 1884.

50. Florida *Times-Union,* February 12,
    1884.

51. *Ibid.,* March 29, 1886.

52. *Ibid.,* March 22, 1886.

53. Atlanta *Journal,* February 16, 1895.

54. Palatka *Daily News,* February 23,
    1886.

55. April 28, 1899.

56. Florida *Times-Union,* February 17,
    1887.

57. New York *Daily Tribune,* Novem-
    ber 17, 1891.

58. The *Tatler of Society* in Florida,
    December 23, 1899. Annual publi-
    cation of St. Augustine, Florida,
    during the 1890's on the coming
    and going of society in Florida.

59. On July 3, 1902, the Plant System was absorbed by the Atlantic Coast Line. The Tampa *Weekly Times* July 3, 1902, had this to say: "Hail and farewell to the Plant System . . . it is a part of the past we all love, and it passes out of life in fact as well as in name."

60. Tampa *Morning Tribune,* November 19, 1898.

CHAPTER THIRTEEN

1. Much of the first section of this essay is taken from, John E. Talmadge, "Rebecca Latimer Felton, Georgian," *Georgia Review,* IX (1955), 65-73.

2. Charles Latimer to C. R. Hanleiter, Man 26, June 11, 1858, in Felton Collection, University of Georgia Library.

3. An example of this technique is an undated clipping from the Atlanta *Constitution* of a letter from her to the editor, *ibid.* "Why a Columbiad was rolled out of the state house to blow off the head of a gray-haired woman—a Methodist, a wife and a mother—I leave the public to guess."

4. Hoke Smith to Rebecca Felton, August 2, 17, 1899, *ibid.*

5. Louis Griffith and John Talmadge, *Georgia Journalism, 1763-1950* (Athens: University of Georgia Press, 1951), 103, 104, 133. C Vann Woodward, *Tom Watson, Agrarian Rebel* (New York: The Mcmillan Company, 1938), 373-376.

6. *Ibid.,* 332; Amanda Johnson, *Georgia, As Colony and State* (Atlanta: W. W. Brown, 1938), 646-648.

7. Newspaper clipping on inside cover of Scrapbook XXXII. Mrs. Felton's scrapbooks are numbered from one to thirty-two. The number of the scrapbook will be cited hereinafter in Roman numerals, the pages in Arabic numerals. Since none of the files of the semi-weekly issue of the Atlanta *Journal* has been located, the hundreds of clippings in the scrapbooks will be used. Many of the letters referred to later in this essay were published in her columns and will be also cited by scrapbook number and page number. All scrapbooks are in the Felton Collection.

8. XXIV, 89; XXXI, 91.

9. XXXII, 10; XXIV, 99, 129.

10. *Ibid.,* 25, 13, 67, 10, 120; XXXI, 91.

11. XXIV, 24, 28; XXX, 15; XXXII, 185.

12. XXIV, 96, 18, 126.

13. *Ibid.,* 18, 99; XXXII, 7, 27; XXXI, 65, 3, 28.

14. IX, 99; XXIV, 13; XXXII, 198.

15. IX, 99; XXIV, 13, 182.

16. XXXII, 184, 49; XXIV, 82.

17. XXXI, 25; XXXII, 39; XXIV, 24.

18. XXXII, 39.

19. IX, 53; XXIV, 26, 144.

20. *Ibid.,* 66; IX, 9.

21. XXIV, 5, 116, 107; XXXII, 27.

22. XXIV, 70, 5; IX, 87.

23. XXIV, 70, 5; IX, 87.

24. XXXII, 44; XXIV, 29.

25. *Ibid.,* 70, 137, 90.

26. *Ibid.,* 29.

27. *Ibid.,* 136, 123; XXI, 36.

28. XXIV, 194, 174.

29. *Ibid.,* 60.

30. *Ibid.,* 152, 165; XXXII, 5.

31. IX, 6; V, 88; XXIV, 97.

32. *Ibid.,* 158, 162; XXXI, 13.

33. V, 45; XXIV, 7, 110; XXXII, 34.

34. *Ibid.,* 181.

35. *Ibid.,* 200, 1, 204-205.

36. XXI, 38; IX, 15, 29.

37. *Ibid.,* 15, 20; XIX, 20; XXIV, 4; XIII, 31; XXIV, 22.

38. XXXII, 8; XXXI, 99; W. C. Dodson to Rebecca Felton, November 3, 1902, in Felton Collection.

39. Virginius Dabney, *Liberalism in the South* (Chapel Hill: University of North Carolina Press, 1932), 191; clipping in Felton Collection.

40. XXIV, 78; XXXII, 14, 37; clipping in Felton Collection.

41. XXXII, 13; XXXVIII, 10; IX, 159-160.
42. XXIV, 80; XXX, 39; XXXI, 37, 77; XXVI, pages unnumbered.
43. XXIV, 41; IX, 67, 147.
44. The Atlanta *Journal,* August 12, 1897, November 11, 1898; Hugh T. Lefler and Albert R. Newsome, *North Carolina, The History of a State* (Chapel Hill: University of North Carolina Press, 1954), 522.
45. IX, 51; XI, 33; XXIV, 128, 222.
46. *Ibid.,* 74; XXX, 15.
47. Clipping December 1, 1881 in Felton Collection; V, 95; XI, 11.
48. XXIV, 106, 15; XXXI, 1.
49. XI, 11; IX, 43; XXIV, 120, 187.
50. *Ibid.,* 73; XI, 37; XXXII, 145.
51. XXIV, 4; XXXII, 197.
52. *Ibid.;* XI, 38; XXXI, 47; V, 46.
53. XXIV, 91; XXX, 28, 45; XVII, 215; Atlanta *Georgian,* October 5, 1920.
54. XXIV, 49; X, 114; XXI, 24; XXIV, 5.
55. *Ibid.,* 35,9.
56. *Ibid.,* 11, 12; XXI, 31.
57. Talmadge, "Rebecca Latimer Felton, Georgian," *loc. cit.,* 71-72.
58. Rebecca Felton to James Gray, February [?], 1919, in Felton Collection.
59. *Ibid.*
60. XXIV, 68.
61. XXXII, 180, 219; XVII, 214; XXIV, 183, 107.
62. XXXII, 219, 204, 29, 207; XXX, 10.
63. IX, 55, 142, 18; XXIV, 39.
64. XXXI, 77, 39; IX, 62, 168; XXXII, 15.
65. XXIX, 140; XXIV, 59, 110; IX, 145.

66. *Ibid.,* 40; XXXII, 13; Helen McAfee to Rebecca Felton, October 10, 1920, in Felton Collection; Mrs. G. W. Lockey to *id.,* December 31, 1911, *ibid.*
67. IX, 46, 65; clipping in Felton Collection; XXXII, 180.
68. *Ibid.,* 14, 180; XXXI, 57, 77; W. L. Garren to Rebecca Felton, undated, in Felton Collection.
69. XXXII, 181; IX, 93; XXXI, 91; clipping in Felton Collection.
70. In scrapbook XXXII there are twelve unnumbered pages before page one. The clipping cited here is on the eleventh of these unnumbered pages. See also IX, 21, 60.
71. XXXII, 214, 8, 2, 25, 33, 182.
72. *Ibid.,* 200, 209.
73. *Ibid.,* 1, 209, 181, 199, 204; IX, 1.
74. *Ibid.;* XXXII, 185, 8.
75. Mary Felton Ramsey to Rebecca Felton, March 28, 1920, in Felton Collection; XXIV, 182, 184, 66, 110.
76. XXXII, 28, 2; IX, 71; XXIV, 184; Ulysses Roach to Rebecca Felton, October 7, 1922, in Felton Collection; Nola Wooten to *id.,* undated, *ibid.;* Mary Felton Ramsey to *id.,* March 28, 1920, *ibid.;* Mrs. C. O. McMichael to *id.,* November 29, 1918, *ibid.;* T. Walt White to *id.,* December 23, 1911, *ibid.;* A. J. Alford to *id.,* April 11, 1903, *ibid.*
77. IX, 57; XXIV, 68.
78. Atlanta *Journal,* undated clipping, in Felton Collection.

CHAPTER FOURTEEN

1. Robert Preston Brooks, "Hoke Smith," in Malone and Johnson, eds., *Dictionary of American Biography,* XVII, 280-282. This is an excellent short summary of Smith's career.
2. Dewey Grantham, "Hoke Smith: Representative of the New South," unpublished doctoral dissertation, University of North Carolina, 1950, 4-6.

3. Hoke Smith Scrapbook, University of Georgia Library, unnumbered vol., 296. See also John Chalmers Vinson, "Hoke Smith, Cleveland's Secretary of the Interior," unpublished masters thesis, University of Georgia, 1944. The Scrapbooks are the most important source of material. For the most part they are made up of newspaper clippings. There is little personal material included.

4. J. H. T. McPherson, "Hoke Smith," in Walter L. Fleming, ed., *The South in the Building of the Nation*, (Richmond: Southern Publishing Society, 1909. 12 vols.), XII, 403-404.

5. Raymond B. Nixon, *Henry Grady, Spokesman of the New South* (New York: Simon Schuster, 1943), 255-257.

6. Alex M. Arnett, *The Populist Movement in Georgia* (New York: Columbia University, 1922), 104-116.

7. Josiah Carter, "Hoke Smith," in Northen, ed., *Men of Mark in Georgia*, IV, 3.

8. Allan Nevins, ed., *The Letters of Grover Cleveland* (New York: Houghton Mifflin Company, 1933), 242, 245, 246, 283-284; Northen, ed., *Men of Mark*, IV, 4.

9. Smith Scrapbook, unnumbered vol. This entire volume is a collection of letters written Gordon by Smith's friends.

10. *Ibid.*, unnumbered vol., 13.

11. *Ibid.*, L, 116.

12. *Ibid.*, XLVIII, clipping enclosed in flap inside back cover of volume.

13. *Ibid.*, XLIX, 66.

14. *Ibid.*, unnumbered vol., 219.

15. Northen, ed., *Men of Mark*, IV, 3-4.

16. Smith Scrapbook, XLIX, 16.

17. *Ibid.*, unnumbered vol., 219.

18. *Ibid.*, XLIX, 76.

19. *Ibid.*, unnumbered vol. 219.

20. *Ibid.*, 219.

21. *Ibid.*, 3, 4, 10.

22. *Ibid.*, 3, 6, 7, 9, 40, 65.

23. *Ibid.*, 9.

24. John Chalmers Vinson, "Hoke Smith and the Battle of the Standards," *Georgia Historical Quarterly*, XXXVI (1952), 201-219.

25. E. P. Oberholtzer, *A History of the United States Since the Civil War* (New York: The Macmillan Company, 1937. 5 vols.), V, 402.

26. Smith Scrapbook, unnumbered vol., 203ff.

27. Thomas H. Martin, *Atlanta and its Builders* (Atlanta: Century Memo-rial Publishing Company, 1952. 2 vols.), II, 374.

28. Smith Scrapbook, unnumbered, 1893-1896, clipping from Washington *Star*, August 3, 1893.

29. Grantham, "Hoke Smith," 260.

30. New York *Times*, November 28, 1931.

31. Atlanta *Journal*, December 4, 10, 18, 1901.

32. Smith Scrapbook, clipping from Augusta *Labor*, November 3, 1901; Atlanta *Constitution*, July 26, 1904.

33. *Ibid.*, XXXVIII, 26, 41.

34. *Ibid.*, 3, 4, 30, 40; Atlanta *Journal*, April 5, 1905.

35. *Ibid.*, XXXVIII, 35.

36. New York *Tribune*, July 8, 1900.

37. Atlanta *Journal*, August 25, 1905.

38. Smith Scrapbook, LXIV, 63.

39. *Ibid.*, CVIII, 37-39.

40. New York *Tribune*, November 2, 1904.

41. Atlanta *Journal*, May 21, 1905.

42. *Ibid.*, June 3, 1905.

43. Atlanta *Constitution*, February 22, 1906.

44. Woodward, *Tom Watson*, 370-371.

45. Grantham, "Hoke Smith," 349.

46. Atlanta *Journal*, June 9, 1906.

47. Atlanta *Constitution*, September 2, 5, 6, 9, 1905.

48. *Ibid.*, January 17, 1906.

49. Atlanta *Journal*, September 24, 1907.

50. *Executive Minutes of Georgia* (1907-1909), 4-14.

51. *Outlook*, (August 10, 1907), 757-758.

52. Smith Scrapbook, 1906-1907, 91.

53. Atlanta *Georgian and News*, August 19, 1907.

54. Atlanta *Journal*, July 30, 1907; *Georgia House Journal, 1907*, 928-929.

55. August 14, 1907.

56. Grantham, "Hoke Smith," 332.

57. *Ibid.*, 335.

58. *Executive Minutes of Georgia* (1907-1909), 7-10, 134-141.

59. Grantham, "Hoke Smith," 343.

60. Francis Beach Hudson, "The Smith-Brown Controversy," unpublished masters thesis, Emory University,

1929-30, presents a thorough study of this interesting feud in Georgia's history.

61. Woodward, *Tom Watson*, 386-392.
62. Grantham, "Hoke Smith," 387-389.
63. Atlanta *Constitution*, May 29, 1908.
64. *Ibid.*, June 23, 1910.
65. *Ibid.*, July 29, 1910.
66. Smith Collection, University of Georgia Library. Miscellaneous Papers.
67. Atlanta *Journal*, August 26, September 1, 1910.
68. *Ibid.*, July 12, 1911; Atlanta *Constitution* June 25, 1911; Jackson Perry Speer, "Hoke Smith, Georgia Progressive," unpublished masters thesis, University of Georgia, 1947.
69. Grantham, "Hoke Smith," 427-429.
70. *Cong. Record*, 62 Cong., 2 Sess., 1.
71. Atlanta *Journal*, March 10, 11, 31, May 29, 1912.

72. J. C. Welliver, "Leaders in the New Congress," *Munsey's Magazine* (February, 1913), 728.
73. Grantham, "Hoke Smith," 446.
74. *Cong. Record*, 64 Cong., 1 Sess., 7390-7393.
75. *Cong. Record*, 63 Cong., 2 Sess., 1947, 2288, 2744, 3046, 3130, 9503; Speer, "Hoke Smith," gives the most complete account of the Smith-Lever and Smith-Hughes acts.
76. New York *Times*, October 24, 1914, June 26, 1915.
77. Atlanta *Constitution*, August 21, 1914.
78. *Cong. Record*, 66 Cong., 1. Sess., 6271-6272.
79. *Ibid.*, 8278, 8786.
80. Grantham, "Hoke Smith," 450.
81. December 8, 1931.

INDEX